NATURE'S NATION

Nature's Nation

Perry Miller

The Belknap Press

OF

HARVARD UNIVERSITY PRESS

CAMBRIDGE, MASSACHUSETTS

Second printing, 1974

Library of Congress Catalog Card Number 67-17316

ISBN 0–674–60550–0

Printed in the United States of America

FOREWORD

In his Preface to the volume of essays entitled *Errand Into the Wilderness,* published in 1956, Perry Miller wrote that he had "put together those that seem to add up to a rank of spotlights on the massive narrative of the movement of European culture into the vacant wilderness of America." It may then be appropriate to describe the present volume, in words of the first piece here included, as concerned with "the problem of American self-recognition," with how companies of immigrants became "parts of the landscape" in that same wilderness. The rapidity with which the settlers began comporting themselves, not simply as sojourners in a remote outpost, but as men who, in Increase Mather's words, here found "land and elbow-room enough in the World," can still astound.

The detailed story of the transformation of the inherited European culture into a provincial mentality is the subject of *The New England Mind: From Colony to Province.* The first group of essays in this collection, although chronologically related to that study, still have their focus on the becoming rather than the inherited, on adaptation rather than preservation, even when the process affects the guise of ancestral piety. Certain doubts as to the suitability of including these essays, concerned as they are with topics examined in the earlier work, were resolved by colleagues and students who urged the usefulness of their extended treatment and detailed annotation for future students of the way in which English provinces became an American nation.

Most of the pieces, however, treat of the concerns of a people who, while clearly recognizing where they were, still entertained certain anxieties as to who they were. Whether such self-recognition was to come from a new, "awakened" sense of man's relation to the Deity, whether from correspondence with "Nature," or whether from a literature that would enable the nation "to see something original and beautiful disengage itself from our ceaseless ferment and turmoil," the urgency of the question was not resolved by the "more perfect union" or by a surrender at Appomattox Court House. The last three essays, here published for the first time, move back and forth in time, from practitioners of the Puritan mode to the twentieth century, and thus reflect the continuity of the search for an answer, if not an answer itself. The three to some extent overlap in that they treat often of the same writers. The angle of perspective varies, however, and they illustrate ways in which Perry Miller was thinking of themes intended for examination in the final sections of *The Life of the Mind in America.*

In the preparation of these pieces for present publication, a few repetitious passages have been deleted, together with occasional topical references irrelevant for the general reader. And, of course, misprints have been corrected and form regularized. Permission to republish has been graciously granted by the *New England Quarterly* for "The Shaping of the American Character," "Emersonian Genius and the American Character," and "Thoreau in the Context of International Romanticism"; by the *Proceedings of the American Antiquarian Society* for "Declension in a Bible Commonwealth"; by the *Journal of the History of Ideas* for "Preparation for Salvation"; by the *Harvard Theological Review* for "Theodore Parker: Apostasy Within Liberalism," and "The Romantic Dilemma in American Nationalism"; by the *Harvard Divinity School Bulletin* for "The Insecurity of Nature"; by *The Virginia Quarterly Review* for "Melville and Transcendentalism"; by Princeton University Press for "From the Covenant to the Revival," reprinted from *Religion in American Life,* 1961; by *Encounter* (Duke University) for "The Great Awakening: 1740-1750"; by Doubleday & Company, Inc., for "The Location of American Religious Freedom," from the book *Religion and Freedom of Thought,* by Perry Miller, Robert L. Calhoun, Nathan M. Pusey, and Reinhold Niebuhr, copyright 1954 by The Union Theological Seminary. Lines from T. S. Eliot's *The Waste Land* on page 282 are reprinted by permission of Faber & Faber and Harcourt, Brace & World; lines on page 288 from Ezra Pound's "Hugh Selwyn Mauberley" in *Personae* by permission of Faber & Faber and New Directions.

ELIZABETH W. MILLER
Cambridge, Massachusetts

March 1, 1967

CONTENTS

INTRODUCTION

BY KENNETH B. MURDOCK

Nature's Nation is much more than a collection of essays by a great scholar. It is, I think, an indispensable guide to full understanding of Perry Miller's achievement, in effect a summary of the basic elements of his thought. The essays it contains, some of them published before but not given the attention they deserved and others now printed for the first time, reveal the variety of his interests, the wide range of his knowledge, his literary taste and stylistic skill, and his brilliance as a teacher.

I know of no other volume of his which so clearly and succinctly discloses his central ideas and his scholarly principles. In it one can trace the development of his thinking from the day when, still a young student in college, he worked his way on a freighter to the banks of the Congo and there dedicated himself to the task of expounding "the innermost propulsion of the United States"—a task he devoted himself to for the rest of his life. In 1933 in *Orthodoxy in Massachusetts,* his first book, he wrote facetiously that he was "so very naive as to believe that the way men think has some influence upon their actions." Twenty-three years later in *Errand into the Wilderness* he declared: "I have difficulty imagining that anyone can be a historian without realizing that history itself is part of the life of the mind; hence I have been compelled to insist that the mind of man is the basic factor in human history."

The "new historians" of the 1920's and 30's, who insisted that men's economic motives and material successes and failures accounted for all their actions, seemed to Miller to be on the wrong track. "They were not getting at . . . *the* fundamental theme, assuming that such a theme even exists." He continued: "I am the last to decry monographs on stoves or bathtubs, or tax laws, banks, the conduct of presidential elections, or even inventories of artifacts. All this is the warp and woof of American history . . . It is true that the outside world cannot judge America unless it knows about the Wilmot Proviso and the chain store." But, he said, "I was condemned to another (I do not say a better) sort of quest."

This quest he felt must "begin at the beginning," and he chose to concentrate first on the Puritan migration to New England. He recognized the priority of the settlement of Virginia but he wanted "a coherence with which" he "could coherently begin." This he found in the ideas of the settlers in the northern colonies, ideas which, for a time at least, dominated their political and social as well as their ecclesiastical organization. In so doing, of course, he ran afoul of the "new historians." They in general

left out of account the Puritans' religious professions, their doctrinal platforms, and their learning, and argued that they came to the chilly shores
of Massachusetts because there were fortunes to be made in fishing, lumber-
ing, and shipping—implying that hypocritically they masked greed under
a cloak of pretended piety. Miller saw deeper, but by no means completely
condemned such historians as Parrington or James Truslow Adams. He
was as eager as they to dispel the "conception of Puritan history which
had settled like a cloud of patriotic obscurantism" over some earlier historians. As he put it, "In the 1920's a few strident and derisive voices,"
such as those of H. L. Mencken and Adams, "got the vaporous mass to
moving." Miller acknowledged the liberation he owed to these "violators
of the temple, for without them, I and my generation might have lacked
the temerity to undertake a fresh and profane examination." He joined
Parrington and Adams in shaking "a few complacencies" of earlier writers.
But when they "conspired to present Thomas Hooker as a sort of John
the Baptist to Thomas Jefferson," Miller rebelled. His "historical conscience" was outraged. He did not blame the two historians he named
but their times and the state of scholarship when they wrote, which, he
said, "was so demoralized" that sincere students and men of stature "could
solemnly make irresponsible statements about the differences between
Lutheranism and Calvinism, let alone about those between Separatists and
Nonseparatists, which clearly betrayed that they did not comprehend such
matters."

His historical conscience demanded that he go farther. He was not
stimulated by any affection for the Puritans or by any filio-pietistic desire
to defend them, but by his conscientious determination not to praise or
vilify them until he was sure that his verdict was supported by impeccable
evidence. His vow to ferret out "the innermost propulsion of the United
States" demanded a thorough examination of the propulsion of the
Puritans. It might or might not prove enlightening, but to neglect the
possibility that it might would have been to falter in his mission. He could
not in honesty accept glib clichés as sufficient definitions of the Puritan mind.

In the first of his series of lectures on "An American Language," written
in 1958 but now first published, he said: "I would like to think that the
time has long since passed when we have to blame some 'fabricated monster
of Puritanism' for a blight that has supposedly fallen upon the American
spirit." The passage continues with a temperate summary of what he had
come to believe the Puritans really were—flesh-and-blood men, by no means
sexually starved, frankly fond of rum, and capable of "indulging in petty
animosities, village gossip, and displays of sheer spite." This was not the
portrait of a community of superhuman saints. The New England settlers'
influence on our literature was bad, not because of what they were but
because genteel writers of the nineteenth century tried to reshape them
in their own image. Miller quotes Ernest Hemingway's comment that the
creators of the image were all gentlemen, all respectable, with small, dried

wisdoms. "Nor would you gather that they had bodies. They had minds, yes. Nice, dry, clean minds." Miller knew that the Puritans had minds, but denied that they were nice, dry, clean ones. Thomas Hooker, he knew, did not try "to prove himself a gentleman. The hazards of living were too important" for that.

Determined investigation of the Puritans led to other discoveries, and Miller destroyed many myths long cherished by earlier writers. Edmund Morgan in his "Perry Miller and the Historians" pointed out that Miller "changed in many ways the standard picture of early New England." He proved that the "founders of Massachusetts were non-separating Congregationalists," that the exodus of some of them to Connecticut was not inspired by zeal for democracy, that "the Antinomian controversy involved a dispute between John Cotton and other ministers in which Cotton was defeated," that the devout in early New England "made the covenant of grace the central doctrine of their system, and that Jonathan Edwards repudiated that doctrine." To this list should be added Miller's teaching his readers to understand typology—a method of interpreting the Bible dear to the Puritans and many other scholars in the seventeenth century. Based on the idea that the Old Testament foreshadowed the New, it enabled typologists to find in the knottiest chapters of the first part of the Bible symbolic meanings which they believed were perfectly consonant with the teachings of Christ and the Apostles. Miller's exposition made it possible for hosts of modern readers to understand for the first time many pages in the work of seventeenth-century writers which had been previously unintelligible and had led to crucial misinterpretations of their authors' meaning. A shining example of the importance of a knowledge of typology is Miller's reinterpretation of Roger Williams' intellectual position and the rock on which he founded his argument against the Massachusetts which exiled him as a heretic.

It is to be hoped that *Nature's Nation* may at last make plain the folly of those who have persisted in trying to fit all its author's work into Procrustean categories. Scholars quite naturally love neat classifications, each neatly ticketed with a title which too often clouds rather than clarifies. Thus we find Miller described simply as a "historian of New England" or "of the Puritans," or as their "advocate." Nearer the mark, he was called simply an "intellectual historian." But why did this "historian of New England" stray into writing two essays on early Virginia, or bother with such themes as "The Romance and the Novel," and devote to Mark Twain, Melville, Cooper, and the English romanticists as much attention as he did to any New Englander? If he was an "intellectual historian," why did he not follow more closely the pattern of earlier writers dignified by that name? And why did he call his magnum opus, which he did not live to finish, "The Life of the Mind in America" rather than "The Intellectual History of America"? If he was an apologist for the Puritans, why did he so trenchantly describe the "Declension" of their Bible Commonwealth?

The table of contents of *Nature's Nation* is enough to show the wide range of his scholarly quest; to read the essays the book contains is to see the depth and breadth of his scholarship.

The strangest label ever given to him seems to me "conservative historian." The only excuse for it I can think of is that he did not agree with the ideas of the "new historians" of two or three decades ago and was unable to accept completely their "debunking" of the Puritans. To me it seems that conservatism is perhaps the last word to apply to Miller, who was an atheist and an iconoclastic assailant of cherished interpretations of history which seemed to him products of fantasy rather than sound knowledge.

The only sense in which he was ever "conservative," unless the word is to be deprived of its ordinary meaning, is that he never wavered from his belief in the age-old principle that a scholar's creed requires careful study of all the evidence relevant to his theme and, so far as is humanly possible, mastery of all the knowledge which in any way might shed light on the interpretation of it. Only when every tree had been identified and studied could the full grandeur of the forest be seen.

Few historians have ever excelled Miller in devotion to this principle. He was a professor of literature as well as a historian, and found the classics of Greece and Rome, the writings of the Middle Ages, and the whole range of literature, American and foreign, past and present, necessary for any approach to comprehension of the past and present history of his country.

In many respects his greatest achievement was the quality and range of his teaching. He gave courses in the divinity school at Harvard as well as in the college and the Graduate School of Arts and Sciences. He skillfully taught and examined not only graduate students but fledgling undergraduates, and liked each year to devote part of his teaching to the history and literature of countries other than his own. He strove constantly to lead his pupils to share his own crusading spirit and to rise above the "sluggish intellect" of their compatriots. In his essay on Theodore Parker he wrote, "We have not leisure, or the patience, or the skill, to comprehend what was working in the mind and heart of a then recent graduate of the Harvard Divinity School who would muster the audacity to contradict his most formidable instructor" at the School. "What indeed *has* happened to us?"

By and large Miller was gentle with his students. There were moments, however, when they provoked him to wrath by revealing their lack of patience or skill and a lackadaisical attitude toward learning. On occasion, an intelligent and hard-working student, educated in American history or literature but with only a smattering of instruction in the history or culture of other countries, presented to him an excited announcement of a discovery of a brilliant and highly significant phrase in Melville, John Wise, or even Increase Mather and he had to explain that both the phrase and its significance had been commonly known and expounded throughout the centuries since Plato or Aristotle or Montaigne. In such cases Miller usually managed to cover his despair with a patient and brief lecture, but now and then his woe was too bitter to endure without a denunciation as angry as any of those which Cotton Mather and other Puritan divines bestowed on young New Englanders who went to sea as pirates or refused to learn their catechisms. But even those students whom he most bitterly chastised, and those who were most annoyed by the contemptuous tone he sometimes used when he discovered how little they had read, often came to admire him. Many who were at first most critical of his ideas and most eager to refute them became in time disciples whose master he was proud to be.

One secret of his power as a teacher and his influence on his pupils was his readiness to admit his own faults and errors. He was not always right, and in 1956 wrote that he had published some articles and sentences that he wished he had not. He declared that in an essay he had published in 1935 he had been guilty of a total miscomprehension and had "miserably spoiled in the saying" what he had meant to say. Some of his work received reviews he called "sullen"; some critics went farther and launched bitter attacks. Students as well as professional reviewers now and then took him to task. He treated all his critics, young or old, in essentially the same fashion. If the comment displayed its author's ignorance of the data on which he had based his statements he was content merely to laugh; if, however, the criticism came from someone well informed, according to his high standards, he plunged eagerly into discussion, more often in correspondence than in print. If his adversary could show him evidence that he had neglected to take into account or demonstrate that he had failed to prove his point. he confessed his errors as promptly and publicly as he could. No doubt such confessions were sometimes painful, but they also gave him joy of a sort. He was as eager to learn as to teach; a new idea given him by a critic was as pure gold as any discovery of his own.

A special value of *Nature's Nation* is its inclusion of many essays which were originally delivered as lectures and initially designed for speech rather than print. All of them were written out in advance and delivered with the manuscript before him. But it is certain that once on the platform he altered them here and there. An audience inspired him; no one who ever heard him lecture can have forgotten the magic of his talk. During the years of his absence from college on his search for adventure he was for a time an actor, playing minor roles and learning the difficult art of the theater. The cunning with which in his lectures he changed his pace, his swift darts of irony, and the sparks of wit which blazed up even more in his speech than in his writing—all reflected his histrionic training. Although the lectures in this volume do not reproduce precisely what his listeners heard when he lectured, they give its flavor.

Now and then his love for the platform led him astray. In some of his lectures, as in some pages of his books, his eagerness to dramatize betrayed him into exaggeration. In his "Theodore Parker: Apostasy within Liberalism," he is perhaps a little too "excited" and possibly overemphasizes Parker's tendency to weep—but Parker was a skillful orator and knew that his lachrymose outbursts might conquer the hearts of his audience; Miller in stressing them had the same end in view. Faced with a crowded auditorium, he felt his task was to stir his listeners emotionally so as to capture their attention. How otherwise could they be brought to listen closely enough to understand all that he was passionately striving to tell them? How else could he effectively wage his battle against their smug indifference and their willingness to accept easy definitions and superficial solutions of the grave problems he was trying to solve? A bit of hyperbole could do good rather than harm if it waked those who were sleepily content with misleading popularizations and comfortably phrased half-truths. But Miller was never a charlatan, and he never forgot his responsibility as a scholar. He once wrote that it was hard for any historian to restrain "his prejudices and to exercise the sort of historical imagination" required, for example, in his own effort to understand "a portion of the past according to its own intentions." Difficult as it was, he steadfastly maintained the necessary restraint.

There is no need here to comment systematically on the essays which follow in this volume. Elizabeth Miller's preface outlines their basic themes and suggests their scope and depth. Miller saw that "the problem of American self-realization" could not be solved or even understood without "gigantic labor." Study of the meaning of America meant venturing into an interminable field. His determination to expound his America to the twentieth century forced him to trace a path through a labyrinth and to undertake a deeper probing of the American past and present than any work definable merely as intellectual history could provide.

He was convinced that to be an American was indeed, as Henry James said, "a complex fate." It was, in Miller's view, an amazing experience. "Being an American," he said, "is not something inherited but something to be achieved." And in "Emersonian Genius and the American Democracy" he praised Emerson's understanding of the "difficult ordeal," the "magnificent but agonizing experience of what it is to be, or to try to be, an American."

In the course of his effort to elucidate the experience and the ordeal, driven on by his pressing need to reveal his America to his compatriots, he came to see that the need might be impossible to satisfy. Certainly no simple formula could define the American "life of the mind," past or present. "The Puritans' cherished covenant theory," he wrote, "broke down because it tried to stereotype the image of America, to confine it to . . . a priori conceptions." "He who would endeavor to fix the personality of America in one eternal, unchangeable pattern . . . comprehends little of how this nation has come along this far." "He who would fix the pattern of decision by confining the American choice to one and only one mode of response—whether this be in politics, diplomacy, economics, literary form, or morality itself—such a one, in the light of our history, is the 'truly Un-American.' " And Miller unhesitatingly admitted that "the meaning of America is simply that its meaning cannot be fixed." But nonetheless he pursued unflinchingly the investigation to which he had dedicated himself.

Donald Fleming, in a perceptive essay, "Perry Miller and Esoteric History," pointed out that Miller had an aptitude for social history but valued it only when it was "tightly held in the matrix of the history of thought." In all his writing "the unmistakable impulse at work" was "to get beneath the surface of his materials and reveal an esoteric pattern." One method he often used in his effort "to get beyond appearances to some deeper reality" is admirably described by Professor Fleming. It was "to take the men of the past at their word, but patiently to explicate this word, turn it about till every facet caught the light—perhaps for the first time in centuries—and then implicate it in a vanished or unsuspected context of ideas." But study of the past alone could not suffice. Standing "on the threshold of an inconceivable age," Miller felt he must test the firmness of his footing. Not only the past but the present—perhaps even the future— demanded devoted attention. The obstacles he faced and the knowledge that his goal might prove unattainable did not daunt him. The search itself was exciting, an adventure he rejoiced in.

He was impressed by a passage from Werner Heisenberg's *Philosophic Problems of Nuclear Science:* "Faced with essentially new intellectual challenges," scientists should "follow the example of Columbus, who possessed the courage to leave the known world in the almost insane hope of finding land again beyond the sea." Heisenberg was addressing himself to scientists. Miller was himself persuaded that "natural science . . . added a dimension" which "a student of the American mind must reckon with," and planned to devote the third part of *The Life of the Mind in America* to "Science—Theoretical and Applied." Only three of the proposed sections were finished before his death, but they are sufficient to show the gusto with which he extended his careful exploration to meet the "new intellectual challenge" which modern science presented to his own age and the future.

It seems to me that he was, in Heisenberg's terms, a Columbus himself, embarked on voyages of discovery in hitherto uncharted worlds. The world might be an area of American thought in the past, neglected by others, or the world in his own day, in which he saw new challenges for old standards, the worship of new gods, and new modes of behavior, all rich with poten- tialities for good or evil. Whatever unknown land there was, he longed to discover and explore it.

Miller had no interest in the hollow rewards which often seem to pass for success in our society; the success he sought was not of that sort. His Columbus-like voyages were not undertaken for praise or material profit. They called for both courage and devotion—the more so since he knew that they might never lead him to a "new world" or even to discovery of the meaning he sought for in an old one. Alan Heimert reports that when Miller was asked by a student whether he intended to write "the 'last word' on everything that had ever been said or written in America," he was both amused and shocked. "He didn't think he had written the 'last word' on anything." He was satisfied with some of his books but always delighted when his pupils went farther than he had, and he constantly urged them to do so. Their achievement was perhaps the success he most valued.

He was not only an explorer as Columbus was but a crusader, determined to vanquish those of his countrymen who refused to face squarely America's problems. He inspired scores of those he taught to join him and to carry on the battle when he could fight no longer. His hope was that they, even though their swords might be bent and their shields dented, would carry their pilgrimage to Jerusalems he never saw and find in their crusade the joy he had experienced in his own.

NATURE'S NATION

THE SHAPING OF
THE AMERICAN CHARACTER

IN 1867 Walt Whitman brought out a revision of *Leaves of Grass*. He was constantly revising; this was the fourth version. The first had been in 1855, the second in 1856, the third in 1860. Virtually all approved and respectable critics of the time who even bothered to consider Whitman were hostile; they believed a "poetry" that could be so recklessly revised to be obviously no poetry at all. Nowadays there are many who regard him as our greatest poet; when Lucien Price asked Alfred North Whitehead what, if anything, original and distinctively American this country has produced, the philosopher answered without hesitation, "Whitman." I suspect that Whitman, at this moment, is not so popular as he was thirty years ago; if I am right, then this is a sign of the times, one which I must consider ominous. But be that as it may, Whitman's successive revisions, Whitman being what he was, are apt to come not from a heightened sense of form or from a quest for more precise language, but simply out of his constantly changing sense of the American destiny. He could never make up his mind, though at each point he had to pretend that he did and so declaim with a finality whose very flamboyance betrays the uncertainty.

In 1856 he printed one of his most interesting songs, the one called in the collected works, "As I Sat Alone by Blue Ontario's Shore." In this version, and again in 1860, the poem is an exaltation of the role he assigned himself, the poet-prophet of democracy. But by 1867 he had lived through the central ordeal of this republic, the war we call variously "Civil" or "Between the States." Something profoundly disturbing had happened to Walt Whitman; it is expressed not only in poems written directly out of his experience, like "Drum-Taps" and "When Lilacs Last in the Dooryard Bloom'd," but in the revisions of previous utterances. In 1856 and 1860, for instance, one line of "By Blue Ontario's Shore" had read, "Give me to speak beautiful words! take all the rest." In 1867 this became "Give me to sing the song of the great Idea! take all the rest." After the war, he would celebrate the democracy itself, not merely the poet. These changes, commentators theorize, record a chastening of Whitman's egotism; they indicate his belated realization that this country is bigger than any man, even a Whitman, and from the realization he learned humility.

However, the sort of humility one acquires only from discovering that

Address given at the conference on "Values in the American Tradition" on October 12, 1954, at Wellesley College. Published in *The New England Quarterly*, vol. XXVIII, no. 4 (December, 1955), pp. 435-54.

his nation is large and he himself small is by definition suspect. In Whitman, there are some curious additions to the postwar announcement of self-abnegation. This couplet, for example:

> We stand self-pois'd in the middle, branching thence over the world;
> From Missouri, Nebraska, or Kansas, laughing attack to scorn.

Or, still more striking, this verse:

> America isolated I sing;
> I say that works made here in the spirit of other lands, are so much poison in The States.
> (How dare such insects as we assume to write poems for America?
> For our victorious armies, and the offspring following the armies?)

Recently a French critic, commenting on this passage, has called it the tirade of a narrow and contemptuous isolationism.[1] Perhaps a Frenchman at this point in history has a reaction different from ours to a boast about the offspring following our victorious armies!

In the light of M. Asselineau's opinion, it is of some significance that Whitman himself, in the 1881 revision of *Leaves of Grass,* suppressed these pieces of strident isolationism. By then he had received further lessons in humility, not from victorious armies but from the stroke that paralyzed him; the last poems, as has often been remarked, show an aspiration toward universality with which the mood of 1867 was in open opposition. However, of one fact there can be no doubt: Walt Whitman, self-appointed spokesman for America, found himself responding in a fashion which may, indeed, be characteristic of the patriot in any country, but has been most conspicuously characteristic of the American: exulting in military victory, he proclaimed that an isolated America has nothing and should have nothing to do with the rest of the world.

This episode in the history of the text is only one out of a thousand which underscore that quality in *Leaves of Grass* that does make it so peculiarly an American book: its extreme self-consciousness. Not only does Whitman appoint himself the poet-prophet of the nation, and advertise to the point of tedium that he sings America, but in the incessant effort to find out what he is singing, what America is, he must always be revising his poems to suit a fluctuating conception. As Archibald MacLeish wrote in 1929 (he as much as Whitman shows how acutely self-conscious about nationality our artists must be), "It is a strange thing—to be an American":

> This, this is our land, this is our people
> This that is neither a land nor a race.

Whether the American public dislikes Whitman or is indifferent to him, still, in this respect he is indeed the national poet Mr. Whitehead called

---

[1] Roger Asselineau, *The Evolution of Walt Whitman* (Cambridge, Mass., 2 vols., 1960, 1962).

him. So, if we then examine closely this quality of Whitman's awareness, even though we do not pretend to be professional psychologists, we are bound to recognize that it emanates not from a mood of serene self-possession and self-assurance, as Whitman blatantly orated, but rather from a pervasive self-distrust. There is a nervous instability at the bottom of his histrionic ostentation—an anxiety which foreign critics understandably call neurotic. In fact these critics, even our friends, tell us that this is precisely what Americans are: insecure, gangling, secret worriers behind a façade of braggadocio, unable to live and to let live.

Some of the articles in the massive supplement on *American Writing To-Day* which the *Times* of London brought out in September 1954 are by Americans, but one called "A Search for the Conscience of a People" sounds as though of English authorship; either way, it declares an opinion I have frequently heard in England and on the Continent. Americans, particularly from the early nineteenth century on, have been in search of an identity. "The Englishman," says the writer, "takes his Englishness for granted; the Frenchman does not constantly have to be looking over his shoulder to see if his Frenchiness is still there." The reason for this national anxiety is that being an American is not something to be inherited so much as something to be achieved. This, our observer concludes, is "a complex fate."

Surely it is, as complex for a nation as for a person. Yet what compounds complexity is that all the time we are searching for ourselves we keep insisting that we are a simple, uncomplicated people. We have no social classes, our regional variations are not great compared with those of France or Germany, no weight of tradition compels us to travel in well-worn ruts. From coast to coast we all buy the same standard brands in chain stores built to a standard pattern, we see the same television shows, laugh at the same jokes, adore the same movie stars, and hear the same singing commercials. How, then, can we be complex? Europe is complex—it is civilized, old, tormented with ancient memories, but we are as natural as children. Then, why are we so nervous? Why do we so worry about our identity? One can imagine an English college setting up a conference on the constitutional principles of the Cromwellian Protectorate, or on the issues of the Reform Bill of 1832, but never, I am sure, one entitled, "On Values in the British Tradition." At Oxford and Cambridge those would be so much taken for granted that even to mention them aloud would be bad form, and to insinuate that they needed discussion would become indecent exposure.

As far as I read the history of the West, I find only one other great civilization that faced an analogous predicament, and that was the Roman Empire. Not the Republic: the original Rome emerged gradually, as have the modern nations of Europe, out of the mists of legend, mythology, vaguely remembered migrations of prehistoric peoples. The Republic had traditions that nobody created, which had been there beyond the memory of mankind, atavistic attachments to the soil. But after the murderous civil wars and wars of conquest, the old Roman stock was either wiped out or so mixed with the races of the Mediterranean that the Empire had become as conglomerate a population as ours, the social cohesion as artificial. As with us, there was not time to let the people fuse by natural and organic growth over several centuries: Rome was no longer a country but a continent, no longer a people but an institution. The aggregation would have fallen apart in the first century B.C. had not somebody, by main force, by deliberate, conscious exertion, imposed unity upon it. Julius Caesar attempted this, but his nephew and ultimately his successor, Augustus Caesar, did it.

This analogy, as I say, has often struck me, but I should be hesitant to construct so seemingly far-fetched a parallel did I not have at least the authority of Alfred North Whitehead for entertaining it. Actually, it was a favorite speculation with Mr. Whitehead, and I may well have got it from him in some now forgotten conversation. However, it comes back to us, as though Whitehead were still speaking, in Lucien Price's *Dialogues*. Augustus Caesar's foundation of an empire would not, Whitehead agrees, satisfy our ideal of liberty, yet it saved civilization. It is, in the very deliberateness of the deed, a complete contrast to the unconscious evolution of the English constitution. Nobody, Whitehead remarks, can say at exactly what point the idea of a limited monarchy came in; the conception originated with no one person nor at any specific time, and even today no scientifically precise definition is possible. Though the Roman Empire was not the result of any long-range plan, once it existed, it was recognized as being what it had become, and systematically organized; the British acquired their empire, as the saying goes, in a fit of absence of mind, and have never quite found a way to administer the whole of it. So they surrender to nature and let irresistible forces guide it into forms that are not at all "imperial."

Now Whitehead's point is that the only other creation of a nation and an administration by conscious effort, the only other time statesmen assumed control of historic destinies and, refusing to let nature take its course, erected by main force a society, was the American Revolution and the Constitutional Convention. To read the history of the first sessions of the Congress under President Washington in 1789 and 1790 is to be driven either to laughter or to tears, or to both. Even more than in the first years of Augustus' principate, I suspect, it presents the spectacle of men trying to live from a blueprint. The document prescribed two houses of legislators, a court, and an executive; as men of cultivation they had some knowledge of parliamentary procedure, but beyond such elementary rules of order they knew not how to behave. They did not know how to address the President, and nobody could figure in what manner a cabinet officer was related to the Congress. That is why, although certain customs have been agreed upon, such as "Senatorial courtesy," we do not have the immemorial traditions that govern, let us say, conduct in the House of Commons. Hence, when one of our customs appears to be violated, we behold a Select Committee of Senators trying to find out what the Senate is. We can do nothing by instinct.

As a matter of historical fact, Professor Whitehead might have pushed that moment of conscious decision further back than the Constitutional Convention. Settlers came to the colonies for a number of reasons that were, so to speak, in the situation rather than in their minds, yet none came without making an anterior decision in his mind. They may have been forced by famine, economic distress, a lust for gold or land, by religious persecutions, but somewhere in their lives there had to be the specific moment when they said to themselves or to each other, "Let's get out, let's go to America." The only exception to this rule is, of course, the Negroes; they came not because they wanted to but because they were captured and brought by force. Maybe that is why they, of all our varied people, seem to be the only sort that can do things by instinct. Maybe that is why Willie Mays is the greatest of contemporary outfielders.

Also, the Indians did not come by *malice prepense*. They are the only Americans whose historical memory goes back to the origin of the land itself; they do not have to look over their shoulders to see if their Indianness is still there. So, they astonished the first Americans by acting upon instinct. One of the most charming demonstrations of this native spontaneity was Pocahontas' rush to the block to save Captain John Smith from having his brains beaten out. Later on, Indian rushes were not so charming, but even in warfare they exhibited a headlong impetuosity that bespoke an incapacity to make deliberate plans. They could never construct an assembly line or work out a split-second television schedule.

As for Captain John Smith himself, we may doubt that this impetuous adventurer came at first to America out of the sort of conscious decision Whitehead had in mind. To begin with, America meant no more to him than Turkey, and Pocahontas no more than the Lady Tragabigzanda, who inspired his escape from slavery in Constantinople—at least, so he says. But even he, who became a temporary American by accident, after a brief two-years' experience of the land, realized that here lay a special destiny. The initial disorders at Jamestown—which were considerable—convinced him that God, being angry with the company, plagued them with famine and sickness. By the time he was summoned home, the dream of an empire in the wilderness was upon him, and he reviewed these afflictions not as merely the customary and universal rebukes of providence upon sinners, but as ones specially dispensed for the guidance of Americans. He spent twenty-two years selflessly propagandizing for settlement. By 1624, after he had digested the lesson of his intense initiation, he had thoroughly comprehended that migrating to America was serious business, much too strenuous for those he called the "Tuftaffaty" gentlemen who had come along, as we might say, only for the ride, in the expectation of picking up easy gold from the ground. No. Mere tourists, traveling nobles, would not build an empire; it needed people who, having decided to remove, would as a consequence of decision put their backs into the labor. In 1624 he reprinted and emphasized a cry he had written to the company back in 1608, when the lesson was just beginning to dawn upon him:

> When you send againe I intreat you rather send but thirty Carpenters, husbandmen, gardiners, fisher men, blacksmiths, masons, and diggers up of trees, roots, well provided; then a thousand of such as we haue: for except wee be able both to lodge them, and feed them, the most will consume with want of necessaries before they can be made good for any thing.

Smith was more prophetic than even he comprehended: America has not time to make people good for anything; they have to be good for something to start with.

The outstanding case of the conscious act of decision was, we all know, the Puritan migration to New England. Whenever we find the religious incentive strong among immigrating groups, something of the same history can be found, but the New Englanders were so articulate, produced so voluminous a literature in explanation of their conduct, and through the spreading of the stock across the continent have left so deep an impress on the country, that the Puritan definition of purpose has been in effect appropriated by immigrants of other faiths, by those who in the nineteenth century left lands of a culture utterly different from the English. The act was formally committed to paper by the "Agreement" signed and ratified at Cambridge in the summer of 1629. The great John Winthrop, the Moses of this exodus, was able to give full expression to the idea even before he set foot ashore; he did it by preaching a lay sermon aboard the flagship of the fleet, on the deck of the *Arbella,* when still in mid-ocean. It was published under the title "A Modell of Christian Charity," in 1630. Chronologically speaking, Smith and a few others in Virginia, two or three at Plymouth, published works on America before the "Modell," but in relation to the principal theme of the American mind, the necessity laid upon it for decision, Winthrop stands at the beginning of our consciousness.

We wonder whether, once Southampton and Land's End had sunk beneath the eastern horizon, once he had turned his face irrevocably westward, Winthrop suddenly realized that he was sailing not toward another island but a continent, and that once there the problem would be to keep the people fixed in the mold of the Cambridge Agreement, to prevent them from following the lure of real estate into a dispersion that would quickly alter their character. At any rate, the announced doctrine of his sermon is that God distinguishes persons in this world by rank, some high, some low, some rich, some poor. Ostensibly, then, he is propounding a European class structure; but when he comes to the exhortation, he does not so much demand that inferiors remain in pious subjection to superiors, but rather he calls upon all, gentlemen and commoners, to be knit together in this work as one man. He seems apprehensive that old sanctions will not work; he wants all the company to swear an oath, to confirm their act of will. This band have entered into a covenant with God to perform the specific work: "We have taken out a Comission, the Lord hath giuen vs leaue to drawe our owne Articles, we haue professed to enterprise these Accions vpon these and these ends." Because this community is not merely to reproduce an English social hierarchy, because over and above that, more important even than an ordered way of life, it has a responsibility to live up to certain enumerated purposes. Therefore this society, unlike any in Europe, will be rewarded by divine providence to the extent that it fulfills the covenant. Likewise it will be afflicted with plagues, fires, disasters, to the extent that it fails. Profound though he was, Winthrop probably did not entirely realize how novel, how radical, was his sermon; he assumed he was merely theorizing about this projected community in relation to the Calvinist divinity, absolute sovereign of the universe. What in reality he was telling the proto-Americans was that they could not just blunder along like ordinary people, seeking wealth and opportunity for their children. Every citizen of this new society would have to know, completely understand, reckon every day with, the enunciated terms on which it was brought into being, according to which it would survive or perish. This duty of conscious realization lay as heavy upon the humblest, the least educated, the most stupid, as upon the highest, the most learned, the cleverest.

There is, I think all will acknowledge, a grandeur in Winthrop's formulation of the rationale for a society newly entered into a bond with Almighty God to accomplish "these and these ends." However, enemies of the Puritans even at the time did more than suggest that the conception also bespeaks an astounding arrogance. Who was Winthrop, critics asked, and who were these Puritans, that they could take unto themselves the notion that the Infinite God would bind Himself to particular terms only with them, while He was leaving France and Germany and even England to shift for themselves? One can argue that coming down from this Puritan conception of America's unique destiny—"Wee must consider," said Winthrop, "that wee shall be as a Citty vpon a Hill, the eies of all people vppon us"—has descended that glib American phrase, "God's country," which so amuses when it does not exasperate our allies. But the important thing to note is that after a century or more of experience on this continent, the communities, especially the Puritan colonies, found the covenant theory no longer adequate. It broke down because it tried, in disregard of experience, in disregard of the frontier and a thriving commerce, to stereotype the image of America, to confine it to the Procrustean bed of a priori conception. Not that the theology failed to account for empirical phenomena; only, the effort to keep these aligned within the original rubrics became too exhausting. The American mind discarded this notion of its personality because the ingenuity required to maintain it was more than men had time or energy to devise.

The little states suffered many adversities—plagues, wars, crop failures, floods, internal dissension. According to Winthrop's reasoning, the communities could not accept these as the normal hazards of settling a wilderness or augmenting the wealth; they had to see in every reverse an intentional punishment for their sins. By the time they had undergone several Indian wars and frequent hurricanes, a tabulation of their sins would obviously become so long as to be crushing. We can imagine, for instance, what Cotton Mather would have made in his Sabbath sermons, morning and afternoon, each over two hours in duration, of the fact that New England was struck in the year 1954 by not one but *two* hurricanes, and that the first, proceeding according to divine appointment, carried away the steeple of his own church, the Old North. He would perfectly understand why, since the population did not immediately reform their criminal habits, even upon such a dramatic admonition, another storm must come close upon the first. Were we still livingly persuaded that we actually are God's country, we would not in the aftermath of hurricanes argue with insurance companies or complain about the Weather Bureau, but would be down on our knees, bewailing the transgressions of New England, searching our memories to recall, and to repent of, a thousand things we have contrived to forget. We would be reaffirming our Americanism by promising with all our hearts to mend the evil ways that brought upon us the avenging fury of hurricanes Carol and Edna.

In pious sections of America at the time of the Revolution some vestiges of the covenant doctrine remained. Historians point out how effective was the propaganda device employed by the Continental Congresses, their calling for national days of fasting and humiliations. Historians regard these appeals as cynical because most of the leaders, men of the Enlightenment, were emancipated from so crude a theology as Winthrop's. Certainly you find no trace of it in the Declaration of Independence. Yet I often wonder whether historians fully comprehend that the old-fashioned religious sanction could be dispensed with only because the Revolutionary theorists had found a substitute which seemed to them adequate to account for a more complex situation. Being classicists, they read Latin; while nurtured on authors of Republican Rome, they were as much if not more trained in the concepts of the Empire, not only in writers like Tacitus and Marcus Aurelius, but in the Roman law. Which is to say that the imperial idea, as Augustus made it manifest, was second nature to them. Whether Madison appreciated as keenly as Whitehead the highly conscious nature of Augustus' statesmanship, he had no qualms about going at the business of constitution-making in a legal, imperial spirit. The problem was to bring order out of chaos, to set up a government, to do it efficiently and quickly. There was no time to let Nature, gradually, by her mysterious alchemy, bring us eventually to some such fruition as the British Constitution; even so, had time not been so pressing, Madison and the framers saw nothing incongruous in taking time by the forelock, drawing up the blueprint, and so bringing into working operation a government by fiat. Analysts may argue that separation of powers, for instance, had in practice if not in theory come about by historical degrees within the colonial governments, but the framers did not much appeal to that sort of wisdom. They had a universal rule: power must not be concentrated, it must be divided into competing balances; wherefore America decrees its individuality through a three-fold sovereign, executive, legislative, and judicial, and then still further checks that authority by an enumerated Bill of Rights.

The Revolutionary chiefs were patriots, but on the whole they were less worried by the problem of working out an exceptional character for America than the spokesmen of any other period. Patriotism was a virtue, in the Roman sense, but one could be an ardent American without, in the Age of Reason, having to insist that there were special reasons in America, reasons not present in other lands, why citizens must inordinately love this nation. Franklin, Jefferson, Madison were as near to true cosmopolitans as the United States has ever produced. But on the other hand, in order to win the war, pamphleteers for the patriot side did have to assert that the Revolution carried the hopes not only of America but of the world. The immense effectiveness of Thomas Paine's *Common Sense,* for example, consisted not so much in its contention that independence of England made common sense as in its implication that only America was close enough to Nature, only these simple people were sufficiently uncorrupted by the vices of civilizations to permit common sense to operate at all.

It is a fanciful speculation, but suppose that the intellectual world of the late eighteenth century had persisted unchanged from 1776 to the present. In that case, through one and three-quarters centuries we should have had a steady and undisturbing task: merely refining on and perfecting the image of ourselves we first beheld in the mirror of the Declaration of Independence. Had there been no Romantic poetry, no novels by Scott, no railroads and steam engines, no Darwin, no machine gun, no dynamo, no automobile, no airplane, no atomic bomb, we would have had no reason to suppose ourselves other than what we were at Concord and Yorktown. We would remain forever formerly embattled farmers listening complacently from our cornfields to the echoes rolling round the world of the shot we fired, without working ourselves into a swivet worrying about whether we should again shoot. However, even before Jefferson and Adams were dead in 1826, the mind of America was already infected from abroad with concepts of man and nature which rendered those of the patriarchs as inadequate as the covenant theology, while at the same time the nation itself was being transformed by an increase of population and of machines, and so had to rethink entirely anew the question of its identity. The French Revolution and the Napoleonic Wars, it is a truism to say, aroused all over Europe a spirit of nationalism which the eighteenth century had supposed forever extinct. One manifestation of the new era was an assiduous search in each country for primitive, tribal, barbaric origins. Germans went back to medieval legends, to the Niebelungen Lied, to fairy tales. Sir Walter Scott gave the English a new sense of their history, so that the ideal British hero was no longer Marlborough or Pitt, but Ivanhoe, Rob Roy, and Quentin Durward, while the yeomen suddenly gloried in having come down from Gurth the Swineherd. Realizing that the evolution of English society as well as of the Constitution had been organic, natural, spontaneous, illogical, the English renounced reason; they challenged America to show what more profound excuse for being it had than a dull and rationalistic convention. All at once, instead of being the hope of the enlightened world, America found itself naked of legends, primitive virtues, archaic origins. It might be full of bustle and progress, but romantically speaking, it was uninteresting, had no personality.

Americans tried to answer by bragging about the future, but that would not serve. In the first half of the nineteenth century many of our best minds went hard to work to prove that we too were a nation in some deeper sense than mere wilfulness. At this time Europeans began that accusation which some of them still launch, which drives us to a frenzy: "You are not a country, you are a continent." Not at all, said James Fenimore Cooper; we too have our legends, our misty past, our epic figures, our symbolic heroes. To prove this, he created Natty Bumppo—Leatherstocking the Deerslayer, the Pathfinder, the embodiment of an America as rooted in the soil, as primordial as the Germany that gave birth to Siegfried.

Professor Allan Nevins recently brought out a selection from the five Leatherstocking volumes of the portions that tell the biography of Natty Bumppo, arranged them in chronological order instead of the sequence in which Cooper composed them, and thus reminded us that Cooper did create a folk-hero, achieving in his way a success comparable to Homer's. Modern readers have difficulty with Cooper's romances because they do seem cluttered with pompous courtships and tiresome disquisitions; these were not annoyances to readers in his day (though I must say that even then some critics found his women rather wooden), so that they had no trouble in appreciating the magnificence of his Scout and of Chingachgook. Mr. Nevins says that when he was a boy, he and his companions played at being Natty and Chingachgook; children nowadays do not read Cooper— I am told that if they can so much as read at all, they peruse nothing but comic books—and they play at being Superman and space cadets. But for years Cooper more than any single figure held up the mirror in which several generations of Americans saw the image of themselves they most wished to see—a free-ranging individualist, very different from Winthrop's covenanted saint or from Paine's common-sensical Revolutionary.

Cooper persuaded not only thousands of Americans that he was delineating their archetype but also Europeans. One does not readily associate the name of Balzac with Cooper, but Balzac was an enthusiastic reader of Leatherstocking and in 1841 wrote a resounding review, praising the mighty figures but explaining what was an even more important element in Cooper's achievement:

> The magical prose of Cooper not only embodies the spirit of the river, its shores, the forest and its trees; but it exhibits the minutest details, combined with the grandest outline. The vast solitudes, in which we penetrate, become in a moment deeply interesting. . . . When the spirit of solitude communes with us, when the first calm of these eternal shades pervades us, when we hover over this virgin vegetation, our hearts are filled with emotion.

Here was indeed the answer to the problem of American self-recognition! We may have come to the land by an act of will, but despite ourselves, we have become parts of the landscape. The vastness of the continent, its very emptiness, instead of meaning that we are blank and formless, makes us deeply interesting amid our solitudes. Our history is not mechanical, calculated; it is as vibrant with emotion as the history of Scott's Britain.

On every side spokesmen for the period between Jackson and Lincoln developed this thesis; by the time of the Civil War it had become the major articulate premise of American self-consciousness. Let us take one example. George Bancroft's *History of the United States* had a success with the populace at large which no academic historian today dares even dream of. When he came to the Revolution, he recast it into the imagery of nature and instinct, so that even Jefferson became as spontaneous (and as authentic a voice of the landscape) as Natty Bumppo:

> There is an analogy between early American politics and the earliest heroic poems. Both were spontaneous, and both had the vitality of truth. Long as natural affection endures, the poems of Homer will be read with delight; long as freedom lives on earth, the early models of popular legislation and action in America will be admired.

So, for Bancroft and his myriad readers, the lesson of the Revolution and the Constitution was precisely opposite to what Whitehead sees in the story. Prudent statesmanship, Bancroft says, would have asked time to ponder, "would have dismissed the moment for decision by delay." Conscious effort "would have compared the systems of government, and would have lost from hestitation the glory of opening a new era on mankind." But the common people—the race of Natty Bumppo—did not deliberate: "The humble train-bands at Concord acted, and God was with them."

We can easily laugh at such language. We may agree that Cooper and Bancroft were noble men, patriotic Americans, but to our ears something rings terribly false in their hymns to the natural nation. Perhaps the deepest flaw is their unawareness of, or their wilful blindness to, the fact that they are constructing in a most highly conscious manner an image of America as the creation of unconscious instinct. They apply themselves to supplying the country with an archaic past as purposefully as General Motors supplies it with locomotion. They recast the conception of America into terms actually as a priori as Winthrop's covenant, and then do just what he did: they say that these spontaneous and heroic terms are objectively true, fixed and eternal. Within them and only them America shall always make decisions, shall always, like the train-bands at Concord, act in reference to their unalterable exactions. We are what we have always been, and so we are predictable. He who acts otherwise is not American.

Behind the Puritan, the Revolutionary, and the Romantic conceptions of social identity lies still another premise; in all these formulations it is *not* articulated. I might put it roughly like this: they all take for granted that a personality, a national one as well as an individual, is something pre-existing, within which an invariable and foreseeable pattern of decision reigns. If, let us say, a man is brave, he will always act bravely. If a nation is proud, chivalric, religious, it will be Spanish; if it is frivolous, amatory, cynical, it will be French. I need hardly remind you that a powerful movement in modern thought has, in a hundred ways, called in question this "deterministic" method. There may be, and indeed there are, physical conditions, such as sex or size, such as climate or mineral resources; but these are not what make the personality we deal with, the nation we must understand. What constitutes the present being is a series of past decisions; in that sense, no act is spontaneous, no decision is imposed, either by the covenant, by common sense, or by Nature.

In the later nineteenth century, as Romantic conceptions of the universe died out, another determined effort was made to recast the image of America, this time in the language of Darwinian evolution. In this century, as the faith weakened that evolution would automatically carry us forward, we have, in general, reformulated our personality into a creature preternaturally adept in production—the jeep and the know-how. Each successive remodeling retains something of the previous form: we echo the covenant not only in the phrase "God's country," but when we pray for the blessing of heaven upon our arms and our industries; we invoke Revolutionary language in our belief that we, of all the world, are pre-eminently endowed with common sense; we also, by calling ourselves "nature's noblemen," imagine ourselves possessed of the pioneer virtues of Natty Bumppo, yet simultaneously suppose ourselves evolving into an industrial paradise, complete with television and the deep freeze. When we try to bundle up these highly disparate notions into a single definition, we are apt to come up with some such blurb as "The American Way of Life."

I am attempting to tell a long story in too short a compass, but I hope my small point is moderately clear. As a nation, we have had a strenuous experience, as violent as that Walt Whitman records; he spent a lifetime trying to put America into his book, only to discover himself bedeviled by changing insights, buffeted by unpredicted emotions, rapid shifts, bewildered by new elements demanding incorporation in the synthesis. He who endeavors to fix the personality of America in one eternal, unchangeable pattern not only understands nothing of how a personality is created, but comprehends little of how this nation has come along thus far. He who seeks repose in a unitary conception in effect abandons personality. His motives may be of the best: he wants to preserve, just as he at the moment understands it, the distinctive American essence—the covenant, common sense, the natural grandeur, the American Way of Life. But he fools himself if he supposes that the explanation for America is to be found in the conditions of America's existence rather than in the existence itself. A man *is* his decisions, and the great uniqueness of this nation is simply that here the record of conscious decision is more precise, more open and explicit than in most countries. This gives us no warrant to claim that we are higher in any conceivable scale of values; it merely permits us to realize that to which the English observer calls attention, that being an American is not something inherited but something to be achieved.

He says this condemns us to a "complex fate." Complexity is worrisome, imparts no serenity, only anxiety. It keeps us wondering whether we might now be something other, and probably better, than we are had we in the past decided otherwise, and this in turn makes decision in the present even more nerve-wracking. Trying to escape from such anxiety by affixing our individuality to a scheme of unchanging verities is a natural response. Yet our national history promises no success to the frantic gesture. Generalizations about the American character can amount to no more than a statistical survey of the decisions so far made, and these warrant in the way of hypotheses about those yet to be made only the most tentative estimates. However, if my analysis has any truth in it, a back-handed sort of generalization does emerge: he who would fix the pattern of decision by confining the American choice to one and only one mode of response— whether this be in politics, diplomacy, economics, literary form, or morality itself—such a one, in the light of our history, is the truly "Un-American."

DECLENSION IN A BIBLE
COMMONWEALTH

EVEN a Puritan society, even a people chosen of God, if they undertake to settle a wilderness, will meet with hardship and sometimes with disaster. Leaders will die, since men cannot live forever; winds and earthquakes strike equally the chosen and the unchosen; caterpillars will consume the grain of the righteous unless God contrive a very exceptional providence to divert them, while saints no less than other men must run the hazard of pestilence, drought, the measles, or shipwreck. When such afflictions overtake a community of the unregenerate, they know not what to do. They put the blame upon second causes or upon blind chance; they have no way to overcome the evil and must either endure or perish. But a holy commonwealth of Puritan saints is fully equipped with a method for meeting emergency. At the first flick of the lash, the whole body politic assembles for a ceremony of public humiliation and communal repentance, wherein the people take the responsibility for the disaster upon themselves, asserting that the fault is entirely theirs and that God has punished them justly and necessarily for their sins. Thereupon the way for accomplishing their relief becomes obvious: they must resolve to mend their ways and beseech the Lord to look with favor upon their reformation. Whole days should be officially set apart for these observances, called in New England "days of humiliation" or "fast days," to be observed not with complete fasting—that extremity was Popish superstition—but with abstinence from all but the essentials of life, even, according to one instruction, from the pleasures of marriage. The principal action of the day should be the delivery of a public sermon before all the society, in which the minister, the spokesman for the community, would set forth the issues of the occasion, review the affliction, and make articulate the determination of the group henceforth to banish whatever sins had brought the distress upon it.

From the beginning Puritan settlements employed this method, and at first with spectacular success. At Plymouth in July 1622 the colony was suffering from a drought which, continued a few days more, would have reduced it to starvation; the authorities appointed a day of humiliation and the next day rain fell, whereupon a second day was set apart for universal thanksgiving.[1] The advance guard of the Massachusetts Bay

Published in the *Proceedings* of the American Antiquarian Society, April 1941, pp. 3-60.

[1] W. DeLoss Love, *The Fast and Thanksgiving Days of New England* (Boston, 1895), pp. 81-85.

Company, even before it reached American shores, was saved from storms and seasickness whenever the Reverend Mr. Higginson bade them observe a fast aboard ship.[2] The procedure worked a memorable result at the Bay in February of 1631: when the fleet had landed the previous June, the canny Winthrop had realized that there was not enough food for the winter and hastened the *Lyon* back to England; by February provisions were almost exhausted and the people appointed a day of solemn humiliation, with the result that the *Lyon* immediately hove into sight. The colony hastened to celebrate a day of thanksgiving, not to Winthrop—who was but the instrument of providence—but to the Lord Himself, who brought the *Lyon* safely into Boston Harbor, no doubt in direct response to the ceremonial humiliation.[3]

The meticulous promptness with which God answered these early fasts left an indelible impression upon the New England mind and furnished the models for later imitation. For a time there seems to have been some indecision as to who should issue the summons. Ideally the call ought to come from the churches, since it was in the churches that men would confess their sins and pray for relief. At the Bay they did originally determine the event, and when the General Court first took the initiative, on September 3, 1634, it contented itself with expressing merely a "generall desire" that a day of humiliation be observed throughout the several plantations.[4] For years many congregations went through the form of voting to concur in fasts proclaimed by the state, and the politicians were always assumed to be acting at the desire of the churches, many fasts being ordained explicitly "upon the motion of the elders."[5] Yet gradually, because public distresses affected all alike, the legislatures assumed the function of calling the people to repentance, and soon entrusted to governors and councils the right to proclaim fasts during the recess. The General Court in Massachusetts first openly commanded a fast in 1637 when it designated a day on which all inhabitants should bewail the Antinomian dissensions[6]—the occasion on which Wheelwright delivered his "incendiary" sermon and almost frustrated the purpose of the Lord. Antinomianism so obviously endangered the whole body politic that it behooved the central government both to take over the one method that would insure the public safety and to make certain that all the public took part. The Plymouth codification of 1636 officially required the governor and assistants to command days of fasting and thanksgiving "as occasion shall be offered."[7] In Connecticut, as in Massachusetts, the churches first determined the

---

2 *Ibid.,* pp. 95-96.

3 *Ibid.,* pp. 103-06; *Winthrop's Journal,* ed. J. K. Hosmer (New York, 1908), vol. I, pp. 57-59.

4 *Records of the Governor and Company of the Massachusetts Bay,* ed. N. B. Shurtleff (Boston, 1853-1854), vol. I, p. 128.

5 Love, *Fast and Thanksgiving Days,* pp. 221-24, 237-38.

6 *Mass. Records,* vol. I, p. 187.

7 *Records of the Colony of New Plymouth* (Boston, 1855-1861), vol. II, p. 18.

days, but gradually the General Court assumed the power of choosing those observed by the whole colony, and in 1655 delegated it to the magistrates during the intervals between sessions.[8] However, particular churches were everywhere free to observe fasts in order to deal with local difficulties, and during the English Civil Wars, when colonial governments were obliged to tread softly lest their sympathy with Parliament cause them to offend the King, they ordered few public observances and left the churches to keep their own as they saw fit.[9]

Thus the colonies settled upon a ritual, and the custom throve through the seventeenth century. Whatever afflicted them or grieved them became the occasion for a day of communal humiliation, when worldly pursuits were laid aside and the people gathered in the churches to acknowledge their sins, to promise reformation, and to pray for relief. Fasts were proclaimed because of dissensions and evil plots, "to prepare the way of friends which wee hope may bee upon comeing to us," for lack of rain or too much rain, for excessive snow, cold or heat, for hailstorms, fires, winds, plagues, pests, the smallpox or witchcraft, for the deaths of leaders or ominous prodigies like eclipses or comets. Some of the later days were not quite so clearly and decisively rewarded as were the first. December 13, 1638, for example, appointed as a fast day after the Hutchinson party were banished, was followed the next night by a tempest of wind and snow in which many lives were lost. The shock was so great that some momentarily lost faith in the method and ventured to ask if there were no better way of seeking the Lord, "because he seemed to discountenance the means of reconciliation." The Court hurriedly sought the advice of the elders who, after deliberation, concluded that by no means should the practice be abandoned, but rather that a second day should be kept "to seek further into the causes of such displeasure."[10] Innumerable colonial and local fasts were observed during the dark months of King Philip's War, and theological perplexities sprouted anew as day after day was followed by military disaster, but the clergy had a ready explanation: the people had not sufficiently abased themselves or truly repented. Therefore they should keep not fewer but still more days of public humiliation.[11]

Behind the practice of these fasts lay a conscious theory, which in the first place was an inevitable corollary of Calvinism, and in the second was for these colonists immeasurably reinforced by the peculiar theology of New England. In Calvinist eyes the physical universe is under the continuous and unceasing direction of God's providence. Whatever comes to pass, a rainstorm, an attack of the smallpox, an earthquake, does not result from mere natural law; it is an event specifically ordained by an

---

[8] Love, *Fast and Thanksgiving Days*, p. 145; *Public Records of the Colony of Connecticut*, ed. J. H. Trumbull (Hartford, 1850-1890), vol. I, pp. 98, 277.

[9] Love, *Fast and Thanksgiving Days*, p. 156.

[10] *Winthrop's Journal*, vol. I, p. 291.

[11] Love, *Fast and Thanksgiving Days*, pp. 192-200.

intelligent being for intelligible reasons. Afflictions do not just happen, but are sent from on high; public calamities are moral judgments upon a sinful people, literally "acts of God." The moral status of a people is therefore written out in events: if they are sinful, they suffer; if they are virtuous, they prosper. For this reason all Calvinists objected strenuously to annual celebrations, to religious feasts, like Christmas, that came about merely through the mechanical revolution of the calendar. Such days could take no account of the moment, whereas the proper time could be discovered only by a careful study of God's providence as it unrolled in daily events; whenever these revealed Him tending toward either anger or benevolence, men were immediately to respond with lamentation or with joy, "pro temporibus et causis." To fix upon any one date for a recurrent festival of humiliation, the Puritan said, was "will-worship," and a pious people may solemnize a fast only for a demonstrable cause— "when there is some notable or eminent publick Danger."[12] A people would outrage God should they humiliate themselves when He was smiling upon them, and be guilty of blasphemy did they rejoice while He was chastising them. When they come under the rod of His wrath, and then foregather for repentance, He may listen to their prayers and grant them deliverance. When He is pleased to bless them, if they promptly show their gratitude in a day of thanksgiving, He is the more likely to continue their felicity. In the forefront of the Calvinist mind was the conception of an absolute sovereign whose will decreed the smallest event, and therefore Calvinists devised the ceremonial of a public humiliation as the best and surest method of relieving public misfortunes.

In the colonies this general Calvinist conception of providence was further particularized, and thereby further implicated in the career of the societies, by certain additions which New England theologians made to the original idea. Long before they came to America, they had become members of a school of doctrine now known as the "federal" or "covenant" theology. They revised or amplified pure Calvinism by defining the relationship between the predestined elect and his God not merely as the passive reception of grace, as did Calvin, but as an active covenant, after the model of that between Abraham and Jehovah in the Book of Genesis. According to this doctrine, the saint was redeemed not simply by an infusion of grace, but by being taken into a league with God, an explicit compact drawn up between two partners, wherein the saint promised to obey God's will and God promised infallibly to grant him salvation. Starting with this notion of a personal and inward covenant, the theologians extended it to the church and the state. They argued that a nation of saints, all of whom were personally in covenant with God, would also be in covenant with Him as a body politic, that as each individual had inwardly subscribed the bond, so a society formed by their regenerate action would swear to the covenant in outward unison. Hence, not alone

---

[12] Thomas Thacher, *A Fast of Gods Chusing* (Boston, 1678), p. 5.

in the privacy of their devotions, but in the forum of the commonwealth they would draw up a concrete treaty, they and God setting down the terms they would observe each toward the other, they promising to obey His law and He to reward their obedience. Under these happy conditions the New Englanders believed that their governments, alone among the nations of the earth, had been founded, and the circumstances of settlement lent plausibility to their belief. The idea that a whole nation might be taken into covenant with God had been invented by the English originators of the theology and was then taken up by their pupils, who later led the migration. At first, in the 1620's, they endeavored to argue that England had once entered into such a covenant, in which it had promised to erect the true polity, and so they had made capital out of England's economic and military reverses, proclaiming them a fitting punishment for a nation that was failing its plighted word. Thomas Hooker explained, while still at Dedham in Essex, that when a people flee the command of the Lord and break His bonds, "when we walke after our own wayes, are not governed by God, and content to be ruled by his holy word in all things, then are we said to forsake his covenant."[13] But no one could point to the precise time and place in which England had taken the covenant; individual saints might be in the covenant of grace, yet the majority of people obviously were not, and hence could hardly be thought of as in a national covenant with God. The New England communities of the 1630's were another story. Here the people entered into a holy society upon their own volition, inspired by their devotion to the word of God and their desire for pure ordinances; they joined in the migration deliberately in order to found sanctified commonwealths, and by that very act swore a covenant with God not merely as individuals but as a people.[14] The first and the unquestioned premise of the New England mind was the conviction that unlike other states these had not come into being through accident, by natural growth or geographical proximity, but were founded in the conscious determination and the free will of saints, who had migrated for the specific ends of holy living. Voluntarism was reconciled with authoritarianism, in politics as in private life, by the hypothesis that none should have the benefit of the law but those who had subjected themselves to it. Just as the liberated will of the saint is at once submitted to the rule of the Bible, so the sovereign power of the holy commonwealth is committed through a national covenant to performing only those actions which God commands, while God will be the patron only of such nations as freely put themselves under His sway.

The covenant of God and the nation was necessarily different from the covenant of God and the individual in one important respect: a society cannot receive the rewards of obedience in another world, for only particular

13 Thomas Hooker, *The Faithful Covenanter* (London, 1644), p. 11.
14 *Winthrop Papers* (Boston, 1931), vol. II, p. 294.

individuals can be translated to heaven. Consequently, the compensations of social rectitude must be given here and now, in the tangible form of material success and victory over enemies. Of course a Calvinist God was originally free to dispense misery and happiness according to no rule but His tyrannical pleasure. He still deals with heathen nations just as He wishes, though He is apt to observe a few principles of common equity and will generally give more prosperity to the sober and industrious than to the violent and rapacious. With a Christian people who are not yet in covenant with Him, He is equally free to behave as He likes, and may afflict them when they are virtuous and prosper them when they are sinning, though with Christians He is more apt to accord His dispensations to their behavior, and we may be fairly certain that a sinning nation will sooner or later come to grief. But the situation is altered when a nation is formally in covenant with God. Then the master of the universe, the absolute monarch of creation, has limited His awful power to the terms of the covenant; He is bound by His own consent, but nevertheless He is bound. Thereafter He can inflict punishment only when the society has deserved rebuke. A nation so fortunate as to be in His covenant is no longer exposed to inexplicable and irrational distress; its public welfare will wax or wane with its morality, and it will receive nothing either of good or evil but what it merits. The saints had been reluctantly forced to admit that God's dispensations with England seemed to come under the head of His dealing with a heathen people rather than with a Christian society, let alone with a covenanted tribe. Hence nothing could be accomplished there, for God was not bound to treat England by any rule of justice, but in New England, as Winthrop told the settlers, men would always know where they stood: after God ratifies this covenant, which He will do by bringing us safely to Massachusetts Bay, if then we strictly perform the articles of our bond, all will go well with us, but if we neglect the ends we ourselves have propounded, if we "shall fall to embrace this present world and prosecute our carnall intencions," the Lord will break out in wrath against us as a perjured people.[15] The founders of New England imprinted this conception upon the New England mind. John Cotton declared that wherever God's servants may be, because they have a covenant with Him, when they "crave a blessing, and mourne for the want of it, God will provide it shall be stretched forth upon the whole Country they live in,"[16] and He will provide not only spiritual benefits but also "whatsoever is good in the creature."[17] If a covenanted people are true to their bond, said Cobbet, God "will tender them deliverances as their federall right"; all peoples, even pagans, are sometimes delivered by "common providences" which spring from the simple mercy of God,

---

15 *Winthrop Papers* (Boston, 1931), vol. II, p. 294.
16 John Cotton, *The Way of Life* (London, 1641), p. 74.
17 Cotton, *Christ the Fountaine of Life* (London, 1651), p. 33.

but these are not the sort of special providences that rescue a covenanted nation from affliction, "such as spring from the vertue of the Covenant."[18] But on the other hand, just "As all good things are conveyed to Gods people, not barely by common providence, but by speciall Covenant," so whatever evils they meet with in this world, "upon narrow search will be found to arise from breach of Covenant more or lesse."[19] Thus to the federal theology, which presided over the founding of New England, crop failures, epidemics, massacres were not harsh decrees of an absolute Jehovah, but just penalties brought upon the populace by their own sins. God did not punish these folk out of spite or rancour or caprice, but in accordance with their deserts. Consequently, when they had violated the agreement, and were reminded of their lapse by the sudden descent of a whirlwind or a plague, there was but one way in which a covenant people could find deliverance, by admitting their fault, undertaking to reform their errors, and begging God to remember His covenant. The ceremony necessarily had to be a public one, with the entire society participating, because God had covenanted with the whole people. When He will not look at us any more and exposes us to evil, said Cotton, if now "we returne and bewaile our breach of Covenant with God, how little good we have done, and how little serviceable we are, then is he wont to let us see, that his Covenant was never so far broken, but he can tell how to be good to us, for the Lord Jesus Christs sake."[20] Unless men push their violations so far that God is obliged to annul the covenant entirely, they can always come back into the benefits of the promise by renewing the letter of their bond. Hence the necessity for setting aside a day of public humiliation and for enacting a renewal of the covenant by the whole society, for only thus could God be induced to become once more the ally of the society, as He had been at the founding, and be persuaded to withdraw whatever terrors the sins of the people had caused Him to send amongst them.

For two decades after 1630 both the theory and practice of the fast day remained exactly as the founders first worked them out, and the effectiveness of the rite was amply attested. John Hull remembered that in those years the Lord "was wont to hear before we called, when we did but purpose to seek God." He frequently chastened them by "nurturing, lopping, and pruning his poor children, by his own fatherly hand, for their good," yet in the main He was pleased to bless the colonies "with great prosperity and success, increasing and multiplying, protecting and defending from all mischievous contrivances, supplying and furnishing with all

---

[18] Thomas Cobbet, *A Just Vindication of the Covenant and Church-Estate of Children of Church-Members* (London, 1648), p. 40.

[19] Thomas Shepard, "To the Reader," in Peter Bulkeley, *The Gospel-Covenant* (London, 1651), p. B2 recto.

[20] Cotton, *Christ the Fountaine of Life*, p. 39.

necessaries, maugre all adversaries."[21] The ceremonial of the humiliation day, being proved the right method for securing such blessings, was quickly standardized. The formula can be seen, for example, in the call issued by the General Court of Massachusetts in 1648. First the afflictions were recited, in this case the distractions in England, an unknown disease which the Lord had visited upon New England, a drought that was endangering the corn, and the mortality of our countrymen in the West Indies; this was followed by the resolution that these matters be "intimated" to the churches; then came the appointment of a day to be kept as a day of humiliation, and finally the peremptory order, "all p[er]sons are here[by] required to abstaine from bodily labor that day, & to resort to the publike meetings, to seeke the Lord, as becomes Christians in a day of humiliation."[22] In 1648, as in previous years, the rite worked the desired result, at least as far as New England health and corn were concerned.

In this proclamation, as in all the earlier ones, a meticulous distinction was observed between the physical afflictions, the disease and the drought, and the sins of the people which were assumed to have produced the afflictions. The theory held that travails were sent upon mankind to remind them of their obligation, whereupon they were to bethink themselves of their sins and take to repentance. However, in the Massachusetts proclamation for October 1652, a subtle modification of the formula was introduced: a fast was ordered for a number of reasons, most of them conventional—storms and rains, wars in England, the growth of heresy—but at the same time, among the provoking occasions for this fast were listed "the worldly mindednes, oppression, & hardhartednes feard to be amongst us."[23] For the first time, the sins themselves were enumerated as evils from which the society was suffering along with such external afflictions as hitherto had furnished the causes for a ceremony. The original theory held that sensible deprivations were a just retribution for the people's sins; it looked upon them as reminders through which God made the people aware of what they had been doing. The Puritans, in other words, had first conceived the relationship between God and the society in objective terms, and looked outward to read their inward condition by the course of events. At this point they began to turn their eyes from external happenings to internal misgivings, and to transfer the sins of the people into the column of causes in a way that had not been contemplated in the original theory. The modification in the formula, the shift from regarding a sin as something to be reformed *after* the physical affliction to considering it as in itself a sufficient reason for ceremonial mortification, is so slight that it would hardly deserve our notice did not this instance mark the beginning of an alteration that

21 John Hull, "Diaries," *Archæologia Americana, Trans. and Coll. Amer. Antiq. Soc.,* vol. III (1857), pp. 185, 168-69.
22 *Mass. Records,* vol. II, pp. 229-30.
23 *Mass. Records,* vol. III, p. 287.

grew perceptibly with the years. Within a decade the formula was completely transformed, and the implications of the new version were subtly but profoundly different from the old. The proclamations steadily and increasingly listed sins rather than manifest troubles; though such calamities as King Philip's War still furnished occasions for fasts, the announcements of the '60's and '70's became progressively recitals of spiritual shortcomings rather than catalogues of misfortunes. Hardheartedness, security, sloth, sensuality, lack of zeal among the rising generation, declension from "primitive affections," formality, hypocrisy were intruded among what had originally been the sole kind of provocations, such as mildew, droughts, caterpillars, shipwrecks, and other such visible "tokens of God's displeasure." Very shortly the visible tokens were offered as distinctly secondary to the sins. There was, in short, a steady drift toward emphasizing the subjective factors before the objective; the focus of attention was turned inward, and the authorities were more apprehensive over the hearts of the people than over their sufferings in the flesh. The significance of this transformation is not lessened by the fact that in all probability it was wrought unconsciously; it was in effect a silent revolution within the New England mind, or at least within the New England sensibility, with the result that between 1660 and 1690 the relationship of the society to God came to be felt in terms that practically reversed the primitive conception.

The altered emphasis of the proclamations was encouraged, if not actually instigated, by the clergy. In the first decades they had naturally devised a special kind of sermon to be delivered upon fast days. Inevitably it arraigned the sins of the society and exhorted the people to repentance. It was bound to present the state of affairs in a grave light and to persuade audiences that without reform still more serious consequences would follow. For the first ministers the delivery of fast-day sermons had been but a small part of their intellectual activity; they were engrossed in the larger issues of theology and of international Protestantism, and their energies were principally devoted to the complicated question of church polity. They had not fled into a provincial solitude but had moved to America in order to carry on the great struggle of the Reformation, to produce the model of a perfect church which all Europe was to imitate. After 1660 such matters were of less concern to the New England clergy, but the spiritual health of their own societies was all-important. Protestantism did not heed the New England model, and after the Restoration the colonies had perforce to rest content with their modest provincial status. Meantime their theology, having been vindicated against all possible heretics, Arminians or Antinomians, was codified in the Westminster Confession which the Synod of 1648 adopted as its own, so that there was no longer urgent need for constructive thinking in affairs of doctrine. But with the isolation of New England, everything now depended on the maintenance of zeal and devotion among the people, for these societies had been founded upon the assumption that they were in covenant with God and would forever be active in His service. Hence the later ministers concentrated upon the fast-day sermon, the call to humiliation and repentance, not only in the towns but above all in the General Court either on days of humiliation or on the annual days of election. They developed, amplified, and standardized a sermon devoted exclusively to an analysis of the sins of the people. Year after year they preached it, and directed their energies less to reciting the judgments of God than to denouncing the spread of corruption. The visible tokens of divine displeasure were used chiefly to underline the mounting evidences of decay or to foreshadow the still more awful afflictions that could be expected unless the zeal of the people was rekindled. Through a succession of these fast-day and election sermons, in the proclamations, histories and tracts, a standard theme began to emerge, to become the recurrent moral of all these utterances: New England is steadily declining from the high purity of the founders. Where the characteristic writings of the first generation were learned treatises upon polity or such profound musing upon the labyrinth of sin and regeneration as the great studies of Hooker, Shepard, and Cotton, the pre-eminent productions of the second generation—and also after 1660 of those of the first who, like Richard Mather or John Davenport, outlived their contemporaries— fall mainly into the category of the jeremiad. The most polished, thoughtful, and impressive creations of these decades, with few exceptions, are lamentations over the "declension" of New England and tirades against its lengthening list of sins. The pattern of the jeremiad took shape as a public review of the shortcomings of the society, designed to be spoken on formal occasions, when the people or their representatives were met together, and the form soon became as fixed and stereotyped as the funeral sermon or Latin oration. The people gathered year after year, doubtless knowing in advance exactly what they would hear, and every General Court, as soon as it had assembled in the spring, would listen once more to an arraignment of public evils before settling down to business. On these occasions the greatest of the jeremiads were delivered, which were generally printed and circulated throughout the colonies; the local ministers took more pains with their fast-day sermons than with any other, so that when a congregation subscribed to have something of their parson's published, they generally selected his raciest jeremiad. Hence the published remains of the period 1660 to 1690 give a very one-sided picture of what was actually preached on ordinary Sabbaths, and manuscript notes taken by faithful listeners show that normally the general doctrines of theology and morality were exhaustively discussed. Yet the fact remains that on the great occasions of communal life, when the body politic met in solemn conclave to consider the state of society, the one kind of sermon it attended was not an exposition of doctrine, not a description of holiness or of grace, not a discourse on what had once been the preoccupation of New England, the reformation of polity, but instead was a jeremiad in which the sins of New England were tabulated over and over again, wherein the outward judgments which God already had inflicted were held to presage what He would increase in violence unless New England hastened to restore the model of holiness.

Michael Wigglesworth sketched out the pattern of the jeremiad in his best verse, "God's Controversy with New England," in 1662. Higginson's election sermon of 1663, *The Cause of God and His People in New England,* approaches the form which achieved definitive shape with Jonathan Mitchell's *Nehemiah on the Wall* in 1667 and William Stoughton's *New Englands True Interests* in 1668. Thereafter the type lay ready to hand for every preacher, and was assiduously imitated in every pulpit. Later practitioners improved upon Mitchell and Stoughton only by extending the list of sins, by going into greater detail. Year by year the stock enumeration grew, and once a new sin was added to the series it kept its place in subsequent renditions. The great jeremiads of the 1670's were the literary triumphs of the decade and deserve to rank among the achievements of the New England mind; some of them made so deep an impression that they were cited and quoted down to the eve of the Revolution. Along with Mitchell's and Stoughton's the most important and elaborate were Samuel Danforth's *A Brief Recognition of New England's Errand into the Wilderness* in 1670, the younger Thomas Shepard's *Eye-Salve* in 1672, Urian Oakes's *New England Pleaded with* in 1673, William Hubbard's *The Happiness of a People* in 1676, Increase Mather's *The Day of Trouble is Near* in 1673, and his *A Discourse Concerning the Danger of Apostacy* in 1677. All but Mather's *Day* were election sermons, and though many similar works by other preachers, before the General Court, the Artillery Company, their own congregations or on lecture days, were published, these were considered the outstanding examples. Fifty years after the Great Migration, the literary form in which the New England mind found its most appropriate expression was a jeremiad. By 1680 forensic indictments of an apostatizing New England in the name of an idealized picture of its primitive sanctity had already become traditional and conventional.

Year after year the sins of New England were catalogued, the expanding list testifying to a steady deterioration. Though the preachers still dwelt upon calamities, and continued to point out that these were inflicted for breach of contract, their first concern was to press home the vast array of the sins themselves, and days of humiliation were celebrated not half so much because of losses to life and property as because of an acute self-consciousness among the children that they could not measure up to their fathers. That the religious interest "hath been for many years languishing and dying," that this is "the observation of all men that have their hearts exercised in discerning things of this nature,"[24] such was the unceasing refrain, and the transgressions of the people were painfully inventoried to prove that they should humble themselves much more for their lack of a godly frame than for their crop failures or diseases. Consequently,

[24] Increase Mather, in Samuel Torrey, *A Plea For the Life of Dying Religion* (Boston, 1683), p. A2 recto.

in the sequence of these jeremiads the social evolution of New England can be traced step by step as it was registered upon the minds of the leaders. As the ministers took cognizance one by one of the defections, they unwittingly recorded the progression of the communities from primitive simplicity to complexity and diversity. Through the screen of clerical denunciation appears the curve of an economic expansion that was annually and inevitably increasing the need for humiliation because it was irresistibly carrying the society away from the original dedication to holiness and the will of God. In 1679, after even an Indian war had not caused New Englanders to reverse their descent, the leaders assembled in Synod at Boston for a supreme effort to remedy what for years they had been condemning. By now they were wholly concentrated upon the offenses and very little occupied with the punishments, which were assumed to be obvious. They issued a report that epitomized and systematized the contents of the jeremiads. More faithfully than could any traveler or royal commission, the clergy here composed a study of social trends in New England, except that, being federal theologians, they cast their findings into the form of an enumeration of the accumulated misdeeds, which they offered in part as an explanation for financial and military reverses, but more importantly as an inducement to public sorrow. That the compilers disapproved of everything they saw, and vainly called upon the populace to forsake its ways in an effort to reachieve the spirit of 1630 does not interfere with the accuracy or the historical validity of their description. Nor was their statement the superficial work of a moment, for they drew upon the jeremiads in which the story had been minutely and continuously documented.

The authors of the Synod's *Result,* of whom Increase Mather was the chief penman, were trained in the logic of Ramus and knew that when they subjected the themes of the jeremiads to the rules of "method" they should place the most important first; first on their list, therefore, was "a great and visible decay of the power of Godliness amongst many Professors in these Churches."[25] In a Puritan state, as Urian Oakes made clear in 1673, a spiritual apathy among the saving remnant of the righteous, even though it produced no overt crimes, was more dangerous than the most flagrant of immoralities. The worst charge that could be brought against a covenanted people was that the "professors," even though they might not "make any notorious and scandalous Digression and Diversion from the good wayes of God," were yet become weary and drowsy, formal and customary, were "drudging and plodding on in a visible regular course of Obedience and Profession: yet behold, *what a weariness is it?*"[26] No more awful failure could overtake a covenanted society than to stop pressing toward the mark of genuine holiness. "A cooling of former life & heate in spiritual communion," "a careless, remiss, flat, dry, cold dead frame of

[25] Williston Walker, *The Creeds and Platforms of Congregationalism* (New York, 1893), p. 427.
[26] Oakes, *New-England Pleaded with* (Cambridge, 1673), p. 27.

spirit," security "in the Land of Rest, Quietness, and Fulness of Spiritual Enjoyment," "heart Apostasy" whereby men cease to fear and trust God "but take up their contentment and satisfaction in something else"—these are the revealing phrases heaped up in the jeremiads and proclamations. It was not that all the citizens were actively evil: "Many have gone a great way by civill honesty and morality," but that those who went thus far were generally "accounted to be in a state of salvation."[27] There is risen up a generation, said Increase Mather in 1674, "who give out, as if *saving Grace and Morality* were the same." No doubt, he countered, morality is necessary, but by itself it is not enough; a godly education is a great help, but if it alone is rested in, "without experience of a regenerating work of the Spirit, then a man's case is sad,"[28] and in New England of the 1670's he found too many born of Christian parents, baptised and educated in religion, who grew up to profess what they had been taught and who thought they needed no other conversion. What for ordinary nations would constitute virtue and civility was miserable inadequacy in a covenanted folk; they must hunger and thirst after the rich provisions of the house of God, they must not be, as Stoughton said many had now become, "empty outside Custom-born Christians," whose feeble profession of faith "hath run it self out of breath, and broke its neck."[29] Could the founders have imagined a more ghastly mockery than that their descendants should be carried to religious duties "from external considerations only, by a kind of outward force without any spiritual life or vigour or delight in them."[30] Yet to such a melancholy state were the posterity descending, and "clear sound Conversions" were becoming rare.[31] Urian Oakes set forth with fervent eloquence the most appalling manifestation of the decline:

> . . . there is great reason to conceive that many Professors may be grown Sermon-proof, that we had as good preach to the Heavens and Earth, and direct our discourse to the Walls and Seats and Pillars of the meeting house, and say, Hear, O ye Walls, give ear O ye Seats and Pillars, as to many men in these Churches, that are deaf to all that is cried in their ears by the Lords Messengers, and are indeed like Rocks in the Sea, not to be stirred and moved by the beating and dashing of these waters of the Sanctuary, or by the strongest gust of rational and affectionate discourse that can blow upon them.[32]

[27] Charles Chauncy, in "Abstracts of Sermons . . . Dec. 25, 1670 to April 2, 1671" (MS. in Harvard College Library).

[28] Increase Mather, *Some Important Truths Concerning Conversion* (London, 1674), 2nd ed. (Boston, 1684), pp. 46-48.

[29] William Stoughton, *New-Englands True Interest* (Cambridge, 1670), p. 27.

[30] William Adams, "Sermons on Sacrament Days, 1678-1684" (MS. in Harvard College Library).

[31] Increase Mather, *Pray for the Rising Generation* (Cambridge, 1678), 3rd ed. (Boston, 1685), pp. 181-82.

[32] Oakes, *New-England Pleaded with,* p. 25.

From this basic defect flowed at once the most serious of all sins, according to the Puritan ethic: pride, manifesting itself variously as a rebellion of subordinates against superiors, as contention in the churches, and, most shockingly, as extravagance in apparel. Concepts of sin are subject to the vagaries of circumstance, and in ages of scarcity or in pioneer societies, frippery in dress is an especially heinous offense; in the Puritan colonies it was still more serious because by indulging in this vice the lower orders pressed upon the upper and endangered the stratified structure of the state. "Servants, and the poorer sort of People," said the Synod, are the most notorious offenders in this regard, endeavoring in their costume to "goe above their estates and degrees, thereby transgressing the Laws both of God and man."[33] However, according to the ministers, there was "excess, gaudiness & fantasticalness in those that have estates," as well as much striving "to make themselves as brave as they can" among those that have none.[34] During the war with Philip the leaders were sure that this offense above all others had let loose the rage of the heathen, and they attributed the defeats of the army to silks, "monstrous and horrid Perriwigs . . . Borders and False Locks and such like whorish Fashions."[35] The same spirit of sinful pride manifested itself in the congregations during the hot disputes over the Half-Way Covenant that embroiled the churches in the 1660's and almost produced open conflict in 1670, when the Old South seceded from the First Church of Boston. The original assumption of the New England order had been, said Stoughton, that in all disagreements "strict and impartial Examination would yield large matter of uncontrollable Conviction," but when saints degenerate and are content with a formal piety, they no longer can be persuaded by even the most infallible syllogisms.[36] The third evil, according to the Synod, was a direct consequence: the appearance of heresies and errors, not merely those imported by Quakers and Anabaptists but those emanating from formal professors who "hearken & adhere to their own fancyes & Satans delusions."[37]

From this point on, the Synod came down to specific practices. The increase of swearing, which in 1676 Increase Mather said had gone so far that even children in the streets were guilty, was naturally associated with the vice of cards or dice and with the vicious habit of sleeping at sermons. The fifth evil was Sabbath-breaking. "Since there are multitudes that do profanely absent themselves or theirs from the publick worship of God, on his Holy day, especially in the most populous places [of] the land,"[38] and

---

[33] Walker, *Creeds and Platforms*, pp. 427-28.
[34] William Adams, "Sermons on Fast Days, 1678-1684" (MS. in Harvard College Library).
[35] Increase Mather, *An Earnest Exhortation To the Inhabitants of New-England* (Boston, 1676), p. 7.
[36] Stoughton, *New-Englands True Interest*, p. 19.
[37] Walker, *Creeds and Platforms*, p. 428; William Adams, "Sermons on Fast Days."
[38] Walker, *ibid.*, p. 429.

there was a steady lament that on the "night after the Sabbath . . . there is more wickedness committed usually . . . than in all the week besides."[39] The Puritan Sabbath began at sundown on Saturday and ended the next evening, and the pent-up energies of a rebellious generation seemed particularly explosive on Sunday nights. In the sixth place there was the sad decay of family government; heads of families were accused of no longer praying or reading the scripture, of becoming "cockering" parents, indulging their children in licentious freedoms, "letting them have their swinge, to go and come where and when they please, and especially in the night."[40] Seventhly, there was the rank flowering of inordinate passions into innumerable lawsuits, with a frequent resort to lawyers, in spite of the Puritan belief that attorneys ought to be suppressed because they "will for their own ends espouse any Case right or wrong."[41] The eighth head of the Synod's *Result* incorporated material which always bulked large in the jeremiads, the sins of alcohol and of sex. Increase Mather heard some say by 1673 that more wine was drunk in Boston than in most towns of its size in the Christian world,[42] and certainly, if the ministers are to be believed, militia training days had become such occasions as are not traditionally associated with the word "Puritanical": "every Farmers Son, when he goes to the Market-Town, must have money in his purse; and when he meets with his Companions, they goe to the Tavern or Ale-house, and seldome away before Drunk, or well tipled."[43] Taverns, of course, had long been looked upon askance, but the Synod was forced to the admission that they were frequented not alone by "town-dwellers" but even by "church-members" who misspent their time there to the dishonor of the gospel and the setting of bad examples.[44] About the beginning of King Philip's War the preachers first discovered that the demon rum was becoming responsible for a new offense, that traders in the back country were using it to debauch the Indians and take advantage of them, which was a particularly crying sin, the Synod declared, because the planters came to this colony with a design to convert the heathen.[45] As for sexual morality, the proclamations and sermons would give the impression of a rapidly thriving promiscuity. Fornication in 1665 was "much increasing among us,"[46] and in 1668 the General Court was obliged to take some means "for the easing of tounes where bastards are borne";[47] in 1672 "the sinn

[39] Increase Mather, *A Discourse Concerning the Danger of Apostacy*, 2nd ed. (Boston, 1685), p. 123.

[40] Samuel Willard, *Useful Instructions for a professing People* (Cambridge, 1673), p. 38.

[41] Samuel Arnold, *David serving his Generation* (Cambridge, 1674), pp. 17-18.

[42] Increase Mather, *Wo to Drunkards* (Cambridge, 1673), p. 20.

[43] Samuel Nowell, *Abraham in Arms* (Boston, 1678), p. 15.

[44] Walker, *Creeds and Platforms*, p. 430.

[45] *Ibid.*; Increase Mather, *A Brief History of the War with the Indians* (Boston, 1676), ed. S. G. Drake (Boston, 1862), p. 99; *Earnest Exhortation*, pp. 10, 15.

[46] *Mass. Records*, vol. IV, pt. 2, p. 143.

[47] *Ibid.*, pp. 393-94.

of whoredom & uncleanes growes amongst us, notwithstanding all the wholesome lawes made for the punishing & suppressing such land defiling evills,"[48] and in this year Alice Thomas made the first recorded attempt to supply Boston with a brothel, "giving frequent secret and unseasonable Entertainmen[t] in her house to Lewd Lascivious & notorious persons of both Sexes, giving them opportunity to commit carnall wickedness."[49] She was taken and whipped through the streets, but that was small comfort to the ministers, who were forced to suspect that if so much fornication had been publicly discovered, "how much is there of secret wantonness & wicked dalliances?" The Puritans were wise enough to know that in any society "that which is seen is nothing in comparison of that which is not."[50]

The ninth and tenth of the Synod's findings testify, in the fashion of the jeremiads, to a growing worldliness that was the moral consequence of an increase in wealth. The ninth told of frauds and deceits invented by a shrewd people in their business affairs, and commenced an indictment of the Yankee trader which many other critics were soon to take up. Still more significant for the student of the social history was the tenth topic: "inordinate affection to the world." The first comprehensive meditation on this theme had appeared in Higginson's election sermon of 1663: the Lord stirred up the founders to come to this land not for worldly wealth or a better livelihood for the outward man; there were no "rationall grounds to expect such a thing in such a wilderness as this," but God has blessed us with many earthly comforts and many "have encreased here from small beginnings to great estates." But it followed, said Higginson, that our prosperity is not the result of our efforts or our resources, but of our piety, and if our piety fails so then will our comforts. New England, he declared in words that were to be quoted for a century, was "originally a plantation of Religion, not a plantation of Trades. Let Merchants and such as are increasing Cent per Cent remember this." If any among us make religion as twelve and the world as thirteen, "let such an one know he hath neither the spirit of a true New-England man, nor yet of a sincere Christian."[51] But alas! the breed of true New-England men seemed to be dying out; in 1674 Samuel Torrey of Weymouth was sure that they were steadily deserting the religious interest and espousing a worldly one, and in the late '70's William Adams said all discerning observers had concluded that the world had so far got into New England's constitution "that there is no likelihood of getting it out till God pull us in pieces."[52] The founders themselves had been aware of the danger that to land-hungry Englishmen, even to tried and approved saints, the prospect

---

[48] *Mass. Records*, vol. IV, pt. 2, p. 513.

[49] *Records of the Suffolk County Court*, ed. Zechariah Chafee, Jr. (*Col. Soc. Mass. Pub.*, vol. XXIX, 1933), vol. I, pp. 82-83.

[50] William Adams, "Sermons on Fast Days," p. 8.

[51] John Higginson, *The Cause of God and his People in New-England* (Cambridge, 1663), pp. 10-11.

[52] William Adams, "Sermons on Fast Days," p. 9.

of vast reaches of land to be had for the clearing might eclipse all other visions. John Cotton had detected as early as 1642 a popular disposition to figure "if we could have large elbow-roome enough, and meddow enough, though wee had no Ordinances, we can then goe and live like lambs in a large place." If this, he promised, should become your frame of mind, "you may have part in Reformation of Churches, but no part in the resurrection of Christ Jesus."[53] But New England elbows grew sharper and longer with the years, and the Synod professed for all the world to read, "There hath been in many professors an insatiable desire after Land."[54] "Land! Land! hath been the Idol of many in New-England," cried Increase Mather; whereas the first planters were satisfied with an acre a person and twenty for a family, "how have Men since coveted after the earth, that many hundreds, nay thousands of Acres, have been engrossed by one man, and they that profess themselves Christians, have forsaken Churches, and Ordinances, and all for land and elbow-room enough in the World."[55] Charles Chauncy became aware in 1655 that there were men in New England who would prefer to settle far into the wilderness without any ministry or schools or means of civilization if they might have their liberty; untroubled by strict sabbaths they could then follow their worldly interest any time, "and their children may drudge for them at plough, or hough, or such like servill imployments, that themselves may be eased."[56] The lament over frontier plantations, where no ministry was settled, swelled to a constant cry in the next decades.

Meanwhile, as the frontier was extended, trade increased. Even in 1639 certain of the magistrates had protested against the fining of Robert Keayne for having dared to buy as cheaply as he could and to sell for the highest price he could get; they objected that in spite of all learned cogitation on the question, "a certain rule could not be found out for an equal rate between buyer and seller."[57] It had taken all the authority of John Cotton and the Word of God to silence them, to make the community accept the rule of the "just price." The later ministers repeated Cotton's dicta, but they were no longer able to force them upon the citizens. And still more horrifying was the fact that the lower orders, comprehending what treatment they were receiving from their employers, had begun to reply in kind. Oakes could tell in 1673 of much "Griping, and Squeezing, and Grinding the Faces of the poor";[58] what wonder that by 1679 "Day-Labourers and Mechanicks are unreasonable in their demands"?[59] "Suppose a poor man," said Chauncy in 1655, "wants a pair of shoos, or other clothes

[53] John Cotton, *The Churches Resurrection* (London, 1642), p. 26.
[54] Walker, *Creeds and Platforms,* p. 431.
[55] Increase Mather, *Earnest Exhortation,* p. 9.
[56] Charles Chauncy, *Gods Mercy Shewed to His People* (Cambridge, 1655), p. 16.
[57] *Winthrop's Journal,* vol. I, p. 316.
[58] Oakes, *New-England Pleaded with,* p. 32.
[59] Walker, *Creeds and Platforms,* p. 431; *cf.* E. A. J. Johnson, *American Economic Thought in the Seventeenth Century* (London, 1932), pp. 207-11.

to cover his nakedness, that hath no silver: truely he must be fain almost to sell himself, to get some mean commodities."[60] The poor man was apparently no better off in 1676; the merchants set such prices on their goods, Increase Mather observed, "it is enough to bring the Oppressing Sword." "And what a shame is it that ever that odious sin of Usury should be pleaded for, or practised in New-England?"[61] How far New England in fact had departed from the theory in which it had been conceived can be seen by comparing the censure of Keayne in 1639 with Mather's lament in 1674, "A poor man cometh amongst you and he must have a Commodity whatever it cost him, and you will make him give whatever you please, and put what price you please upon what he hath to give too, without respecting the just value of the thing."[62] The medieval and scholastic concept of the just price, like the medieval attitude toward usury, was simply dropping out of the economic code of New England, though the ministers were still, in the name of the original ideal, fulminating against a process that they could not hinder.

The last of the Synod's paragraphs described the fatal unwillingness of the people to reform, even after the Lord had called upon them in a series of severe judgments, and the corresponding decay of what in the seventeenth century was called "public spirit," which meant a disinclination to pay the public charges, a neglect of education, and a reluctance to support the ministry. At this point the ministers were clearly fighting for the Puritan intellectual ideal, for the existence of a religious leadership that would be learned as well as pious, scholarly as well as fervent, against a spreading disposition among the people to prize education less than profits, and an academic discourse less than emotional rant. "Young men prefer cheap knowledge, easily come by, to wholesome wisdom."[63] The jeremiads ceaselessly bewailed the state of "inferiour schools" and of "the Colledge," that "School of the prophets," without which religion would fail and the light of the sanctuary flicker out. Furthermore, Puritan scholars had to be maintained not only at school but in their libraries, for the pursuit of learning in the Puritan code was a lifetime occupation. The people no doubt are "generally poor and low enough," Oakes admitted, but if the "Common Wealth of Learning" is once allowed to languish, there will be an end also of our civil and ecclesiastical state; unless there is a supply of learned men, and unless learned men are paid in the proper style, "who sees not what Ignorance, and Rudeness, and Barbarism will come in like a Floud upon us?"[64] "Should Academical Learning fall in this land," Increase Mather joined in the chorus, "darkness shall then cover the earth,

[60] Chauncy, Gods Mercy, p. 20.
[61] Increase Mather, Earnest Exhortation, p. 11.
[62] Increase Mather, The Day of Trouble is near (Cambridge, 1674), p. 22.
[63] Publ. Col. Soc. Mass., vol. XXVIII, p. 23; cf. Samuel Eliot Morison, Harvard College in the Seventeenth Century (Cambridge, 1936), pp. 329-34.
[64] Oakes, New-England Pleaded with, pp. 57-58.

and gross darkness the people."[65] Not that the Holy Spirit was "locked up in the narrow limits of Colledge learning," but assuredly ministerial gifts were not to be acquired "in a Shoemakers Shop."[66] To the last ditch the Puritan ministers would defend the ideal of learning and scholarship, even after they were induced to surrender the doctrine of the just price and to countenance the taking of interest, but there were forces at work in their society as early as the 1670's which were challenging the ideal and creating a demand for religion more adapted to the appetites of an unlearned, land-grabbing, hard-drinking, and excitable people.

The Synod did not pretend that its digest of offenses was an original document. "The things here insisted on," it declared, "have . . . been oftentimes mentioned and inculcated by those whom the Lord hath set as Watchmen to the house of Israel, though alas! not with that success which their Souls have desired."[67] Even its systematic and devastating presentation appears to have wrought little of the success desired by the watchmen, and after the *Result* was published in 1680 they resumed the preaching of jeremiads. But now a new theme appeared along with the enumeration of particular breaches of conduct: a frank recognition that the jeremiad had become a kind of literary stereotype. With the models of the '60's and '70's before them, and the report of the Synod on their desks, the clergy openly acknowledged, as did Willard in 1682, that they were repeating a form which long since had come to be a set-piece. The Synod supplied a tabloid content for more and more jeremiads, and many preachers simply retailed from their pulpits the substance of the *Result,* mechanically and in the same sequence. The pattern had become conventional, and the preachers were compelled to admit that the people were getting bored. There were some, apparently, who grumbled that the jeremiads were "nothing else but the mistakes of an irregular (though well minded) zeal, or the dumps and night visions of some melancholick spirits." Yet, though such sermons were "condemned by some, contemned by many more, scarcely believed by any,"[68] and though the ministers had to confess as much, they resolutely persisted through a further succession of fast days and days of election. The best works of the 1680's were, monotonously, jeremiads: Willard's *The Only Sure Way to Prevent Threatened Calamity* in 1682, Samuel Torrey's *A Plea for the Life of Dying Religion* in 1683, and William Adams's *God's Eye on the Contrite* in 1685. The line was interrupted by the revocation of the charter and the establishment of the Dominion of New England, during which the ministers had to restrain their denunciations. But no sooner was Andros deposed than the provisional government of the saints met once more to hear a jeremiad, delivered by the young Cotton Mather and com-

[65] Increase Mather, *Earnest Exhortation,* p. 24.
[66] Samuel Willard, *Ne Sutor ultra Crepidam* (Boston, 1681), p. 26.
[67] Walker, *Creeds and Platforms,* p. 425.
[68] Samuel Willard, *The Only Sure Way To Prevent Threatened Calamity,* printed with *The Child's Portion* (Boston, 1684), pp. 179, 180.

plete with all the old array of sins. Under the new charter the form was cultivated with new vigor, and persisted well into the eighteenth century, although from time to time an election preacher might lay it aside and devote himself to discussing the principles of political science. Except for a few such deviations, election sermons continued to be cast in the form of the jeremiad, and colonial or local fast days still produced them by the hundreds. Year after year denunciations of wrath against vicious and unclean practices, against a lifeless frame and flaccid zeal, sounded in the ears of New Englanders; time after time they were exhorted to repent and reform lest God in His anger destroy them utterly, but still they declined. Suddenly in 1740 the people took fire again, and a revival of fervor swept the back country and the lower classes, but in a fashion that proved not at all to the liking of many who had preached the most stirring jeremiads.

We must, of course, make allowance for ministerial exaggeration when we go to the jeremiads for a picture of life in the seventeenth century. Also we must remember that a group of worried preachers calling upon the people to repent were not chronicling the history of their times in a scientific and objective spirit. Yet the sequence of their denunciations does provide a neat chronological summary of a chapter in the economic growth of New England. What they called sins are recognizable as manifestations of social change, and the phenomena they singled out are equally important to the modern historian. The jeremiads tell the story of a society that had been founded by men who believed, rightly or wrongly, that it was motivated solely by religion and was dedicated to realizing on earth the explicit revelation of God, a society organized on theological principles and ruled by an economic code that was a survival from the Middle Ages. They further testify that, in the course of the century, by the very necessities of its predicament, the society became increasingly involved in the work of settlement, of fishing and of trade, that it emerged by slow and insensible degrees into the now familiar outlines of a commercial and capitalist economy. The jeremiads are evidences of the grief and bewilderment that this uncomprehended evolution caused the leaders, who were conscious only of their inability to resist it. But the modern observer cannot help being struck with one remarkable fact about the whole series of denunciations: while the ministers were excoriating habits and tempers that were the direct result of the process, while they were lamenting the worldly spirit of merchants and frontiersmen and demanding that they come to humiliation, they at no time condemned the pursuit of wealth or the expansion of the frontier. They berated the consequence of progress but never progress itself. They deplored the effects of trade upon men's religion, but they did not ask men to cease from trading.[69] They arraigned men of great estates, but not the estates. Jonathan Mitchell said that a people needed for their temporal

[69] Johnson, *American Economic Thought,* pp. 141-42, 205-07.

welfare safety, honesty, civil privileges, and orthodox religion, and also—
"Prosperity in matters of outward Estate and Livelyhood."[70] His colleagues
bemoaned the demoralizing influences of the frontier, but they did not
call a halt to the march of settlement. In the midst of denunciation, colonial
Jeremiahs continued their hearty endorsement of the precepts of pious
labor and of the exploitation of worldly opportunities which had always
been central teachings in Calvinism. New England merchants, farmers,
and shipbuilders increased "cent per cent," and the results were a decay
of godliness, lust for possessions, class antagonisms, expensive apparel, and
a lessened respect for learning. In these respects New Englanders seemed to
be deserting the great tradition of their fathers. But they would have deserted it still more had they not labored in their callings with a diligence
that was bound to increase their estates and widen the gulf between the
industrious and the shiftless, the rich and the poor, between those who
made money and those who borrowed it—and paid the interest!

That every man should have a calling in this world and should work
in it faithfully was a first premise of Calvinism and Puritanism. William
Ames, whose textbook of ethics was standard in seventeenth-century New
England, laid down the dictum that even he who has an income must nevertheless work in a calling; each man has a talent for something, whether
for government or banking or ditch-digging, which is given him of God.[71]
It is no disgrace according to Ames's teachings for a man to suffer poverty
if the circumstances are beyond his control, for then the bad fortune is
sent from God as a correction or a trial, but it is a loathsome crime for a
man to accept poverty which he could avoid or remedy.[72] As the Puritan
conceived the order of things, God had cunningly contrived that men, if
they would live at all, must seek the physical necessities of life in the earth
or the sea, but in His benevolence He also provided that the objects of
their search are there to be found, if men will only bestir themselves to
hunt. "Whatsoever we stand in neede of," John Winthrop meditated
before he set out for New England, "is treasured in the earth by the
Creator, & to be feched thense by the sweate of or Browes."[73] Riches are
ordained for use; they are dangerous temptations, but the path of the saint
is beset with temptations, to be overcome and not to be fled. Private property is founded "not onely on humane, but also on naturall and divine
right,"[74] and just as the laborer is worthy of his hire, so fidelity in one's
occupation, if performed in the fear of God, will in the course of providence
lead to wealth. These teachings were never challenged or altered in seven-

[70] Jonathan Mitchell, *Nehemiah on the Wall* (Cambridge, 1671), pp. 3-5.
[71] William Ames, *Conscience with the Power and Cases thereof* (London, 1643),
bk. 5, pp. 248-50.
[72] Ames, *Conscience*, bk. 5, pp. 251-54.
[73] Robert C. Winthrop, *Life and Letters of John Winthrop* (Boston, 1869), vol. I,
p. 315.
[74] Ames, *Conscience*, bk. 5, p. 222.

teenth-century New England, and they reappear in the very preachers who gave themselves most energetically to the composition of jeremiads. William Adams, for example, could explain that while in one sense the "world" means opposition to God, in another it may signify that which is good, beautiful, amiable, and necessary, and when it is thus comprehended, "the believer is not to be crucifyed to the world: But hath much business to do in & about the world which he is vigorously to attend, & he hath that in the world upon which he is to bestow affection."[75] Ames's doctrine was recapitulated at the end of the century by Samuel Willard in his immense *summa* of all Puritan knowledge, *A Compleat Body of Divinity*, wherein Puritans were informed that they were bound by their allegiance to God to engage themselves in an outward calling, for "Man is made for Labour, and not for Idleness."[76]

John Cotton composed the finest exposition in the authentic language of New England Puritanism of what, since Max Weber, has come to be generally called the "Protestant ethic." He made abundantly clear that Puritan philosophy did not expect men to desist from profit-making—on the contrary, it positively encouraged them—but it did expect them to get the profits without succumbing to the seductions. Civil life in the world, no less than the life of contemplation, is lived by faith, Cotton declared, and just as soon as a man finds faith in his heart he is drawn to live in "some warrantable calling," "though it be but of a day-labourer."[77] The true Christian does the work that providence sets before him sincerely and faithfully, not shirking the most homely or difficult or dangerous tasks. "If thou beest a man that lives without a calling, though thou hast two thousands to spend, yet if thou hast no calling, tending to publique good, thou art an uncleane beast."[78] But the distinctive cast of the Puritan theory —in which it contrasts radically with the prevalent assumptions of the nineteenth century—appears first in Cotton's emphasis upon "the publique good" and second in his insistence that though a man have great gifts for his calling, he depend not upon his own powers but upon God for rewards and profits. The Puritan conception was far from "rugged individualism"; a man might not make all the money he could or spend it as he chose, for he was bound to serve the good of the whole, else he was an unclean beast. Furthermore, he was obliged to keep constantly in mind that his gifts were from God and that the providence of God governed his success or failure, not the state of the market or the rate of exchange. If the saint worked at his business in such a spirit, he could not be corrupted by success. He would take all good fortune, according to Cotton, "with moderation,"[79]

[75] Adams, "Sermons on Sacrament Days," p. 178.
[76] Samuel Willard, *A Compleat Body of Divinity* (Boston, 1726), pp. 691-95.
[77] John Cotton, *The Way of Life*, pp. 437, 438.
[78] *Ibid.*, p. 449.
[79] Cotton, *The Way of Life*, p. 446.

he would be an ascetic in the midst of prosperity, and no matter how much he outstripped the fathers of New England in wealth he would not fall below them in piety.

The Puritan ideal can be perceived in dramatic form in a little allegory that enjoyed great popularity among Puritans of both Englands during the seventeenth and even into the eighteenth century. *A Rich Treasure At an easy Rate; or, The ready Way to true Content,* purportedly by one "N. D.," was first published in London in 1657 and reissued in Boston at least in 1683 and again in 1763. According to this simple narrative, at one end of town lives Poverty with his wife Sloth, "in a sorry ruinous Cottage; which shortly after fell to the ground, and he was never able to repair it,"[80] while at the other end dwells Riches with his servants Pride, Oppression, Covetousness, Luxury, and Prodigality. He once had two sons, Honour who died young and Ambition who came to an untimely end; his daughter Delicacy has a bastard child Infamy, and daughter Avarice produced Misery, while his chaplain, Sir John Reader, stumbles through the prayers in a book and then gives himself to drinking and swearing. Into town comes Godliness, with his servants, Humility, Sincerity, Repentance, Experience, Faith, Hope, Charity, Temperance, and Sobriety. He tries living first beside Riches and then beside Poverty; Riches insults him, and Poverty raises such a hullabaloo by coming home every night from the ale-house drunk as a beggar that Godliness is in despair. For a time he is tempted to go into a cloister, but he remembers—and here we have the essence of the Protestant ethic—"that Man was made for Society" and that he is bound "to honour God, as much as was possible, by doing good to humane Society."[81] At this juncture he meets with Gravity, who advises him to live in the middle of the town, halfway between Riches and Poverty, beside old Labour, the best housekeeper in the parish, and his good wife Prudence. Godliness and Labour get on famously, with the help of Labour's servants, Forecast, Diligence, Expedition, Cheerfulness, and Perseverance, "early Risers and at their work." As soon as Labour becomes the friend of Godliness, he prospers marvellously. Godliness teaches him to pray, and Labour's estate increases still more, until at last Content comes to live with him, bringing in his train Justification, Adoption, Assurance and Sanctification. Labour's happiness knows no bounds: "he had never prayed before, but now *Godliness* had thoroughly instructed him, and taught him a better Art, and the way of thriving."[82]

This all too transparent allegory might be taken for a symbolic rendering of the lives of a thousand New Englanders in the age of the jeremiads, most notably, perhaps, for the career of the mintmaster, John Hull. He was no child of "Riches," for his father was a blacksmith, and he had but little "keeping" at school; he hoed corn for seven years, until "by God's good

[80] *A Rich Treasure* (Boston, 1763), p. 4.
[81] *A Rich Treasure,* pp. 20-21.
[82] *Ibid.,* p. 32.

hand" he was apprenticed to the trade of a goldsmith.[83] At the age of twenty-three he joined hands with "Godliness," for the Lord had brought him under very choice means, the ministry of John Cotton, and had made the means "effectual"; so he found "room in the hearts of his people" and was received into the fellowship of the First Church of Boston.[84] The economic virtues that waited upon both Labour and Godliness were all his; he was an early riser and at his work, "and, through God's help, obtained that ability in it, as I was able to get my living by it."[85] He kept his shop so well that shortly it not only kept him but supplied him a surplus to invest in ships and land, and John Hull became one of the first merchant princes of Massachusetts. But always, whether tradesman or merchant or banker, he went in the fear of God, looking to Him for all rewards and submitting everything to His will. When the Dutch got his ships, he knew where to seek for consolation: "The loss of my estate will be nothing, if the Lord please to join my soul nearer to himself, and loose it more from creature comforts."[86] However, when his foreman at Point Judith Neck stole his horses, the Puritan saint knew what to say to him: "I would have you know that they are, by God's good providence, mine."[87] Business and piety mingled in his instructions to his captains; the Lord should be worshipped in his vessels, sabbaths sanctified, and all sin and profaneness suppressed. "That the lords prescence may bee with you & his blessing bee upon you . . . is & shall be the prayer of yor friends & owners,"[88] but also, he wrote with the same pen, "Leave noe debts behind you whereever you goe."[89] He would tell his captains to follow their own judgment, knowing that businessmen must make the most of providential chances: "but indeed it is hard to forsee what will bee & therefore it is best willing to submit to the great governing hand of the greate Governer of all the greater and lesser revolutions that wee the poore sons of men are involved in by the invoyce you see the whole amounteth to £405:16:3." There is no full stop in this passage, but every threepence is accounted for. In his old age he prepared for death, and would not send a venture to the Canaries because he was "desirous to be more thoughtfull of Lanching into that vast ocion of Eternity whether we must all shortly bee Carried,"[90] but one would hardly describe him, or the ethic he practiced, as "otherworldly." Religion to a man of his temperament meant precisely seizing the main chance and getting ahead in the world, and sin was synonymous with wasted opportunities. He took into his shop two apprentices, Jeremiah Dummer

---

[83] Hull, *Diaries*, p. 142.

[84] *Ibid.*, p. 145.

[85] *A Rich Treasure*, p. 142.

[86] *Ibid.*, p. 146.

[87] *Ibid.*, p. 127.

[88] Hermann F. Clarke, *John Hull a Builder of the Bay Colony* (Portland, Maine, 1940), p. 52.

[89] William Weeden, *Economic and Social History of New England* (Boston, 1891), vol. I, p. 250.

[90] Weeden, *Economic and Social History of New England*, vol. I, p. 249.

and Samuel Paddy; by Puritan standards Dummer was a good boy, but Paddy was a wastrel, and after Master Hull was compelled to turn him out he went, as was to be expected, from bad to worse. There was no mercy for the prodigal in the heart of John Hull; years afterward he told Paddy off in a severe letter embodying the grim contempt of the successful Puritan for those who do not unite godliness and labor in their callings: "Had you abode here and followed your calling you might have been worth many hundred pounds of clear estate and you might have enjoyed many more helpes for your sole. Mr. Dummer lives in good fashion hath a wife and three children and a good estate is a member of the church and like to be very useful in his generation."[91] John Hull died worth some six thousand pounds, and would have been worth twice that had he not supported the colonial treasury out of his own pocket. Samuel Willard preached his funeral sermon, reciting his many virtues but saying this outshone them all, "that he was a Saint upon Earth; that he lived like a Saint here, and died the precious Death of a Saint." However, he was a Puritan saint, and no Papist devotee who fled into the unproductive solitude of a desert or a cloister; no, though he lived "above the World" and kept "his heart disentangled," he was always "in the midst of all outward occasions and urgency of Business," and Parson Willard did not hesitate to mention, among his accomplishments, "Providence had given him a prosperous and Flourishing Portion of this Worlds Goods."[92]

Thanks to this spirit among its citizens, to the fact that there were many Hulls and Dummers as well as Paddys, providence blessed New England with a flourishing portion of this world's goods, much more, as Higginson remarked in 1663, than could have been expected from its slim resources and stony soil. The amazing truth is simply that the society denounced continuously in the jeremiads was not economically declining but advancing. There were a few bad years, of which pious conservatives like John Hull as well as the ministers would make the most; he gloomily recorded in 1664 that there was a smite upon all employments, "at least in general, all men are rather going backward than increasing their estates," but the same year he noted also that about one hundred sail of ships had come into Boston harbor, "and all laden hence."[93] Where there were ships there were profits, and New England businessmen got their share. For the first ten years New England lived happily and comfortably off its immigrants, the newcomers bringing in foreign goods and at the same time providing the market for New England produce. It can hardly be too much stressed that the orthodoxy of New England, the "New England Way" both in church and state, was formed during the halcyon decade of 1630–1640 when the economic problem took care of itself, in what

[91] Clarke, *John Hull,* p. 133.
[92] Samuel Willard, *The High Esteem which God Hath of the Death of His Saints* (Boston, 1683), pp. 16-17.
[93] Hull, *Diaries,* pp. 214, 215.

Hubbard called "the first and golden age in this new world,"[94] and the New England mind bore the impress of its origins in its inability thereafter to comprehend how any economic question could ever rise into such prominence. But this happy era was brought abruptly to an end when the calling of the Long Parliament shut off immigration and threatened New England with starvation. Then, for the first time, the colonies perceived the situation into which the providence of God had led them: they were in desperate need of English wares which they could not manufacture for themselves and without which they would not survive, but at the same time they possessed a limited and inadequate number of articles that could be sold in England; therefore, in order to live, they had to find some way of converting their fish, lumber, wheat, flour, and livestock into a means of paying for English cloth and tools. For reasons best known to Himself, God had not laid before His saints the easy problem He set the Godless Virginians, who found at their doorsteps a crop that could be marketed in London, and needed only to harvest it. The New Englanders had to learn commerce or perish. They did not perish, though once again they professed that they were not indebted solely to their own ingenuity or their capacity for hard work: "when the first way of supply began to be stopped up, God in his merciful providence opened another, by turning us into a way of Trade and Commerce, to further our more comfortable subsistence."[95] However, this way of trade and commerce was no half-time occupation. There would be a limit to the number of hours a man could spend meditating upon an intricate distinction between works as a condition of the Covenant of Grace and the Papal heresy of justification by works, when he was compelled to spend almost all his waking hours amid, according to an almanac jingle of 1648, "Heaps of wheat, pork, bisket, beef and beer. Masts, pipe-staves, fish, should store both far and near, which fetch in wines, cloths, sweets and good tobac."[96] "Our Maritan Towns began to encrease roundly,"[97] wrote the pious historian in 1650, but he had seen only the beginning; the Restoration was a grievous setback for the Puritan orthodoxy, and John Hull was among the most depressed, for he found "the face of things looking sadly toward the letting-in of Popery";[98] yet he and his commercial colleagues had little cause to complain of the government of Charles II. The Navigation Acts and the exclusion of the Dutch created a golden opportunity for the merchants of New England, and in this ironic fashion, at the hand of the most flagrant immoralist of the age, the providence of God compensated Puritan colonies for the ravages of King Philip. In 1691, when the spokesmen for Massachusetts

[94] William Hubbard, *A General History of New-England* (*Mass. Hist. Soc. Coll.*, 2nd ser., vol. V), pp. 158, 247-48.
[95] Hubbard, *The Benefit of a Well-Ordered Conversation* (Boston, 1684), p. 97.
[96] Weeden, *Economic and Social History of New England*, p. 152.
[97] Edward Johnson, *The Wonder-Working Providence of Sions Saviour*, ed. J. F. Jameson (New York, 1910), p. 247.
[98] Hull, *Diaries*, p. 196.

were defending their society against criticism from the outside, they could conveniently forget the burden of the jeremiads and announce to the world that the people of New England had shown "that Necessity and Freedome could do wonders," that they in a few years had grown to a height and greatness that had brought more riches, industry, and glory to the English nation than ever any colony had done.[99] Thus wealth did in fact accumulate, and if a man had the right spirit, if he rose early and worked in his calling, if he trusted to God for the return, he was almost certain not to be disappointed. Men who started as millers, being paid in grain, were compelled to find buyers and so grew to be traders, perceiving therein the guiding hand of providence; men who started as artisans settled down in workshops, took apprentices, and shortly were capitalists. Merchants imported the indispensable stocks and advanced them to farmers and frontiersmen on credit and so became bankers, and could crack the whip of discipline over their inefficient debtors, as did John Hull: "I am afraid lest by keepeing a drinkeing House you learn to tipple yor selfe and thereby stifle the voice of yor Conscience that else would call upon you to bee Righteouse me thinks some fruits might have come to mee last winter."[100] They bought up the fishing fleet as soon as God had made clear that the cod was to be the mainstay of Massachusetts, and by the beginning of the eighteenth century a few capitalists dominated the industry. By that time also the merchants had taken hold of their providential opportunities with such forecast, diligence, expedition, and perseverance that not only had they succeeded the Dutch as the principal competitors of the English merchants but also they were steadily draining the interior of whatever had a market value, syphoning off money from Newfoundland, bringing in cargos from southern Europe, diverting the coinage of the Caribbean into their pockets, and finally, to cap the climax of their brilliance, earning the freight charges on everything they handled and then selling their very ships at a handsome profit! The great statesmen who led the migration lost money in the enterprise, and if their estates were worth a thousand pounds at their deaths, God had been merciful. But Robert Keayne the merchant, even though he was prohibited by his church from charging as high a price for his goods as he might have got, left over four thousand pounds in 1656, and John Holland, who fitted vessels for the cod fisheries, had amassed more than that by 1653. Increase Mather cried that land had become the idol of many; to judge from the records, the many were church members, leading citizens, and the saintliest figures of the second or third generation. Bellingham, Endecott, and Willoughby in Massachusetts, Wyllys and John Winthrop, Jr., in Connecticut had engrossed "many hundred, nay thousands of Acres." By 1670 there were said to be thirty merchants in Boston worth from ten to thirty thousand pounds; they modestly denied that they had yet reached such figures, yet by the end

[99] *The Andros Tracts*, vol. II (1869), p. 243.
[100] Weeden, *Economic and Social History of New England*, p. 250.

of the century the families of Lillie, Faneuil, Belcher, Foster, Phillips, Wharton, Clarke, Gallup, Sewall, were a long way from penury, and Ned Ward reported that "In the Chief, or high Street there are stately Edifices, some of which cost the owners two or three Thousand Pounds." He held that these illustrated the adage of a fool and his money being soon parted, "for the Fathers of these Men were Tinkers and Peddlers";[101] the fact is that the merchants of Boston were generally no such fools as to build bigger houses than they could afford, but that many of them had come up in the social scale, and had come a long way, there could be no denying. The holy commonwealth was turning into a commercial society, so much so that the very language of piety was affected, and even those ministers who denounced worldliness expounded their theology in the imagery of trade. Joshua Moody, for example, would deliver a Thursday lecture in which he declared that salvation yielded a hundred per cent clear gain, and "It is rational that Men should lay out their Money where they may have the most suitable Commodities and best Pennyworths"![102] Samuel Willard's *Heavenly Merchandize* in 1686 was exactly what the title indicates, and Boston merchants could easily grasp every sentence. The Puritan tenet that men must know the conditions of redemption in addition to believing the Gospel came out as: "A prudent buyer will see his wares, & try them before he will buy them"; that one effect of sin is to make men try to haggle with God over the terms of salvation was thus expounded: "He that really intends to buy, will first cheapen; every one hath such a principle, that he could buy at the best rates; to have a thing good, and have it cheap, is most mens ambition." Willard concluded that Christ was a good buy and could be had not too dearly.[103]

The question thus is forced upon us, why did New England of the late seventeenth century express itself most frequently and most earnestly in elaborate self-denunciation? Why did the spokesmen for a society that had triumphed over the frontier and the sea, that was piling up money and building more stately mansions on the high street, incessantly call upon that society to abase itself before the Lord, as though it were a loathsome and contagious leper? And why did the people listen, why did they read such jeremiads, why did they fill up their own diaries with similar meditations and include themselves in the general condemnation, even when, like John Hull or Samuel Sewall, they were fast progressing along the road to wealth? We must remember that the jeremiad sermons were delivered always on the most formal occasions, when the whole people assembled with the conscious purpose of taking stock of their condition. And always, either in their churches or in the General Court, they heard

[101] Edward Ward, *A Trip to New-England* (London, 1699), ed. G. P. Winship (Providence, 1905), pp. 38-39.

[102] Joshua Moody, *A Practical Discourse Concerning the Choice Benefit of Communion with God in his House* (Boston, 1685), 2nd ed. (1746), p. 14.

[103] Samuel Willard, *Heavenly Merchandize: or the Purchasing of Truth Recommended, and the Selling of it Disswaded* (Boston, 1686), *passim*.

what already they had been told a thousand times, the only variation being that year after year the number of their sins increased. These ceremonies were obviously formal purgations of some sort, periodic gatherings for the solemn purpose of self-condemnation; the rite was kept up with gusto for a generation and was still being practiced, though with lessening conviction, a century later.

Explanation would be easy if the jeremiads had been directed solely at non-church members. Occasionally the ministers did bewail the presence of Philistines among the children of Israel. There were always a few dissolute persons like Peter Bussaker in Connecticut, who was whipped for "his fillthy and prophane expressions (viz that hee hoped to meete some of the members of the Church in hell err long, and hee did not question but he should),"[104] and Increase Mather complained in 1673 of unregenerate rogues who took particular pleasure in luring church members into the taverns and making them drunk, "which argueth a strange degree of impiety."[105] Urian Oakes dared to admit in 1682 that some New Englanders were weary of the "theocracy,"[106] and by 1691 Joshua Scottow tried to argue that the more spectacular enormities had been perpetrated by the mixed multitude that came not over with the saints.[107] But had the sins of New England, enumerated in the jeremiads, proclaimed in the fast-day bulletins, and tabulated by the Synod, been merely the sins of the reprobate, all would have been well. Instead, however, there was a universal confession that the saints themselves were guilty, that they especially furnished examples of declining zeal, security, hardheartedness, and the like, for only the regenerated could exhibit these particular declensions.[108] The sins of pride and contention were more evident inside the churches than without. The decay of New England was definitely not a matter merely of the multitude; it was a backsliding of the children of the covenant.

Whereupon a second hypothesis suggests itself: did anybody really believe in the declension? Were the jeremiads merely rhetorical gestures? Was this one more instance, in the long history of sanctimonious pretense, of a confession of sinfulness on Sunday to be followed on Monday by raising the interest rate or foreclosing a mortgage? Did the people listen on the day of humiliation to an attack on their fine apparel when they had come to church in order to exhibit it? To some extent this may have been true, but Puritan diaries and other evidences do not as a whole bear out such an impression. On the contrary, they show a people who were sincerely and genuinely overwhelmed with a sense of their own short-

104 *Records of the Particular Court of Connecticut (Conn. Hist. Soc. Coll.,* vol. XXII, 1928), pp. 54-55.
105 Increase Mather, *Wo to Drunkards,* p. 21.
106 Urian Oakes, *A Seasonable Discourse* (Cambridge, 1682), p. A2 verso.
107 Cf. Joshua Scottow, *Old Men's Tears For their Own Declensions* (Boston, 1691).
108 Cf. Cotton Mather, *Magnalia* (Hartford, 1853-1855), vol. II, pp. 493-94.

comings. The mixture of business and piety in Hull's instructions to his captains was not hypocrisy, it was the natural expression of a man to whom religion and business were equally real, and he humbled himself most ardently on the days of fasting. The jeremiads bespoke something deeper than a pious fraud; they were the voice of the community, and they patently proceeded from some more profound anxiety, some apprehension of the spirit and trouble of the heart that needed constant and repeated assuaging.

The problem becomes more complex if we ask whether there really was in fact so terrible a degeneration as the jeremiads portrayed. If we took them at face value, we should conclude that New England was swept with what in modern parlance would be called a crime wave that lasted over forty years, and would expect that by 1700 it had become complete chaos. When Hutchinson reviewed the literature and studied the Synod of 1679, judging by the worldly and secularized standards of an eighteenth-century gentleman, he was compelled to interpolate, "we have no evidence of any extraordinary degeneracy."[109] No doubt one could collect enough instances from the court records to create the impression of extensive depravity, but the point would have to be made that these crimes were the exception rather than the rule and that even in the supposedly decayed state of public morality they still were punished. As for the mass of the people, whether full members or Half-Way members or merely inhabitants, they were hard at work, raising their families, clearing the land, attending church, searching their souls, praying for the grace of God, and humbling themselves for their unworthiness. Above all, in accordance with the dominant ethic of the society, they were at work; they were obeying the Biblical injunction to increase and multiply, and they were, with some interruptions, receiving the rewards of pious industry in the form of material prosperity.

But as the rewards came in, and New England adjusted itself to different circumstances, it was perforce compelled to take cognizance of other matters than sanctity and polity. The truth of the matter seems to be not that New England was declining but that it was changing; it had become something other than it had started out to be, in spite of the fact that many who were responsible for the change still desired with all their hearts that it remain unchanged. The orthodox colonies were, as they themselves proudly admitted, "theocracies," which meant that they were medieval states, based upon the fixed will of God, dedicated to the explicit purposes of Revelation, that they were societies of status and subordination, with the ranks of man arranged in a hierarchical series, the lower obedient to the higher, with gentlemen and scholars at the top to rule and direct. They were to be governed with a view to the religious end of mankind, not to the profit motive. Things were right or wrong intrinsically, not

109 Thomas Hutchinson, *The History of the Colony and Province of Massachusetts Bay,* ed. L. S. Mayo (Cambridge, 1936), vol. I, p. 274.

relatively, and a just price for all merchandise could be determined absolutely by theologians. The ideal was not mere theory; it was implemented by such prosecutions as that of Robert Keayne and by repeated legislation fixing the prices of commodities and the wages of workers. Three generations of experience in a changing world that would not remain obedient to the prescriptions of the founders could not shake the faith of the clergy in their code of social regulation, which Samuel Willard reproduced in the last decade of the century as part and parcel of the "body of divinity." From the textbook of Ames to the folio of Willard[110] all agreed that rights to property were invalid if founded only upon "civil law" and not at the same time upon natural and divine law, which meant upon the moral law as well. All the relations of life, natural, economic, ecclesiastical, were held to be fully covered by the rules of the Bible, and especially the social, which by divine appointment were always to take the form of an orderly progression of ranks, classes, and degrees. Condemnations of excesses in apparel were careful to point out that there was a lawful distinction to be observed between the dress of the upper and the lower orders, for "one end of Apparel is to distinguish and put a difference between persons according to ther Places and Conditions."[111] The jeremiads constantly endeavored to hold up in the face of a changing society the ancient ideal of a due subordination of Superiors and Inferiors, the static hierarchy of gentlemen, priests, scholars, burghers, and peasants. The most eloquent on this subject was William Hubbard's remarkable *The Happiness of a People* in 1676, which, though betraying on every page an awareness of altering conditions, of internal divisions and conflicts, pled fervently for the primitive conception of "order." The infinite and omnipotent creator had made the world of differing parts, "which necessarily supposes that there must be differing places, for those differing things to be disposed into, which is Order." Especially must this subordination be observed in the political world, and "whoever is for a parity in any Society, will in the issue reduce things into an heap of confusion."[112] The angels in heaven are not all of one rank, and if we look at the firmament, "the pavement of that glorious mansion place . . . may we not there see, one star differing from another in glory?" Does not the eagle surmount "the little choristers of the valleys"? Therefore, "It is not then the result of time or chance, that some are mounted on horse-back, while others are left to travell on foot." The Lord appoints her "that sits behind the mill" and "him that ruleth on the throne"; the greatest part of mankind are but "tools and instruments for others to work by," rather than "proper agents to effect any thing of themselves," and they "would destroy

---

[110] Cf. Ames, *Conscience*, bk. 5, pp. 236-39; Cotton, in *The Hutchinson Papers* (Albany, 1865), vol. I, pp. 193-94; Willard, *A Compleat Body of Divinity*, pp. 696-721.

[111] Oakes, *New-England Pleaded with*, p. 34.

[112] William Hubbard, *The Happiness of a People In the Wisdome of their Rulers* (Boston, 1676), p. 8.

themselves by slothfulness and security" were they not driven to labor and supervised by their betters. "In fine," Hubbard concluded, "a body would not be more monstrous and deformed without an Head, nor a ship more dangerous at Sea without a Pilot, nor a flock of sheep more ready to be devoured without a Shepheard, then would humane Society be without an Head, and Leader in time of danger." And though he disagreed with other preachers on many points, Hubbard was at one with them in contending that religion alone held such a society together, bound rank to rank, kept each in its place, and made all work toward the same inclusive end.[113] "The Interest of Righteousness in the Common wealth, and Holiness in the Churches are inseparable," said Urian Oakes. "The prosperity of Church and Common wealth are twisted together. Break one Cord, you weaken and break the other also."[114]

By this ideal the jeremiads judged the society, and by this standard they found it failing. They testify, therefore, to the fact that the reality was corresponding less and less to theory and that men were conscious of the discrepancy even while they were unable to cope with it. The change came on apace, irresistible and terrifying, for no one could see where it was leading, though all could see it coming. Instead of zeal there was simple piety and industry; scholars became less influential as the pioneer and the businessman became more important. Class lines drawn upon the basis of inherited status had to be redrawn on the basis of wealth. The social leadership of New England was later to become very adept at receiving into its ranks new men of wealth or ability, but it could do so with ease only after New England put aside its original social theory and gave itself entirely to the ethic of a commercial age. In the seventeenth century the shock was great when some fine names were dimmed and upstart families, Symonds, Brattles, and Whartons, forged ahead. In vain Samuel Willard preached that a civil deference ought to be paid to the gentlemanly class, "tho' the Providence of God may bring them into Poverty";[115] by 1689 Cotton Mather could only shake his head in amazement over the changes New England had seen: "If some that are now rich were once low in the world, 'tis possible, more that were once rich are now brought very low."[116] Nor did a family have to work its way to the very top of the social scale in order to upset the religious hierarchy. It was enough if a Robert Turner, for instance, admitted as an indentured servant to the church of Boston in 1632, should become the master of the tavern, "The Sign of the Anchor," and die in 1664 with an estate of sixteen hundred pounds, or if a John Kitchin should start as the servant of Zachery Bicknell, and his grandson Edward be a merchant prince the equal of the Endecotts. Samuel Shrimpton began as a brazier, but he ended by owning

---

113 *Ibid.*, pp. 9-10.
114 Oakes, *New-England Pleaded with*, p. 49.
115 Willard, *A Compleat Body of Divinity*, p. 643.
116 Cotton Mather, *Magnalia*, vol. I, p. 104.

a large part of Beacon Hill, while Thomas Savage, the son of an English blacksmith, began as a tailor, then erected wharves on Fleet Street, and finally made £2500.[117] The social structure refused to stay fixed, and classifications made by God Himself were transgressed with impunity. Thanks to the pious industry of the saints, or the near-saints, New England ceased to be a holy city set upon a hill, where men remained forever in the station to which they were born, where all ranks meekly submitted to the dictation of gentlemen and scholars.

Of course, had the fluctuation meant merely that a few social leaders were recruited from the abler among the lower ranks, it would not in itself have endangered the Puritan social ideal. But the process by which the successful businessman rose in the world played havoc with the primitive constitution of the society. John Josselyn sagely observed that in New England the diligent hand made rich, but that those of a "droanish disposition" became wretchedly poor.[118] If there were men like Turner and Savage and Hull who left a long inventory of property, there were others whose whole estate did not go beyond that of Thomas Turvill in Newbury: "An old worne out coat and briches with an old lining £0 6s 0d; A thread bare, tho indifferent close coat and doublet with an old wast coat, 1:00:00; Two shirts and a band, 11s; a pair of shoes, 4s; An old greasy hatt, 6d, a pair of stockings, 1s; An old doublet, an old wast cote and a pair of old sheep skin briches, 0:04:00."[119] In the first decades New England had thought it might be an exception to the prophecy that the poor would always be with us, but by the end of the century it knew better. Still worse, however, the process which built up the fortunes of the few worked hardship not only upon the droanish poor, but upon the yeomen farmers, men of virtue and industry, who were permitted by the providence of God to accumulate estates worth no more than two or three hundred pounds. The workings of the economic system forced them to pay a reluctant tribute to the merchants, millers, and shipbuilders. They went into debt for the imported goods; they paid the merchants with their produce, but they received only the first cost and their little store of cash flowed into Boston coffers. The rural districts were reduced to trading on a commodity basis, in what was called "country pay," which figured prices at a higher rate than the goods would fetch in sterling, yet the merchants collected their debts at the rate of sterling and not at the higher level, and the back country began to agitate for cheap money. The class antagonism and the regional hostility which the jeremiads deplored were not figments of an overheated imagination, they were bitter realities, becoming more bitter with the years, and they were tearing the holy and

---

[117] For examples of shift in social status in seventeenth-century New England I am indebted to an unpublished dissertation by Mr. Norman H. Dawes.

[118] John Josselyn, *An Account of Two Voyages to New-England* (London, 1675), Boston, 1865, p. 129.

[119] Joshua Coffin, *A Sketch of the History of Newbury* (Boston, 1845), pp. 89-90.

united commonwealth apart. As the lines were more sharply drawn, even the upper class of inherited position, the sons and daughters of Winthrops, Nortons, Dudleys, Saltonstalls, Bradstreets, became less dedicated leaders of a religious crusade and more a closed corporation of monopolists. They married among themselves, Winthrops with Bradstreets, Dudleys with Saltonstalls, while ministerial families also intermarried extensively and each group took on the character of a caste. Though the church always offered an avenue of escape to the abler youth of the lower orders, to such men as John Wise, the son of an indentured servant, or Thomas Barnard, the son of a maltster of Hartford, yet the ministers of New England no less than the magistrates and the merchants were formed into a vested interest by the end of the seventeenth century—which was not exactly what the founders had envisaged.

The new men, especially the new men of wealth, came up by a different ladder from that which Winthrops and Cottons had ascended, and they showed the effects of their training almost at once. Edward Johnson was horrified as early as 1650 to discover that merchants and vintners "would willingly have had the Commonwealth tolerate divers kinds of sinful opinions" because they were more interested in increasing the population, "that their purses might be filled with coyne," than in upholding an orthodox regime.[120] Thirty years later the merchants of Boston and Salem were generally eager to come to terms with the English government even to the extent of surrendering the sacred charter. A Samuel Shrimpton would as soon serve as a councillor for Andros as an assistant for the commonwealth, and Thomas Maule, who started as a cloth worker in Salem and grew to be a large importer and exporter, was actually a Quaker. But even if the new men were loyal to the theocracy, they would not abide by its regulations in matters of business. The long succession of laws in which the Puritan authorities attempted to fix wages and prices, to decree proper fashions in dress for the different classes, and to hold the merchants in check as John Cotton had restrained Robert Keayne, fell to the ground. "Those good orders," Hubbard sighed, "were not of long continuance, but did expire with the first and golden age in this new world." In 1639, he noted, to seek a profit "above 33 per cent" had been to invite exemplary punishment, but "since that time the common practice of the country hath made double that advance no sin."[121] On this point John Dunton seems to have spoken with greater accuracy than on some others: "Their Laws for Reformation of Manners," he said, "are very severe, yet but little regarded by the People, so at least as to make 'em better, or cause 'em to mend their manners,"[122] while the ministers themselves could see no moral to the story but that "there are more divisions

---

[120] Edward Johnson, *Wonder-Working Providence,* ed. Jameson, p. 254.
[121] Hubbard, *History,* vol. I, pp. 158, 248.
[122] John Dunton, *Letters Written from New England, A.D., 1686,* ed. W. H. Whitmore (Boston, 1867), p. 71.

in times of prosperity than in times of adversity, and when Satan cant destroy them by outward violence he will endeavour to undo them by Strife and variance."[123] It was a complete defeat for the original plan of New England that frontier towns should be settled without a ministry, but, as Cotton Mather declared in 1690, the insoluble problem was how "at once we may Advance our Husbandry, and yet Forbear our Dispersion; and moreover at the same time fill the Countrey with a Liberal Education."[124]

And all this time, when the advance of husbandry and the increase of trade was dispersing the society and dividing the classes, husbandmen and traders were constantly encouraged by the code of Puritanism itself to do exactly those things that were spoiling the Puritan commonwealth. They worked in their callings, and they created multiplicity instead of unity; they waited upon God for the reward and they became social climbers instead of subordinates; they took advantage of their opportunities and they brought about *laissez faire* instead of sumptuary regulation. But in so doing they were blessed, for the injunction they obeyed was as much derived from the primitive creed as was the ethic of regulation and subjection. The more the people worked in the right spirit, the more they transformed the society into something they never intended; the more diligently they labored on the frontier, in the field, in the countinghouse, or on the banks of Newfoundland, the more surely they produced what according to the standards of the founders was a decay of religion and a corruption of morals.

The jeremiads, therefore, were more than a complaint of the saints against worldlings in their midst, more than a hypocritical show, more than a rhetorical exercise. They were necessary releases, they played a vital part in the social evolution because they ministered to a psychological grief and a sickness of the soul that otherwise could find no relief. They were the profession of a society that knew it was doing wrong, but could not help itself, for the wrong thing was also the right thing. They were social purgations, enabling men to make a public expiation for sins that they could not avoid committing, freeing their energies to continue working with the forces of change. A predicament that was produced by the providence of God, a declension that was aggravated at every point by a precise obedience to the edicts of God, could be faced by a bewildered people only with a humbling of themselves before the inexplicable being who brought them into it. From such ceremonies men arose with new strength and courage; they had done the best they could, they had acknowledged what was amiss, they could now go back to their fields and benches and ships, trusting that the covenanted Lord would remember His bond, but when again they grew apprehensive they could look into

---

[123] John Allin, in "Sermons, Sept. 19 to Dec. 15, 1689" (MS. in Harvard College Library).

[124] Cotton Mather, *The Serviceable Man* (Boston, 1690), pp. 50-51.

their own hearts, read what was amiss there, and hasten once more to cleanse their bosoms of poison by public confession. The jeremiads called over and over for reformation, not merely for humiliation and repentance, but for an actual change in the social habits; they produced nothing of the sort, but only more days of humiliation. They did not really signify a resolution to reform, because the people were powerless to resist the march of events. Hence, knowing their impotence, the people needed some method for paying the necessary tribute to their sense of guilt and yet for moving with the times. They knew inwardly that they had betrayed their fathers, or were betraying them; they paid homage to them in the ceremony of humiliation and thus regained something of their self-respect, though paradoxically they had to acquire it by confessing their iniquities.

A literary form does not come into flower unless it answers some necessity in the emotional and social environment. The drama was a true expression of Elizabethan society and the jeremiad sermon was a perfect articulation for the little societies in New England, once the first rush of settlement was over and they were caught in the web of colonial economy. The form perfectly suited the needs of the moment, for on the one hand it satisfied the passionate desire to remain loyal to the Puritan tradition and on the other it sanctioned the pious ethic of godly labor which was destroying the tradition. Devotion to business, the accumulation of riches, the acquisition of houses and lands, these were the duties of all Christians, and what they earned in the way of elegance or luxury was the just reward of their holy diligence. But business and riches meant devotion to the world, and luxury was also a symbol of pride. The sins lamented in the jeremiads were not those of the notoriously scandalous, but such sins as were bound to increase among good men who worked in their callings according to the right Puritan ethic, even though the results of their labor had to be condemned by the ideal which engendered it. Hence these sins had to be professed and denounced, the more so because they were incurable. After the proper obeisance had been offered to an ideal that it was abandoning, the society then had deferred to the past, and so was the more prepared to march into the future.

"PREPARATION FOR SALVATION" IN SEVENTEENTH-CENTURY NEW ENGLAND

I N T H E second half of the seventeenth century the clerical and political leaders of the Puritan colonies in New England became convinced that their societies were steadily degenerating. In 1679 the ministers met at Boston in a formal Synod, drew up a systematic survey of the evils, and launched a vigorous campaign to incite the people to recovery.[1]

Whether the colonies had in fact so woefully fallen off need not concern us. The point is that the ministers, and in all probability most of the people, believed that the case was desperate, and the staggering tabulation of sins, crimes, and offenses published by the Synod in 1679 furnished sufficient documentation. What does concern us is that the leaders of these Calvinist communities, believing that they were faced with destruction, called upon their people to reform, although not a man among them yet entertained any serious doubts about the doctrine of divine determinism. They maintained the absolute sovereignty of God and the utter depravity of man; they held that whatever came to pass in this world was ordained by providence, and they attributed the success of the founders not to human abilities or to physical opportunities, but solely to God, who had furnished the abilities and brought about the opportunities by His providential care. Therefore the question was bound to present itself to divines and statesmen of the second generation, could any merely human effort arrest the moral decline? Was not it a fact in the irresistible plan of God, just as the triumph of the first generation had been decreed in heaven? If God was withholding His grace, could the people be expected to become saints, and if He was depriving them even of "restraining grace," could they possibly avoid yielding to every temptation? And if God, even while rendering them powerless to resist, was at the same time augmenting the temptations, what point could there be in summoning the society to repent?

Any other nation, having such absolute control over all the agencies for molding public opinion, might have gone directly to work. But a Puritan state, anxious though it was to excite the populace, could not merely preach repentance and expect the mass of men to obey. Before it could call upon them to reform, it had first to prove that there were legitimate provisions in the accepted theory of the community for assuming that they could if they would. Was there any authorization in the Word

Published in the *Journal of the History of Ideas,* vol. IV, no. 3 (June 1943), pp. 253-86.
[1] *Cf.* Williston Walker, *The Creeds and Platforms of Congregationalism* (New York, 1893), pp. 427 ff.

of God—as it had been definitively expounded by the founders—for summoning the populace to this work? For the Puritan, this was the all-important question. If he could not prove that the founders had bequeathed him a principle to serve in the emergency, he could not invent one of himself, for that would be to commit the horrid crime of "innovation."

Unfortunately the leaders in the second half of the century were aware that in one fundamental respect their situation differed from anything the founders had foreseen. John Winthrop had declared that the societies of New England were in a direct covenant relationship with Jehovah, exactly as the chosen people of the Old Testament had been; they had agreed with Him to abide by the rules of righteousness, to practice the true polity, to dedicate themselves to doing His will on earth. If they lived up to their promise, He would reward them with material prosperity; if they faltered, He would chastise them with physical affliction until they reformed. When he proclaimed this national covenant, Winthrop had not been troubled by the fact that a majority of the settlers were presumably not regenerated. Only one-fifth of the adult population could give such evidence of their sanctification as would admit them to the covenant of a particular church, but Calvinist theory did not prevent the remaining four-fifths, even though unnumbered among the visible saints, from sharing in the covenant of the nation or from acting their part in its fulfillment. According to the doctrine of all Reformed communities, there existed a realm of conduct which was within the competence of a merely "natural" ability, wherein unregenerate men could be expected to behave one way rather than another because of ordinary pressures, the law, the police, moral persuasion, or the promptings of their conscience. Whether they were saints or not, all men could be required to furnish the state a purely "external" obedience, to abstain from murder or theft, to take no usury and to pay their debts. A holy state, received into a covenant with God, differed from an uncovenanted one not because all its citizens were saints but because therein saints could determine and administer the laws and the natural inhabitants be either incited or compelled to obey. In Massachusetts and Connecticut these conditions were fulfilled. The mass of the planters were earnest beings who, by voluntarily migrating, demonstrated that they were eager to do whatever was within the command of their "natural ability." Furthermore, the leadership was a monopoly of certified saints, who were enabled through grace not only to practice good laws but to enforce obedience upon the body politic. Thus the terms of the national covenant could be complied with, though but a small minority were capable of entering the personal covenant of grace. The national covenant bound men only to "external" righteousness, without presuming the essential sanctity of every individual. In his great oration of 1645 Winthrop explained that all those who enter a civil society—he obviously meant both the godly and the ungodly—no longer have the right to exercise their impulses to evil, but are now committed, by their own assent, to obeying the authority which is set over them for their own good, and to doing only that which is inherently good, just, and honest. Hence he could summon all inhabitants, church members or not, to a public repentance. The national covenant obliged the community only to an outward rectitude, and required that God punish all violations with a physical affliction, but it also promised that an outward reformation would procure an immediate deliverance. No doubt God would never consent to take a society into such a national covenant which did not contain some men sanctified by the Spirit, inwardly as well as externally, but a core of them was adequate as long as they were in control.

For the founders there did exist a real distinction between the realms of nature and of the Spirit, and such actions as required no supernatural assistance were altogether sufficient to insure the public welfare. The original saints could earn their liberation from all social distresses by carrying their unconverted neighbors to at least a constrained compliance with the good, just, and honest—which would fully satisfy the public justice of God. But thirty or forty years later the ministers had built up the picture of a universal depravity, and it seemed clear that the society was no longer responding to providential corrections, let alone to the laws against usury and excessive apparel. They put the blame upon all alike, and called for action from all. One of their principal complaints was the infrequency of sound conversions, and the purely numerical consideration, which had been of no consequence to John Winthrop, thus became tremendously important. It was now absolutely imperative that the vast number of nonmembers, who had supposedly committed themselves to the extent of their natural ability (or been committed by their fathers), who were regularly convened on the days of humiliation and urged to repent, be assured that they could do something. The children of the saints were troubled about their own calling and election, which to many was not so "sure" as that of their fathers had been; a large number were members by only a "Half-Way Covenant" which left their inward condition in some perplexity, and they also had to be convinced, whether they were truly regenerate or not, that they could achieve at least the external obedience. Certainly the mass could no longer be carried or driven by the saints, for the saints were not equal to the task. Had it been merely a matter of recalling approved Christians from temporary lapses, the clergy would have had clear sailing, but in 1679 they had to face the fact, by their own admissions, that the whole body politic was in a bad way, and that a reform which touched only a segment would not be enough. In order to effect a national recovery, the whole nation had to be recovered; the declension was a social phenomenon, and it semed to bring social consequences, plagues, wars, and famines. Hence these determinists were the more obliged to find some method for appealing to natural men, for persuading the unregenerate that they could achieve enough sanctity to preserve the society, though they might never be able to save their souls. The whole people, citizens and inhabitants, church members and non-members, recorded their vow to repent and reform on the many days of humiliation, but their promise would remain an empty gesture unless they could be convinced that they did have the power to keep it without first having to be numbered among the spiritually elect.

It might seem, when the leaders returned to first principles and studied the works of their fathers, that they were caught in the inexorable logic of Calvin. All things in their world were ordained by God, and if He decreed that a people were to decline, no human hand could fend off the appointed outcome. So the founders had conceived the world. They had, it is true, carved out a small island of liberty in the sea of determinism, which was the covenant of grace, but even that covenant was a very slight curtailment of God's awful despotism. The great English theologians from whom New England learned the "federal" doctrine had delivered themselves without equivocation. William Perkins, for instance, condemned all "Pelagians" who would seek the cause of predestination in men, as if God ordained them only after He foresaw which would receive or reject the offer of salvation. The decrees have no cause beyond God's arbitrary pleasure, and Perkins dismissed as "subtile deuices" all attempts to mitigate this "hard sentence."[2] William Ames worked out more carefully the rationality of the covenant, but he always insisted upon the irrationality of a transcendent might behind it, and agreed that no foreknowledge of God should ever be presupposed to His determinations.[3] John Preston would argue that according to the logic of the covenant men were justly condemned for not doing what they could do, but he would also declare, "God hath kept it in his power to draw whom he will, to sanctifie whome he will," and would expound the natural freedom of men with this qualification, "yet it is not in any mans power to beleeve, to repent effectually."[4] Hence John Ball's *A Treatise of the Covenant of Grace,* published in 1645, in some respects the most daring excursion in the whole literature, could not avoid the embarrassing question: "To what end doe the promises and threatenings [of the covenant] tend . . . if God doe worke all things by his effectuall power in them that believe?" Ball could not answer his own question, and took refuge in the conventional distinction between God's revealed and hidden will. Openly He demands obedience of all men, but secretly He gives the ability only to the few already elected: "That is, he invites many in the Ministry of his Word, and externall administration of the Covenant, whom he doth not inwardly instruct and draw." If you concluded, therefore, that the offer of the covenant was a "giftelesse gift," Ball could reply only that you were an unthankful

[2] William Perkins, *Works* (London, 1612-13), vol. I, pp. 107-11.
[3] Ames, *The Marrow of Sacred Divinity* (London, 1643), p. 105.
[4] John Preston, *The Saints Qvalification* (London, 1633), pp. 236, 237.

servant and perverse being.[5] But the ministers of New England by 1679 had to deal with a race of the unthankful and perverse.

The founders faithfully echoed such teachers. Cotton pointed out that God could pour His grace upon the most abominable sinners, so that "If he take pleasure to breathe in a man, there is nothing can hinder him, it will blow upon the most noysome dunghill in any place, and be never a whit the more defiled." Logic compelled him to suggest that the best way to become a saint might be "to have run a lewd course of life," since a Calvinist God would then be the more challenged to show His power,[6] but such reflections were sadly out of order in 1679. Thomas Hooker seemed to be no more helpful: man is darkness and God is light, he said, and darkness is unalterably opposed to light: "Thou canst resist a Saviour, but not entertaine him, doe what thou canst."[7] In fact, the ministers, who in the *Result* of the Synod bade all men reform, also renewed their allegiance to the *Westminster Confession,* which explicitly stated that "God from all eternity did by the most wise and holy Counsel of his own Will, freely and unchangeably ordaine whatsoever comes to pass," and further declared that until grace comes the natural spirit must be "passive" and utterly incapable of moral action. "A natural man being altogether averse from that good, and dead in sin, is not able by his own strength to convert himself, or to prepare himself thereunto."[8] With what right, therefore, could the divines rally depraved generations to repent in the name of the fathers, who had taught that a people to whom God chooses not to give His grace are impotent? If men may sit all their lives under the most clear dispensations of the Gospel and yet remain impenitent—Samuel Willard testified at the end of the century, "woful experience tell[s] us that there are a great many that do so"[9]—with what face could the ministers preach reformation? What inducement could they offer the average man or what hope of success could they hold out?

It was at this point that the second and third generations began to perceive the advantages in an idea which the founders themselves had devised, which they had heroically vindicated against all opposition and bequeathed to their children as an indispensable part of New England orthodoxy. Though Calvinism pictured man as lifeless clay in the potter's hand, and the *Westminster Confession* asserted that the natural man could not convert himself or even "prepare himself thereunto," the New Englanders had been able to maintain that there did exist a state of "preparation for salvation." We should note at once that the seeds of this difficult and dangerous idea are to be found in the writers whom the New Englanders studied even before the migration. Perkins, Preston, and Ames

[5] Ball, *A Treatise of the Covenant of Grace* (London, 1645), p. 343.

[6] Cotton, *The way of Life, or Gods VVay and Course* (London, 1641), pp. 113, 117.

[7] Hooker, *The Soules Vocation* (London, 1638), pp. 230-31.

[8] Walker, *Creeds and Platforms,* pp. 370-71, 377-78.

[9] Willard, *A Compleat Body of Divinity* (Boston, 1726), p. 427.

were Calvinists, and undoubtedly had no intention of propounding any belief at variance with the accepted creed, but they were also the formulators of the covenant or "federal" version of Calvinism, in which they managed to present Jehovah as consenting to deal with sinners according to the terms of a covenant.[10] As soon as the relationship of God to man was conceived in this fashion, the corollary became obvious that the terms of a covenant may be known in advance. Men must still receive grace, which is dispensed arbitrarily according to sovereign decrees, but the very fact that God does propose terms means that there may be a moment in time between absolute depravity and the beginning of conversion in which the transaction is proposed. Men may not be able to do anything until they are regenerated, but until then they can listen and meditate. Grace is a covenant, and the essence of a covenant, these theologians never wearied of explaining, is an agreement between two agents, both of whom must know the conditions. If election be a flash of lightning that may strike at any moment, men cannot place themselves in its path, nor cultivate any anticipatory attitudes, but when it comes as a chance to enter a contract, they must first of all learn what is to be contracted. Though God gives His son freely, Preston said, "yet except we take him, that gift is no gift; therefore there must be a taking on our part."[11] A man must have his quill sharpened for the signature and the wax warmed for his seal. God has graciously put aside His overwhelming might in order to treat with men in a rational negotiation, "that we might know what to expect from God, and upon what termes."[12] If we may know the terms, we may be encouraged, in advance of our conversions, even while we possess nothing more than our "natural gifts," to commence a course of obedience. Once regeneration was conceived not as a sudden prostration but as a gradual process commencing with an initial stage of negotiation, it became possible, even probable, that men should undergo a preliminary state of "preparation" before they actually were called.

The English formulators were concerned chiefly to establish the fact that regeneration is a process in time, capable of being analyzed into temporal units. They concentrated attention not so much on the crisis of conversion but on the moment just preceding it, when the covenant of grace was being tendered to a sinner but was not yet taken up. In Perkins the idea of preparation first appeared as little more than a conventional instruction to preachers that they should spare no pains with their people: "This preparation is to bee made partly by disputing or reasoning with them, that thou mayest thorowly discerne their manners and disposition, and partly by reproving in them some notorious sinne, that being pricked in heart and terrified, they may become teachable."[13] Among his successors

---

[10] Cf. Perry Miller, The New England Mind (New York, 1939), ch. 13.
[11] Preston, The Nevv Covenant, or The Saints Portion (London, 1629), p. 172.
[12] Obadiah Sedgwick, The Bowels of Tender Mercy (London, 1661), p. 6.
[13] Perkins, "The Art of Prophecying," Works (London, 1631), fol. 670.

the idea took on increased dimensions. We can trace through their works an expanding realization that previous to the signing of a covenant there must be a period in which man is instructed and solicited, that before a simple regeneration he may be careless but before a covenant he must learn to stipulate. The federalists denounced Arminianism because they said that no amount of good works merited any consideration from God, but at the same time they taught sinners provisions for their possible conversion. Preston, for example, said that the worst of sinners may be called without any antecedent humbling of the heart, just as a sick man does not need a sense of sickness in order to be cured, but nevertheless "if he be not sicke, and have a sense of it, he will not come to the Physitian."[14] Coming to the physician will not in itself work a cure, but it may be "a preparative sorrow." Though a reprobate may have the sense and yet never be saved, the elect are seldom taken into the covenant of grace until after they too have had it. In general the evidence indicates that these theologians had succeeded, even before 1630, in investing the word "preparation" with a distinct connotation, making it mean a period in time during which men could acquire a "sense" which was not yet an actual conversion but which might be a forerunner of it, an experience that all men might have, since it was not limited merely to the elect,[15] which could be construed as a hopeful augury of ultimate success and could be demanded of all men, whereas an authentic work of the Spirit would have to wait upon the disposition of God.

To establish this thesis the covenant theologians undertook a labor which won them fame throughout Protestant Europe and which was assiduously carried on by their New England disciples, a subtle analysis of the temporal process of regeneration, so that they were able to give elaborate descriptions of every step, beginning with the most minute diagnosis of the dawning of a premonition. Yet all this while, their loyalty to the basic Protestant doctrine of salvation by faith required them to insist that, no matter how slight this first movement might be, it should be attributed to no effort of man but solely to the grace of God. Hence their conception of a state of preparation, as something that came before even the most infinitesimal rumble of faith, was exceedingly welcome. Preparation did not need to be called a saving act of the human will; it could be set forth as no meritorious work in any Arminian sense, not even as part of faith at all, but as a mere inclination to accept faith, should faith ever come. This much a corrupt man might do, for it was really no motion of his soul; it was no lifting of himself by his own bootstraps, but simply an attitude of expectancy. Had the mechanism of regeneration

---

[14] Preston, *The Breast-Plate of Faith and Love* (London, 1630), p. 13.

[15] *Cf.* Preston, *Remaines* (London, 1637), p. 193: "The preparative sorrow is nothing else but a sorrowing for sinne, as it causeth punishment, or a sorrowing for some Iudgement likely to ensue, and pronounced against him, but this is not the true sorrow: a reprobate may have this sorrow, which shall never be saved . . . it hath his originall from nature."

still been phrased exclusively in the language of Calvin, as a forcible seizure, a holy rape of the surprised will, there would have been no place for any period of preparation, which would have been conceivable only as the first moment of an effectual calling. But when regeneration was understood to be the offer and acceptance of a covenant, even though the power to accept it must come from God, men could make themselves ready to entertain it, since they could know in advance what form it would assume and what response it would entail. Though God might do as He pleased, it was noted that normally those who most strove to prepare themselves turned out to be those whom He shortly took into the covenant of grace.

So far as the somewhat obscure passages from the early writers can now be made out, they do not exhibit any interest in the social implications of the idea. These writers still assumed the distinction between the realms of nature and of grace; at this point they were concerned with salvation, not with politics. The conduct of society, the observance of the moral law in domestic and business affairs, was to them a matter of regulation and compulsion. Good laws were to be enforced, and even the most drastic forms of Calvinism always assumed that men had the physical power to obey whatever laws the state imposed. Such actions had nothing to do with salvation, and were not a part of preparation. Of course a saint would endeavor to be a good citizen, but the performance of his civic duties did not earn his redemption. The idea of preparation, as formulated by Perkins, Preston, and Ames, met a spiritual need; it encouraged men to seek holiness in the midst of a determined universe. But almost as soon as the idea was propounded, it began to reveal that it did in fact have social as well as spiritual consequences, for while a man was undergoing a work of preparation in the hope that it might be followed by a conversion, he would be making every effort, out of his own volition, to perfect his external behavior. He would have a positive incentive to righteous conduct, although he could not yet be said to be a true saint or even to have a hope of salvation. But though he might finally go to hell, if while he lived in this world he prepared himself, he would *ipso facto* fulfill the terms of the national covenant. Thus the rapid development of the idea, first among the theologians of English Puritanism and then among the leaders of New England, is a symptom of the change that came over the Puritan movement as it became concerned more with the conquest of power than with the pursuit of holiness. Sixteenth-century Puritans were driven by one consideration above all others, the salvation of their souls, and they set out to cleanse the church as a proof of their sainthood, but in the seventeenth century Puritans became organized into a political party and thereupon had to take more thought for the strategy of winning a political victory. The problem of determinism never bothered men who were already convinced of their election, for they were free to do God's will; but when saints banded together to capture the English state, or after they had captured the new states in New England, they had to find more effective means of getting all the people, the mass of the unregenerate whom they were now to govern, started on the road they had traveled in the sheer exuberance of zeal. In the practical terms of social regulation, their problem now was to excite the people to moral action. Almost from the beginning the leaders perceived that to depend merely upon the sanctions of the law, upon the coercion of natural abilities was not enough. Yet according to Calvinist doctrine, if men were ever to perform anything beyond the limits of nature, they had to be supplied with grace. Hence for the sake of the social welfare, as much as for the welfare of particular souls, it became necessary that men be made gracious. Yet grace was dispensed only by God, according to the secret pleasure of His will, and men could not be converted by any amount of external compulsion. But preparation was not a supernatural work. All men could achieve it, and all men therefore could be called upon to prepare for grace, and thereby to exert themselves in precisely such a course of moral conduct as was required of all the society by the national covenant.

We should not be surprised that Thomas Hooker, the virtual dictator of Connecticut and one of the most socially minded among the early ministers, should be also the greatest analyst of souls, the most exquisite diagnostician of the phases of regeneration, and above all the most explicit exponent of the doctrine of preparation. Thomas Shepard and Peter Bulkeley followed his lead. All three agreed that preparation was not a meritorious work; they took infinite precautions lest their doctrine be construed in any Catholic or Arminian sense. Hooker would explain that no natural action can prepare for supernatural grace, and that the effectual operation of the Word must never be thought to depend upon anything that a man may do by himself, "not upon any preparation which was done, nor any performances . . . but meerly upon the power and good pleasure of the Lord."[16] After justification the will has acquired a new power, "whereby it is able to set forth it selfe into any holy action," but in the first stage it is merely wrought upon, "and I am a patient and doe onely endure it: but I have not any spirituall power to doe any thing of myself."[17] Bulkeley put it in the language of the federal theology: after God has taken us into a covenant with Him, He requires a positive performance of its terms, but "first the Lord doth dispose us and fit us to a walking in Covenant with him," and in these hours we must remain passive.[18] In fact Hooker and his friends were so eager to prove their orthodoxy that they would indulge in statements as extreme as any to be found in the history of New England, and consequently their real position has been generally misrepresented.[19] Since the sinner must be at first

[16] Hooker, *The Application of Redemption,* 2nd ed. (London, 1659), pp. 297-98.
[17] Hooker, *The Soules Preparation for Christ* (London, 1632), p. 156.
[18] Peter Bulkeley, *The Gospel-Covenant* (London, 1651), p. 319.
[19] *Cf.* Frank H. Foster, *A Genetic History of the New England Theology* (Chicago, 1907), pp. 26, 31-35.

"meerly patient," said Hooker, God is at liberty to give or to deny grace to whom He pleases, and may justly refuse it to the most prayerful and conscientious, *"for it is not in him that wils and runs, but in God that shews mercy."*[20] By the same token God may bestow it "upon such who neither prize nor profit at al they have." The Puritan God was a capricious Jehovah whose favor did not follow upon any good work of man—it "hangs not upon that hinge."[21]

We may very well ask what Hooker and his group could conceivably accomplish when they prefaced the doctrine of preparation by such qualifications. To appreciate the significance of their work we must remember that had they definitely broken with the Calvinist system, had they openly advocated the natural freedom of men to perform deeds that would secure salvation, they would have been branded as Arminians. So Hooker was extremely careful to insist upon the natural impotence of the unregenerate. He was not endeavoring to preach even the possibility that holy actions might be performed by natural men, but he was endeavoring to mark off a number of chronological phases in the sequence of regeneration and then to argue that the first might be undergone by some who ultimately did not continue through the others, who finally proved to be reprobates. The important point was to establish the factual existence of this probationary period, to demonstrate that regeneration was not a precipitate or instantaneous transformation and that the first degree did not always or necessarily lead to the second. There is an "order" in God's proceedings, Hooker said: first He takes away the resistance of the soul by an irresistible operation, whereupon the soul "comes to be in the next passive power" and is disposed to a spiritual work—*"vult moveri."*[22] In his preface to Rogers' *Doctrine of Faith,* a handbook much prized among the people, Hooker called attention to a passage wherein Rogers wrote that we cannot tell exactly when faith is born, whether after a man has fully apprehended Christ or when he first hungers for Him; this, Hooker remarked, ought to settle all disputes about preparation, for all should agree that in the first stage "there is as it were the spawne of Faith, not yet brought to full perfection."[23] But this first conviction need not be regarded as a "fruit" of faith, only as a preliminary negotiation. Of course such beginnings must be initiated by the Lord—"I have no power of my selfe, but onely receive it from the Lord";[24] when the will is first turned toward God, it is "not onely the bare power and faculty of the natural will" at work, but that will turned by God's efficiency, yet at this point God is still acting from the outside, as when He moves any object in nature, not from within as He does after He has filled the heart with His Spirit.[25] Hence there is a space between

---

[20] Hooker, *The Application of Redemption,* p. 309.
[21] *Ibid.,* p. 299.
[22] *Ibid.,* pp. 395-96.
[23] John Rogers, *The Doctrine of Faith* (London, 1629), p. A10.
[24] Hooker, *The Soules Vocation* (London, 1638), pp. 204-05.
[25] Hooker, *The Unbeleevers Preparing for Christ* (London, 1638), p. 32.

depravity and sanctity, a hiatus during which the human will is being influenced but is not yet transformed, a state which Hooker characteristically illustrated in a metaphor, comparing it to the moment when a clock that was running out of order is stopped but not yet repaired. At that moment, "the clocke is a patient, and the workman doth all," yet whenever the workman is the Holy Ghost and "where ever it is soundly wrought," the operation "will in the end be faith and grace."[26] Hooker's reputation among Puritans was great because he was the expert chronometer of regeneration, offering the most acute discriminations of preparation, vocation, justification, adoption, and sanctification, but his most impressive thought was devoted to the first action in the series. Through this doctrine he did more than any other to mold the New England mind.

However, his teachings were not universally accepted by all Puritans. They were opposed even by some of the federalists, who saw in them, despite Hooker's elaborate safeguards, a sophistical form of Arminianism. Pemble, for example, without mentioning Hooker by name, attacked his doctrines in the *Vindiciae Gratiae,* declaring that such actions as Hooker identified with preparation could not be encompassed by the unconverted. "They are not antecedents, but consequents and parts of true conversion," whereas any preparative actions produced merely by human efforts could be "no efficient causes to produce grace of conversion."[27] Giles Firmin attacked both Hooker and Shepard specifically, on the ground that their doctrine caused seekers after God much unnecessary discouragement since it made them distrust the first acting of the Spirit for fear it might prove no more than an abortive preparation. They demanded more of men than God required and called upon them not merely to repent but to go beyond repentance, whereas according to Firmin the battle was won just as soon as men were able to lament their sins.[28]

The majority of New England divines followed Hooker, but there was one ominous exception. John Cotton generally figures as the chief "theocrat" of Massachusetts and is popularly remembered as the dictator of its intellect, yet in fact he differed widely from his colleagues, and his dissent came near to causing his ruin. On this fundamental point Hooker's influence eclipsed Cotton's, and his share in the formation of American Puritanism is correspondingly the larger. The full story of the opposition is difficult to reconstruct, because the authorities made every effort to play it down; nevertheless, the noise of their disagreement resounded through the Calvinist world. Enemies of the New England Way were quick to make the most of it, the Presbyterian Baillie, for instance, scoring a blow when he sneered that Winthrop and Welde, in their narrative of the Antinomian episode, did all they could "to save Mr. *Cottons* credit," yet they could not so falsify the story but what "they let the truth of Mr. *Cottons* Seduc-

---

[26] Hooker, *The Sovles Preparation for Christ,* pp. 157-58.
[27] William Pemble, "Vindiciae Gratiae," *Workes* (Oxford, 1659), pp. 78, 81-84.
[28] Giles Firmin, *The Real Christian* (London, 1670), "To the Reader."

tion fall from their Pens."[29] The halting sentences in which Cotton endeavored to reply do more to confirm our suspicions of a difference than to persuade us of the asserted agreement, nor do we need to search very far into his writings to find the theological basis for his divergence.

Cotton's position was simplicity itself. Though he was a "federalist," he was first of all the man who sweetened his mouth every night with a morsel of *The Institutes*. He was persuaded that between the natural and the regenerate man lay a gulf so immense that only divine grace could bridge it. If a man performs a single action appropriate to the elect, he has then and there become one of them. There can be no halfway conversion; a man is either one or the other, and those who once receive grace will infallibly persevere through all shortcomings to an ultimate glorification. Therefore what Hooker and Shepard called preparation was for Cotton simply the impact of grace, and the prepared were already saints. "A man is as passive in his Regeneration, as in his first generation."[30] If we are "fitted" for good deeds, the first motion must be a work solely of God, who alone can fit us, and once He gives the smallest competence, He has thereby signified His irrevocable favor. Hence, as Cotton saw it, the first motion no less than the last is "true spirituall Union between the Lord & our souls"; define it as closely as possible, it is still from God.[31] The natural heart is totally "drowsie," and "for our first union, there are no steps unto the Altar."[32] Can a blind man prepare himself to see?[33] Hooker's doctrine creates a false sense of security, for it tells men that preparation consists in a disposition to wait upon Christ, and those who have brought themselves by their own efforts to such a seeming surrender thereupon give over striving. The supreme refinement of deceptive faith has always been a self-induced determination to wait upon Christ: "there is no promise of life made to those that wait & seek in their own strength, who being driven to it, have taken it up by their own *resolutions*." Should we try to reassure ourselves by reflecting that if we cannot work we can believe, or that if we cannot believe we can wait until we come to believe, "here is still the old roote of *Adam* left alive in us, whereby men seeke to establish their owne righteousnesse."[34] There can be no safe building upon such resolves, for they are produced by mechanical causes, even when induced by the persuasive eloquence of the pastor at Hartford.

Cotton was the better Calvinist, and he knew it: not only would he plead the authority of federalists like Pemble in rejecting preparation, he would also cry out, "Let *Calvin* answer for me."[35] Nevertheless Hooker

[29] Charles Francis Adams, *Antinomianism in the Colony of Massachusetts Bay, 1636-1638* (Prince Society, Boston, 1894), p. 364.
[30] Cotton, *The New Covenant* (London, 1654), p. 55.
[31] *Ibid.*, pp. 28-29.
[32] *Ibid.*, p. 54.
[33] Cotton, *The way of Life* (London, 1641), p. 182.
[34] *The New Covenant*, pp. 196-97, 182; cf. pp. 19-25, 54-55, 58-80.
[35] *Gospel Conversion* (London, 1646), p. 22; cf. pp. 18-19, 30, 46.

triumphed in New England, for the good and sufficient reason that Cotton's doctrine fathered the awful heresy of Antinomianism. Modern historians often find the technicalities of this dispute so abstruse as to lead them comfortably to conclude that it was meaningless, but its social consequences became immediately apparent when Mrs. Hutchinson declared that she had come to New England "but for Mr. Cotton's sake" and added, "As for Mr. Hooker . . . she said she liked not his spirit."[36] Mr. Hooker, it will be remembered, aided by Shepard and Bulkeley, was the principal prosecutor in her trial before the Synod, and did not check the expression of his satisfaction upon her expulsion.

Anne Hutchinson took her stand upon Cotton's doctrine of a radical distinction between regeneration and unregenerateness, asserting that in no sense whatsoever could works have anything to do with justification, that they could not even be offered as "evidence," and that a true saint might consistently live in any amount of sin. She wiped out all Hooker's fine-spun discriminations between a state of preparation and a state of adoption; she presented the clear-cut alternatives of an absolute union with Christ or an utter disseverance. Her followers regarded preparation as the most offensive among the tenets of the New England clergy, and cited Hooker and Shepard as proof positive that the ministers were preaching a "covenant of works." If Hooker would allow that a man could do something, anything, before he was redeemed, which could also be done by those who eventually went to perdition, what was this but Popery? The Antinomians emphatically declared that the sinner, "for his part, must see nothing in himselfe, have nothing, doe nothing, onely he is to stand still and waite for Christ to doe all for him."[37] They disapproved any preaching of the "law," any pressing of duties upon the unconverted, any calling them to faith and prayer; to exhort even the elect to fulfill their obligations was superfluous, not because saints would be perfect but because those who are concerned about their conduct are still under the obsolete covenant of the law. To them it seemed that Hooker, though he professed the impotence of nature, set men to work of themselves and promised the unconverted that somehow they might take the first step toward grace if only they would try; therefore, as Anne Hutchinson saw it, the people were misled into thinking themselves justified no further than they could perceive themselves enabled to perform good works, although the essence of Protestantism was the assurance of justification through the free promise of forgiveness. Election did not admit of degrees proportioned to the extent of the endeavor, nor could any amount of sin reverse the divine decree; justification was absolute and final, in and by itself.

Anne Hutchinson announced that she had learned her doctrine from Cotton, and throughout her ordeal wrapped herself in the mantle of his authority, to the consternation of the authorities. Even after the Anti-

36 Adams, *Antinomianism*, p. 272.
37 *Ibid.*, p. 74.

nomians were exiled, and Cotton had utterly renounced them, they would not give him up. In the heat of the conflict the elders brought Cotton to a conference, "drew out sixteen points, and gave them to him, entreating him to deliver his judgment directly in them." Winthrop remarks that many of his reply "were dispersed about"; seven years later, one Francis Cornwell published in England what purported to be an authentic version, with a dedication to Sir Harry Vane—for that erstwhile friend of Mrs. Hutchinson was now a power in the land. The book was so popular that two more editions appeared in 1646 and a fourth in 1647,[38] and when copies were brought to Boston there must have been anguish in the parsonage of the First Church. Winthrop says that at the conference Cotton cleared some doubts, "but in some things he gave not satisfaction";[39] in Cornwell's version he appears to have given none at all. The issue in 1637, says the editor, came down to this: the renegade clergy "would not believe themselves justified, no further than they could see themselves work; making their Markes, Signes, and Quallifications, the causes of their Justification," whereas the Antinomians upheld the true Protestant position that the evidence of justification is to be discerned "onely by Faith in the Free Promise."[40] Cornwell exhibited Cotton adhering to the Antinomian sense. Being asked whether there are any conditions in the soul before faith "of dependance unto which, such promises are made," he replied roundly, no: "To works of creation there needeth no preparation; the almighty power of God calleth them to be his people, that were not his people."[41] In other answers, still according to Cornwell, Cotton asserted that to evidence one's justification by his sanctification is Popery, that "Such a Faith as a practicall Sillogisme can make, is not a Faith wrought by the Lords Almighty power," that no conviction wrought by natural means, even by evangelical preaching, should be confounded with a true work of faith, for "the Word without the Almighty power of the Spirit is but a dead Letter," that God does not give His grace upon condition of our becoming prepared, because "it is not his good pleasure to give us our first comfort . . . from our owne righteousnesse."[42] In these words the Antinomians were content that their cause be stated; they then appealed to the judgment of Protestantism whether the divines in New England, following the way of Hooker and of preparation, had not betrayed the Bible Commonwealth.

Anne Hutchinson said that but one minister besides Cotton remained

---

[38] *Sixteene Questions of Seriovs and Necessary Consequence, Propounded unto Mr. John Cotton* (London, 1644); *A Conference Mr. John Cotton held at Boston* (London, 1646); *Gospel Conversion* (London, 1646); *Severall Questions* (London, 1647).

[39] John Winthrop, *Journal,* ed. J. K. Hosmer (New York, 1908), vol. I, pp. 203, 207.

[40] *Gospel Conversion,* p. A5.

[41] *Ibid.,* pp. 1, 5.

[42] *Ibid.,* pp. 6, 16-17, 18, 28.

faithful, her brother-in-law, John Wheelwright, who came to grief when, on the fast day appointed for a public lamentation over the controversy, he delivered a sermon which the authorities found "incendiary." The text of that discourse does not immediately suggest, to an age insensitive to the fine shading of theological dispute, exactly wherein it was subversive, but if it be read in the light of the times, in view of the then agitated state of the question of preparation, its inflammable substance becomes all too evident. Wheelwright later repudiated Mrs. Hutchinson, or at least the errors charged upon her; yet like Cotton he opposed the doctrine of preparation and therefore by implication accused his colleagues of apostasy. "To preach the Gospell," he declared, "is to preach Christ . . . & nothing but Christ . . . so that neither before our conversion nor after, we are able to put forth one act of true saving spirituall wisdome, but we must haue it put forth from the Lord Jesus Christ, wth whom we are made one."[43] Hooker, Shepard, and Bulkeley were bending all their ingenuity to tabulating the successive periods of conversion, but Wheelwright flatly announced that when the Lord converts a soul, He "revealeth not to him worke, & from that worke, carieth him to Christ, but there is nothing revealed but Christ, when Christ is lifted vp, he draweth all to him, that belongeth to the election of grace." If men think they are on the highway to salvation after they have traversed the first mile but are not yet united to Christ, "they are saued wthout the Gospell." "No, no," he exclaimed, "this is a covenant of works."[44] If so, then the ministers of New England were not Protestants, and the friends of Wheelwright might warrantably conclude that Christians should refuse them a hearing, that they might take even more violent measures against them.

Therefore Wheelwright was banished, but John Cotton was not. There were many reasons why the authorities were unwilling to send away their most renowned scholar, but one is forced to suspect that he owed his preservation to the fact that he was still more reluctant to go. Wheelwright would disown the extravagances of the Antinomians,[45] but he would not compromise on preparation; Cotton bent before the storm and saved his standing in the holy commonwealth at the expense of his consistency. Perhaps this statement is too severe, for in works presumably written after 1638 Cotton still stressed the strictly Protestant version of the covenant of grace, which, he said in a book published five years after his death, "is not of our will, but of the Lords, that takes away our strong heart, and gives us a soft heart before any preparation."[46] Nevertheless, it is clear that Cotton learned at least a degree of caution from his unhappy experience, and his subsequent references inevitably suggest that he so moderated his

---

[43] Charles H. Bell, *John Wheelwright* (Prince Society, Boston, 1876), p. 163.
[44] *Ibid.*, p. 164.
[45] *Ibid.*, p. 199.
[46] Cotton, *An Exposition upon The Thirteenth Chapter of the Revelation* (London, 1656), p. 211.

opinions as to make himself no longer able to speak frankly. The account which he gave in his reply to Roger Williams is so patently evasive, so utterly fails to correspond to the narrative of Winthrop, and is so denuded of feeling that every line rings with a hollow sound. He had never, according to his own account, given any countenance to the "sundry corrupt, and dangerous errors" of the "Familists," but instead had publicly preached against them. The orthodox brethren had then said to the erring party, "See, your Teacher declares himselfe clearely to differ from you," and they had replied, "No matter . . . what he saith in publick, we understand him otherwise, and we know what he saith to us in private." On no other grounds than these was bred a "jealousie" in the country "that I was in secret a Fomenter of the Spirit of Familisme, if not leavened my selfe that way."[47] In this account and in others he confessed that he had meditated fleeing from Massachusetts, since in the opinion of many, "such a Doctrin of Union, and evidencing of Union, as was held forth by mee, was the *Trojan* Horse, out of which all the erroneous Opinions and differences of the Country did issue forth,"[48] yet, he protested, he did not have to go, not because he changed his mind, but because "private conference with some chiefe Magistrates, and Elders" revealed the welcome fact that he was in essential agreement with them after all! At the Synod he at last discovered the "corruption of the Judgement of the erring Brethren" and saw the fraudulence of their pretense of holding forth nothing but what they had received from him, "when as indeed they pleaded for grosse errors, contrary to my judgment," and therefore he "bare witnesse against them."[49] This happy resolution was not a matter of his being recovered, but "the fruit of our clearer apprehension, both of the cause and of the state of our differences, and of our joynt consent and concurrence in bearing witnesse against the common heresies, and errors of Antinomianisme, and Familisme, which disturbed us all."[50] Therefore he could reply to Baillie that there had never been any question of his "Seduction"—all of us hold Union with Christ, and evidencing of Union by the same Spirit, and same Faith and same holinesse."[51]

But what of Cornwell's embarrassing pamphlet? Cotton could do nothing but denounce it as a forgery and publish what he swore were the replies he had given in the cross-examination of 1637. The student finds himself wondering how, if Cornwell's version is accurate, Winthrop could have said at the time that Cotton cleared some doubts, or how, if Cotton's own version is true, Winthrop should have added that in other things he gave no satisfaction. At any rate, what Cotton now presented sounds strangely different from his previous statements. He described himself replying to

[47] Cotton, *A Reply to Mr. Williams* [1647] (*Publications of the Narragansett Club*, vol. II, Providence, 1867), pp. 80-84.
[48] Adams, *Antinomianism*, p. 360.
[49] *A Reply to Mr. Williams*, p. 83.
[50] *Ibid.*, p. 376.
[51] *Ibid.*, p. 362.

the question of whether our union with Christ be complete before and without faith, that though from one point of view we are united to Christ as soon as He elects us, "yet in order of nature, before our faith doth put forth it self to lay hold on him," we may be among the elect without a final union—an admission that gave Hooker every right to introduce a period of preparation. When asked if justification could be evidenced by a "conditionall" promise—a word he formerly had denounced—he hedged: "The Spirit doth Evidence our Justification both wayes, sometimes in an absolute Promise, sometimes in a conditionall," and though he would still hestitate to take "saving qualifications" as a "first evidence" of justi-fication, he would generously grant that "A man may haue an argument from thence (yea, I doubt not a firm and strong argument)."[52] Since Hooker had carefully defended his thesis against Arminian constructions, Cotton could seek refuge in the same disavowals; the promises of the covenant, he could say, have no efficacy in themselves to bring men to faith unless the Spirit accompanies them, "yet this is the end to which God giveth them, to stir up the Sons of men."[53] Consequently, men are not to rest but are to be exhorted "to provoke themselves and one another, to look after the Lord." He would still insist that in the first work of conversion a man must be passive; nevertheless, urged on by his colleagues, he would say, "There are many sins which a man lives in, which he might avoid by very common gifts, which would he renounce, God would not be wanting to lead him on to further grace."[54] This was exactly what Hooker meant by "preparation."

Cotton was much too valuable to be sacrificed unnecessarily, and in the 1640's he vindicated the wisdom of the authorities by rendering the New England Way yeoman service in its dispute with the Presbyterians, but on this point he never dared again to speak with authority. If he touched upon it, he would preface his remarks, "Reserving due honour to such gracious and precious Saints, as may be otherwise minded."[55] Eager as he

---

[52] Cotton, *The Way of Congregational Churches Cleared* (London, 1648), pt. 1, pp. 41-47.

[53] Cotton, *The New Covenant*, p. 89.

[54] Cotton, *Christ the Fountaine of Life* (London, 1651), p. 174.

[55] This phrase occurs in *A Treatise of the Covenant of Grace* (London, 1671), p. 35; this volume is the third edition of *The New Covenant* (London, 1654). In the first version the courteous gesture is lacking; an objection is propounded, "whether doth not the Lord give us some saving Preparations before Jesus Christ?" and to this question itself is appended an explanation for its existence, "for there be those that are gratious Saints, that have conceived that there are some gratious Qualifications, which the Lord giveth to prepare for Jesus Christ." Cotton is here represented as replying in a short and positive dictum, that such a notion "would be prejudiciall unto the grace and truth of Christ" (p. 53). In the revised text of 1671 the question stands alone, without the explanation, and Cotton begins his reply by first expressing due honor to the precious saints who disagree with him; he humbly professes that he cannot "discern" any preparation and modestly suggests that the idea "seemeth to be" prejudicial to the Gospel. Both editions were printed after Cotton's death; Allen says in his preface to *The New Covenant* that the text was "taken from the Authors mouth in Preaching, was afterward presented

was to prove the basic unanimity of New England, he could not altogether conceal his well-known opinions, and he had to admit a degree of difference: "though some may conceive the Union wrought in giving the habit, and others rather refer it to the act: and some may give the second place to that, whereto others give the first."[56] Yet his strategy was always to minimize the importance of these differences; he went conspicuously out of his way to approve the treatises of Shepard and Hooker, particularly Hooker's *The Sovles Preparation,* and smoothed over his former objections with the mild qualification, "wherein . . . they sometime declare such works of Grace to be preparations to conversion, which others do take to be fruits of conversion."[57] In every case, he protested that he and they were entirely at one upon all essentials, holding alike that whosoever did come under a saving work of the Spirit had to experience a preparation of some sort. His effort to drape the conflict in the robes of harmony was assiduously seconded by the other spokesmen for New England, their deliberate obscurantism indicating not only how wide but how dangerous the breach had been. The issue made a deep impression upon the seventeenth century, and as late as 1690 George Keith, then speaking as a Quaker and hailing in Anne Hutchinson a forerunner of George Fox, embarrassed his New England opponents by reminding them that Cotton had been closer to his doctrine and to hers than to theirs.[58] Even at the end of the century the leaders were maintaining the defensive tactics of the founders; in a preface to Cotton Mather's *The Everlasting Gospel* in 1700, Higginson granted that Cotton had "differed from some of his Brethren in *The Souls Preparation for Christ"* and had contended that "some" took certain works to be *"preparations to Conversion, which others take to be fruits of Conversion";* however, Higginson insisted, the disagreement never became a serious issue, because all agreed that such works must be achieved by every person who undergoes the effectual influence of the Spirit. *"And so the Difference is but Logical, and not Theological."*[59]

The fact of the matter is, however, that in 1637 the difference had been not only theological but social and political, and had Cotton stood his ground either he would have had to flee or the society been torn asunder. He did not stand his ground, and his uneasy references to the affair in subsequent years are oblique admissions that he and not Hooker made the concession. Hooker seemed to be tightening his victory when, in sermons

unto him with desire of his perusal and emendation of it; which being done (and indeed the interlinings of his owne hand doe plainly testifie his correcting of it)," he then delivered the manuscript to a gentleman of Boston who brought it to London (p. A7 verso). Whether the revision of the later edition represents an "interlining" of Cotton's own hand or of his editor's may be questioned, but in either case it testifies to a weakening or blurring of his originally clear-cut opposition.

[56] Adams, *Antinomianism,* p. 362.
[57] *The Way of Congregational Churches Cleared,* pt. 1, pp. 75-76.
[58] Keith, *A Refutation of Three Opposers of Truth* (Philadelphia, 1690), p. 68.
[59] P. B6 verso.

delivered at Hartford in the 1640's, he began an exposition of preparation
with the remark, "I shall not only speak mine own Judgment, but the
Judgment of all my fellow Brethren, as I have just cause, and good ground
to beleeve,"[60] and then proceeded to expound preparation in direct contradiction to the views of Cotton. After guaranteeing their orthodoxy by
a blanket assertion that they were not Arminians, Hooker and his brethren
serenely defined preparation as a work that should be demanded of all
men as a "condition" of their salvation. The Antinomians had succeeded
only in convincing them of the supreme need for a more vigorous pressing
of moral responsibility upon all the people; the horror of Anne Hutchinson's
heresy was simply that "most of her new tenents tended to slothfulnesse,
and to quench all indevour in the creature."[61] She had declared before the
Synod, "The Spirit acts most in the Saints, when they indevour least," and
the Synod had answered, "Reserving the special seasons of Gods pre-
venting grace to his owne pleasure, In the ordinary constant course of his
dispensation, the more wee indevour, the more assistance and helpe wee
find from him."[62] The last embers of Antinomianism had to be beaten
out, and Hooker showed the clergy how to wield the one flail that would
serve, the doctrine of preparation. With Cotton subdued, Hooker preached
repeatedly upon it. "The soule of a poore sinner must bee prepared for the
Lord Jesus Christ, before it can receive him."[63] The people must do something to receive God or else never expect Him: "only he watcheth the time
till your hearts be ready to receive and entertaine him."[64] When the soul
perceives—if it listened to Hooker it could not help perceiving—that it
cannot save itself, it "falls downe at the foot of the Lord, and is content
to be at Gods dispose," and though at that moment it has no dominion over
its sin, "yet it is willingly content that Jesus Christ should come into it."[65]
Hooker never preached long without a metaphor: a sharp sauce, he explained, will not "breed a stomacke, yet it stirres up the stomacke,"[66] and
so a godly preparation, though it may not breed faith, may yet stir up
the stomach of faith—and conduct.

The connection of the Antinomian outburst with the further development of the idea of preparation can be traced explicitly in the works of
Thomas Shepard. When he described a sort of heretics who hold that there
is no sorrow for sin but what is common to both the reprobate and the
elect and who insist that genuine grief can come only after the soul is in
Christ by faith, his listeners had no trouble knowing whom he meant, or
in following his assertion that such heretics are in error because a man
who gives no previous thought to his sins is in no position to receive grace,

[60] *The Application of Redemption*, p. 309.
[61] Adams, *Antinomianism*, p. 163.
[62] *Ibid.*, p. 109.
[63] *The Unbeleevers Preparing for Christ*, p. 2.
[64] *The Sovles Implantation* (London, 1637), pp. 47-48.
[65] *Ibid.*, pp. 85, 34.
[66] *Ibid.*, p. 234.

even the irresistible grace of God. No doubt it would be Pelagian to say that a man can dispose himself of his own power, but some antecedent disposition is necessary; a form cannot be joined to matter until the matter is prepared, until it is made "such a vessel which is immediately capable" of the union.[67] Shepard acknowledged that this is a difficult doctrine; even angels may be "posed" by the problem of explaining how men may yield themselves to Christ so that all their fruit comes from Him and not from themselves, but Shepard was certain that before any soul experiences a supernatural change it must learn to "lie like wax" beneath the seal.[68] This learning was what he and Hooker understood by preparation.

The real import of a Puritan doctrine is seldom found in the formal statement. To protect their orthodoxy, theologians would hedge every proposition with innumerable qualifications; but once they had proved and vindicated a doctrine, they were free to reveal its true meaning in their "applications." In their exhortations Hooker and Shepard disclosed the great utility of the doctrine of preparation, namely, that they could demand of every man, no matter how sinful, that he make the requisite and feasible preparations, and they could blame him for his own damnation if he refused. Of course, Hooker would explain, if a man's relief depended upon his own endeavors, he would certainly fail: the soul cannot choose Christ "out of the power of nature"; nevertheless, an inn must be prepared to receive the guest, else He will pass by to another lodging.[69] In another characteristic simile, he declared that it is with the soul as with a woman in childbirth: "when her throwes come often and strong, there is some hope of deliverance; but when her throwes goe away, commonly the child dies, and her life too."[70] If a man should argue, "I can do nothing for my self, therefore I will take a course that no man shall do any thing for me," humanity would call him mad; instead, he can and must conclude, since he is able to do nothing of himself, "therefore I must attend upon God in those means which he useth to do for all those he useth to do good unto."[71] Assuredly, unregenerate though he be, a man can avoid the grosser temptations; it is not in your power to make the Gospel "effectual," but it is in your power to doe more than you doe, your legs may as well carry you to the word, as to an Ale-house." You can read pious books as well as "Play-books"; "you may sing as well Psalmes as idle songs." By the doctrine of preparation, in short, the people of New England, nominally professing a rigid Calvinism, could still be told, "doe what you are able to doe, put all your strength, and diligence unto it."[72] At the very least, if they could not resist the ale-house and the play-book, they could "wait" upon God:

[67] Thomas Shepard, *Works*, ed. John A. Albro (Boston, 1853), vol. I, pp. 160-63.
[68] *Ibid.*, vol. III, pp. 307-08.
[69] *The Unbeleevers Preparing for Christ*, p. 40.
[70] *The Sovles Preparation for Christ*, p. 189.
[71] *The Application of Redemption*, p. 320.
[72] *The Saints Guide* (London, 1645), p. 117.

It is true indeed, we cannot doe it, but by Christ, it is the grace of Christ, the power of Christ, the spirit of Christ that doth help us to get our selves from under iniquitie; yet notwithstanding we must labour to get our selves from under it, and Christ will help us. . . . It is the Lords Almighty power that hath possesst us with this libertie and freedome from iniquitie, but yet notwithstanding before we can come to inioy a full libertie from all iniquitie, we must fight for it, and wage the battels of the Lord.[73]

The people could not excuse themselves by pleading that they were disabled, for with the very argument they showed that they were *"not yet* WILLING *to be made* ABLE."[74] Hooker never hesitated to exhort the unregenerate: "It is possible for any Soule present (of ought I know or that he knows) to get an humble heart."[75] The customary ending of a Hooker sermon was an encouragement to all men "that you would indeavour, and be perswaded to get an interest in Christ."[76] Likewise, Thomas Shepard held it a "slothful opinion" to believe that since no activity of grace can be received except from God, men should attempt nothing.[77] Peter Bulkeley indicated the connection of the doctrine with the federal theology by reasoning that, since grace is an offer of a contract, a man can humble himself before God, confess his depravity, and entreat God for a chance to enter the covenant. Generally, Bulkeley promised, God will receive those who come to Him, and "Thus you see the way to enter into Covenant with God."[78]

Here at last was a fulcrum for the lever of human responsibility, even in a determined world. Here was something a man could do, here was an obligation that could be urged upon him, no matter how impotent his will. He could at least prepare, he could wait upon the Lord. Of course, his preparation would be worthless if it did not lead to faith, but it was not, like faith itself, so far above the reach of a mortal being that he could do nothing toward attaining it. Whatever was lost or gained in this restatement, one thing was sure: it ruled out all forms of Antinomianism. In 1657 Hooker's fellow Congregationalists in England, Goodwin and Nye, published his *Application of Redemption* with their hearty endorsement, admitting that Hooker had been accused of "urging too far, and insisting too much upon that as *Preparatory,* which includes indeed the beginnings of true Faith," but they were now ready to agree with him, because they in England were suffering what New England had endured in 1637, a wave of Antinomian fanaticism, and they hoped that Hooker's volume would set to rights "those that have slipt into *Profession,* and Leapt over all both *true* and *deep Humiliation* for sin, and *sence of their natural Con-*

[73] *The Saints Dignitie, and Dutie* (London, 1651), p. 38.
[74] *The Application of Redemption,* p. 143.
[75] *The Sovles Hvmiliation* (London, 1638), p. 207.
[76] *The Saints Dignitie, and Dutie,* p. 118.
[77] *Works,* vol. II, p. 401.
[78] *The Gospel-Covenant,* p. 51.

dition."[79] With this to recommend the doctrine, that it provided both an antidote to Antinomianism and a working basis for stirring up the sinful will without running to the opposite extreme of Arminianism, no wonder it became a prized possession of the New England mind! And no wonder that as the decades passed and the leaders became more and more worried over the declension, as they were obliged to find means for stimulating the zeal of the flagging generations, they enlarged and magnified the scope of preparation.

The next stage in the development of the doctrine is marked by John Norton's *The Orthodox Evangelist,* published in 1657, which was a treatise upon the particular "evangelical truths" that were then being widely opposed "in this perilous hour of the Passion of the Gospel." There were many Antinomians, mystics, seekers, and Quakers abroad, and therefore Norton devoted three long chapters to preparation; he did not so much extend Hooker's idea as give it systematic formulation, but by that very act, by stripping off Hooker's rhetoric, he caused further implications to emerge. He was compelled, for instance, to distinguish between works which are preparatory in the sight of God—which are achieved only by the elect—and those judged by man, which are to be measured by the rule of charity and to be considered in many cases merely as grounds for hope, not as the signs of a completed redemption. Leaving secret things to God, Norton was able to insist that preparatory works in the second sense might legitimately be required of everybody. His definitions emphasized the temporal element, making preparation a period in which a man is neither a sinner nor a saint, but in some tentative halfway condition: "By preparatory Work, we understand certain inherent qualifications, coming between the carnal rest of the soul in the state of sin, and conversion wrought in the Ministry." It is a "common work of the Spirit," whereby "the soul is put into a Ministerial capacity of believing immediately," whereas the unprepared soul is incapable of directly receiving faith.[80] He stressed constantly that God works conversion not by a violent invasion of the psyche but by degrees: " 'Tis in the works of Grace, as we ordinarily see in the works of Nature; God proceeds not immediately from one extream unto another, but by degrees."[81] Norton again recited all the safeguards against Arminianism; he denied that preparatory works have any causal influence upon vocation, and repeated that even the preparing soul is passive. Yet he carried the analysis so far beyond Hooker that not only was he able to describe preparation as a part of the process of conversion, but to dissect preparation itself into a process, with an array of component stages: believing in the holiness of the law, realizing the nature of sin, learning the message of Christ, comprehending the need for repentance, and finally waiting upon Christ in the use of means under the Gospel Covenant. All

---

[79] *The Application of Redemption,* p. C2 verso.
[80] John Norton, *The Orthodox Evangelist* (London, 1657), p. 130.
[81] *Ibid.,* p. 135.

this, let us remember, was presented as pertaining only to preparation, during which the soul remains passive! Preparation, as Norton said, "worketh not any change of the heart, yet there are in it, and accompanying of it, certain inward workings, that do dispose to a change."[82] He did not demand that every individual run through all the stages he marked out; in fact, he declared, the least measure is enough to put a soul into a "preparatory capacity," and since certainty of election is not always possible in this life, a work of preparation among the as yet unconverted, even if it be not followed by a visible operation of the Spirit, must still be taken as a hopeful sign. In any event, it was clear that preparation could be accomplished by the unregenerate. Arminians and Pelagians allowed too much to preparation—one wonders what more they could allow!—but Norton's chief concern was to counter those "Enthusiasts" who were denying the usefulness or indeed the very existence of any preparation. Hence the conclusion for him, even more explicitly than for Hooker, was the moral duty of all men to seek for preparation, even though it would not guarantee their salvation: "That it is the duty of every one that hears the Gospel to believe, and that whosoever believeth shall be saved; but also it ministers equal hope unto all (answerable to their preparatory proceeding) of believing, and being saved."[83] That the soul should first be prepared and then called to faith, instead of being called without warning, "is the method of the Gospel, ought to be the direction of the Ministry, and course of the Soul; Christs own way, and therefore the most hopefull and most speedy way for attaining of faith and salvation thereby."

Increase Mather came back to Boston in 1661, believing it the last stronghold of Protestantism and resolved to maintain all doctrines in their most rigorous form; just as he at first opposed the Half-Way Covenant, even though his father was a principal advocate, so also he held to Cotton's views on preparation. In 1669 he declared conversion a miracle, far beyond the power of nature to produce or even approach,[84] and in 1674 was preaching "men are altogether *passive* in their *Conversion*."[85] But meanwhile New England sank into the mire of apostasy, and he above all others thundered the need for reform. Very shortly he found himself obliged to remodel his thinking, starting not from abstract doctrines but from the facts with which he was contending. He changed sides on the Half-Way Covenant, and before long he also altered his views of preparation, declaring that while the gate is indeed strait, yet God requires men to strive for entrance, and consequently "they should do such things as have a tendency to cause them to Believe."[86] Others in his generation, under the same circumstances, likewise found charms in the same thought. Samuel

---

[82] *Ibid.*, p. 154.

[83] *Ibid.*, p. 171.

[84] Increase Mather, *The Mystery of Israel's Salvation* (London, 1669), p. 90.

[85] *Some Important Truths about Conversion* (London, 1674), 2nd ed. (Boston, 1684), p. 5.

[86] *Sovl-Saving Gospel Truths* (Boston, 1703), 2nd ed. (Boston, 1712), pp. 22-27.

Willard was too skilled in the traditional theology ever to lose sight of natural inability; he would explain that when a man repents, "it is God by his Spirit that enforms him with this power and grace," and he held it an error to "put a Divine honour upon Moral swasion, as if it could of it self attract and draw the heart after it,"[87] yet whenever he exhorted the congregations, he pointed out that in preparation, as apart from regeneration, they have a power of working upon themselves. "It is one of Satans cheats, to tell us we must wait before we resolve."[88] In his *Compleat Body of Divinity* he defined preparation as that time in which the soul is not yet redeemed but is merely in *"a posture and readiness for the exerting of the act of Faith, which follows thereupon."*[89] Even at this date there were debates among the orthodox, and many whom Willard respected still denied the existence of any preparatory works; but he repeated the arguments of Hooker and Norton, and added a few of his own, to prove once more that men may be called upon to prepare themselves if not to convert themselves.[90] In 1690 a committee of ministers attempted to moderate the confusion that followed the revolution against Andros by issuing a manifesto of the ancient creed of New England; admitting that men are saved or rejected entirely by the will of God, they hastened to insist, nevertheless, that there are "some previous and preparatory common works" which may be accomplished by all, though in those who afterwards fall away "we deny them to be the beginnings of true justifying or saving faith."[91] Most sermons in the last decades of the century exhibit the same alternation between an assertion of human impotence and an incitation to preparation, and in one breath denounce the "insignificant and unsavoury" belief that men's efforts have any value while in the next they exhort men to greater efforts. The inconsistency no longer bothered the preachers, and once having stated the conventional inability, they were at liberty to press upon their congregations an obligation to act, as though John Calvin had never lived. If accused of Pelagianism they answered that preparation was not salvation and therefore not a matter of grace. How may I know that I have Christ? the people would ask, and Samuel Mather could reply, "As Your *Conviction* is, such your faith is: as is the preparation work, such is the closing with Christ. It is a *sure rule;* and this is the reason why we so much, and so often press for *preparation* work. . . . And there is more *preparation* needful, than many think for."[92]

The culmination of this development, the enlargement of preparation to a point beyond which it could not be extended without bursting the bonds of orthodoxy, is to be seen in the writings of Cotton Mather. Even

[87] Willard, *Mercy Magnified on a penitent Prodigal* (Boston, 1684), p. 212.

[88] *Ibid.,* pp. 215-16.

[89] *A Compleat Body of Divinity* (Boston, 1726), p. 435.

[90] *Ibid.,* pp. 434-36.

[91] Allen, Moody, Willard and Cotton Mather, *The Principles of the Protestant Religion Maintained* (Boston, 1690), p. 110.

[92] Samuel Mather, *A Dead Faith Anatomized* (Boston, 1697), p. 87.

at the beginning of his career he was so far heedless of first principles as to represent his brother Nathaniel entering into a covenant with God *before* being converted, which then became "an influence into his *Conversion* afterwards."[93] Cotton Mather never had any other conception of grace than as a process that could be "cherished and promoted"; though he paid the usual lip service to total depravity, he always heartily exhorted depraved men to set their house in order, and their provisions, according to his instructions, would have included almost every action of the religious life. "You may make a *Tryal";* there can be no harm in trying, for "Never, I am perswaded, never any Soul miscarried, that made such Applications."[94] True, God has not promised to give grace to those who seek it; nevertheless—there is always a "nevertheless" in Cotton Mather's discourse—" 'Tis many ways Advantageous, for an *Vnregenerate* Man, to Do as much as he *can,"* for "there is a probability that God intends to help him, so that he shall *do* more than he *can."* Certainly, if a man makes his *"Impotency* a Cloak for his *Obstinacy,* it will Aggravate his Condemnation at the Last." The way to be recovered—"the way of the *New-Covenant"*—is very simple: *"Try* whether you can't give that Consent; if you *can,* 'tis done!"[95] By the beginning of the eighteenth century, preparation had come to mean, for all practical purposes, that every man was able to predispose himself for grace, that his fate was in his own hands, even though grace was given of God. The memory of John Cotton's dissent remained a monitor of caution, but the preachers were no longer capable of comprehending why he had dissented.

The premise of clerical thinking in the new century remained ostensibly what it had been in the old, the inherent nature of a covenant, whether among men or between man and God. But in the later treatment, the fact that a covenant not only permits but requires a preliminary negotiation and that the terms of salvation must therefore be known to every sinner, became not a condescending mercy of God but a utilitarian convenience. The federal theology began by permitting what strict Calvinism would not, some sort of anticipatory behavior among those who desired redemption, but successive theologians steadily enlarged the field of such behavior by shifting the focus of attention from the awful majesty of God to the concrete and manageable propositions of a business transaction. "For this reason," Willard put it in 1700, "the *Gospel Promises* are exhibited on terms; and these terms therein proposed, do not only tell us what it is that God requires of Sinners in the treaty of Peace which he opens and manageth with them . . . but they do also give us to understand after what manner God will by his Grace convey a pardon to Sinners."[96] Puri-

[93] Cotton Mather, *Early Piety, Exemplified in the Life and Death of Mr. Nathanael Mather* (London, 1689), p. 20.
[94] *Batteries upon the Kingdom of the Devil* (London, 1695), p. 108.
[95] *The Seriovs Christian* (London, 1699), pp. 21-24.
[96] Willard, *A Remedy against Despair* (Boston, 1700), pp. 42-43.

tans of the seventeenth century always assumed that God alone could fully enable men or nations to take up a covenant, but from the beginning the federalists had insisted that there is "an order in which he brings them to a participation";[97] hence the rationalizing, secularizing tendencies of the age did not need to appear in New England as a frontal attack upon the terrible decrees of election and reprobation, but could be satisfied by a cautious translation of the initial action in the order of grace into the language of a commercial parley. The infusion of grace itself, said Cotton Mather, is immediately done by God's almighty arm, "But then, the Spirit of God, because He will deal with us as *Rational Creatures,* He also puts forth a *Moral Efficiency* for our *Conversion;* We are capable of *Treaties,* of *Proposals,* of *Overtures;* and He therefore *Exhorts* us, and Uses a variety of *Arguments* to perswade us."[98]

Once more, we must remark that the first federal theologians set forth the idea that conversion is a logical process following a discernible "order," beginning with a period of preparation, not for social but for evangelical reasons. They wished to incite men to preparedness, not in order that laws might be obeyed, but that souls might be saved. Yet they did dignify certain motions, admittedly within the attainment of the unregenerate, as the prologues to conversion. Thereupon they made the national covenant a logical possibility, for not only God but all the people could bear their part: "As in a Covenant there are Articles of agreement betweene party and party; so betweene God and his people."[99] To become a holy society, a people must know the terms of holiness and be able to observe them; the doctrine of preparation secured both conditions, and so Massachusetts and Connecticut could conceive of themselves as societies in which all men, saints or not, were pledged to observe the externals of religion. But once these societies began to decline, the inhabitants to grow remiss and be duly punished by plagues and financial losses, they could all be informed: "they shall seek to him for a pardon, and upon their so doing, they shall find it."[100] Within a few decades the preparation that was first urged upon all men for the salvation of their souls was being pressed upon them for the preservation of the state. They could do what was required, and though they might miss their redemption they could reform their manners. There were still limits to what men could do merely in a way of preparation, but by staying away from the alehouses and putting off their luxurious clothes they could make the difference between social prosperity and ruin.

But at this point a new question intruded itself upon the leaders: would men bestir themselves in order to save the society when they had no hope of escaping hell? Might not the unregenerate understandably object that there was no reason why they should strive for a goal they could not

[97] *Ibid.,* p. 44.
[98] Cotton Mather, *A Letter to Ungospellized Plantations* (Boston, 1702), pp. 12-13.
[99] Hooker, *The Faithful Covenanter* (London, 1644), p. 12.
[100] Willard, *A Remedy against Despair,* p. 44.

attain merely in order that the saints might grow rich? That this question, in some form, could not be avoided is abundantly testified by the sophistries of Cotton Mather, and in him the worst forebodings of Anne Hutchinson were finally vindicated, for he began, though in the most tentative fashion, to suggest that whoever would prepare himself would almost certainly go to heaven! First of all, he was concerned that men keep up the outward observances. "Men have a *Natural Power, as to the External part of Religion*"—there was no longer any qualification in his mind. Therefore it followed, "If men do not in Religion, what they have a *Natural Power* to do, they cannot with any modesty complain of the Righteous God, that He does not grant them the *Higher Power,* to Exert those Acts of Religion, which are Internal."[101] By the same token it followed that those who did exercise the lower power were practically assured of receiving the higher: "If men did in Religion, more than they do, & *All* that they could by a *Natural Power* do, there would be a greater Likelihood, (I say not, a *Certainty,* but a *Likelihood,*) that God would grant them that *Higher Power.*"[102] The founders had taken for granted that a holy society could force the proper manners upon the unregenerate; Cotton Mather could not persuade the unregenerate to mend their manners without luring them with the promise of an almost sure chance of salvation, even though they still were deficient in grace and faith.

It was but a short step from such thinking to an open reliance upon human exertions and to a belief that conversion is worked entirely by rational argument and moral persuasion. The seeds of what Jonathan Edwards was to denounce as "Arminianism" in the mid-eighteenth century were sown in New England by Hooker and Shepard, who, ironically enough, were the two most evangelical among the founders and the most opposed to seventeenth-century forms of Arminianism. The subsequent development of their doctrine is not a mere episode in the history of a technical jargon. It is nothing less than a revelation of the direction in which Puritanism was traveling, of the fashion in which the religious world of the seventeenth century was gradually transformed into the world of the eighteenth. A teleological universe, wherein men were expected to labor for the glory of God, wherein they were to seek not their own ends but solely those appointed by Him, was imperceptibly made over into a universe in which men could trust themselves even to the extent of commencing their own conversions, for the sake of their own well-being, and God could be expected to reward them with eternal life. Even while professing the most abject fealty to the Puritan Jehovah, the Puritan divines in effect dethroned Him. The fate of New England, in the original philosophy, depended upon God's providence; the federal theology circumscribed providence by tying it to the behavior of the saints; then with

---

[101] Cotton Mather, *A Conquest over the Grand Excuse of Sinfulness and Slothfulness* (Boston, 1706), p. 28.
[102] *Ibid.,* p. 29.

the extension of the field of behavior through the elaboration of the work of preparation, the destiny of New England was taken out of the hands of God and put squarely into the keeping of the citizens. Even while invoking the concept in an effort to stem the tide of worldliness, the ministers contributed to augmenting the worldly psychology: if the natural man was now admittedly able to practice the external rules of religion without divine assistance, and if such observance would infallibly insure the prosperity of society and most probably the redemption of souls, if honesty would prove the best policy and if morality would pay dividends, then the natural man was well on his way to a freedom that would no longer need to be controlled by the strenuous ideals of supernatural sanctification and gracious enlightenment, but would find adequate regulation in the ethics of reason and the code of civic virtues.

THE GREAT AWAKENING
FROM 1740 TO 1750

THOMAS AQUINAS, having to define theology in the very first question of the *Summa,* with characteristic skill resolved on the eighth article the problem of to what extent sacred doctrine is "argumentative." His judicious conclusion is that sacred scripture can dispute with one who denies its principles "only if the opponent admits some at least of the truths obtained through divine revelation." If the opponent believes nothing, there are then no means of proving articles of faith; Christians have only the negative capability of answering objections. That is to say, we can only show the opponent that, while we cannot convince him of our truth, he has no leg of his own to stand upon. If he can be reduced to recognizing his incompetence, then perhaps the way will be opened for a work of conviction; but that will have to be a work of divine illumination, not of human persuasion.

Inheritors of the Protestant tradition frequently come upon this introductory passage with a feeling of relief—at least, I have found that some students, approaching the *Summa* for the first time, do breathe such a sigh. It says that they do not have to worry about arguing with Thomas; they do not need to fear that he will undermine their commitments. They can settle back to enjoy the subtle play of the Thomistic dialect as they might delight in the development of a fugue. But, on the other hand, in a short time they become obscurely uncomfortable: if sacred doctrine is to be spun out to the length of the *Summa* only for delectation of those who already believe in divine revelation, what becomes of that long chapter in Protestant history which we call "missions"? If this is what theology really is, how could there ever have been any evangelists? If, properly speaking, we can preach only to the converted, how did Christianity, even from the beginning, make converts?

In the *Summa* Thomas was not required to give historical explanations for the spread of Christianity through the Roman Empire, or for such mass conversions as that of the Franks. It was enough that martyrs had witnessed to the faith that Thomas was expounding. One of the greatest of living theologians, Paul Tillich, remarks that a *summa* by definition deals with all the actual and many of the potential problems of theology, and so suggests that in the thirteenth century the *summa* was the predominant form primarily because it suited the needs of the time. That is, at a moment when the universal, united, catholic church seemed to

Published in *Encounter* (Divinity School, Duke University), March 1956, pp. 1-12.

cover the civilized areas of the earth, there was no need for a genetic account of how it came to be. What was wanted, and what was a joy to supply, was the fascinating statement of what it then stood for. But at the beginning of the modern period, Tillich continues, the situation became so altered as to call no longer for any *summa,* but for the essay, that which "deals with *one actual* problem." Calvin may have dreamed that in composing the *Institutes* he was producing a Protestant *summa,* and the enlargements in successive editions pushed the book toward such comprehensiveness. The final version retains a memory of that supreme grandeur, but the book tacitly confesses on every page that it is at best no more than, in Tillich's terms, an essay on the Calvinistic manner of reading scripture, as opposed to both the Catholic and the Lutheran.

Hence in the vast literature of Protestantism, the typical work of the theologian is not something to stand beside Thomas or Bonaventura, but the specific treatise on some "great point" in divinity: the atonement, irresistible grace, the covenant. Protestant polymaths who still attempted a summary of actual and potential problems were likely, in the seventeenth century, to prove such academic compilers as Petro van Mastricht, whose 1300-page *Theoretica-Practica Theologica* could with difficulty be read by only a few Cotton Mathers; the most that busy pastors could afford in the way of summation was John Wollebius' *The Abridgment of Christian Divinity,* the very title of which confesses how far it was from even pretending to be a *summa.* Jonathan Edwards cherished the comprehensive dream, and throughout his life piled up notebooks for an ultimate synthesis; but circumstances in America compelled him, as circumstances in Protestant countries also obliged his fellows, to issue *ad hoc* essays on specific problems: the religious emotions, original sin, the freedom of the will, true virtue. In the nineteenth century it became the custom for long-lived professors in theological seminaries to labor toward the crowning achievement of their career, a ponderous "system of theology." But these were always regarded as Professor Hodge's or Professor Strong's private organizations of the universe. And these were read, if at all, only by a few of the professor's most devoted students; otherwise they gathered dust, and today can be picked up, by those whose curiosity goes so far, on the miscellaneous tables of secondhand book stores for twenty-five cents a volume. The effective books in American Protestantism of the nineteenth century were essays: Charles Grandison Finney's *Lectures on Revivals,* Nathaniel Taylor's *Concio ad Clerum,* Lyman Beecher's *The Faith Once Delivered to the Saints,* Horace Bushnell's *Christian Nurture,* John H. Nevin's *The Anxious Bench,* William Ellery Channing's Baltimore sermon, Josiah Strong's *Our Country.* These were all argumentative, and all strove, with varying vehemence, to overcome the heretic whether or not he originally made any concessions to divine revelation. We may say that the essay, in this sense, comes to its climax in the sermons of such urban revivalists as De Witt Talmage and Dwight Moody, the formal premise of which is that the majority of the audience do *not* accept a single doctrine of Christianity and so must be persuaded against their wills. The prevailing assumption is that somehow the book or the preacher can overwhelm the opponent by conveying to him the necessary conviction. Actually, this presumption was as much a part of Channing's reasoned statement or of Bushnell's exposition of the Trinity as of Peter Cartwright's frontier exhortations.

Paul Tillich is one of several who have announced that by now the era of the essay has come to an end, that it can no longer deal with what Tillich calls "the chaos of our spiritual life." But this chaos makes equally impossible the creation of a *summa*. Therefore Tillich addresses himself to composing a *Systematic Theology*. Curiously enough, in this system Tillich, in his "existential" terminology, finds himself virtually reiterating the initial concession of Thomas' intellectualist *Summa*. "The knowledge of revelation," Tillich says, "can be received only in the situation of revelation, and it can be communicated—in contrast to ordinary knowledge—only to those who participate in this situation."

Of course, Thomas Aquinas did not mean that nothing at all could be said to unbelieving opponents. Quite the contrary: if he wrote the *Summa Theologica* for those who agreed, at least in part, upon the scriptures, he also wrote the *Summa Contra Gentiles* for those who would accept nothing of them. For those who are not Thomists, this work generally proves the more absorbing reading, if only because it is the supreme example in literature of arguing a case not by trying to prove it but by demonstrating that those who deny it have no case of their own. It leaves the gentiles no alternative. Still, I suppose that many read it with fascination and yet remain unconvinced, or at least undisturbed, because to modern temperaments it appears that Thomas enjoyed too facile a method for establishing his *quod erat demonstrandum,* the classical distinction between essence and existence. I would not vulgarize a magnificent train of thought, but at the risk of vulgarization let me say that it may seem a simple business, once you have got the gentile to acknowledge that the "essence" of man includes everything that might be imagined of archetypal man, to then prove that his own particular existence falls short, and always will fall short, no matter how much existence he takes unto himself, of such essential perfection. From there the argument runs smoothly that man's ultimate happiness can not possibly be found in this life, that it can be attained only when the intellect sees the divine essence (in whom alone are existence and essence synonymous), and that since the created intellect needs the assistance of the divine light in order so to behold God in His essence, the obvious implication follows (though it need hardly be stated) that only Christianity offers the requisite assistance. The gentile is thus left to search frantically for a similar possibility in his own existential theology, which obviously he cannot find; the Christian theologian, having put the poor fellow in this predicament, can afford to wait patiently until the distracted being comes of himself to beg admission to the true church.

Protestantism, it is customary to say, rent the unity of the medieval church. Modern Thomists, especially those who call themselves "Neo-Thomists," often justify their "Back to Thomas" slogan with a plea for rediscovering the unity of the *Summa,* sometimes appearing to hunger after the comprehensiveness quite apart from any profession of faith. However, to the cold eye of history, it may well seem that the subtle coherence of the Thomistic *Summa* had been torn apart by the scholastic disputes of the fifteenth century, long before Luther was born, and that Protestantism may be interpreted as a violent effort to reassert a singleness of view by Biblical dogmatism rather than by finespun logic. Be that as it may, the point I wish to make is that Protestants seldom or never attributed the spread of the Reformation across Europe to the efficient power of their own arguments. They denounced the corruptions of the medieval church, and they published thousands of tracts refuting the Council of Trent and defending their positions, and then they published thousands more expounding variations among themselves, but all the while they attributed the progress of the Reform to God. It was "a work of the Holy Spirit." The Protestant preacher, especially the Calvinist, did not conceive of himself as a missionary. He bore witness to God's truth, and then the truth worked of itself in this or that listener. William Bradford started his history *Of Plymouth Plantation* with that moment of "the first breaking out of the light of the Gospel in our honourable nation of England." Satan immediately raised an opposition, but according to Bradford the light of the Gospel continued to spread because the cause was "watered with the blood of the martyrs and blessed from Heaven with a gracious increase." In describing the gathering of the Scrooby congregation, Bradford does recognize the instrumentality of men: "When as by the travail and diligence of some godly and zealous preachers." But their activity is not so much the provoking cause as merely an incidental circumstance: along with (rather than because of) their labors, "many became enlightened by the Word of God, and had their ignorance and sins discovered unto them, and began by His grace to reform their lives and make conscience of their ways." Edward Johnson well knew at what a cost of organizing, scheming, raising funds, the Massachusetts Bay Company was launched; yet as he told the story in 1654, in *Wonder-Working Providence of Sions Saviour,* he declared that in this critical time "Christ the glorious king of His Churches, raises an Army out of our *English* Nation," that "Christ creates a New *England* to muster up the first of his Forces in." Johnson even represents the summons as being broadcast through the land by a herald, crying "Oh yes! oh yes! oh yes!"

Of course, all English colonists advertised that they intended to convert Indians. However, we have to be wary of interpreting their profession in a nineteenth-century spirit. In the first place, critics of both Virginia and New England accused the settlers of doing little or nothing. In the second place, as we can see most clearly in John Eliot's activity in Massachusetts, the conception of the manner in which conversion was to be wrought did not mean sending circuit riders into Indian territory, but rather gathering a few tractable Indians into a community, like that of Natick, where within the confines of a settled existence, to the accompaniment of steady preaching, the light of the Gospel might (should God be willing) break also upon them, but break out of and by itself.

Essentially this same assumption was at the bottom of all the Protestant colonies, the Dutch Reformed and the Scottish Presbyterian as well as the New England Puritans. There may be exceptions here and there, but in general the aim was to hew a civilization out of the wilderness, to put a church into the center of the new community, and then to pray that the grace of God would flow through these channels as already it had flowed through the societies of Europe and Britain. Hence in 1740, when that commotion started which we call the Great Awakening, all parties began with the ancient assumption that this was a recognizable "pouring out of the grace of God upon the land." It was the long-prayed-for, the overdue "supernatural work." George Whitefield, Jonathan Edwards, Gilbert Tennent were not instigators, not fomenters; they were simply eager Christians whose hopes were being miraculously realized, as though by no action of their own, and they fell upon the opportunity providentially given. In their conception, Christ's herald was again crying "Oh yes! oh yes! oh yes!"

Historians have variously pointed out that the decade of the Awakening, 1740 to 1750, is a watershed in American development. They have difficulty putting their fingers on just precisely what the transformation was, since there were no revolutionary changes in political institutions. Except for the splintered churches of Pennsylvania, New Jersey, and New England, the social scene in 1750 seems fairly much what it was in 1740. And yet you feel, the moment you go to the sources, that after 1750 we are in a "modern" period, whereas before that, and down to the very outburst, the intellectual world is still medieval, scholastic, static, authoritarian. Before 1740 ministers labored in their communities, but their effort could still be described by what Thomas had defined as the only legitimate function of sacred doctrine—that is, to use human reason and the liberal arts, "not, indeed, to prove faith (for thereby the merit of faith would come to an end), but to make clear other things that are set forth in this doctrine." After 1750, whole segments of Protestant America have made the fatal break: they have dared to say, or at least to act as though they had said, that the merit of faith is not one whit diminished if a passionate preacher arouses, excites, creates the faith in an opponent. The immensity of this revolution becomes apparent the moment we recognize that it did not come to an end in 1750, that it contained a dynamic that took fifty years to work itself out. After a lull, which can be accounted for by the distraction of the War for Independence, the spiritual revolution again went forward in the Second Great Awakening of 1800. Whitefield on the Boston Common, Edwards at Enfield, the Tennents at the Log College, point the way inevitably toward the first gigantic mass meeting at Cane Ridge in 1801, where some twenty thousand people assembled on August 11 and by night three thousand of them had fallen in a trance to the ground, while hundreds were "jerking, rolling, running, dancing and barking."

This revolution wrought between, let us say, the evangelism of the English Puritans or the French Huguenots and that of Francis Asbury, Barton Warren Stone, or Alexander Campbell is so fundamental and pervasive, and yet so amorphous, that the historian has a problem in taking stock of it. It is everywhere, and yet it is nowhere. It can be described, but can it be analyzed? Social historians and sociologists do, of course, explain it as a cultural phenomenon. From their point of view the frontier is the environmental factor—though as Whitefield first suggested and as Finney later proved, the revival technique could be carried into the city as well as to the fire-lighted camp meeting. But there is another question to be asked, toward the answering of which sociologists are of no help at all. That question is what did it mean for Protestantism in this country, and what does it still mean for American Protestantism, in a purely *religious* sense, to have gone through this revolution? By this I mean to ask not what it did to the denominations, not what it signified in numbers, organizations, controversies, attitudes toward slavery, and so on, but what the reorientation did to the religious mentality itself.

Naturally, one has to point out that a great change also took place, in varying degrees, in some Protestant quarters of Europe. We can say that all the many movements on the Continent which we lump together as Pietism—to distinguish them from sixteenth-century expressions—are analogies to the American revival and camp meeting. And then there is the Wesleyan revival of eighteenth-century England, which exhibits many of the phenomena to be noted in America, which indeed fed the American flame, at first through Whitefield and then through the pioneer Methodist missionaries. But over against Pietism and Methodism in Europe there always stood powerfully entrenched institutions, the Catholic Church on the Continent and the Established Church in England, which kept the new conception from spreading like the wildfire of the Great Awakening and the wilder fire of the second revival. Also, older forms of Protestantism there clung to their Reformation heritages, and resisted the sheer emotionalism of these newer energies. And finally, the hold of the Enlightenment on the educated classes meant that in Europe the revival remained primarily a lower-class affair. When it did win a few aristocratic converts, like the Countess of Huntington's "connexion," these moderated its more violent tendencies. So, if there was a new logic conceived in the Great Awakening which had to force itself to an ultimate conclusion, only in America was the opportunity provided. Across the mountains lay the wilderness of

Kentucky, Indiana, Illinois: in this wilderness there was no established church to hinder, no cultivated aristocracy to sneer, and into it swept hordes of simple, excitable, optimistic people, and with them came the revival, the shouting and the gesticulating. Out of their ecstatic experience emerged, without anybody's quite formulating it, a stalwart conviction that Christ can be preached to unbelievers in so aggressive a manner that they will be swept into faith, will-they nill-they.

It must be said, or at least whispered, that when the sensitive Protestant of today looks back upon the period from 1800 to the Civil War, the period when the evangelical revolution triumphed and dominated the churches, he is bound to feel uncomfortable. Considered as a chapter in the history of the Christian spirit—aside from what it amounts to in the statistical increase of professions—it is often a melancholy spectacle. Compared with almost any chapter in the history of Protestantism in the time of Luther or Calvin, or in that of the Puritans, it is vulgar, noisy, ignorant, blatant. In a perceptive enumeration of the elements in this chaotic situation, Professor Sidney Mead [in an essay in *Lively Experiment*], distinguishes an anti-historical sectarianism, a voluntary principle, a missionary zeal, a cult of revivalism with a consequent oversimplification of traditional theological problems for the sake of results, a general flight from reason, and a ruthless competition among the denominations. Taking all these factors or forces together, and watching them at work in simultaneous frenzy, a tender sensibility cannot find the resulting picture pretty. Professor Mead entitles his essay "Denominationalism: The Shape of Protestantism in America." To the extent that the shape given in the pre-Civil War period is still with us, we should not be surprised that some of our best minds look back with nostalgia to the comparatively dignified unification of the individual and the community at which Puritanism aimed, or even to the serene syntheses of the Middle Ages.

The difficulty is that, however dramatic or heroic figures like Lyman Beecher, Peter Cartwright, James McGready may be as personalities, we can hardly give them much intellectual respect. At the same time, a student of the period receives little spiritual sustenance by turning from these rowdy figures to the cold rationality of an Andrews Norton. Many of us sympathize with Horace Bushnell in his effort to find a way out of the sterility of revivalism without having to settle for "the corpse-cold Unitarianism of Brattle Street and Harvard College"—to use Emerson's devastating phrase. Still, admirable as Bushnell is, he is a limited figure; his culture was starved and narrow, and his formulations seldom seem profound enough to become more than historical curiosities. Indeed, the mighty pundits of Andover Theological Seminary had brains, and they used them—Leonard Woods, Moses Stuart, Calvin Stowe, Edwards A. Park—and there are also the ponderous tomes of Nathaniel Emmons. But who today can read these dinosaurs with anything like an assurance that from their pages emerges such a sense of genuine Christian piety as speaks directly to us from the works of Thomas Hooker, of Thomas Shepard, or of Job Scott?

The worst of it is that in this period these proliferating Protestant churches almost wrecked the American mind. The dismal consequences for education are just now tabulated by Richard Hofstadter and Walter Metzger in *The Development of Academic Freedom in the United States*. This volume is more than a history of academic freedom in the technical sense; it is a highly literate history of education. The chapter on "The Old-Time College," in the years 1800-1860, is a bitter pill that should be resolutely prescribed to all those suffering under the illusion that the pioneer colleges of that era, especially the denominational ones, were something glamorous. They were a national disaster, from the ravages of which we have only partially recovered. The anger of the authors is barely held in check, and they say with studied moderation: "The worst thing that can be said of the sponsors and promoters of the old colleges is not that they failed to foster sufficiently free teaching and research in their own colleges, but that when others attempted to found freer and more advanced institutions the denominational forces tried to cripple or destroy their work." For page after page there comes the shameful story of the clergy raising a cry of "Godless" against state universities, of the bleak intolerance of organized piety, of presidents and professors humiliated, of curricula stuffed with sectarian bigotry, of the inhibition of science, and of the deadly pall of doctrinal moralism. And out of these pages emerges the anguished wail of good men defeated and chagrined—not merely deistical rationalists like Jefferson, but sincere religionists like J. M. Sturtevant. Out of sad experience Sturtevant wrote in 1860 that this spirit of sect "elevates minor denominational peculiarities into tests of fitness for the highest and most dignified stations; it tends to fill the most important chairs of instruction with men of inferior talents and attainments, because they are supposed to be right in the matter of denomination, and thereby to impair the efficiency of the Institution in the discharge of its appropriate function." No modern can frame a more damaging indictment of the era.

What then should we do with this early national epoch in American Protestantism? Should we shudder over it, turn our backs upon it, and try to forget it? Perhaps the haunting memory of this unlovely spectacle excites many students to greet as glad tidings Paul Tillich's thesis that the Protestant era is at an end, that the work of the Reformers is accomplished, that a new prospect of theological enterprise is beginning in which we can justifiably free ourselves from the clutch of evangelical ancestors. It is certainly interesting, and I think significant, to see how Tillich's audience—and he is not an easy author to comprehend—is steadily expanding. However, he is not the only one who lately has sketched the outline of a new "shape"—I am not forgetting Reinhold Niebuhr or Richard Niebuhr. But there is discernible in many Protestant centers a growing feeling that, though we may still pay our respects to Luther, to Calvin, and to the Puritans, the descendants of those prophets who held sway in the nineteenth century were a decadent lot, and they have nothing whatsoever to say to us.

Even if you think this is overstating the case, you can, I am sure, see that here we confront a predicament. None of us likes to repudiate his grandfathers; the churches were so eminently successful in keeping up with the march of the frontier, and they put up so valiant a struggle to civilize the wilderness, that we seem to have no right to berate them for failing at the same time to create a great theological literature. But I am ready to insist that there is something more to be said, something that, if it can be properly put, will help us to perceive that this era in American Protestantism was not so much the decline of an older epoch as it was the birth pangs of a new. Something was then wrought in the religious life of this nation that is entirely without precedent in the Christian past, which can not be paralleled in Europe.

Let me try, for simplicity's sake, to put my argument bluntly. The Great Awakening of 1740 was at first hailed by its partisans, we have seen, as a supernatural work. Hence much of the effort in the first delirious months went into formulating the signs or symptoms of authentic conversion, this being still conceived as a seizure from above. The sermon that Edwards delivered on September 10, 1741, at New Haven, entitled *The Distinguishing Marks of a Work of God,* is the best memorial of this early conception, though similar essays were produced by the Tennents. But even in this year, opponents of the Awakening were starting their attack, and everywhere their main charge became that, far from being a supernatural work, the outburst was criminally excited by artificial stimulations. Charles Chauncy's *Seasonable Thoughts on the State of Religion,* published in 1743, is the principal indictment, but the "Old Lights" and the "Old Side" repeated it again and again. They accused the revivalists of abusing human nature under a pretense that God Himself was working the harm. Consequently the revivalists, led by Edwards, were obliged to answer that their techniques did not do violence to the human constitution, either physically or psychologically. Though to the bitter end they contended that the Awakening was a pure act of God, they had progressively so to expound it that in effect they represented Almighty God as accommodating His procedures to the faculties and potentialities of His creature. From the time of Calvin, the focus of Calvinist and of most Protestant thinking had been the will of God; the great divide that we call the Awakening forced both American parties, whether proponents or opponents, to shift the focus of analysis to the nature of man.

As has been often demonstrated, the line of development from Charles Chauncy to William Ellery Channing is direct. Hence Channing does summarize a century of reorientation when, upon collecting his papers in 1841, he said of them that they are "distinguished by nothing more than by the high estimate which they express of human nature." He recognized that many would call him a romancer or, what is worse, one who exalted man against God and so pandered to moral vanity. But he was determined not to permit such striking contrasts between man and God as would imply that man had no ground for hope; instead, he would show forth the "likeness" between the Creator and the creature. His is the ultimate rejection of Calvinism because his motive was to keep man from being swallowed up in the absolute. "By looking at the sun," he said, "we lose the power of seeing other objects." Therefore, he concluded, "The finite is something real as well as the infinite."

Yes, one may say, Channing here made articulate certain qualities of the age and of this country; nevertheless, he spoke for a relatively restricted number of persons in eastern New England. The majority of Protestants, whether orthodox Congregationalists in New England or revivalists in Illinois, were incited by the spectacle of Unitarianism not to exalt man but to humble him even more, to insist officially upon the dreadful reality of natural depravity and to cultivate still more energetic methods for exciting conversion. Peter Cartwright, for instance, defended the jerks—though he disapproved of the more histrionic "exercises"—because he saw in them a judgment from God and also a demonstration "that God could work with or without means, and that he could work over and above means, and do whatsoever seems to Him good, to the glory and salvation of the world." Indeed, this thesis the revivalists advanced over and over again; yet the same Peter Cartwright once found himself forbidden by a Presbyterian minister to form a Methodist society within the area of his church, and to him Cartwright answered, "The people were a free people, and lived in a free country, and must and ought to be allowed to do as they pleased." When the Presbyterian cleric still endeavored to suppress the Methodists, Cartwright relates that members of his own congregation objected on the grounds that he was un-American. "I told them," Cartwright continues, "that my father had fought in the Revolution to gain our freedom and liberty of conscience; that I felt that my Presbyterian brother had no bill of sale for the people."

Here, I suggest, we get a sudden insight into the paradox really at work within the heart of the period. On the whole, the great figures of the era are men of ebullient spirits, vigorous men, far from being cloistered and neurotic scholars. It is customary to say that the Awakenings of 1800 were a reaction to what seemed to good Christians the threat of an advancing infidelity, of French deism or even atheism. There is undoubtedly much truth in this version, even though the orthodox may have much exaggerated the ravages of the Enlightenment among the masses. Still, even if they did exaggerate, they were sincerely convinced in 1800 that the country hovered on the brink of disaster. Hence the pronounced anti-intellectual character of their counterreformation. As Peter Cartwright always contended, there was then no time for the devout to train themselves for their task by dallying with education: "If Bishop Asbury had waited for this choice literary band of preachers, infidelity would have swept these United States from one end to the other." But what Cartwright unwittingly confesses in this remark is that when a situation seems so desperate, Christians do not retire to their chambers, get down on their knees and pray that God may pour out His grace upon the land: they gird up themselves, and they go out to do something about it. Though they go forth in the name of the Lord, preaching the sinful inability of man and the necessity of supernatural salvation, yet they also go on the tacit premise that man in America, having fought for liberty in the Revolution, is the sort of creature who can be wrought upon by evangelists.

We must never forget that the great revival was enacted in an arena where the conception of religious liberty was so taken for granted that it had hardly ever to be stated. Therefore, in this open field, the very competition among the denominations which Professor Mead emphasizes as the fundamental characteristics of the time becomes, to the analytical eye, not so much a manifestation of individuality as a curious, one might say an almost unconscious, method of maintaining some perverse form of solidarity. Rivalry among the churches, even while appearing as contention, proclaimed that they were all members of one single society, that they were not disparate atoms but all conjoined in emulation.

The vehemence of the Protestant counteraction does seem, viewed simply as a historical phenomenon, out of all proportion to any real danger that America might become a nation of Voltaires and Tom Paines, or even of Jeffersons. No doubt, still speaking historically, we can comprehend how the pitch of intensity was kept up by the churches' fear lest the wild West lapse into pagan barbarism. But neither these nor any other historical influences fully explain the depth and passion of the religious anxiety unleashed by the Second Awakening. There was at the center of the impulse a motive that can not be explained by any configuration of environmental factors: there was a spontaneous movement of the people to redress the balance of a religious life fragmented into the most incoherent individualism the Protestant world had yet confronted. It was an instinctive, and in that sense a profound maneuver, to redress the balance by carrying the general desire for a living religion into cultural forms. In these circumstances, such concrete embodiments had perforce to be competing churches; but in the whole panorama of unending competition there was, by the very similarities among the denominations—if only by their universal acceptance of ecclesiastical rivalry as the law of institutional life—a kind of achieved stability. In effect, the United States built out of potential chaos a state church, the internal law of which is competition.

It is the obvious thing to say, yet it cannot too often be said, that in the effort to meet the challenge of Tom Paine, of the masses of the unchurched, of the immense spaces of the West, the Protestant churches found their instrument in revivalism. Thereupon, it is fitting and proper to raise the question, as for example does Jerald Brauer in his *Protestantism in America,* of whether, once the churches thus found ways of answering the needs and prejudices of the frontier, they also could carry with them resources to judge and criticize. In the shape that Protestantism took during these decades of the nineteenth century are many components that must appear to most of us repulsive: village censoriousness, crabbed sectarianism, an ignorance of and contempt for the continuity of the historic church, and above all a dumb hostility to the religious intellect. To the extent that these qualities are still with us, we have a problem. However, it ill behooves us, even if we deplore their persistence, to pronounce a blanket condemnation upon the situation of a hundred years ago. Actually, these traits are in substance crude consequences of an effort to discover modes of solidarity. Once they are seen in this light, they take on more meaning than when they are written off as mechanical results of a frontier environment.

There is a sense in which historic Christianity, in every age and throughout changing situations, has driven a wedge between man and man, painfully forcing upon each his individuality. Yet on the other hand, it has with equal force inculcated participation, the collective, the community. When challenged by a revolution, a frenzy, a new technology, or by the fall of an empire, Christian leaders have struggled—often without quite knowing what they were doing—to preserve both the poles of their antinomy, to prevent the one extreme from detaching itself from the other, to keep religion from becoming demonic, as it assuredly would should either prevail to the exclusion of the other. Faced by the stupendous challenge of continental America, with the sudden and convulsive opening of the West, the churches responded. They too hardly knew what they were doing, and the reasons they gave for themselves are pitifully unperceptive. These have to be studied deeply in order to yield up that which churchmen could never quite say. In this perspective both their successes and their uglinesses remain, it is true, data for history, but they also become symbolical renderings, in a concrete situation, of the ever-changing and yet always unchanged terms of man's relation to the divine life.

FROM THE COVENANT TO THE REVIVAL

O N JUNE 12, 1775, the Continental Congress dispatched from Philadelphia to the thirteen colonies (and to insure a hearing, ordered the document to be published in newspapers and in handbills) a "recommendation" that July 20 be universally observed as "a day of publick humiliation, fasting, and prayer." The Congress prefaced the request with a statement of reasons. Because the great "Governor" not only conducts by His providence the course of nations, "but frequently influences the minds of men to serve the wise and gracious purposes of his providential government," and also it being our duty to acknowledge his superintendency, "especially in times of impending danger and publick calamity"—therefore the Congress acts.

What may elude the secular historian—what in fact has eluded him—is the mechanism by which the Congress proposed that the operation be conducted:

> that we may with united hearts and voices unfeignedly confess and deplore our many sins, and offer up our joint supplications to the all-wise, omnipotent, and merciful Disposer of all events; humbly beseeching him to forgive our iniquities, to remove our present calamities, to avert those desolating judgments with which we are threatened. . . .

The essential point is that the Congress asks for, first, a national confession of sin and iniquity, then a promise of repentance, that only *thereafter* may God be moved so to influence Britain as to allow America to behold "a gracious interposition of Heaven for the redress of her many grievances."[1] The subtle emphasis can be detected once it is compared with the formula used by the Virginia House of Burgesses in the previous month, on May 14:

> devoutly to implore the Divine interposition for averting the heavy calamity which threatens destruction to our civil rights, and the evils of civil war, to give us one heart and one mind firmly to oppose, by all just and proper means, every injury to *American* rights. . . .

Jefferson testifies that in Virginia this measure was efficacious. The people met with alarm in their countenances, "and the effect of the day through the whole colony was like a shock of electricity, arousing every man and placing him erect and solidly on his centre."[2] However gratify-

Published in *Religion in American Life* (Princeton University Press, 1961), vol. I, pp. 322-68.
[1] B. F. Morris, *Christian Life and Character of the Civil Institutions of the United States* (Philadelphia, 1864), p. 525.
[2] *Ibid.*, pp. 526-27.

ing the local results might be, it should be noted that this predominantly Anglican House of Burgesses, confronted with calamity, made no preliminary detour through any confession of their iniquities, but went directly to the throne of God, urging that He enlist on their side. The Virginia delegation in Philadelphia (which, let us remember, included Patrick Henry but *not* Jefferson) concurred in the unanimous adoption of the Congress' much more complicated—some were to say more devious—ritualistic project. Was this merely a diplomatic concession? Or could it be that, once the threatened calamity was confronted on a national scale, the assembled representatives of all the peoples instinctively realized that some deeper, some more atavistic, search of their own souls was indeed the indispensable prologue to exertion?

The question is eminently worth asking, if only because conscientious historians have seen no difference between the two patterns, and have assumed that the Congressional followed the Virginian.[3] And there are other historians, who may or may not be cynical, but who have in either case been corrupted by the twentieth century, who perceive in this and subsequent summonses to national repentance only a clever device in "propaganda."[4] It was bound, they point out, to cut across class and regional lines, to unite a predominantly Protestant people; wherefore the rationalist or deistical leaders could hold their tongues and silently acquiesce in the stratagem, calculating its pragmatic worth. In this view, the fact that virtually all the "dissenting" clergy, and a fair number of Anglicans, mounted their pulpits on July 20 and preached patriotic self-abnegation, is offered as a proof that they had joined with the upper middle class in a scheme to bamboozle the lower orders and simple-minded rustics.

This interpretation attributes, in short, a diabolical cunning to the more sophisticated leaders of the Revolution, who, being themselves no believers in divine providence, fastened onto the form of invocation which would most work upon a majority who did believe passionately in it. This reading may, I suggest, be as much a commentary on the mentality of modern sociology as upon the Continental Congress, but there is a further observation that has been more cogently made by a few who have noted the striking differences in phraseology: the Congressional version is substantially the form that for a century and a half had been employed in New England.[5] Hence some analysts surmise that the action of the Congress, if it was not quite a Machiavellian ruse for hoodwinking the pious, was at best a Yankee trick foisted on Virginia and New York. Leaving aside the question of whether, should this explanation be true, it might just as well have been a Virginian fraud, one which cost Patrick Henry and Peyton

[3] *Cf.*, for instance, Arthur M. Schlesinger, *Prelude to Independence* (New York, 1958), pp. 31-32.

[4] Philip Davidson, *Propaganda and the American Revolution* (Chapel Hill, 1941), *passim.*

[5] Perry Miller, *The New England Mind: From Colony to Province* (Cambridge, Mass., 1953), pp. 19-26.

Randolph nothing, perpetrated to keep the New Englanders active, the simple fact is that unprejudiced examination of the records of 1775 and 1776 shows that New England enjoyed no monopoly on the procedure. The House of Burgesses might suppose it enough to petition Almighty God to redress their wrongs; the churches of the dissenters, and indeed most Anglican communities, already knew, whether in Georgia, Pennsylvania, or Connecticut, that this was not the proper way to go about obtaining heavenly assistance. The Biblical conception of a people standing in direct daily relation to God, upon covenanted terms and therefore responsible for their moral conduct, was a common possession of the Protestant peoples.

However, there can be no doubt that New England had done much more than the other regions toward articulating colonial experience within the providential dialectic. Because, also, presses were more efficient there than elsewhere, and Boston imprints circulated down the coast, it is probable that the classic utterances of Massachusetts served as models for Presbyterians and Baptists as well as for "low-church" Anglicans. For many decades the Puritan colonies had been geographically set apart; the people had been thoroughly accustomed to conceiving of themselves as a chosen race, entered into specific covenant with God, by the terms of which they would be proportionately punished for their sins.[6]

In that sense, then, we may say that the Congressional recommendation of June 12, 1775, virtually took over the New England thesis that these colonial peoples stood in a contractual relation to the "great Governor" over and above that enjoyed by other groups; in effect, Congress added the other nine colonies (about whose status New Englanders had hitherto been dubious) to New England's covenant. Still, for most of the population in these nine, no novelty was being imposed. The federal theology, in general terms, was an integral part of the Westminster Confession and so had long figured in the rhetoric of Presbyterians of New Jersey and Pennsylvania. The covenant doctrine, including that of the society as well as of the individual, had been preached in the founding of Virginia,[7] and still informed the phraseology of ordinary Anglican sermonizing. The Baptists, even into Georgia, were aware of the concept of church covenant, for theirs were essentially "congregational" polities; they could easily rise from that philosophy to the analogous one of the state. Therefore the people had little difficulty reacting to the Congressional appeal. They knew precisely what to do: they were to gather in their assemblies on July 20, and inform themselves that the afflictions brought upon them in the dispute with Great Britain were not hardships suffered in some irrational political strife but intelligible ordeals divinely brought about because of their own abominations. This being the situation, they were

[6] Perry Miller, *The New England Mind; The Seventeenth Century* (New York, 1954), pp. 464-84.

[7] Perry Miller, *Errand into the Wilderness* (Cambridge, Mass., 1956), pp. 119-22.

to resolve, not only separately but in unison, to mend their ways, restore primitive piety, suppress vice, curtail luxury. Then, and only thereafter, if they were sincere, if they proved that they meant their vow, God would reward them by raising up instruments for the deflection of, or if necessary, destruction of, Lord North.

Since the New Englanders were such old hands at this business—by exactly this method they had been overcoming, from the days of the Pequot War through King Philip's War, such difficulties as the tyranny of Andros, smallpox epidemics, and parching droughts—they went to work at once. For the clergy the task was already clear: beginning with the Stamp Act of 1765, the clerical orator who spoke at every election day, in May, surveyed the respects in which relations with England should be subsumed under the over-all covenant of the people with God. Charles Chauncy's *A Discourse on the good News from a far Country,* delivered upon a day of "thanksgiving" (the logical sequel to several previous days of humiliation) to the General Court in 1766, explained that repeal of the odious Stamp Act was a consequence not of any mercantile resistance but of New England's special position within the covenant of grace.[8] As the crisis in Boston grew more and more acute, successive election orators had an annual opportunity to develop in greater detail proof that any vindication of provincial privileges was inextricably dependent upon a moral renovation. Following the "Boston Massacre" of 1773, anniversaries of this atrocity furnished every preacher an occasion for spreading the idea among the people. The form of these discourses was still that of the traditional jeremiad, but by the time the Congress issued its wholesale invitation, the New England clergy had so merged the call to repentance with a stiffening of the patriotic spine that no power on earth, least of all the government of George III, could separate the acknowledgment of depravity from the resolution to fight.

Everything that the Congress hoped would be said in 1775 had already been declared by the Reverend Samuel Cooke of the Second Church in Boston at the election of 1770.[9] If that were not precedent enough, the General Court on October 22, 1774, confronting General Gage and the Boston Port Bill, showed how double-edged was the sword by proclaiming not a fast day but one of thanksgiving; it was illuminated by the sermon of William Gordon, from the Third Church in Roxbury, which was all the more memorable because Gordon had been English-born.[10] On May 31, 1775, six weeks after Lexington and Concord, Samuel Langdon, President of Harvard, put the theory of religious revolution so completely before the Court (then obliged to meet in Watertown) that the doctrine of political resistance yet to be formulated in the Declaration seems but

[8] John Wingate Thornton, *The Pulpit of the American Revolution* (Boston, 1860), pp. 105 ff.

[9] *Ibid.,* pp. 147-86.

[10] *Ibid.,* pp. 187-226.

an afterthought.[11] A few weeks before that assertion, on May 29, 1776, Samuel West of Dartmouth made clear to the General Court that what was included within the divine covenant as a subsidiary but essential portion had been not simply "British liberties" but the whole social teaching of John Locke.[12] After the evacuation of Boston, both Massachusetts and Connecticut were able to assemble as of old, and comfortably listen to a recital of their shortcomings, secure in the knowledge that as long as jeremiads denounced them, their courage could not fail. The fluctuations of the conflict called for many days of humiliation and a few for thanksgiving; in Massachusetts, the framing of the state constitution in 1780 evoked another spate of clerical lectures on the direct connection between piety and politics. Out of the years between the Stamp Act and the Treaty of Paris emerged a formidable, exhaustive (in general, a repetitious) enunciation of the unique necessity for America to win her way by reiterated acts of repentance. The jeremiad, which in origin had been an engine of Jehovah, thus became temporarily a service department of the Continental army.

The student of New England's literature is not astonished to find this venerable machine there put to patriotic use; what has not been appreciated is how readily it could be set to work in other sections. On this day of humiliation, July 20, 1775, Thomas Coombe, an Anglican minister at Christ's Church and St. Peter's in Philadelphia, who once had been chaplain to the Marquis of Rockingham, explained, in language which would at once have been recognized in Connecticut, that our fast will prove ineffectual unless we execute a genuine reformation of manners (interestingly enough, the printed text is dedicated to Franklin):

> We must return to that decent simplicity of manners, that sober regard to ordinances, that strict morality of demeanor, which characterized our plain forefathers; and for the decay of which, their sons are but poorly compensated by all the superfluities of commerce. We must *associate* to give a new tone and vigor to the drooping state of religion among ourselves. We must support justice, both public and private, give an open and severe check to vices of every sort, and by our example discourage those luxurious customs and fashions, which serve but to enervate the minds and bodies of our children; drawing them off from such manly studies and attainments, as alone can render them amiable in youth or respectable in age.[13]

This Philadelphia Anglican combined as neatly as any Yankee the call for patriotic resistance and the old cry of Cotton Mather that the people respond to a jeremiad by implementing *Essays To Do Good*. By Coombe's standard, Quaker Philadelphia would appear to be a Babylon, but the opportunity for salvation was at last providentially offered: "Let such

[11] *Ibid.*, pp. 227-58.
[12] *Ibid.*, pp. 259-322.
[13] Thomas Coombe, *A Sermon* (Philadelphia, 1775), pp. 11-12.

persons, however, now be told, that patriotism without piety is mere grimace."[14]

Thus we should not be surprised that Jacob Duché, preaching on this same July 20 before not only his Anglican parish but the assembled Congress, portrayed the whole trouble as "a national punishment" inflicted on "national guilt." He surveyed, as did all "Puritan" speakers, the manifest favors God had shown the colonies, and then diagnosed their present affliction as centering not on the iniquity of the British Cabinet (iniquitous as it undoubtedly was) but rather on the infidelity of Americans:

> have we not rather been so far carried away by the stream of prosperity, as to be forgetful of the source from whence it was derived? So elevated by the prospect, which peace and a successful commerce have opened to us, as to neglect those impressions of goodness, which former affections had left upon our hearts.

Was it not palpably for this reason, and this alone, "that the Almighty hath bared his arm against us"? If so, the answer for Duché, as for President Langdon, was clear: by reformation of manners, by a return to primitive piety, we would, as a united people, win the cause of American liberty. "Go on, ye chosen band of Christians," he cried to the Congress.[15] The fact that after the Declaration Duché lost heart and turned Loyalist does not make his *The American Vine* any less a spiritual jeremiad of the sort that most invigorated patriot courage.

The way the war went, and especially the British occupation of Philadelphia, prevented among the middle states the copious displays that flowed from the presses of Boston and Worcester. Even so, there was some sort of printing shop in Lancaster, and there in 1778 Hugh Henry Brackenridge brought out *Six Political Discourses Founded on the Scripture.* Known to fame—such fame as he has—for his picaresque novel of the 1790's, *Modern Chivalry,* Brackenridge figures in our histories as a Jeffersonian rationalist. So profound is the spirit of the Enlightenment displayed in this work that we are convinced that he could not have later imbibed it, but must have learned it at Princeton, where he was classmate and friend of Madison and Freneau. In 1778, however, he was an ordained Presbyterian minister; hence this fugitive publication is of more than passing interest as illustrating the continuation, three years after the first day of national humiliation, of the religious conception of the struggle. George III, declares Brackenridge, was instigated by Satan; divine providence must perforce be on the patriot side. "Heaven hath taken an active part, and waged war for us." This he can say, even when the British hold Philadelphia! However, he can produce Saratoga for evidence. Hence it is clear that "Heaven knows nothing of neutrality," providence is the

[14] *Ibid.,* p. 15.
[15] Jacob Duché, *The American Vine* (Philadelphia, 1775), pp. 24-26.

agency of God, and "there is not one tory to be found amongst the order of the seraphim." For our reverses we must have only our own sins to blame, and the surest way to victory is our conversion: "it becomes every one in the day of storm and sore commotion, to fly swiftly to the rock of Christ Jesus!" Granted that a man like Brackenridge might cleverly play upon these stops to excite a pious auditory, still it is evident that these were the appeals even a rational patriot would need to sound.[16]

To glance for a moment at the other end of the geographical spectrum: the people of Georgia had so far in their brief history found few opportunities to promote themselves into the role of an elected community; certainly the saints of Connecticut would never suppose Georgians equal in standing before the Lord with themselves. Still, when the Provincial Congress of Georgia met in 1775, before proceeding to support the Revolution they first listened to a clerical address—for all the world as though they were in Connecticut—by the Reverend John J. Zubly. It was printed in Philadelphia as *The Law of Liberty*.

Zubly reproduces the pattern of New England argumentation, though perhaps with somewhat less provincial egotism. These Americans are the result of a consecutive unfolding of God's covenant with mankind, now come to a climax on this continent; for Americans, the exercise of liberty becomes simply the one true obedience to God. This is not license, but resistance to sin; those who do not combat depravity will be judged:

> We are not to imagine because the gospel is a law of liberty, therefore men will not be judged; on the contrary judgment will be the more severe against all who have heard and professed the gospel, and yet walked contrary to its precepts and doctrines.

By this logic, once more, patriotic resistance to England is a way—the only way—to avert the wrath of Jehovah.[17]

If anywhere among the states the lineaments of Puritan federal theology would be dim, one might suppose that place to be Charleston, South Carolina. Legend continually obscures for us, however, how profoundly Protestant the culture of that region was at this time and for several decades afterwards. In 1774 William Tennent, son of the great William of Log College, expounded to planters and merchants that they were threatened with slavery because of their transgressions. The first dictate of natural passion is to imprecate vengeance upon the instruments of our torment, to resolve to endure hardships rather than surrender the privileges of our ancestors. But this, Tennent explained, is the wrong procedure. The first duty of good men is to find out and bewail "the Iniquities of our Nation and country," which are the true causes of the dismal catastrophe about to befall us.[18]

---

[16] H. H. Brackenridge, *Six Political Discourses Founded on the Scripture* (Lancaster, 1778), pp. 50-61.

[17] John J. Zubly, *The Law of Liberty* (Philadelphia, 1775), p. 6.

[18] William Tennent, *An Address, Occasioned by the Late Invasion of the Liberties*

Though by now the Revolution has been voluminously, and one might suppose exhaustively, studied, we still do not realize how effective were generations of Protestant preaching in evoking patriotic enthusiasm. No interpretation of the religious utterances as being merely sanctimonious window dressing will do justice to the facts or to the character of the populace. Circumstances and the nature of the dominant opinion in Europe made it necessary for the official statement to be released in primarily "political" terms—the social compact, inalienable rights, the right of revolution. But those terms, in and by themselves, would never have supplied the drive to victory, however mightily they weighed with the literate minority. What carried the ranks of militia and citizens was the universal persuasion that they, by administering to themselves a spiritual purge, acquired the energies God had always, in the manner of the Old Testament, been ready to impart to His repentant children. Their first responsibility was not to shoot redcoats but to cleanse themselves, only thereafter to take aim. Notwithstanding the chastisements we have already received, proclaimed the Congress on March 20, 1779—they no longer limited themselves to mere recommending—"too few have been sufficiently awakened to a sense of their guilt, or warmed with gratitude, or taught to amend their lives and turn from their sins, so He might turn from His wrath." They call for still another fast in April 1780: "To make us sincerely penitent for our transgressions; to prepare us for deliverance, and to remove the evil with which he hath been pleased to visit us; to banish vice and irreligion from among us, and establish virtue and piety by his Divine grace." And when there did come a cause for rejoicing (almost the only one in four or five years that might justify their using the vestibule of thanksgiving, the surrender of Burgoyne), patriots gave little thought to lengthening lines of supply or the physical obstacles of logistics; instead, they beheld providence at work again, welcomed Louis XVI as their "Christian ally," and congratulated themselves upon that which had really produced victory—their success in remodeling themselves. Now more than ever, asserted the Congress on October 31, 1777, we should "implore the mercy and forgiveness of God, and beseech him that vice, profaneness, extortion and every evil may be done away, and that we may be a reformed and a happy people."[19]

Historians of English political thought have reduced to a commonplace of inevitable progression the shift of Puritan political philosophy from the radical extreme of 1649 to the genial universals of 1689. John Locke so codified the later versions as to make the "Glorious Revolution" seem a conservative reaction. As we know, Locke was studied with avidity

of the American Colonies by the British Parliament (Philadelphia, 1774), p. 11. Tennent must have charmed his Carolinian audience by exclaiming (p. 17) that if these judgments have begun in New England, the bulwark of piety, those awaiting the profane South would be "more dreadful calamities."

[19] Morris, pp. 533-36.

in the colonies; hence the Congress used consummate strategy in presenting their case to a candid world through the language of Locke.

Nevertheless, we do know that well before the Civil War began in England, Parliamentarians—and these include virtually all Puritans—had asserted that societies are founded upon covenant; that the forms of a particular society, even though dictated by utilitarian factors, are of divine ordination; that rulers who violate the agreed-upon forms are usurpers and so to be legitimately resisted. This complex of doctrine was transported bodily to early Virginia and most explicitly to Puritan New England. The turmoils of Massachusetts Bay—the expulsion of Roger Williams and Anne Hutchinson, the exile of Robert Child, the disciplining of the Hingham militia, and the first trials of the Quakers—whatever other issues were involved in them, were crises in the political creed. Governor Winthrop was not much troubled, though possibly a bit, when he told the men of Hingham that in signing the covenant they had agreed to submit to rulers set over them for their own good—unless they could positively prove that their rulers were the violators!

The development of New England, however, steadily encouraged the citizens to deduce that they themselves, in framing the compact, had enumerated the items which made up their good. John Cotton and John Winthrop, having entirely accepted the contractual idea, were still making within it a last-ditch stand for medieval scholasticism by contending that the positive content of the magisterial function had been prescribed by God long before any specific covenant, whether of Israel or of Massachusetts, was drawn up. By the mid-eighteenth century, even in "semi-Presbyterial" Connecticut, good Christians were certain they could designate both the duties and the limitations of magistrates. In basically similar fashion, though not so easily traceable, the same transformation was wrought among the Protestant, or at least among the "Calvinistic," elements of all the communities. To put the matter bluntly, the agitation which resulted in the War for American Independence commenced after an immense change had imperceptibly been wrought in the minds of the people. That they needed from 1765 to 1776 to realize this was not because they had, under stress, to acquire the doctrine from abroad, but because they did have to search their souls in order to discover what actually had happened within themselves.

Consequently, every preacher of patriotism was obliged to complicate his revolutionary jeremiad by careful demonstrations of exactly how the will of Almighty God had itself always operated through the voluntary self-imposition of a compact, how it had provided for legitimate, conservative resistance to tyrants. Early in the eighteenth century, John Wise prophesied how this union of concepts would be achieved, but he seems to have had no direct effect on the patriot argument. Jonathan Mayhew was far ahead of his fellows; after his death in 1766 the others required hard work to catch up. In general it may be said that they started off serenely confident that of course the philosophy of the jeremiad, which required abject confession of unworthiness from an afflicted people, and that of the social compact, which called for immediate and vigorous action against an intruding magistrate, were one and the same. Then, discovering that the joining required more carpentry than they had anticipated, they labored for all they were worth at the task. Finally, by 1776, they triumphantly asserted that they had indeed succeeded, that the day of humiliation was demonstrably one with the summons to battle.

Political historians and secular students of theory are apt to extract from the context those paragraphs devoted solely to the social position, to discuss these as comprising the only contribution of the "black regiment" to Revolutionary argument.[20] To read these passages in isolation is to miss the point. They were effective with the masses not as sociological lectures but because, being embedded in the jeremiads, they made comprehensible the otherwise troubling double injunction of humiliation and exertion. In this complicated pattern (which could be offered as the ultimate both in right reason and in true piety), the mentality of American Protestantism became so reconciled to itself, so joyfully convinced that it had at last found its long-sought identity, that for the time being it forgot that it had ever had any other reason for existing.

A few examples out of thousands will suffice. Gordon's *Discourse* of December 15, 1774, runs for page after page in the standardized jeremiad vein: "Is not this people strangely degenerated, so as to possess but a faint resemblance of that godliness for which their forefathers were eminent?" Is it not horrible beyond all imagination that *this* people should degenerate, seeing how scrupulously God has befriended them according to the stipulations of their covenant with Him? Yet the ghastly fact is "that while there is much outward show of respect to the Deity, there is but little inward heart conformity to him." And so on and on, until abruptly, with hardly a perceptible shift, we are hearing a recital of the many palpable evidences that divine providence is already actively engaged in the work. Only by the direct "inspiration of the Most High" could the unanimity of the colonies have been brought about. From this point Gordon's cheerful jeremiad comes down to the utilitarian calculation that Americans are expert riflemen, wherefore "the waste of amunition will be greatly prevented"; after which he concludes by urging the people to "accept our punishment at his hands without murmuring or complaining"![21]

The elements woven together in this and other speeches can, of course, be separated one from another in the antiseptic calm of the historian's

---

[20] For example, Alice Baldwin, *The New England Clergy and the American Revolution* (Durham, N.C., 1928), a pioneer work of great value, but upon which later historians have unhappily depended. In this view, I should take Clinton Rossiter, *Seedtime of the Republic* (New York, 1953), as representing the strain of obtuse secularism.

[21] Thornton, pp. 208, 212, 225.

study, and the whole demonstrated to be an unstable compound of incompatible propositions. What may be left out of account is the impact of the entire argument, the wonderful fusion of political doctrine with the traditional rite of self-abasement which, out of colonial experience, had become not what it might seem on the surface, a failure of will, but a dynamo for generating action.

President Langdon's sermon of May 1775 played a slight variation on the theme by suggesting that the notorious crimes of England had brought these troubles as a divine visitation on *her!* Other preachers occasionally toyed with this device, but obviously it was not the full-throated note the populace expected and wanted. Langdon returned to the really effective music when he justified the afflictions of America:

> But alas! have not the sins of America, and of New England in particular, had a hand in bringing down upon us the righteous judgments of Heaven? Wherefore is all this evil come upon us? Is it not because we have foresaken the Lord? Can we say we are innocent of crimes against God? No surely.

After several pages of such conventional self-accusation, the moral emerges as easily in 1775 as it used to flow from the mouth of Cotton Mather: "However unjustly and cruelly we have been treated by man, we certainly deserve, at the hand of God, all the calamities in which we are now involved."[22]

Then follows a turn which is indeed novel, which reveals the subtle yet largely unconscious transformation that the Revolution was actually working in the hearts of the people. Langdon concludes his jeremiad by calling upon Americans to repent and reform, because *if* true religion can be revived, "we may hope for the direction and blessing of the most High, while we are using our best endeavors to preserve and restore the civil government of this colony, and defend America from slavery."[23]

Here, in exquisite precision, is the logic of the clerical exhortation which, though it may seem to defy logic, gives a vivid insight into what had happened to the pious mentality of the communities. For, Langdon's argument runs, once we have purged ourselves and recovered our energies in the act of contrition, how then do we go about proving the sincerity of our repentance (and insuring that divine providence will assist us)? We hereupon act upon the principles of John Locke! At this point, and not until after these essential preliminaries, Langdon turns to his exposition of Whig doctrine:

> Thanks be to God that he has given us, as men, natural rights, independent of all human laws whatever, and that these rights are recognized by the grand charter of British liberties. By the law of nature, any body of people, destitute of order and government, may form themselves into

[22] *Ibid.,* p. 247.
[23] *Ibid.,* p. 249.

a civil society according to their best prudence, and so provide for their common safety and advantage. When one form is found by the majority not to answer the grand purpose in any tolerable degree, they may, by common consent, put an end to it and set up another.[24]

The next year, Samuel West of Dartmouth persuaded the General Court of Massachusetts, not to mention readers elsewhere in the colonies, that the inner coherence of the thesis was maintained by these two combined doctrines: while, because of our abysmally sinful condition, we must obey magistrates for conscience' sake, we also find "that when rulers become oppressive to the subject and injurious to the state, their authority, their respect, their maintenance, and the duty of submitting to them, must immediately cease; they are then to be considered as the ministers of Satan, and as such, it becomes our indispensable duty to resist and oppose them."[25] What we today have to grasp is that for the masses this coalescence of abnegation and assertion, this identification of Protestant self-distrust with confidence in divine aid, erected a frame for the natural rights philosophy wherein it could work with infinitely more power than if it had been propounded exclusively in the language of political rationalism.

There were, it should be pointed out, a few clerics who could become patriots without having to go through this labyrinth of national humiliation. But in the colonies they were a minority, and they came from a Protestantism which had never been permeated by the federal theology—which is to say, they were generally Anglicans. The most conspicuous was William Smith, later Provost of the College of Philadelphia. When he responded to the Congressional recommendation, on July 20, 1775, at All-Saints in Philadelphia, he emphasized his dissent from the covenantal conception at once:

> I would, therefore, cherish these good dispositions; and what may, peradventure, have begun through Fear, I would ripen into maturity by the more cheering beams of Love. Instead of increasing your afflictions, I would convey a dawn of comfort to your souls; rather striving to woo and to win you to Religion and Happiness, from a consideration of what God hath promised to the Virtuous, than of what He hath denounced against the Wicked, both through Time and in Eternity.[26]

A historian not versed in the discriminations of theology may see little difference, considered as propaganda, between Provost Smith's form of Christian exhortation and President Langdon's, since Smith also aligns the providence of God on the side of resistance. But for men of 1775—that is for most of them—there was a vast gulf between Smith's conception and that of the New Englanders, of Coombe, of Duché, of Zubly. The really effective work of the "black regiment" was not an optimistic appeal to the

24 *Ibid.*, p. 250.
25 *Ibid.*, p. 296.
26 *The Works of William Smith, D.D.* (Philadelphia, 1803), vol. II, p. 119.

rising glory of America, but their imparting a sense of crisis by revivifying Old Testament condemnations of a degenerate people.

Smith's method, however, did have one advantage: more readily than the Puritans and Presbyterians, he could promise that God would bless a victorious America with prosperity, with that "happiness" which the Declaration said all men had a natural right to pursue. Smith did note in passing that we must repent and sincerely reform our naughty manners,[27] but his recruiting sermons pay much more attention than do those of New England or of the back country to the strictly legal contention. These generally conclude, as did one to a battalion of militia on June 25, 1775, with the earthly rewards in prospect:

> Illiberal or mistaken plans of policy may distress us for a while, and perhaps sorely check our growth; but if we maintain our own virtue; if we cultivate the spirit of Liberty among our children; if we guard against the snares of luxury, venality and corruption; the Genius of America will still rise triumphant, and that with a power at last too mighty for opposition. This country will be free—nay, for ages to come a chosen seat of Freedom, Arts, and Heavenly Knowledge; which are now either drooping or dead in those countries of the old world.[28]

Surely Smith's logic is straightforward. On December 28, 1778, he preached before a Masonic chapter and dedicated the sermon to Washington. There is no mention in it of affliction; hardships, even unto death, are to be borne in a spirit of Christian fortitude, and Christians are simply to fight the good fight, confident that when they die they shall have full scope for the exercise of charity.[29] But, though Smith's form of Christianity, with its piety hardly more than a species of Stoicism, might appeal to Washington and prove unobjectionable even to Jefferson, and though Smith delivered a heartfelt eulogy on Benjamin Franklin,[30] it was neither Smith's genial Anglicanism nor the urbane rationalism of these statesmen which brought the rank and file of American Protestants into the war. What aroused a Christian patriotism that needed staying power was a realization of the vengeance God denounced against the wicked; what fed their hopes was not what God promised as a recompense to virtue, but what dreary fortunes would overwhelm those who persisted in sloth; what kept them going was an assurance that by exerting themselves they were fighting for a victory thus providentially predestined.

To examine the Revolutionary mind from the side of its religious emotion is to gain a perspective that cannot be acquired from the ordinary study of the papers of the Congresses, the letters of Washington, the writings of Dickinson, Paine, Freneau, or John Adams. The "decent respect" that these founders entertained for the opinion of mankind caused them to put

---

[27] *Ibid.*, pp. 123, 138.
[28] *Ibid.*, pp. 283-84.
[29] *Ibid.*, p. 67.
[30] *Ibid.*, vol. I, pp. 44-92.

their case before the civilized world in the restricted language of the rational century. A successful revolution, however, requires not only leadership but receptivity. Ideas in the minds of the foremost gentlemen may not be fully shared by their followers, but these followers will accept the ideas, even adopt them, if such abstractions can be presented in an acceptable context. To accommodate the principles of a purely secular social compact and a right to resist taxation—even to the point of declaring political independence to a provincial community where the reigning beliefs were still original sin and the need of grace—this was the immense task performed by the patriotic clergy.

Our mental image of the religious patriot is distorted because modern accounts do treat the political paragraphs as a series of theoretical expositions of Locke, separated from what precedes and follows. When these orations are read as wholes, they immediately reveal that the sociological sections are structural parts of a rhetorical pattern. Embedded in their contexts, these are not abstractions but inherent parts of a theology. It was for this reason that they had so energizing an effect upon their religious auditors. The American situation, as the preachers saw it, was not what Paine presented in *Common Sense*—a community of hard-working, rational creatures being put upon by an irrational tyrant—but was more like the recurrent predicament of the chosen people in the Bible. As Samuel Cooper declared on October 25, 1780, upon the inauguration of the Constitution of Massachusetts, America was a new Israel, selected to be "a theatre for the display of some of the most astonishing dispensations of his Providence." The Jews originally were a free republic founded on a covenant over which God, "in peculiar favor to that people, was pleased to preside." When they offended Him, He punished them by destroying their republic, subjecting them to a king. Thus while we today need no revelation to inform us that we are all born free and equal and that sovereignty resides in the people— "these are the plain dictates of that reason and common sense with which the common parent has informed the human bosom"—still scripture also makes these truths explicit. Hence when we angered our God, a king was also inflicted upon us; happily, Americans have succeeded, where the Jews did not, in recovering something of pristine virtue, whereupon heaven redressed America's earthly grievances. Only as we today appreciate the formal unity of the two cosmologies, the rational and the Biblical, do we take in the full import of Cooper's closing salute to the new Constitution: "How nicely it poises the powers of government, in order to render them as far as human foresight can, what God ever designed they should be, power only to do good."[31]

Once this light is allowed to play on the scene, we perceive the shallowness of that view which would treat the religious appeal as a calculated propaganda maneuver. The ministers did not have to "sell" the Revolution

[31] Samuel Cooper, *A Sermon Preached . . . October 25, 1780* (Boston, 1780), pp. 2, 8, 11, 14, 15, 29.

to a public sluggish to "buy." They were spelling out what both they and the people sincerely believed, nor were they distracted by worries about the probability that Jefferson held all their constructions to be nonsense. A pure rationalism such as his might have declared the independence of these folk, but it could never have inspired them to fight for it.

This assertion may seem too sweeping, but without our making it we can hardly comprehend the state in which American Protestantism found itself when the victory was won. A theology which for almost two centuries had assumed that men would persistently sin, and so would have to be recurrently summoned to communal repentance, had for the first time identified its basic conception with a specific political action. Then, for the first time in the life of the conception, the cause was totally gained. Did not a startling inference follow: these people must have reformed themselves completely, must now dwell on a pinnacle of virtuousness? But there was no place in the theology of the covenant for a people to congratulate themselves. There was a station only for degenerates in need of regeneration, who occasionally might thank God for this or that mercy He granted them, forgiving their imperfections. Where could Protestantism turn, what could it employ, in order still to hold the religious respect of this now victorious society?

An Anglican rationalist, as we have seen with William Smith, would have no difficulty about the sequence of statements which said that by resisting England we would assure the future prosperity of the republic. The patriotic Jeremiahs also employed the argument, but they had to be more circumspect. Protestant political thinking had never doubted, of course, that God instituted government among men as a means toward their temporal felicity—or, at least toward their "safety." But it always based its philosophy upon the premise of original sin. Since the Fall, had men been left in a pure state of nature, all would have been Ishmaels; no man's life, family, or property would be secure. So, government was primarily a check on evil impulses; its function was negative rather than positive; it was to restrain violence, not to advance arts, sciences, technology. Yet, as Governor John Winthrop agreed during the first years of Massachusetts Bay, because *"salus populi suprema lex,"* there was a corollary (lurking out of sight) that government ought, once it restrained the lusts of these people, to do something more creative about making them comfortable.

In the negativistic emphasis of Protestant teachings, the reason for King George's violence and the consequent righteousness of resisting him were easy to make out. He and his ministers were violating the compact, so that he had become Ishmael. Law-abiding subjects were defending social barriers which, if once broken through, would cease to confine all social passions. By defying Britain they were preserving mankind from a descent into chaos. Resistance to a madman is not revolution; it is, in obedience to God, an exercise of the police power.

Yet what happens to particles of this logic when to it is joined the contention that by such resistance the righteous not only obey God but acquire wealth for themselves and their children? How can the soldier venture everything in the holy cause, after having confessed his depravity, if all the time he has a secret suspicion that by going through this performance he in fact is not so much repenting as gaining affluence for his society?

In most of the patriotic jeremiads the material inducement is adumbrated —sometimes, we may say, smuggled in. It could not be left out. Yet once the machinery of national humiliation proved effective in producing the providential victory of the Americans, were they not bound to the prophecy that by their utilization of the form, they, and they alone, would bring about a reign of national bliss? But in that case how could a confession of unworthiness be sincere?

An uneasy awareness of the dilemma was present even in the early stages of agitation. Listen, for instance, to Samuel Williams, pastor of the church in Bradford, delivering *A Discourse on the Love of Country,* December 15, 1774:

> As what should further confirm our attachment to our native country, it bids the fairest of any to promote *the perfection and happiness of mankind.* We have but few principles from which we can argue with certainty, what will be the state of mankind in future ages. But if we may judge the designs of providence, by the number and power of the causes that are already at work, we shall be led to think that the perfection and happiness of mankind is to be carried further in America, than it has ever yet been in any place.[32]

This passage is only one of hundreds in the same vein, and all wrestle with the same dubious contention: we have sinned, therefore we are afflicted by the tyranny of a corrupt Britain; we must repent and reform, in order to win the irresistible aid of providence; once we have wholeheartedly performed this act, we shall be able to exert our freedom by expelling the violators of the compact; when we succeed we shall enter upon a prosperity and temporal happiness beyond anything the world has hitherto seen. But always implicit in this chain of reasoning was a vague suggestion that the people were being bribed into patriotism. And by universal admission, the occasion for a nation's deserting its Maker and surrendering to sensuality was always an excess of material comforts. So, was not the whole machinery an ironic device for bringing upon the children of the victors judgments still more awful than any that had previously been imposed?

The clergy had, in short, simplified the once massive complexity of the process of social regeneration by concentrating its terrorizing appeal upon a single hardship, the British government. Seventeenth-century theologians would have been more wary. They took pains to keep the list so long—

---

[32] Samuel Williams, *A Discourse on the Love of Country* (Salem, 1775), p. 22.

draught, fires, earthquakes, insects, smallpox, shipwrecks—that while the people by their holy exertions might be let off this or that misery, they were sure to be tormented by some other. The Revolutionary divines, in their zeal for liberty, committed themselves unwittingly to the proposition that in this case expulsion of the British would automatically leave America a pure society. In their righteous anger, they painted gorier and gorier pictures of the depravity of England. Said President Langdon, "The general prevalence of vice has changed the whole face of things in the British government";[33] wherefore it had to follow that the sins of the colonial peoples, which brought down the Intolerable Acts, were in great part "infections" received from "the corruption of European courts." But then, once we inoculated ourselves against these contagions, would we not become a people washed white in the Blood of the Lamb?

The progress of events which led the patriots from their initial defense of "British liberties" to the radical plunge into independence also led them to this doctrinaire identification of religious exertion with the political aim. By 1776 Samuel West made it crystal clear:

> Our cause is so just and good that nothing can prevent our success but only our sins. Could I see a spirit of repentance and reformation prevail through the land, I should not have the least apprehension or fear of being brought under the iron rod of slavery, even though all the powers of the globe were combined against us. And though I confess that the irreligion and profaneness which are so common among us gives something of a damp to my spirits, yet I cannot help hoping, and even believing, that Providence has designed this continent for to be the asylum of liberty and true religion; for can we suppose that the God who created us free agents, and designed that we should glorify and serve him in this world that we might enjoy him forever hereafter, will suffer liberty and true religion to be banished from off the face of the earth?[34]

What else, then, could President Ezra Stiles of Yale College preach upon, before the General Assembly of Connecticut, on May 8, 1783, but *The United States Elevated to Glory and Honor?*

> This will be a great, a very great nation, nearly equal to half Europe. . . . Before the millennium the English settlements in America may become more numerous millions than the greatest dominion on earth, the Chinese Empire. Should this prove a future fact, how applicable would be the text, when the Lord shall have made his American Israel high above all nations which he has made, in numbers, and in praise, and in name, and in honor![35]

Still, the more closely we study this literature of exultation, the more we suspect that the New Englanders were dismayed by the very magnitude of their success. The Middle States were less inhibited. Most revelatory is

[33] Thornton, p. 243.
[34] *Ibid.,* p. 311.
[35] *Ibid.,* p. 440.

George Duffield's *A Sermon Preached in the Third Presbyterian Church* of Philadelphia on December 11, 1783—the day that Congress could at long last conscientiously appoint a "Thanksgiving." It was now abundantly clear, said Duffield, that from the beginning the Revolution had been under providential direction. We have created a nation which shall receive the poor and oppressed: "here shall the husbandman enjoy the fruits of his labor; the merchant trade, secure of his gain; the mechanic indulge his inventive genius; and the sons of science pursue their delightful employ- ment, till the light of knowledge pervade yonder yet uncultivated western wilds, and form the savage inhabitants into men." In the exuberance of triumph, Duffield permitted himself to say, in effect, that the jeremiad had also triumphed, and that we, being a completely reformed nation, need no longer be summoned to humiliation!

> A *day* whose evening shall not terminate in night; but introduce that joyful period, when the outcasts of Israel, and the dispersed of Judah, shall be restored; and with them, the fulness of the Gentile world shall flow to the standard of redeeming love: And the nations of the earth, become the kingdom of our Lord and Saviour. Under whose auspicious reign holiness shall universally prevail; and the noise and alarm of war be heard no more.[36]

In this situation—if all the nation participated, as most of it did, in the assurances of Duffield's *te Deum*—there would be, at least for the moment, no further use for the jeremiad. A few New Englanders, along with Presi- dent Witherspoon of Princeton, cautioned the people that while indeed God had blessed them beyond all expectation, they now had the further responsibility of perpetuating the reformation, but theirs were but feeble admonitions compared with the compulsions of the dark days of 1775. Because the program of salvation had been combined with the struggle for nationhood, American Protestants were obliged to see in the Treaty of Paris the fulfillment of prophecies. Ezra Stiles took as his text Deu- teronomy xxvi:19, a verse that long had done yeoman's service as a club for beating backsliders, and then explained that on this occasion he selected it "only as introductory to a discourse upon the political welfare of God's American Israel, and as allusively prophetic of the future prosperity and splendor of the United States."[37] This by implication does pretend that the reformation had been entirely successful. So, with some reluctance, Stiles suggests that with the finish of the colonial era we have come also to the close of the jeremiad:

> And while we have to lament our Laodiceanism, deficient morals, and incidental errors, yet the collective system of evangelical doctrines, the instituted ordinances, and the true ecclesiastical polity, may be found here in a great degree of purity.[38]

36 George Duffield, *A Sermon Preached in the Third Presbyterian Church* (Philadelphia, 1784), pp. 16-17, 18.
37 Thornton, p. 403.
38 *Ibid.,* p. 473.

Whereupon a chill strikes the exulting heart. If this be so, are we not, under the providence of God, on leaving the exciting scenes both of war and spiritual conflict, now headed for a monotonous, an uninteresting prosperity, the flatness of universal virtue?

These people, however, had for a long time been disciplined to the expectation of woe. The government of the Confederacy became mired in confusion, thus clouding once more any reading of God's design. While the states were devising a constitution to correct this affliction, the blow was struck; but not in America—in Paris. At first, of course, the fall of the Bastille seemed to strengthen the alliance of social doctrine and religious hope. Shortly the fallacy became evident. Not that there was any serious threat in America of a reversion to the depraved state of nature which engulfed France in 1793; yet in this glorious republic the French Revolution brought home to the devout an immediate realization of the need for dissociating the Christian conception of life from any blind commitment to the philosophy of that revolution. Indeed, they had no choice ultimately but to abandon the whole political contention of either of the two revolutions, and to seek at once some other program for Christian solidarity. They did not need to renounce the Declaration, nor even to denounce the Constitution, but only henceforth to take those principles for granted, yield government to the secular concept of the social compact, accept the First Amendment, and so to concentrate, in order to resist deism and to save their souls, upon that other mechanism of cohesion developed out of their colonial experience, the revival.

It took them until about the year 1800 to recast—or, as they believed, to recover—their history. Amid the great revivals which swept over Connecticut, Kentucky, and Tennessee in that year, which expanded into Georgia, Illinois, and for decades burned over northern New York, the Revolution was again and again presented as having been itself a majestic revival. The leadership of Jefferson, Paine, and the rationalists was either ignored or explained away. The "Second Great Awakening" engendered the denominational forms of American Protestantism which still endure, but perhaps equally important was its work in confirming the American belief that the Revolution had not been at all revolutionary, but simply a protest of native piety against foreign impiety.

Denominational historians tell us what the churches had to contend with following the Treaty of Paris. One fact seems indisputable: while Presbyterians and Congregationalists hesitated, Methodist itinerants rushed in. During the 1790's the major churches undertook a radical realignment of thinking, which for a century or more would determine their character.

The factors in this cultural crisis—complex though they were—can be, for narrative purposes, succinctly enumerated.

Despite the warnings of Provost Smith, the Protestant clergy preached so extravagant a Christian utopianism that with the end of the war they could only term what confronted them a demoralization beyond anything they had ever imagined. In 1795, for instance, the Methodist Church was calling for the resumption of fast days because of "our manifold sins and iniquities—our growing idolatry, which is covetousness and the prevailing love of the world . . . the profanation of the Sabbath . . . disobedience to parents, various debaucheries, drunkenness, and such like."[39] Relative to, say, the 1920's, the America of the 1790's may appear a reign of idyllic simplicity, but to organized religion it seemed morally abominable.

Coincident with this internal confusion came the French Revolution, that "volcano," as Robert Baird retrospectively called it in 1844, which "threatened to sweep the United States into its fiery stream."[40] It would not have set off such hysteria had not its excitements coincided with the frightening division of American society into parties, portending in the eyes of many an internal conflict. It is important, if we would make sense out of later developments, to insist that by no means all the religious— call them Calvinist, evangelical, or simply orthodox—went with Hamilton against Jefferson. On the contrary, multitudes were not alienated by Jefferson's deism. The publicity given by Henry Adams to Timothy Dwight's insane fears over Jefferson's election—Dwight's certainty that all the virgins of Connecticut would be raped—has been so played up in our histories that we forget how the evangelicals were worried not so much about the President as about the whole apocalyptical scene. The Presbyterian General Assembly in May 1798 bewailed innovations in Europe, the parades of devastation and bloodshed, but saw these as ominous because along with them had come "a general dereliction of religious principle and practice among our fellow-citizens, . . . a visible and prevailing impiety and contempt for the laws and institutions of religion, and an abounding infidelity which in many instances tends to Atheism itself."[41] By this time the churches supposed themselves once more in the predicament Edwards had diagnosed in 1740: the nation, having prospered, had become slovenly. Each by itself, with connivance, concluded that it was high time for another outpouring of God's Spirit, and then to their surprise found themselves engaged in a common enterprise which owed nothing to political agitation or to governmental encouragement. "We rejoice," said the Stonington Baptist Association in 1798, "that many of our brethren of different denominations have united in concert of prayer, and meet at stated season, to offer up fervent [sic] supplications, that God would avert his judgments."[42]

There was a dimension to their anxiety, however, which had hardly been present in 1740—the terrifying West. Kentucky and Tennessee were opened up, the Ohio Valley was ready for the stampede. The churches—

---

[39] Nathan Bangs, *A History of the Methodist Episcopal Church* (New York, 1839), vol. II, p. 146.

[40] Robert Baird, *Religion in America* (New York, 1844), p. 102.

[41] Quoted in Charles R. Keller, *The Second Great Awakening in Connecticut* (New Haven, 1942), pp. 1-2.

[42] *Ibid.*, p. 191.

Congregational, Baptist, Presbyterian, Lutheran, even the insurgent Methodist—were European institutions. In their several ways they had given religious sanction to the political break with Europe. Then, by 1800 or thereabouts, they had also to realize that they could no longer operate in terms of a provincial society huddled along the Atlantic coast, facing toward Europe; they had to find means for combating what everybody feared would be a plunge into barbarism, on the other side of the Appalachians, in a vast area stretching away from Europe. In the next decades the cry for saving the West swelled to a chorus of incitation infinitely more impassioned than had been the call for resistance to England. A view of the valleys of the two great rivers, said William Cogswell in 1833, is enough to make heaven weep, "enough to break any heart unless harder than adamant, and to rouse it into holy action, unless colder than the grave."[43]

To uncover the mainspring of the "Second Great Awakening" one has to look in these directions, rather than to rest content with the conventional explanation that it was reaction against deism and the Enlightenment. Actually, European deism was an exotic plant in America, which never struck roots into the soil. "Rationalism" was never so widespread as liberal historians, or those fascinated by Jefferson, have imagined. The basic fact is that the Revolution had been preached to the masses as a religious revival, and had the astounding fortune to succeed. In a little more than a decade the Protestant conscience recognized anew that in the spiritual economy victory, especially the most complete victory, is bound to turn into failure. So the struggle had to be commenced once more. James McGready, Barton Warren Stone, and the two McGees were picking up at the end of the 1790's where the patriotic orators had relaxed. They were sustained by a sense of continuity.

There were, nevertheless, a few differences in their comprehension of the task. For these revivalists, it was no longer necessary to find space in their sermons for social theory. They might honor John Locke as much as George Washington, but could at best salute both in passing. Furthermore, they really had no way of holding the entire nation responsible for the observance of a covenant with heaven. Clergymen of 1776 could plausibly present the tight little cluster of colonies as having been somehow all caught up within a special and particular bond, but after 1800, and even more after 1815, the country was too big, too sprawling, too amorphous. No Baptist, Presbyterian, or Methodist could pretend on national holidays to speak for the conscience of all churchmen. These two considerations so altered the bases of their campaign from what had served the First Awakening that they had to devise entirely new ones. They were required to risk an adventure unprecedented in history. Calling upon all the people to submit to a uniform moral law, they at the same time had to concede that American Christianity must and should accept a diversity of churches.

[43] William Cogswell, *The Harbinger of the Millennium* (Boston, 1833), p. 102.

We once, said the *Biblical Repository* in 1832, entertained utopian ideas about great national religious institutions, but neither the state of the country nor the temper of the age will admit them: "Theological peculiarities and sectional feelings call for separate institutions."[44] If this configuration posed a threat of centrifugal force, then that had to be countered by the centripetal power of the revival. Therefore the technique of revivalism had to be remodeled to serve precisely this function. Thus accepting the liberal consequences of the Revolution in the form of republican governments, and so abandoning the dream of theocracy, and equally surrendering (except for rhetorical flourish) the idea of a people in a national covenant with their Maker, these insurgents proposed to salvage the Protestant solidarity by the main force of spiritual persuasion. They summoned sinners to the convulsions of conversion; what in fact they were doing, even though few quite understood, was asserting the unity of a culture in pressing danger of fragmentation.

Of one thing patriotic sermons of the Revolution were supremely confident, even from the first stirrings of violence: with a free United States would dawn the era of religious liberty. Massachusetts and Connecticut might have to construct a curious logic to explain just how this assurance was to be reconciled with their retention of a "standing order," yet whatever the devices by which they apologized for it, they stoutly added that all other denominations could and would enjoy perfect freedom. Samuel Cooper in 1800 betrayed his embarrassment by carefully quoting all the libertarian passages in the new Constitution, and further acknowledging that there exists a diversity of sentiments respecting the extent of civil power in religious matters. He would not enter into disputation, but he could frankly recommend, "where conscience is pleaded on both sides, mutual candour and love, and an happy union of all denominations in support of a government, which though human, and therefore not absolutely perfect, is yet certainly founded on the broadest basis of liberty, and affords equal protection to all."[45] Ezra Stiles permitted himself in 1783 conveniently to ignore the Connecticut system in his enthusiasm for prophesying that with our liberation from the Church of England and our attaining of freedom, we would restore the churches to primitive purity: "Religious liberty is peculiarly friendly to fair and generous disquisition." He was so persuaded that in a free market truth would prevail that he was willing to go to any lengths: "Here Deism will have its full chance; nor need libertines more to complain of being overcome by any weapons but the gentle, the powerful ones of argument and truth. Revelation will be found to stand the test to the ten thousandth examination."[46]

The prospect of glory for America lay not in this or that church, Stiles announced, but in the national virtue of all of them together: "We must

---

[44] *Biblical Repository,* vol. IV (Andover, 1832), p. 79.
[45] Cooper, pp. 36-37.
[46] Thornton, p. 471.

become a holy people in reality, in order to exhibit the experiment, never yet fully made in this unhallowed part of the universe, whether such a people would be the happiest on earth."[47] Outside New England, preachers spoke unequivocally, asserting that all sects stood on a common level and that never again should there be any connection between religious profession and the rights of citizenship. In Connecticut after 1818 and in Massachusetts after 1833, ministers could happily join the chorus of freedom. Those who had fought most stoutly against disestablishment soon professed, as did Lyman Beecher, that it was a blessing to their churches.

Thus it was evident that the salvation of the nation which the revivalists of 1800 and of the following decades burned to accomplish had to be won, if won it might be, by their own exertions, with no assistance from any civil authority. They undertook their task without trepidation. They were aware that they were attempting an "experiment" unprecedented in Christian history, against the success of which past experience testified. This consideration only encouraged them. In the colonies there had come about a multiplicity of churches, a knack of getting along together, and a formal separation of church and state, by a process so natural as to make them see nothing extraordinary in their situation. True, they did recollect that formerly there had been nasty struggles, but these they banished from mind and ceased to dream of an established or uniform orthodoxy. There was clearly no cause to fear that either the federal or state governments, though thoroughly secularized, would ever become enemies of Christianity. If the civil powers could not actively foment a revival, they could likewise not hinder it. So at first the spiritual leaders saw nothing incongruous in their continuing to speak as though the whole nation professed itself still in covenant, as a unit, with providence. Indeed when President Washington proclaimed a day of thanksgiving for the inauguration of the Constitution in 1789, and another in 1795 over the suppression of the whiskey rebellion, the formula of national federation seemed still to prevail, and the churches promptly acted as of old.

The first tremors of disillusionment came when President Adams called for fasts in 1798 and 1799, ostensibly because of such standard afflictions as cholera and yellow fever. In the heat of the political contention, the Jeffersonians saw these gestures not as pious intercessions of the whole people before the throne of grace, but as Federalist plots to ensnare Republicans into praying for John Adams. It is not surprising then that Thomas Jefferson exposed the hollowness of the federal conception in 1802 by taking advantage of an awkward address from the Danbury Baptist Association (this minority in Connecticut was then objecting to being compelled to observe fast days appointed by the standing order) to announce that he would not longer, "as my predecessors did," proclaim such days. As he explained in a much-quoted letter of 1808, he considered

[47] Thornton, p. 487.

the federal government prohibited by the Constitution from intermeddling with religious institutions, and that even to "recommend" a ceremonial observance would be indirectly to assume an authority over religion. It is not for the interest of the churches themselves, he said, "that the General Government should be invested with the power of effecting any uniformity of time or matter among them."[48] Wherefore, if the churches were to save this society and keep it righteous, though they might for a time employ the familiar language (as the Presbyterian Assembly did in 1798: "eternal God has a controversy with this nation"),[49] they soon were forced to recognize that in fact they now dealt with the Deity only as particular individuals gathered for historical, capricious reasons into this or that communion. They had to realize, at first painfully, that as a united people they had no contractual relationship with the Creator, and that consequently a national controversy with Him could no longer exist.

President Madison, despite his scruples, reverted to custom, and actually in 1812 chanted the ancient litany: we must acknowledge "the transgressions which might justly provoke the manifestations of His divine displeasure," we must seek His assistance "in the great duties of repentance and amendment" in order to counter Britain's Acts in Council.[50] But the magic had gone out of the spell. In the first place, the idea of James Madison sincerely using these phrases made it a rigmarole. Second, many good Christians, especially in New England, were so passionately opposed to the policy which was bringing on the hated war that they could not attribute the manifestations of displeasure as due to any transgressions of their own, but solely to the stupidity of the administration. They would respond to such an invitation from the White House not by assembling in churches to renew their covenant with Jehovah, but rather by gathering in a convention at Hartford, in order, if necessary, to break their covenant with anti-Federalist states. How obsolete the pattern had become, how indeed it no longer made sense and had to break up of itself, finally became evident in 1832 when Henry Clay was so misguided as to attempt to convert it into a stick for beating Andrew Jackson.

At the end of June in that year (the election was coming in the autumn), Clay introduced in the Senate a resolution to request that the President recommend a day of humiliation and prayer because the country was threatened with a cholera invasion. Clay had so little knowledge of the proper incantation—in the course of the debate he admitted that he was not a church member, but that even so he had "a profound respect for Christianity, the religion of my fathers, and for its rites, usages and its observances"—that he entirely omitted a recital of the sins of the nation which

<hr />

[48] Anson Phelps Stokes, *Church and State in the United States* (New York, 1950), vol. I, pp. 489-91.

[49] W. W. Sweet, *Religion on the American Frontier*, vol. II, *The Presbyterians* (New York, 1936), p. 55.

[50] Morris, p. 549.

had drawn this visitation upon it. The most liberal of clerical orators in the Revolution would have been horrified at this violation of protocol! Instead, Clay proved at length that the presidential recommendation "would be obligatory upon none," that it should be gratefully received by "all pious and moral men, whether members of religious communities or not."

Significantly enough, the Whigs rushed to Clay's support, even though some of them, like Frelinghuysen of New York, had once been Federalists and had formerly sneered at little Jimmy Madison's effort to play the prophet. But the Democrats would have none of it. Tazewell of Virginia scored heavily as he reaffirmed Jefferson's contention that Congress has no more power to make such a resolution than to enact any law concerning religious matter or right, but he scored more heavily when he denied that there was any threat to the mass of the nation from cholera. Once an affliction becomes so much a matter of debate that there can be no universal and instantaneous agreement upon its severity, then the glorious era of the covenant is terminated. In the House, Davis of South Carolina buried the resolution by branding the custom as "derived from our English ancestors," and said that if it were observed, it would increase alarm and so augment calamity.[51]

Despite the fumbling theology of the Whigs, Clay's resolution got lost in committee (Jackson was prepared to veto it had it ever emerged). However, in August 1861, Lincoln did recommend a day of humility, and some of his language evoked memories of the past. Yet here the "affliction" was manifestly recognizable, and besides, by 1861, a succession of revivals and the prosperity of the "voluntary principle" had so reoriented American Protestantism within an uncovenanted piety that it could respond to the President's proclamation without anybody's giving a thought to the heavenly contract—at least, shall we say, in terms which the Puritan federalists would have recognized. The emphasis of this day of humiliation was not really humiliation but a unanimous prayer "that our arms may be blessed and made effective for the re-establishment of law, order and peace throughout the country." This, of course, makes the fast day frankly an implement of municipal policy, just what the Revolutionary proclamations are accused of being, but which they were only subordinately to their religious directive. The irony is that in 1861 the ceremony could be so openly devoted to the national "happiness," because the religious injunction had for several decades previously issued not from the covenantal relation of the nation to God's designs but from a fervor of individual piety aroused by the revivals and harnessed to religious action, not through an established church but within a bewildering variety of voluntaristic churches.

What gives both meaning and poignance to the story is that at the very moment Lincoln issued his proclamation, in churches to the south of the Mason-Dixon Line—which in theology, polity, and general piety were

[51] *Annals, 22 Congress,* First Series (1832), pp. 1130-32, 3834.

indeed the brethren of those to the north—equally anxious prayers were being offered for a blessing upon Confederate arms, and likewise in the name of law and order. Between the Revolution and the Civil War an alteration was worked in the mind of American Protestantism which is in fact a more comprehensive revolution than either of the military eruptions. With the political order separated from the ecclesiastical, yet not set against it, the problem had become not how to enlist the community into a particular political crusade for any social doctrine, but how to preserve a spiritual unity throughout a multitude of sects amid the increasing violence of political dissension. On the one hand, the revival movement and the extension of the voluntary system could not prevent the Civil War, as conceivably the theology of the covenant might have; but what these forces could do was to formulate a religious nationalism which even the war could not destroy. Whatever blood was shed and scars remained, the battles were fought upon the assumption of a cultural similarity of the contestants, one with another, which could surmount the particular issues in dispute and thus become, after 1865, a powerful instrument of reunification.

I do not mean to assert, as I hope is obvious, that the jeremiad form of the sermon automatically ceased upon the miscarriage of Clay's resolution in 1832. It continued to be a staple in evangelical preaching. But never again would it have the sting of the seventeenth-century exercises, or of those of the Revolution. Without having behind it any living sense of a specific bond between the nation and God, it could survive only as a species of utilitarian exhortation.

For instance, Joel Parker discoursed in 1837 to the Presbyterian Congregation in New Orleans upon the Panic of 1837, which he presented as a novel "yet severe infliction." But when he asked whence it arose, he dwelt not upon the sins of the people, but almost entirely upon the educative effects of the experience. He entitled his homily, "Moral Tendencies of Our Present Pecuniary Distress," and though his adumbration of the moral effects by inference noted those tendencies which hitherto had been immoral, what really bore him up was such a reflection as "Our present pecuniary embarrassments tend ultimately to produce great good, by raising the tone of commercial integrity."[52] In other words, Parker was saying that if the besetting sin had been speculation, now, out of affliction, good men will learn caution, and so quickly step into the places of wealth vacated by the gamblers. Since these by definition will be virtuous, they, even when they become rich, will observe the Sabbath.

Parker's effort is, perhaps, too slight to be taken very seriously, but the logic—or rather the rhetoric—to which it is reduced illustrates the problem that confronted a preacher who in the Jacksonian age endeavored to fire again the once-shattering blunderbuss of the jeremiad, even when he was specially favored by an outburst of cholera or even more by a financial

[52] Joel Parker, *Moral Tendencies of Our Present Pecuniary Distress* (New Orleans, 1837), p. 5.

panic spread across the whole nation. These calamities were not calamitous enough, severe though they were, to overcome the stubbornly persisting premise in the popular mind, deposited there both by the Declaration of Independence and by the successful jeremiads of the Revolution, that this people lived not in fear and trembling before a covenanted Jehovah, but as a race who go through sorrow, distress, reverses, in an ecstatic assurance of "happiness."

Adequately to unravel this tangle would take much space. To some extent it has variously been unraveled, in that analysts have one way or another perceived that the revival, although luridly wallowing in sin and hysterics, was anything but an indulgence in "Christian pessimism."[53] Aside from the obvious fact that revivalists in general—not merely Methodists but those professing, as did Finney, some form of "Calvinism"—so emphasized the ability of the sinner to acquire conversion as in effect to transform Calvinism (everywhere outside Old School Presbyterianism) into an operational Arminianism, even more fundamentally they made religious exultation an adjunct to the national vigor. Not to pile up citations, let us take one single but highly revelatory example, an article in *The Spirit of the Pilgrims* of 1831, entitled "The Necessity of Revivals of Religion to the Perpetuity of Our Civil and Religious Institutions." If one can resist the temptation to marvel that here is a naïve merging of Christianity with the culture beyond anything even imagined by Albrecht Ritschl, he can then decipher that it speaks out of a moment in the religious transformation of the colonies into a nation which remains, to say the least, crucial for all subsequent history of American Protestantism.

What is fascinating about this disquisition—though only because it is more articulate than most in the literature—is its admission that the real issue for American Christianity is "the corrupting influence of a pre-eminent national prosperity." On that basis, the essay accepts the basic challenge: is it a work beyond the power of God "to effect such a change of human character as will reconcile universal liberty and boundless prosperity, with their permanence and purity"? We suppose in advance that the author concludes on a note of Christian triumph. That forensic peroration does not count. What speaks to us is the primary definition, and then the anxiety, impossible to conceal, which gives the argument its thrust.

This anxiety is no longer dismay or pain because of ordeals to which the people have been subjected, not because of plagues or hurricanes, but a dread about the future. Will we be able to endure this prosperity? How can we, in the face of the "appalling" dangers which threaten the United States? And what are these? How deeply altered have become the very circumstances which Ezra Stiles, a half century before, found to be guarantees of American glory: the dangers arise "from our vast extent of territory, our numerous and increasing population, from diversity of local interests,

[53] Most recently and entertainingly by Bernard A. Weisberger, *They Gathered at the River* (Boston, 1958).

the power of selfishness, and the fury of sectional jealousy and hate." The student is perplexed when dealing with such revivalists as Beecher and Finney as to just how much they believed their harvests were wrought by supernatural grace or how much they knew that they themselves stirred them up, engineered them by force of personality and lung power. This exhortation in Beecher's journal—if not actually written by him, then surely it had his approval—suggests a realm of emotion in which the question might be disposed of: the revival could be conceived as neither a descent from on high nor an artificial stimulation because it could be seen as an effort of religion to keep pace with the rush of American progress. It would thus cease to be a means of placating a vengeful deity and become the way so to change the nature of the citizens as to enable them to cope with their colossal nationality. "Let me then call the attention of my readers to our only remaining source of hope—GOD—and the interposition of his Holy Spirit, in great and general Revivals of Religion, to reform the hearts of this people, and make the nation good and happy."[54]

It is hardly too much to say that as the concept of the national covenant dissolved, depriving the jeremiad of its reason for being, the new form of religious excitation, the revivalistic preaching, fed not on the terrors which the population had passed but on the gory prospect of those to come. Concealed within this curious device is a secret assurance that if religion can be identified with nationality, or vice versa, then we can insure both goodness and happiness. When Americans talked to each other, they made a great show of the fear; when they turned to Europe, in order to explain this peculiar and apparently insane American ecclesiastical order, they revealed the confidence which inwardly sustained them. Robert Baird, for instance, had spent years in France as an agent for the Presbyterian Church, before his 1844 publication of *Religion in America*. Since it was addressed to an English and European public, there was no need for him to shout imprecations upon the disastrous consequences of prosperity, but simply and proudly to explain the beauties of American revivals and the efficient workings of the voluntary principle. By the time he was finished, foreign readers might get at least a glimmer of how the miracle operated: in a free democracy, with church and state entirely separated, amid what seemed a chaos of sects and orgiastic convulsions, the society could be called a "Christian" community. In fact, it was more thoroughly imbued with a Christian spirit than any in Europe.[55]

Certainly this paradox required explaining. We may doubt that even the judicious Baird succeeded in making Frenchmen and Englishmen understand. Certainly Alexis de Tocqueville pondered and pondered about the mystery, and his pages on religion in *De la Démocratie en Amérique* are probably the least perceptive he ever wrote. They show that he never could escape the puzzlement which fell upon him and his companion, Gustave de

[54] *The Spirit of the Pilgrims,* vol. IV (Boston, 1831), pp. 467-79.
[55] Baird, pp. 105-29.

Beaumont, shortly after they arrived in 1831 (the year of the piece in *The Spirit of the Pilgrims*), which Beaumont expressed in a letter from New York after learning that at Sing Sing prison there was on successive Sundays a rotation of ministers among the various churches:

> Actually, this extreme tolerance on the one hand toward religions in general—on the other this considerable zeal of each individual for his own religion, is a phenomenon I can't yet explain to myself. I would gladly know how a lively and sincere faith can get on with such a perfect toleration; how one can have equal respect for religions whose dogmas differ; and finally what real influence on the moral conduct of the Americans can be exercised by their religious spirit, whose outward manifestations, at least, are undeniable.

Faced with sociological absurdity, the rational Frenchman could only decide that in American religion there is more breadth than depth, and that the competition among churches must be attributed "to conceit and emulation rather than to conviction and consciousness of the truth."[56] This would not be the last time that Gallic logic failed to encompass the spectacle of American irrationality.

Philip Schaff was German instead of French, and deeply religious instead of priding himself on his liberalism. Furthermore he lived in America, became an American, studied it with affection. He never could approve of the revivals, and since he believed passionately in the unity of Christendom, he was distressed by sectarianism. Yet when, after ten years in this country, he revisited Germany and lectured about American Protestantism in Berlin, the resulting book, translated under the title *America* and published at New York in 1855, lovingly proclaimed that "the United States are by far the most religious and Christian country in the world; and that, just because religion is there most free." His Prussian auditors remained skeptical, but they were shaken when Schaff solemnly informed them that in Berlin, a city of four hundred and fifty thousand, there were only forty churches; in New York, "to a population of six hundred thousand, there are over two hundred and fifty well-attended churches, some of them quite costly and splendid, especially in Broadway and Fifth Avenue." Schaff's book, which has been neglected by historians, is in many respects a more profound, a more accurate work than Tocqueville's overrated one, and the extent to which it achieves profundity is a consequence of his firm conviction that not any one of the present confessions would ever become exclusively dominant in America, "but rather, that out of the mutual conflict of all something wholly new will gradually arise."[57]

But precisely Schaff's use of the future tense was the most difficult thing for the returned German Lutheran to explain to his former colleagues. Whatever may become of venerable Europe, he said, "America is, without

---

[56] George Wilson Pierson, *Tocqueville and Beaumont in America* (New York, 1938), p. 106.
[57] Philip Schaff, *America* (New York, 1855), pp. xii, 94, 97.

question, emphatically a land of the future." He hastened to say that this is not because Americans are more meritorious than Europeans, but because providence has so arranged matters. This should not make Americans vain, but rather humble, "that they may faithfully and conscientiously fulfill their mission."[58] But also, during these years this prospect was what made them anxious. As the tension between the sections mounted, the appeal to religion—to revivalism and to the power of will expressed in free churches—to preserve unity became more and more agonized. No influence but religion, *The Spirit of the Pilgrims* had said in 1831, "can unite the local, jarring interests of this great nation, and constitute us benevolently one." By 1856 a writer in *Bibliotheca Sacra* was pleading:

> Whether we will or not, we have within us a feeling of unity with all associated with us under the same institutions or laws. All are part of one great whole. It is not mere fancy, a mere prejudice; it is ordered so by our Creator; and, when we urge to the cultivation of national feeling, we but carry out His designs.[59]

It is, of course, a matter of historical fact that the slavery question proved so disruptive that not even this fervent religious nationalism could keep the great evangelical bodies from separating into southern and northern opponents. And from those prophetic divisions flowed eventually secession and all its woes. In that sense, the instinct of the revivals had been correct from their beginnings in 1800: that which should terrify religious souls in America was not the past but the future. Men must seek the Lord not because of what they have done or have suffered but so that they may be prepared to endure what is approaching. But the federal theology, the doctrine of the covenant and the call to humiliation as a method of gaining relief from affliction, was a creation of what Schaff called venerable Europe, and was supposedly extracted from the still more venerable Old Testament. Its entire emphasis was retrospective: the covenant had been made with Abraham, John Winthrop had committed the Puritan migration to a covenant back in 1630, the patriots of the Revolution called upon themselves to repent so that God would restore them to a blessing from which their transgressions had led them. The struggle was always to return, to get back to what, theoretically, the people, the communities, had once been. Therefore, among the many transformations wrought in the mentality of America between the Revolution and the Civil War was precisely this turning of the gaze from what had been, and could therefore be defined, to the illimitable horizon of the inconceivable. No doubt, as Schaff remarked, this achievement was not a result of the Americans' being more energetic or cleverer than other people (though they liked to boast that they were), but of circumstances—their isolation, their natural resources, their economic opportunity. Everything

[58] *Ibid.*, p. xvii.
[59] *Bibliotheca Sacra,* vol. XIII (Andover, 1856), p. 201.

thus conspired to work an intellectual and moral transformation. In this drama the religious revolution plays a vital part, because in the prewar society religion was all-pervasive. The piety that arose out of the process could not stave off the bloodshed. Perhaps we may even accuse it of prolonging the strife, of intensifying the ferocity. But it imparted a special character to this war which remains a part of its enduring fascination. Above all, by giving to American Protestantism an absolute dedication to the future, by leading it out of the covenant and into the current of nationalism, the religious experience of this period indelibly stamped an immense area of the American mind.

THE INSECURITY OF NATURE

THE THIRD CHURCH of Boston resulted in 1669-1670 from a fission inside the First Church during the controversy over the Half-Way Covenant. Its minister died in 1678; the church was too important a pivot in the dispute to be entrusted to a raw Harvard graduate, and on March 31, 1678, it ordained Samuel Willard, who from 1663 to 1676 had conducted the Church of Groton. He was an ideal choice: born in Concord, 1639, the son of Major Willard, Harvard Class of 1659, he was absolute master of the vast body of Protestant learning, of that compendium of physics, mathematics, logic, rhetoric which had constituted the European intellect at the time of the Great Migration. In addition, he was a devoted champion of the Half-Way Covenant.

Beginning in 1687 he took upon himself—a voluntary service—to deliver on the first Tuesday of each month a systematic exposition of *The Westminster Confession* and of the *Catechism,* designing "to exercise and entertain the Riper and stronger Minds, of more enlarg'd Capacities and more advanced Knowledge." He kept these up even after he was pressed (1701) into serving as titular vice-president of Harvard (in effect president); at his death (1707) he left a mountain of manuscript. Although the book, said his editors, was "passionately wish'd for," not until 1726 could they add, "this growing Country is become now capable of taking off the Impression of so great a Work, the largest that was ever Printed here, and the first of Divinity in a Folio Volumn." In that year Willard's successors at the Old South, Joseph Sewall and Thomas Prince, brought out *A Compleat Body of Divinity,* a landmark in American publishing and a magnificent summation of the Puritan intellect.

But by this time a disturbing change was taking place in the climate of colonial opinion. In 1707 John Leverett was chosen Willard's successor at Harvard; during his administration, 1707 to 1724, a cleavage was wrought between two groups of New England intellectuals which, it is hardly extravagance to say, has never quite been reconciled. The Mathers hated him and managed to gather about them in the Boston churches young ministers of their complexion, Sewall and Prince along with Joshua Gee, John Webb, William Cooper, and Thomas Foxcroft. Benjamin Colman at Brattle Street was Leverett's friend, but not until three years after Leverett's death did the First Church force upon Foxcroft the acceptance

The Dudleian Lecture on Natural Religion for the academic year 1952-53, delivered in Andover Chapel, Harvard University, April 14, 1953. Published in the *Harvard Divinity School Bulletin,* vol. XIX (1953-54), pp. 23-38.

of Charles Chauncy as colleague-pastor. However, Leverett also had his partisans: Nathaniel Appleton in Cambridge, Edward Wigglesworth, the first Hollis Professor of Divinity, as well as John Barnard, Edward Holyoke, and Ebenezer Gay.

Against these cultivators of what was publicly called the "Catholick Spirit," Sewall and Prince directed Willard's folio, but they were fully aware that to publish in 1726 an exposition of conservative theology in purely seventeenth-century terms was to invite contempt. For Cotton Mather, having long before comprehended the nature of the crisis, had rallied his forces under the banner of him he called "our perpetual dictator," Sir Isaac Newton. *The Christian Philosopher,* published in 1721, made clear, once and for all, that, however it might be done, the orthodoxy of New England would hereafter need to be couched in phrases compatible with the *Principia.*

Sewall and Prince boasted that Willard asserted the good old truths under a lively influence, that he did not (their dig at Leverett, Appleton, and Wigglesworth was clear to the public of 1726) "talk of them as many now adays do in their Theological Treatises, in so cold a manner, as if they were either blind to their Excellence, or in doubt of their Verity, or at least insensible of their great Importance to themselves and others." On the other hand, being pupils of Cotton Mather, and made by him conscious of the flood of recent English publications, they had to confess that Willard was "less exact in his *Philosophical Schemes & Principles*" than would suit the new age. Hence Sewall and Prince took great precaution, their nervousness making a striking contrast to the confidence with which the founders a century before had utilized medieval science: as to "philosophical" terminology, they said, everybody is left to his own freedom—as though, in 1726, there really was any freedom to accept or reject Newton! Even so, they clung to their (momentarily) skeptical position, "that the internal Nature of Things being so extremely incluse and hidden, *many* of our *Philosophical Schemes* have been but mere *Hypotheses* subsisting only in the imaginations of Men, and being unsoundly rais'd from a few imperfect Observations of the Appearances & Events of Nature, have been successively thrown out by *others* as unstable as they." Thus coyly sheltering themselves behind Newton's condemnation of hypotheses, they insinuated that those who were endeavoring to erect a revolutionary or too "catholick" theology on Newtonian science were building on sand. They protested that Willard never took his now discredited physics "into the *System* of Religion, which will for ever remain the same thro' all the successive Changes of Philosophy." Thus they believed that in the name of science itself they could predict that the truths of Westminster would flourish "in these Western Schools and Churches thro out all the successive Changes of external Forms & Languages among them, as long as the Sun and Stars shall shine upon them, and till cloudy transient Time give place to bright & permanent Eternity."

We are obliged to note how ephemeral was the situation to which Sewall and Prince's words were addressed. Their anxiety reflects not only the predicament of Protestantism in general, but a domestic alignment which was in a state of flux. Back in 1718 the anti-Leverett faction had become a powerful, if incongruous, coalition: it contained the Mathers and their cohorts, the House of Representatives (Elisha Cooke, the demagogic tribune, hated his cousin Leverett), the Council (where Judge Sewall predominated), and both the Dudleys, the ex-governor (who died in 1720) and his son Paul, then attorney-general. Leverett would have been utterly defeated had not the royal governor, Samuel Shute, saved him. But in 1723, Shute ignominiously fled; the harassed Leverett died suddenly in his bed, May 3, 1724, convinced that his cause was lost. I think it important, even though unpleasant, to remember that Paul Dudley joined with the family he despised in hounding to death the first great liberal and "Catholick" president of Harvard College.

Leverett's party might have been smashed had there not followed two developments. First, the choice of a compromise candidate, Benjamin Wadsworth (after both Colman and Joseph Sewall declined), and second, the collapse of the confederacy. Dudley and Cooke were inveterate enemies, and no Dudley could for long be a henchman of the Mathers. A new grouping of forces resulted in 1727 when the Anglican pastors, Timothy Cutler and Samuel Myles, demanded places among the overseers. Then Paul Dudley joined with survivors of the Leverett group to resist the Church of England. Out of this experience, having fought both against and for Harvard College, Paul Dudley formed the resolution which became the Dudleian bequest.

He had to ask himself why these factions were tearing New England apart. His enemies accused him of being a "Tory"; when the Mathers were fighting him, which was most of the time, they quoted his unguarded remark that "this country will never be worth living in for lawyers and gentlemen, till the Charter is taken away." Yet he, the proper model of an English gentleman, was a virtuoso who sent contributions to the *Transactions* which won him a Fellowship in the Royal Society. His funeral eulogist says that he had thoroughly studied divinity and also "was well versed in Natural Philosophy." Despite the slurs of his enemies, he had a deep love for New England; he knew that the Matherians had been entirely hospitable to the new science and had suffered in 1721 for supporting inoculation, whereas partisans of Leverett had appropriated more of the tone than the substance of the philosophical Enlightenment.

Undoubtedly his conviction was strengthened as he looked on, dismayed and disgusted, at the turmoil of the Great Awakening. The children of Mather, who had been his allies against Leverett—Sewall, Prince, Foxcroft—went all out for the madness; but the heirs of Leverett—Edward Holyoke, now president of Harvard, Professor Wigglesworth, John Barnard, Nathaniel Appleton, Ebenezer Gay, and above all Charles

Chauncy—resisted it. Meanwhile, despite the extravagances of a few deists, English theology, following the lead of such judicious gentlemen as Richard Bentley, seemed to be proving that a *modus vivendi* among the jarring sects could be formulated upon the proposition that Christian theology, taken in the broadest sense, was so stoutly confirmed by Newtonian physics that such eruptions of enthusiasm as the Great Awakening were entirely uncalled for. True, Jonathan Edwards presumed to employ the Newtonian physics, but in a fashion which to most of the learned seemed baffling and fantastic; all the more reason why the unanimity of New England should be anchored to the positively clear and civilized meaning.

Paul Dudley became chief justice in 1745, and died January 25, 1750. By then he had seen more than enough of human fractiousness. The worries of the transition period, those that in 1726 had beset Sewall and Prince, were a thing of the past; the basic and pressing problems of this provincial culture could now be defined. New England had to reconcile itself to being a self-confessed community of dissenters, its way of life protected against the Church of England only by the Toleration Act of 1689; hence Judge Dudley wanted the fourth lecture to defend the validity of Congregational or Presbyterian—that is, nonepiscopal—ordination, so that students should be immunized against the doctrine of apostolic succession. But New England still belonged to the international community of Protestantism, and so he required that the third lecture be upon the errors of the papacy. Of course, a Protestant country gets its religion from the Bible, wherefore the second should be upon revealed religion. But both in New England and England, there now flourished large and commodious principles of comprehension, upon which lawyers and gentlemen could agree, which quieted all sectarian heats; most divines (if they were also gentlemen) knew what these were. The judge's language is self-explanatory, or at least then was, and for a century was to seem so: "for the proving, explaining, and shewing the proper Use and Improvement of the Principles of Natural Religion, as it is commonly called and understood by Divines and learned men." Hence the first, and indeed the central, lecture was to be on "Natural Religion," which for that age was entirely synonymous with natural theology. Thus the series was to be kept up in never-ending rotation; every four years restitution would be made to the shade of John Leverett, but the manes of Cotton Mather would also be placated.

In 1755 President Holyoke commenced with natural religion, the next year John Barnard spoke on revealed religion, and in 1757 Professor Wigglesworth disposed of papal infallibility. By now it was time that Cotton Mather be remembered, and Prince was asked to speak on ordination; he declined because of his health, and so Nathaniel Appleton, Leverett's own lieutenant, declared Congregational ordination valid. Seventeen hundred and fifty-nine was crucial: natural religion for the second time, and the corporation did the handsome thing: they invited Joseph Sewall. But he, as they may have expected, pled that he was too old, and so the delighted authorities summoned to the desk Ebenezer Gay, to preach *Natural Religion, Distinguish'd from Revealed,* which did nothing to heal and much to widen New England's breach. Not until 1761 did a survivor of the Matherian-revivalist party get a chance, and then it was the aged and half-paralyzed Foxcroft, who soporifically denounced the Pope's supremacy. In 1762 the lecturer was Chauncy, after whom Peter Clark of Danvers, who in 1758 had maintained the doctrine of inherent depravity in a pamphlet debate with Samuel Webster, was allowed to expound *Man's Dignity and Duty as a Reasonable Creature.* He played fair, but a listener aware of the smouldering animosities would have caught certain grim implications. Thereafter, well into the Unitarian period, while some more or less "conservative" divines might give the other lectures, natural religion was entrusted exclusively to the liberal, the "rational" wing—to Andrew Eliot in 1771, to President Langdon in 1775, to Gad Hitchcock in 1778, to Moses Hemmenway in 1783, and so on, down to Henry Ware in 1811, John Gorham Palfrey in 1839, and—culmination of this series—Ezra Stiles Gannett in 1843. I have read through this sequence, and been both fascinated and bored; one generalization can, I believe, be safely made: from 1755 to 1843 the Dudleian Lecture on natural theology struck a single note and kept pounding on it. It was precisely, I am sure, the note Judge Dudley wanted. If the only evidence we had were these lectures, we would never know that by the middle of the period Harvard had become Unitarian. They are a Gibraltar of security throughout a tumultuous epoch, serene, unperturbed and absolutely self-confident.

And yet, they do show signs of inward tension. The patient student is relieved at last in 1847 when William Henry Furness first gently shakes the venerable structure, and breathes freely in 1851 when Frederic Henry Hedge demolishes it entirely. Holyoke, we assume, was close to Dudley; he defined natural religion as "that regard to a Divine Being or God which men arrive at, by mere Principles of natural Reason, as it is improveable, by Tho't, consideration & Experience, without the help of Revelation." There, in short, is the challenge the Dudleian Lecture was bound to deliver to the New England clergy: try, if you can, to defend the faith that is in you, making believe for the moment that you have no help, or never had any help, from supernatural revelation!

Of course, the hazard was not really so great as it might sound, because, in the first place, there was always to be a lecture on revealed religion the year after, which would pick up and repair any broken pieces left by the natural oration. Secondly, the discourse on natural religion was itself only a *tour de force*: as President Holyoke frankly informed the students in his peroration, if they still had doubts, or if he had inadvertently raised any, they might "at all Times apply to those who are able to instruct you, in any Difficulties that may occur to you, in your persual of the

Mind & will of God." In order to understand how and why the Dudleian Lecture on natural religion came into being we must endeavor to realize— the effort is indeed great—that it was conceived out of a sublime confidence in the ability of the Harvard faculty to set the youth of the land to rights about any and every difficulty concerning the mind and will of God.

This confidence in turn was engendered out of the experience of Judge Dudley and his ilk: they could answer the students' questions because Sir Isaac Newton had answered their own. There was no longer the slightest danger, said Holyoke, that a respect for natural religion would lead to any revival of the Stoic worship of a self-sufficing law of nature, for the simple reason that "Sir Isaac Newton . . . chuses to consider & Define God, not as is usually done, from his Perfections, Nature & Existence, & the Like, but from his Dominion." The eighteenth century, especially those elements which in the name of Locke and Newton prided themselves on their modernity, has been accused of elevating the Deity to so remote a region above the creation that He was permitted no further connection with it than that of the watchmaker with a mechanism which forever runs by itself. Edwards was too good a Newtonian to exploit this charge against fellow Newtonians who took care not to become deists, but he vigorously attacked the "Arminians"—meaning precisely the party of President Holyoke—for their tendency to enhance the liberty of man by curtailing the sovereignty of God. Hence the first lectures on natural religion took a highly strategic line: warily avoiding the question of human ability, natural or gracious, and sounding anything but radical, they stressed the thesis that in Newtonian physics the Creator, far from being separated from His creation or Himself subjected to mechanical laws of motion, was more than ever required to be omnipresent and ever-active. Newton had delivered mankind from the temptation to impose rules upon the Divine by conclusively proving the emptiness of ontological reasoning; henceforth the only proof for the existence of God would be the cosmologi- cal, and a first premise of every formulation in the *Principia,* no matter how mathematically demonstrable, was that natural law is an arbitrary edict. Thus the Harvard lectures strove to turn the tables upon Edwards and his disciples by showing that they, and they alone, knew how to main- tain in scientific terminology the orthodox doctrine of an absolutely sovereign Jehovah.

Ebenezer Gay was sure he ran no risk of atheism when saying, "there may be something in the intelligent moral world analogous to Attraction in the material system." With Newton on their side, they could turn back to Calvin and give the lie direct to his assertion, "Vain, therefore, is the light afforded us in the formation of the world to illustrate the glory of its Author." Much to the contrary, Holyoke proclaimed, a self-evident "Elegance & Beauty in all natural things" make them not only evidences of their Author but preceptors of morals. And Ebenezer Gay further reveals that the lecture on natural religion, arrayed in the garments of

Newton, was a weapon against revivalists and enthusiasts, against New Light theologians, against those who still insisted upon a strict construction of the doctrines of total depravity and inherent corruption. Exhorting the students to apply themselves to studies "in natural Philosophy and mathematical sciences," he exclaimed, "Vehemently to decry Reason as useless, or as a blind Guide, leading Men into Error and Hell; and to run down natural Religion as mere Paganism, derogates from the credit of revealed, subverts our Faith in it, dissolves our obligation to practice it."

The march of these eighteenth-century lectures—majestic and stately—deserves deeper study, but allow me this one observation: in the historical perspective, for all their sincerity, they do show themselves to be the instrument of a group, or of an interest. They are successive manifestoes of the liberal, rational—should we say proto-Unitarian?—element. They rest upon the massive authority of Newton, but specifically they are directed against domestic opponents.

Yet, as the inexorable years roll on, the lectures themselves, while piling up evidences of the being and perfections of God out of the works of nature—until, according to Andrew Eliot (who, by the way, is an ancestor of T. S. Eliot), the conclusion should be evident "to the meanest capacity"—betray that one problem was steadily gnawing at the vitals of their security. Substantially the question ran something like this: suppose natural religion be so evident and conclusive, why did not (or do not) heathens live better or more moral lives? Granted there were a few Senecas and Ciceros, there were infinitely more Caligulas and Neros; granted that natural theology is a sort of probationary period before the fullness of revelation, still if the best it can produce is the orgies of Babylon, Alexandria, and Rome, what good is it? In short, the scientific assurance which inspired Dudley's bequest remained steady and unabated, but in the very heart of this optimistic theology there sprouted and persistently spread a doubt about its ethical effectiveness; by the first decades of the nineteenth century the tone had imperceptibly changed from a ringing condemnation of old Calvinists and New Lights to a desperate pleading that there was, or should be, a moral sanction in nature.

Gad Hitchcock shows how far the emphasis was shifting even in 1779 by redefining natural religion not as that which mankind enjoy in the strength of unassisted reason but as that which reason will recognize to be right when confronted with it. This permits him to explain that Greeks and Romans failed to profit from the manifest teachings of nature, not because the universe was less clear in its moral precepts then than now, but because the heathen were sinful. Evidently neither he nor his auditors noted that this was a step backward, in the direction of Calvin. But what to many may seem even more curious, this stress upon depravity as that which stands between man and his reception of natural religion becomes noticeably heavier among the avowed Unitarians. It is Henry Ware, no less, who in 1811 insists that while the design in nature is fully apparent, men are naturally hostile to natural religion because of their wickedness and pride. Where Gay made a perfunctory concession to human imperfection and then grandly asserted that natural deeds cannot be considered worthless in the eyes of God, Ware takes a dimmer view of human nature; he makes the chief value of natural religion the fact that it, by tantalizing us with a rudimentary knowledge, excites us to seek (next year) the higher knowledge of revelation.

I insist that this development will startle only those who forget the actual mentality of the early Unitarians, of a generation in which Norton's *Evidences* was imagined to be genuine Christian apologetics, in which Orville Dewey and Ezra Stiles Gannett preached as dolefully about human depravity as did Lyman Beecher. So much was staked upon the historicity of the miracles that a denigration of natural theology was almost inevitable. There is a much more glowing tribute to the spirituality of nature in Channing's lecture of 1820 on revealed religion—which nevertheless demands factual acceptance of the supernatural miracles—than in James Kendall's timid praise of natural religion the year before. With Gannett's appraisal of the "Value" of natural religion in 1843 the stock seems sadly reduced. Religion, says Gannett, consists of four departments: God, life, duty, sin. Natural religion does speak "intelligibly and decisively" about God, but it is of little help in life, especially on the question of immortality, for it cannot counteract "those appearances of the death-chamber and the grave, which it requires a direct voice from Heaven to pronounce only Superficial." It is woefully inadequate in the matter of duty, and is wholly silent on the subject of sin. It never taught decency to the heathen because it "lacked authority," and in the long run is mainly valuable "in the analogies it furnishes for the relief of difficulties or the elucidation of truths which belong to Revelation."

I like to say that I admire Ezra Stiles Gannett, but I know that when I say this I am obliged to smile, for he perfectly embodies that literal-mindedness, that lack of humor, of imagination, and of any aesthetic sense which gives a sometimes comic cast to the lofty sincerity, the courage, the moral solidity of his group and generation. But it is hard to feel that his lecture in 1843 or the preceding ones by Palfrey in 1839 and Brazer in 1835 are wholly ingenuous. In fact, these sermons could not be, for they proceed on the assumption that Immanuel Kant never existed and, still worse, that there never was such a person as David Hume.

William Henry Furness in 1847 comprehended something of these thinkers, but in 1851—a decade and a half, let us note, after Emerson's *Nature* and thirteen years after *The Divinity School Address*—the Dudleian orator on natural religion bluntly asserted that for fifty years the premise upon which the lecture was originally founded and was all the while being doggedly delivered had become obsolete. This, if true, constitutes a record of imperviousness to ideas which even the University of Oxford might envy!

Hedge's discourse is a remarkable performance; it survives only in manuscript and ought to be published, if only because it is an important document for the Emersonian period. It is also shrewd and tough-minded. It attacks the venerable masquerade of dispensing, on this forensic occasion, with Christianity and seeming to trust to nature; it calls this a miserable trick, "like that of children playing blindfold, and pretending to walk with their eyes covered, while at every turn, they peep beneath the bandage, and by surreptitious observations, furnish themselves with a new direction." Hedge contends that the distinction between natural and supernatural religion is false and absurd; all religions, like thoughts themselves, are simultaneously natural and supernatural, and who can tell which is which? He composes a rich passage on the glories of spring, at the season of Dudleian Lectures burgeoning outside Divinity Hall, and concludes that if we are bereft of those inward, transcendent assurances of the heart, which none can call either natural or supernatural, the so-called natural face of things, the finiteness and frailty of life, is a terrifying prospect. Holyoke and Ebenezer Gay had not fully perceived, had not in fact even guessed, that behind their cosmological assurance lay the epistemological assumption that the natural universe readily yields up moral meanings. Hedge was a better student of Kantian metaphysics than Gannett or Palfrey, yet interestingly enough the distress he confessed to was not so much epistemological as sentimental. The old confidence in meaning had fallen into meaninglessness not because nature had become an unknowable *Ding-an-sich* but because, of and by itself, it had proved inhuman.

For what is our life, this human existence, into which we have come we know not whence nor why, if there be no God, and no immortality? It is an island of small extent, in the midst of a wide, dumb inexorable deep, which is soon to swallow us up. Why we are here, we know not; we only know that we are here, and we make us a home as we can, and store and adorn it as we may. But whenever, in our hurry, we pause to listen, we hear the eternal surf that expects us, and we know that our island is crumbling beneath our feet.

One may well ask, as he ponders the remarkable passage, which here intrudes upon the progression of Dudleian Lectures with the sound of a knell, whether the melancholy it exudes flows from a loss of faith in nature or in revelation. Though Hedge concludes that nothing will avail us in this dire predicament but "Faith," he does not display anything like Holyoke's certitude that next year's lecture on revealed religion is going to arrest the crumbling beneath our feet.

So Hedge introduces us to the second era in the history of the lecture, which extends at least to the present lecturer, during which the speakers have found themselves in the embarrassing position of being unable to execute the will of Paul Dudley; instead, they have had to confess perplexity. For a hundred years they have had to admit that they cannot solve *all* the difficulties concerning the mind and will of God that occur to the youth of Harvard College.

Perhaps fortune was kind in that between 1857 and 1887 Dudleian Lectures were discontinued, while the fund was being repaired. When they were renewed, a tacit agreement had been universally arrived at that on the subject of natural theology the speaker had no obligation beyond proclaiming what faith, if any, was in him. So Samuel McCord Crothers did with a prose poem in 1894, while John Henry Barrows in 1898 discoursed on the Hindus. In 1902 Josiah Royce encompassed natural religion in the dialectical sleight-of-hand of the Absolute; in 1906 Francis Greenwood Peabody not surprisingly discussed *The Social Conscience and the Religious Life,* and in 1911 Dean Fenn, in a noble essay, declared natural theology to be a contradiction in terms, said that there no longer exists any agreement among "divines and learned men," and made a counterassertion that, while natural theology was a defunct conception, among the people at large, outside the churches was growing a wonderful and inspiriting "natural religion" wholly independent of traditional forms.

More recent lectures have, like this discourse, taken refuge in history. But I should like to make two brief comments upon the procession. First, the lectures on natural religion turn out, over and over again, to be pleas, disguised as examinations of nature, for principles to which the speakers are committed on quite other grounds than their knowledge of physics and chemistry. In the first decades the lectures are defenses of a coherent, ultimately a denominational, opinion which, forgetting the warning of Sewall and Prince, asserted a positive congruity of nature with the content of Christianity, or rather with its version of Christianity. When this contention broke down—partly of its own weight, partly because of external criticism—lecturers were left with no alternative except to dress up natural theology in terms of their own prepossessions, and so to make the best of it.

This generalization, which may be a bit extreme, amounts to saying that even when preachers exercised care about reading their subjective commitments into nature, nevertheless they did (even Hedge) try to impress upon it the ethos of their culture. A history of the Dudleian Lectures is in fact an epitome of the modern intellect, at least as that intellect impinged upon Harvard; the crises along the way are crises in secular rather than in theological ideas. After two centuries of this—as it may well seem—unavailing effort, the result is bound to be a discrediting of natural theology; but by the same token, the enterprise becomes a comment upon something else, upon something which, supposedly, was not a subject for discussion: it becomes an involuntary confession that the religious intellect of this community has been protractedly guilty of indolence.

Second, we should note that through all these alterations, speakers assumed that their scientific version of nature was a single, a self-consistent entity. It was either Newtonian mechanism, the Kantian universe, the scheme of the Absolute, the articulated plan of natural evolution, or the creed of humanitarianism. The lecturer's problem was reconciliation; if he could harmonize nature and religion, all well and good; if he could not harmonize, he had to say what a man might believe despite nature. Because from the beginning Dudleian lecturers were hostile to Edwards, there appears very little understanding of his concern that science be regarded not as an alien body requiring incorporation into Christianity, but as a language of God by which men should learn to refashion the language of theology. Again, while all the speakers exhibit courage, we have also to ask whether they were not fundamentally indolent.

Dean Fenn let fall in 1911 one arresting sentence: dismissing the cosmological proof of the first cause as worn out, he said, "Certainly no argument can be pronounced demonstrative which at its conclusion offers us two alternatives both equally inconceivable." From the context it is evident that he would further deny that two contradictory alternatives could simultaneously be held. If antinomy was all nature had to offer, we should cultivate human goodness and a love of beauty.

Surprisingly enough, Pascal was read in the New England of the Mathers. They thought him a Jansenist, and looked upon Jansenism as a stirring of Protestant piety in the midst of Catholicism. But also, at least in that moment when the Scholastic categories were collapsing and the new physics had not yet replaced them, New Englanders could still appreciate Pascal's warnings against natural theology. He stands at the beginning of our age, trying to warn mankind that nature, bounded on every side by the infinites of the Nothing and of the All, can at best devise only temporary systematizations. These Pascal called products of the "imagination," and he prophesied that they would not hold up if regarded as patterns of the cosmos. As for natural law, he said, there is nothing man cannot make natural, nothing natural he cannot make unnatural. He tried to find a precarious safety by confronting one truth with its opposite, both equally inconceivable. "A fine thing," he cried in savage irony, "to tell a man who does not know himself to go by himself to God! And a fine thing to say it to a man who does know himself!"

President James Bryant Conant, not in a Dudleian Lecture but in an address at Columbia University, says in *Modern Science and Modern Man* that there no longer is, or probably ever will be, a unified World Hypothesis, that the intellect of today must entertain as coexistent a series of seemingly contradictory truths. A leading physicist of our day has said that a truth, the opposite of which is untrue, is trivial truth, but a profound truth is one of which the opposite is equally true. Classical physics, we are told by those who should know, turns out to be involved in inner contradictions. In what for me is the most exciting of recent discussions, *Philosophic Problems of Nuclear Science,* Werner Heisenberg writes:

> Now nature, through the medium of modern physics, has reminded us very clearly that we should never hope for such a firm basis for

comprehension of the whole field of "things perceptible." Rather when faced with essentially new intellectual challenges should we continually follow the example of Columbus, who possessed the courage to leave the known world in the almost insane hope of finding land again beyond the sea.

We know, if only from newspaper reports, that Albert Einstein in his last years strove to produce a convincing theory of a unified field, being preconvinced, as he beautifully put it, that God does not play dice with the cosmos. But assuredly the mind can never wholly forget, or recover from, this century's agonizing experience of discontinuity, of indeterminacy in nature. "For the accuracy," says Heisenberg, "up to which it is useful to employ these concepts to describe nature intelligibly is limited by the so-called uncertainty relations." Yet he also tells us, "let us not forget that it is the content not the words which is important in a tragedy or comedy, and that this also holds good for our world."

Wherefore, the failures of our predecessors should warn us against again trying to translate scientific statements directly into theological parables. Mr. Conant concludes that modern physics, arising out of quantum mechanics, can be of no use to modern man in his search for "minimal commitments." But we have also to keep in mind that profundity of Pascal's:

> It is a natural weakness of man to believe that he possesses a truth directly. For that reason he is always ready to deny anything which is incomprehensible to him. Yet, in fact, by nature he knows delusions only, and he ought to regard as genuine only the opposite of those things that seem to him to be false.

I need merely remark, without elaborating, that throughout the centuries, Christian theology has, in the sense of both Pascal and our physicist, set up profound, though inconceivable, truth: the dual nature of Christ, the Trinity, the balance of the attributes, the contradictory yet coexistent elements in the scheme of redemption, the intrusion of eternity into time, the transmission of the sin of Adam, the utter paradox of faith itself. These it has somehow kept alive, if only as exercises of the mind and of the heart; it has withstood the incessant—and natural—propensity of man to reduce these profundities to trivialities. It has, with Pascal, denied that man can *directly* obtain security from nature or from the Bible itself. We stand only on the threshold of an inconceivable age, yet I am persuaded that natural science itself has added a dimension to the situation which theologians ought to have remembered even in the age of Judge Dudley, but did not. As long as no short cuts are imprudently attempted, there is promise of a new era in what may still be called, wryly enough, a theology of nature. Modern physics definitely does *not,* let me repeat, encourage even those who can comprehend the atom to take over into theology scientific propositions as substantial confirmations of theological doctrines; what physics does do is challenge the religious intellect to show whether it has anything like the industry and creativity of the scientific, whether it is prepared to confront, on its own, the antinomies provided by its peculiar and unique insights.

Which brings me back to my text, one that frequently did service in the first decades of my predecessors, but which in the later decades has seldom been cited on these occasions. Overcome as I am by a diffidence which the early and the confident theologians would stigmatize as weakness, I put my text at the end rather than at the beginning: it is, of course, what Paul said about the natural indolence of the Romans: "For the invisible things of him from the creation of the world are clearly seen, being understood by the things that are made, even his eternal power and Godhead; so that they are without excuse."

THEODORE PARKER: APOSTASY
WITHIN LIBERALISM

I AM NOT the first to detect in recent scholarship dealing with the transcendental period of New England a tendency toward vindicating, or at least toward putting in a good word for, the hitherto regularly berated opponents of Emerson and Theodore Parker. Because in the 1830's and 1840's and well into the 1850's the phalanx of those most outspoken in resistance were the Unitarian clergy, the custom has been for chroniclers of the literary and theological radicalism to heap derision upon the men who occupied established pulpits in the neighborhood of Boston and who spoke for the substantial portions of the community. In this indictment it is *de rigueur* to relate that after Parker's South Boston sermon of May 19, 1841, entitled *The Transient and Permanent in Christianity,* only eight of the local ministers would any longer exchange pulpits with him. Furthermore, after the publication in January 1842 of *A Discourse of Matters Pertaining to Religion,* the Boston Association directly challenged Parker to withdraw of his own accord. In the annals of American Protestant "liberality" these actions have long figured, axiomatically, as "persecution." Only within the last decade have voices been hesitantly raised to suggest that possibly something may be said on behalf of the alleged persecutors. Could it be that Unitarian Boston was not quite so bigoted as it has been represented?

Anyone brought up in the prevailing tradition, established by Parker's biographers in the later half of the century—by John Weiss, O. B. Frothingham, John White Chadwick—would assume as a matter of course that in the contests of the 1830's and '40's Emerson was the purest of white and Andrews Norton as black as the pit, that Parker was a gleaming Galahad while the Boston Association, with its eight memorable exceptions, was a nest of vipers. Interestingly enough, gestures toward a revision of this account have come from younger scholars. Possibly this phenomenon is a symptom of that swing toward "conformity" which elders with treasured memories of their own youthful deviations are prone to deplore. If to many fresh eyes Emerson and Parker are beginning to seem too fantastically obstreperous, as they did when judged by the organizational standards of a Samuel K. Lothrop or an Andrew Peabody, then we may no longer hold the comfortable persuasion that the Unitarianism of that time, which proclaimed itself "liberal," was entirely hypocritical.

Published in the *Harvard Theological Review,* vol. LIV (October 1961), pp. 275-95.

What a revolution in our historiography is adumbrated, let alone enacted, by the very raising of this consideration! As early as 1848 James Russell Lowell posed, in *A Fable for Critics,* what had already become the ultra-liberal query which no Unitarian might evade: how could the liberal Christianity conceivably accuse *anybody* of heresy, let alone a man of Parker's manifest sincerity? It should, of course, dissociate itself from professed atheists and deists, but how could there, within the community which owed allegiance to William Ellery Channing, be anything short of deism which deserved to be treated as apostasy? These "Socinians," as Lowell mischievously called them, said they believed something, though he confessed himself baffled as to just what it might be:

> I think I may call
> Their belief a believing in nothing at all,
> Or something of that sort; I know they all went
> For a general union of total dissent:
> He went a step farther; without cough or hem,
> He frankly avowed he believed not in them;
> And, before he could be jumbled up or prevented,
> From their orthodox kind of dissent he dissented.

So the refrain continued even into 1926, with Vernon Parrington's *Main Currents*: Parker spoke out the truth which he had gathered at immense pains, said Parrington, and so was decried as a demagogue and agitator by "ministers and lawyers and merchants and politicians, men in high position, distinguished leaders of Boston society." Parker offended, according to Parrington, the Boston code of good breeding; he "pronounced judgment on Bostonians respected in the Back Bay, mighty in State Street." In 1936 the latest of Parker's biographers, Henry Commager, concluded with the familiar recitation that Parker had the courage as a young man, unknown and friendless, "to meet those black looks, those biting remarks, at the Berry Street Conferences." Parker had the great fortitude to endure the social ostracism, the odium. "Perhaps," mused Commager, "it would have been better if he had not fought back so hard; but he was a fighter, he couldn't help that." From Lowell to Commager, the scoundrels of the piece are the guardians of propriety, and these not the orthodox, not the Calvinists or the Methodists, but the liberal clergy, who, according to the sanctified narrative, turned upon him in a petulant rage which has exposed for all time, even until today, the hollowness of their pretensions to liberality. Instead of proving to be men of authentic probity, they showed themselves close hypocrites. Behind the courteous mask are disclosed the leprous features of what Parker thunderously denounced as "Hunkerism."

By the perfervid eloquence with which Parker presents himself as the martyr—in his public utterances, in his letters and journals—he contrives that any account of him must inescapably exhibit a saint crucified on Boston Common. His appeal overcomes the charges of his critics and

even the frequent admissions of his followers that he obviously relished
the role, that he embraced and exaggerated the contumely of his brethren.
What free spirit among us can help being stirred into adherence by such
a passage as this—announced to his "congregation" of three thousand, all
refugees from conventional churches, in the Music Hall on November 14,
1852?

> With such views, you see in what esteem I must be held by society,
> church, and state. I cannot be otherwise than hated. This is the necessity
> of my position—that I must be hated.

"Call me Ishmael," commenced the author of the most gigantic of American
nonconformities, a romance entitled *Moby-Dick,* published a year before
Parker's "Some Account of My Ministry." For our century, which prides
itself on having re-discovered Melville, on having for the first time
divined the spiritual drive within Melville's diabolism, Parker becomes,
even more dramatically than Frothingham or Chadwick could imagine, an
archangel of dissent. For us, striving to breathe an atmosphere already
filled with the filings of steel and perhaps soon to be permeated with
particles of hydrogen, salvation is sought through vicarious identification
with the figure of the rebel, the outsider, the angry young man—the more
so while we are supinely submitting to the televised Hunkerism of the
singing commercial. Hence Parker still looms for us, along with John
Brown and Henry Thoreau, as one of the majestic nay-sayers in pre-Civil
War America. So, if there are now murmurs against the canonization
which liberals long ago bestowed upon him, we are indeed upon the
threshold of a new crisis—if we have not already stumbled into it—similar
to the agonizing one in which he was a principal actor—and victim.

Undoubtedly we today have to ask whether his habit of sentimentalizing
his ostracism was not a form of self-pity. In his own time his friends
would grant that he did a bit luxuriate in martyrdom, but they could then
rally round what they held were his revolutionary teachings, and so maintain the standard attitude of militant defiance. For us, almost all his
once earth-shaking pronouncements are commonplaces, have become in fact
platitudes. Hence most of us are left sadly unmoved—where his friends
were moved to tears of rage—by the disclosure of this passage from his
journal on the eve of his forty-second birthday:

> Poor dear father, poor dear mother! You little knew how many a man
> would curse the son you painfully brought into life, and painfully and
> religiously brought up. Well, I will bless you—true father and most
> holy mother were you to me: the earliest thing you taught me was
> *duty*—duty to God, duty to man; that life is not a pleasure, not a
> pain, but a *duty*.

Though we can hardly doubt the sincerity of this passage we are almost
bound, I am sure, to detect in it an embarrassing mawkishness, a somewhat
affected posturing before the mirror. And even many of the utterances

to which his admirers have vibrated for a century may well appear to us slightly tinged with the sour envy of the plebeian for the patrician.

I will go eastward and westward, and northward and southward, and make the land *ring*; and if this New England theology, that cramps the intellect and palsies the soul of us, does not come to the ground, then it shall be because it has more truth in it than I have ever found.

The reiterations of biographers and other celebrants—the facility with which they fall into the same incantations of denunciation for the respectable—eventually excite a suspicion among us that Parker seduces us into allegiance precisely because the targets of his most telling abuse are Boston and Harvard College. Satirizing the rigidities and sterilities of these communities has for many years become a sure-fire way of making a hit in Dubuque. They are always good for a laugh, as, to mention only two out of many recent examples, the commercial successes of John Marquand's *The Late George Apley* and Cleveland Amory's *The Proper Bostonians* demonstrate. The characters in such works who are shown in a comic light are almost always Unitarians—or if not, then former Unitarians who have sought a still more placid peace of mind by becoming Episcopalians. They are stereotypes cut from the same cardboard Santayana used for *The Last Puritan*. Therefore persons who are not Bostonians are happy to applaud when they find Parker writing in 1845: "I went to the meeting of the Unitarian Association; a stupid meeting it was, too. The brethren looked on me as the *Beni Elohim* looked on Satan, as he came last of all. However, they shook hands all the more tenderly, because the heart was not in it, and then turned the cold shoulder." However, this sort of thing is so infectious that Bostonians themselves join in the fun and discover a perverse pride in relishing all ridicule of themselves. The Harvard Divinity School has so hugged to its bosom the jibes Parker levied against it that I should perform a work of supererogation were I now to repeat the old chestnuts. Once Parker was safely dead and could no longer make a nuisance of himself, the most proper of Bostonians would graciously accept as the highest of compliments Parker's remark to his fellow agitator, Charles Sumner (whom the same classes also execrated in his life but whom they honored after his death by erecting his statue in Harvard Square), "Boston is a queer little city, the public is a desperate tyrant there, and it is seldom that one dares disobey the commands of public opinion."

Furthermore, as an encouragement to revisionist thinking, it manifestly is fair to admit that any fraternity has a constitutional right to refuse to accept persons it dislikes. The Unitarian clergy were an exclusive club of cultivated gentlemen—as the term was then understood in the Back Bay— and Parker was definitely not a gentleman, either in theology or in manners. Ezra Stiles Gannett, an honorable representative of the sanhedrin, addressed himself frankly to the issue in 1845, insisting that Parker should not be persecuted or calumniated and that in this republic no power to restrain him by force could exist. Even so, Gannett judiciously argued, the association could legitimately decide that Parker "should not be encouraged nor assisted in diffusing his opinions by those who differ from him in regard to their correctness." We today are not entitled to excoriate honest men who believed Parker to be downright pernicious and who barred their pulpits against his demand to poison the minds of their congregations. One can even argue—though this is a delicate matter—that every justification existed for their returning the Public Lecture to the First Church, and so suppressing it, rather than letting Parker use it as a sounding board for his propaganda when his turn should come to occupy it. Finally, it did seem clear as day to these clergymen, as Gannett's son explained in the biography of his father, that they had always contended for the propriety of their claim to the title of Christians. Their demand against the Calvinist orthodoxy for intellectual liberty had never meant that they would follow "free inquiry" to the extreme of proclaiming Christianity a "natural" religion.

Grant all this—still, when modern Unitarianism and the Harvard Divinity School recall with humorous affection the insults Parker lavished upon them, or else argue that after all Parker received the treatment he invited, they betray an uneasy conscience. Whenever New England liberalism is reminded of the dramatic confrontation of Parker and the fraternity on January 23, 1843—while it may defend the privilege of Chandler Robbins to demand that Parker leave the association, while it may plead that Dr. N. L. Frothingham had every warrant for stating, "The difference between Trinitarians and Unitarians is a difference in Christianity; the difference between Mr. Parker and the Association is a difference between no Christianity and Christianity"—despite these supposed conclusive assurances, the modern liberal heaves repeatedly a sigh of relief, of positive thanksgiving, that the association never quite brought itself officially to expel Parker. Had it done so, the blot on its escutcheon would have remained indelible, nor could the Harvard Divinity School assemble to honor Parker's insurgence other than by getting down on its collective knees and crying "peccavi."

Happily for posterity, then, the Boston Association did not actually command Parker to leave the room, though it came too close for comfort to what would have been an unforgivable brutality. Fortunately, the honor of the denomination can attest that Cyrus Bartol defended Parker's sincerity, as did also Gannett and Chandler Robbins; whereupon Parker broke down into convulsions of weeping and rushed out of the room, though not out of the fellowship. In the hall, after adjournment, Dr. Frothingham took him warmly by the hand and requested Parker to visit him—whereupon our burly Theodore again burst into tears.

All this near tragedy, which to us borders on comedy, enables us to tell the story over and over again, always warming ourselves with a glow of complacency. It was indeed a near thing, but somehow the inherent decency of New England (which we inherit) did triumph. Parker was never excommunicated. To the extent that he was ostracized or even reviled, we solace ourselves by saying he asked for it. Yet, even after all these stratagems, the conscience of Christian liberality is still not laid to rest, any more than is the conscience of Harvard University for having done the abject penance for its rejection of Ralph Waldo Emerson's "Divinity School Address" of naming its hall of philosophy after him. In both cases the stubborn fact remains: liberalism gave birth to two brilliant apostates, both legitimate offspring of its loins, and when brought to the test, it behaved shabbily. Suppose they both had ventured into realms which their colleagues thought infidel: is this the way gentlemen settle frank differences of opinion? Is it after all possible that no matter how the liberals trumpet their confidence in human dignity they are exposed to a contagion of fear more insidious than any conservative has ever to worry about?

However, there is a crucial difference between the two histories. Emerson evaded the problem by shoving it aside, or rather by leaving it behind him: he walked out of the Unitarian communion, so that it could lick the wound of his departure, preserve its self-respect, and eventually accord him pious veneration. Parker insisted upon *not* resigning, even when the majority wanted him to depart, upon daring the fellowship to throw him out. Hence he was in his lifetime, as is the memory of him afterwards, a canker within the liberal sensitivity. He still points an accusing finger at all of us, telling us that we have neither the courage to support him nor the energy to cut his throat.

Actually, the dispute between Parker and the society of his time, both ecclesiastical and social, was a real one, a bitter one. It cannot be smoothed over by now cherishing his sarcasms as delightful bits of self-deprecation or by solemnly calling for a reconsideration of the justice of the objections to him. The fact is incontestable: that liberal world of Unitarian Boston *was* narrow-minded, intellectually sterile, smug, afraid of the logical consequences of its own mild ventures into iconoclasm, and quite prepared to resort to hysterical repressions when its brittle foundations were threatened. Parker, along with Garrison and Charles Sumner, showed a magnificent moral bravery when facing mobs mobilized in defense of the Mexican War and slavery. Nevertheless, we can find reasons for respecting even the bigotry of the populace; their passions were genuine, and the division between them and the abolitionists is clear-cut. But Parker as the ultraliberal minister within the pale of a church which had proclaimed itself the repository of liberality poses a different problem, which is not to be resolved by holding him up as the champion of freedom. Even though his theological theses have become, to us, commonplaces, the fundamental interrogation he phrased is very much with us. It has been endlessly rephrased, but I may here put it thus: at what point do the tolerant find themselves obliged to become intolerant? And then, as they become aware that they have reached the end of their patience, what do they, to their dismay, learn for the first time about themselves?

There can be no doubt, the Boston of that era could be exquisitely cruel in enforcing its canons of behavior. The gentle Channing, revered by all Bostonians, orthodox or Unitarian, wrote to a friend in Louisville that among its many virtues Boston did not abound in a tolerant spirit, that the yoke of opinion crushed individuality of judgment and action:

> No city in the world is governed so little by a police, and so much by mutual inspections and what is called public sentiment. We stand more in awe of one another than most people. Opinion is less individual or runs more into masses, and often rules with a rod of iron.

Even more poignantly, and with the insight of a genius, Channing added—remember, this is Channing, not Parker!—that should a minister in Boston trust himself to his heart, should he "speak without book, and consequently break some law of speech, or be hurried into some daring hyperbole, he should find little mercy."

Channing wrote this—in a letter! I think it fair to say that he never quite reached such candor in his sermons. But Theodore Parker, commencing his mission to the world-at-large, disguised as the minister of a "twenty-eighth Congregational Church" which bore no resemblance to the Congregational polities descended from the founders (among which were still the Unitarian churches), made explicit from the beginning that the conflict between him and the Hunkerish society was not something which could be evaporated into a genteel difference about clerical decorum. Because he spoke openly, as Channing had prophesied someone might, with daring hyperbole, Parker vindicated Channing's prophecy that he who committed this infraction of taste would promptly discover how little mercy liberals were disposed to allow to libertarians who appeared to them libertines.

By reminding ourselves of these factors in the situation, we should, I am sure, come to a fresh realization, however painful it be, that the battle between Parker and his neighbors was fought in earnest. He arraigned the citizens in language of so little courtesy that they had to respond with, at the least, resentment. What otherwise could "the lawyer, doctor, minister, the men of science and letters" do when told that they had "become the cherubim and seraphim and the three archangels who stood before the golden throne of the merchant, and continually cried, 'Holy, holy, holy is the Almighty Dollar' "? Nor, when we recollect how sensitive were the emotions of the old Puritan stock in regard to the recent tides of immigration, should we be astonished that their thin lips were compressed into a white line of rage as Parker snarled at them thus:

> Talk about the Catholics voting as the bishop tells! reproach the Catholics for it! You and I do the same thing. There are a great many bishops

who have never had a cross on their bosom, nor a mitre on their head, who appeal not to the authority of the Pope at Rome, but to the Almighty Dollar, a pope much nearer home. Boston has been controlled by a few capitalists, lawyers and other managers, who told the editors what to say and the preachers what to think.

This was war. Parker meant business. And he took repeated care to let his colleagues know that he intended them: "Even the Unitarian churches have caught the malaria, and are worse than those who deceived them"— which implied that they were very bad indeed. It was *"Duty"* he said that his parents had given him as a rule—beyond even the love that suffused his being and the sense of humor with which he was largely supplied—and it was duty he would perform, though it cost him acute pain and exhausted him by the age of fifty. Parker could weep—and he wept astonishingly often and on the slightest provocation—but the psychology of those tears was entirely compatible with a remorseless readiness to massacre his opponents. "If it gave me pleasure to say hard things," he wrote, "I would shut up for ever." We have to tell ourselves that when Parker spoke in this vein, he believed what he said, because he could continue, "But the TRUTH, which cost me bitter tears to say, I must speak, though it cost other tears hotter than fire." Because he copiously shed his own tears, and yielded himself up as a living sacrifice to the impersonalized conscience of New England, he was not disturbed by the havoc he worked in other people's consciences.

Our endeavor to capture even a faint sense of how strenuous was the fight is muffled by our indifference to the very issue which in the Boston of 1848 seemed to be the central hope of its Christian survival, that of the literal, factual historicity of the miracles as reported in the four gospels. It is idle to ask why we are no longer disturbed if somebody, professing the deepest piety, decides anew that it is of no importance whether or not Christ transformed the water into wine at eleven A.M. on the third of August, A.D. 32. We have no answer as to why we are not alarmed. So we are the more prepared to give Parker the credit for having taken the right side in an unnecessary controversy, to salute his courage, and to pass on, happily forgetting both him and the entire episode. We have not leisure, or the patience, or the skill, to comprehend what was working in the mind and heart of a then recent graduate of the Harvard Divinity School who would muster the audacity to contradict his most formidable instructor, the magisterial Andrews Norton, by saying that, while he believed Jesus, "like other religious teachers," worked miracles, "I see not how a miracle proves a doctrine." What indeed *has* happened to us? While we sagely approve this devastation of Parker's, we ourselves are not prepared to make of it a slogan against the miracles. It is worth an hour of our time to summon up the shade of Theodore Parker, if only to let him squarely put the question to us.

For clearly it is not enough to answer that we have exhausted the subject or that it has exhausted us, that we consider it wearisome and no longer worth disputing. That is an easy way out, which enables us to leave our churches on a Sunday morning and go placidly home to an unperturbed dinner. It precludes our having to participate in the ferocity with which Parker propounded, and with which his enemies condemned, the jolting thesis of the South Boston sermon:

> If Jesus had taught at Athens, and not at Jerusalem; if he had wrought no miracles, and none but the human nature had ever been ascribed to him; if the Old Testament had forever perished at his birth—Christianity would still have been the word of God; it would have lost none of its truths.

Either this passage is arrant nonsense or else it reveals that something more incendiary is at work than an academic discourse about the authenticity of the miracles. If the first, then we have gathered today for a ceremonial exhumation, after which we shall seal the coffin for at least another century. If the second, then we are obliged to probe further into hidden chambers and ask what actually was at stake when Parker offended his colleagues over the miracles.

All accounts attest the staggering range of his reading. He was literate in at least twenty languages, he collected an immense library, and he pored over the interminable literature of early nineteenth-century German examinations of the Biblical texts—a jungle which was and which still is impenetrable for most students of theology. Yet in his own publications, and even more in his preaching, he made strikingly little use of this fund of learning. Indeed, the one and only monument to his titanic labors in his library is his version of the treatise on the Old Testament by Wilhelm Martin Leberecht De Wette. Born in 1780 in a town near Weimar, De Wette had known Schiller and Goethe, received his inspiration immediately from Herder. Exiled from Prussia by royal decree in 1819, he was for three decades the entrenched and powerful theologian at Basel, whence he fought against the rationalists on his left and the evangelical pietists on his right. Americans understood little of the European situation, and were instinctively hostile to everything German. They had no awareness of De Wette's position, but they had heard vaguely that he was dangerous to every form of Christianity. Parker entitled his rendition, *A Critical and Historical Introduction to the Canonical Scriptures of the Old Testament.* He completed the first draft in 1837, worked it over and over, added copious notes and comments, and finally put the huge manuscript through the press in July 1843. Apparently it had no effect upon religious thought in America, except to advertise Parker's adherence to Germanism and to insinuate by his use of "Canonical" in the title that he was attempting to shatter the coherence of the Old Testament.

In addition to the translation and the footnotes, Parker also spoke briefly but effectively for himself. If we seek the true grounds for his intransigence, we shall find it in this book rather than in his more diffuse and scandalous declarations about the miracles. Or rather, the latter statements were consequences of what he had learned from his study of De Wette: they were the corollary of his scholarship, though he was sufficiently a child of the New England tradition to know instinctively that in the pulpit the use of art is to conceal art. Verbal though he was—indeed much too profuse—and garrulous as were his publications, he never allowed himself the time to explain precisely wherein his technique consisted in a use of history to destroy historicity. Hence it may be said that he was something of an enigma to his contemporaries, and was even a puzzle to himself. In which case, we must expound more exactly than he ever quite could do, or cared to do, why he is worth remembering a hundred years after he expired in Florence.

We have to attest that despite his omnivorous reading in the Biblical scholars he himself showed little or no originality in the technical areas. That which Emerson said of the whole transcendental group applies even to him: their scholarship exhibited the typically American superficiality. But the square-toed son of a Lexington farmer, and the forthright grandson of the commander of militia on the Lexington Common, could make out, from his service with De Wette, that the education purveyed by the Harvard Divinity School evaded what De Wette termed "negative criticism." The school was always saying—the more nervously because the orthodox accused it of merely negating—that such and such was true. Wherefore it had come, through no other compulsion than its own neurasthenia, to insisting that a man could not be accounted a Christian who disbelieved in the historicity of the miracles, though he might bask in the rays of salvation while serenely rejecting the Trinity. Parker hardly needed De Wette or any Continental scholar to point out the obvious discrepancy, though his Germanic importations supplied him with the authority to denounce it: the bias, not to say the shameless predilection, of his Unitarian elders in favor of the miracles and against the Trinity put blinders on their eyes. They could not freely employ any critical method. If they could not, then wherein were they actually more emancipated than the Calvinists? As Parker strove over and over again to make his point to the association, he was not worried whether they did or did not believe in miracles. What galled him was that they should dogmatize in advance as to the factualness of the performances, and then abhor as an Ishmael any who insisted, as Parker kept insisting, upon the preliminary need for an open-minded examination of the credentials. His apostasy within liberalism centers upon his elevation of this word "criticism," which came to be the term that his Unitarian opponents most detested. This was the more disturbing because they were persuaded that they had practiced all the critical rigor the civilized world any longer required.

Parker strove to demonstrate to the glib American student wherein real erudition consisted by giving translations as well as the originals of Latin,

Greek, and Hebrew quotations. To pile Pelion upon Ossa, or perhaps we should say in order to add insult to injury, he added out of his own reading masses of corroborative materials from patristic and modern commentators. The result was that he produced a De Wette which was nothing like what the *Einleitung* dared to be in its native language. Parker's rendition is a chronicle of how variously the Old Testament has been read by successive ages of Christendom, of how frequently the sense of one century has contradicted that of another. Thus he endeavored to teach the present generation to distrust its own dogmatics. He was, he tells us, tempted to entitle the book an "Introduction on the Basis of De Wette" rather than a "Translation," but he decided the latter more "modest." Yet by publishing this quandary, Parker effectively violated his own modesty, and we may well conclude that in this case arrogance was the better part of valor. Still, he made his critics aware that the two volumes were something more than a literal rephrasing, that they were specifically directed at the vitals of liberality. "I can only hope," he concluded, "the work will direct critical inquiries to a faithful examination of the Bible and that correct views of its origin and contents may at length prevail." This was an oblique way of announcing that so far only incorrect views were in circulation, at the Harvard Divinity School as well as at Andover. Parker's humble profession of hoping to be instrumental "in spreading the light of truth on this subject" could appear to his peers only as a conceited claim that he had a monopoly on that illumination.

He managed to highlight De Wette's basic statement of the method, of its scientific character, as being (the italics are Parker's) *historico-critical.* That is to say, as De Wette contended and as Parker gleefully translated, the Bible is to be considered a wholly historical phenomenon, completely subject to the professional rules of historical inquiry. Consequently, any consideration of it "in a religious view" comes into the range of De Wette's analysis only insofar as the dogma of inspiration and revelation is connected with the origin of the texts. It follows, De Wette put into the crucial sentence, "This dogma itself, therefore, is likewise to be treated historically." What Parker manufactured out of his "translation" thereupon appears in a paragraph of his own composition, which is not so much an addition as a blunt interpolation, which he distinguished from the original by printing it in brackets, and thereby loudly calling attention to it.

"Most of the English and American theologians," he wrote with deceptive calmness, insist that the books of the Bible, especially those of the Old Testament, be considered from a religious point of view, "declaring [again, the italics are Parker's] *dogmatic theology* is the touchstone, wherewith we are to decide between the true and false, the genuine and the spurious." Hence they refuse to examine—or are incapable of examining—the Bible as an historical production. They force themselves to treat it as the highest standard of human faith and life.

Parker does not go out of his way to note that this condemnation applies as well to Andrews Norton's ponderous and stillborn volumes on the *Evidences of Christianity* as to the Calvinistic commentaries of Moses Stuart. But in 1843 everybody in Eastern Massachusetts—and at Yale and Princeton—would know whom he attacked. When either of them, Unitarian or orthodox, approached the books of the Bible as a peculiar phenomenon, not to be judged by the same canons of criticism which apply to all other human writings—say, to the plays of Shakespeare—Parker roundly declared that their supposedly different methods remained in effect a single and erroneously stupid way of exposition—that which "strikes a death-blow to all criticism, and commits the Bible to a blind and indiscriminating belief."

The essence of Parker's thinking is here succinctly stated. We may say that throughout the last two hectic decades he did nothing but ring changes upon it, or merely repeat it. Some may then object that if this is all the shooting was about, then the provocation was trivial, that the whole commotion had better be forgotten rather than celebrated a century after Parker's self-imposed immolation.

I suspect that the issue is not dead. It is not only still with us, but in the era of Niebuhr and Tillich and Barth it has actually become, if anything, more pressing than it was in the 1840's. At any rate, of this we may be assured, that Parker, guided by De Wette and his readings in German romantic literature, faced up to the problem of criticism as no one else in his America did—as Emerson certainly never did and as in fact, strange though the conjunction at first sight appears, only Edgar Allan Poe came near to doing. Yet on second thought the conjunction is not too far-fetched. In the sense in which I use this phrase, "the problem of criticism," and as Parker was trying to spell it out both in the De Wette Introduction and the *Discourse,* it pertains equally to the fields of literary evaluation and Biblical scholarship.

In the *Discourse,* amid what was as usual his too gushing volubility, Parker managed (as occasionally he could) to frame several compact sentences which his opponents never understood and the full implications of which, in all areas of the mind, Parker himself may not have appreciated. For Parker was thinking only of the parochial issue of the miracles when he said that because of a literal belief in the narrative of the Bible, "A deference is paid to it wholly independent of its intrinsic merit." He had in mind mostly, maybe only, the then excitingly new discovery by the Romantic Age that history treated imaginatively need not be fettered by the history of historians when he declared that the mythology of the Bible should be surgically separated from its factual record, so that the critic could "take the Bible for what it is worth." This did not mean that he would reverence the factual and discard the mythological; on the contrary, knowledge of the distinction would make the latter meaningful for the first time in the life of Christianity. So he was speaking only as a Unitarian when he wrote that if we are required to "believe" the whole of the

Bible, absurdities and all—if we stupidly make one part authoritative in the single sense by which we treat another as regulatory—"then we make the Bible our master, who puts Common Sense and Reason to silence, and drives Conscience and the religious Element out of the Church."

But suppose, if this be not too extravagant an interjection, we now substitute in Parker's sentences Hamlet for the Bible, and the cult of Shakespeare for the Unitarian Church. What have we, in either form, but a statement of the ever tormenting question of an individual's relation toward that to which he subjects himself—to that which is over and above him, more powerful than he can ever be, which he deeply loves but also in startling moments of awareness fears—against which he must preserve his own particular being? Parker's effort was to save the human spirit from becoming embalmed in Bibliolatry, just as a major effort of modern criticism has been to rescue living intelligence from Shakespeareolatry. The same obstacles persist: in Parker's day, his opponents did not know their souls had already atrophied amid their gracious conventions, as in our day academic instructors in Shakespeare courses are unaware their lungs have ceased to function. In that sense, Parker's campaign, at the Melodeon and at the Music Hall, was a contest for life against death, in which he used a timeless sense of historical fluctuations as his supreme weapon against the deadly illusion of historical finality.

Yet this is not to conclude—not by any means—that upon our re-examination we should join with Parrington and Commager in elevating Parker once more as the paladin of freedom against repressive Boston. Some of his critics were intelligent enough not to denounce him solely because he divorced belief in Christ from belief in the miracles. A few were astute enough—let this be chalked up to their credit—to note that he was himself guilty of the very crime he charged against them. He delighted, for instance, in disclosing how he, and he alone, had found in the Pentateuch "marks of a distinct plan and design on the part of the compiler." He deciphered the cunning plot, this subtle scheme, as though he were a cryptographer breaking a code—as though he were Edgar Poe constructing and then unraveling a detective story—and so could describe the tremendous fabrication as "artificial." Then, speaking as a modern man of letters, he announced that this was no disparagement of the compiler any more than a similar criticism would be of the legendary compiler known as Homer. Both had constructed a national epic. What Parker would blame was the ridiculous fancy among Christians of thrusting the authorship of the Biblical romance onto the Deity.

Yet Parker was unwilling to note—even though he assured his people that he and they entertained many opinions which future criticism would prove erroneous—that this sort of "historical" method, especially when it exposed some secret design behind an obfuscation of Scripture, was as fully prepared to impose its scheme of interpretation upon the Bible as were Unitarians to impose upon it their fable of the miracles. Parker was ready, in the end of all, to translate the untranslatable into the dreary prose of De Wette, just as any Calvinist had formerly been eager to translate the gospels into the five points of the Synod of Dort. Therefore it is not to be wondered at that there should arise in modern theology, as in modern literary discusion, a tribe of recalcitrants who consign all of Parker's and De Wette's annotations, along with those of Strauss or Baur or Moulton, to the realm of irrelevant footnotes—who proclaim anew the inner coherence of the Bible, just as cognate spirits in the other sorts of criticism summon us to contemplate the "essential" tragedy of Hamlet apart from all historical consideration of Elizabethan manners, diction, or of the belief in the objective reality of ghosts. In a sense, Parker's opponents, standing firm on a principle of interpretation which they would not yield to the formless relativity of historical anthropology, clinging fanatically to the sterile doctrine of the miracles, could rationally insist that they were the ones who came to the Bible for what it was worth, the ones who respected its intrinsic merit; whereas Parker, pretending to separate wheat from chaff, merely extracted verses which suited his preconception, and then called the rest chaff. The Unitarians were saying, as Norton's *Evidences* boldly contended, that the divine relevation could not be made less divine by any amount of explication of the historical circumstances, by any account of tribal customs, or by any demonstrations of how books were compiled or texts interlaced. Employ the *historico-critical* method as rigorously as you will, this generation of Unitarians in effect (though seldom as pungently as they should have) declared, the Bible remains the Bible. And the Bible, though it does not mention the Trinity and so should not bear the burden of this monstrosity, emphatically does tell of the miracles, exactly as Hamlet does contain a ghost. Parker, in their view, was deceiving not only to multitudes who flocked to the Music Hall instead of to decently constituted churches, but also himself. The glad tidings he gave out were not those of release, after all, but of an enslavement to a priori transcendentalism.

Meanwhile, out of his study of the Old Testament under De Wette's tuition, Parker acquired a deep respect for the prophets, even while he was learning an even deeper contempt for the priests. As he taught himself and his people to discard the notion that the prophets had ever pretended to be forecasters of events, he saw with what seemed to him absolute clarity that they had been men who grasped the nature of their social emergencies, who realized wherein lay the sinful complacency of the prosperous. As soon as he conceived the "truth" of the Old Testament in these terms he understood why priests who offered their congregations an explanation of the Bible which purported to be definitive for all time to come would by that very token not be disturbed by slavery, by the flourishing of prostitution in Boston, or by the cheats and hypocrisies of ordinary business conduct. They could not be prophets, for their theology rendered them insensitive to the crises of their time. We may suppose that merely by temperament Parker would have flung himself into all such "causes" as abolition and women's rights, but his doctrine of the prophet as opposed to the priest certainly supplied him with a formal justification. Only a prophet could denounce the rituals of the priests in the name of a Jehovah who was the eternal rule of virtue. The paradox with which the prophets could live but which terrified the sanctimonious priests consisted in the recognition that this standard or righteousness was to be apprehended only through familiarity with the historical, and so with the temporal and fleeting, manifestations of it. History thus elevated its own methodology into a destructive force, which over and over again became the purgation of false religion. Yet destruction was not an end in itself: it was the necessary prologue, age after age, to what Parker, in his most ecstatic moments, hailed as "absolute religion."

It is a distorted image of Parker that the ancient and honorable of Massachusetts held of him during his life, which they cherished after his death, that of the religious demagogue, the brash seeker for publicity by sensationally taking up every disreputable movement for "reform" then being agitated among New England's peculiarly active lunatic fringe. This judgment casts discredit upon the judges, not upon Parker, for it is blind to the majestic nobility of the man. It is, however, an equally distorted portrait that has been created by such libertarians as Parrington, by the epigoni of transcendentalism in the various "free religion" movements, by cantankerous village nonconformists—that of the ever stalwart fighter for freedom in an age and against a society that had surrendered to cowardice. This view is blind to the neurotic compulsions which drove him to his maniacal ransacking of the world's scholarship without enabling him to use it beyond his edition of De Wette, to his pitifully limited aesthetic sense, to the facile nature of his few basic ideas, his intuitive and utterly dogmatic trust in his conception of God and immortality, and the repetitious banality of most of his published works.

Yet both these conceptions become useless once we penetrate to a more important context, because both of them are formulated on superficial levels of conventional categorization which bear only a distant relation to a deeper level wherein the true significance of Theodore Parker resides. On this other plane there is no such fundamental conflict between an oversimplified liberalism and a grotesque conservatism. On this level, both parties were, and in the American Protestant community still are, entangled within the same net of confusion. If we take the term "theological liberalism" to mean roughly the syndrome of propositions Parker put forth— historical criticism of the Bible, rejection of formalized creeds and most especially of the Westminster, assertion of the rights of intuition over speculation and of the heart over the head, along with an elevation of reason over authority, a boundless optimism as to human perfectibility along with a sacred obligation to fight eternally against social evils—then we may conclude that Parker dramatized the hitherto concealed terror within the assurance of progress. An advancing liberalism, he demonstrated, even though this was not his intention, is bound, the more it forges ahead, the more to slacken its attack on the enemy at its front and to turn back, in order to dismantle the great bastions it had formerly erected on what had been frontier outposts, beyond which it has passed. In practice, then, it can never entertain the prospect of ultimate or final victory, or any resting place. It can enjoy no surcease from insecurity and anxiety. Where the orthodox conservative must murder the Lamb of God, where Oedipus must murder his father, in order to enter their inheritance, the liberal has no time for either diversion. He is too busy killing himself. Or, more precisely, in slaying the previous incarnation of himself, as we in this present ceremony are dismembering Theodore Parker. The history of liberal religion is one of perpetual suicide.

Amid these tensions Parker strove to maintain his tremulous balance; amid these he suffered, until at last they did destroy him. What he demands of us is not so much love or even sympathy—though these are rewarding exercises of the spirit when extended to him—but more than these, a full and just comprehension of his and of our own predicament.

THE LOCATION OF AMERICAN
RELIGIOUS FREEDOM

IN JULY 1849, George P. Putnam published a romance written by a doctor, one William Starbuck Mayo, weirdly entitled *Kaloolah*. For the firm, the book was a risk, since the story was, in substance, similar to a romance that had appeared earlier that year, written by Herman Melville and as weirdly entitled *Mardi*. Both works told of an adventurer's long quest for a mysterious white girl, Melville's amid the brown-skinned savages of Polynesia and Mayo's among the brown-skinned Bedouins of the Sahara. Two years before, Melville had made a sensation with his supposedly autobiographical account of life among the cannibals. Mayo was accused of imitating him, especially as his book clearly had a somewhat autobiographical character. Mayo indignantly denied that he was copying Melville, though we may easily believe that he was. However that may be, the literary gods, or rather the public, were capricious. Melville's book was a dismal failure, while *Kaloolah* was a success, running rapidly through several editions. There was then no "best-seller list," but for months it would have topped any bookseller's report. Today *Kaloolah* is remembered, if at all, only for its analogies to Melville, but in 1849 it hit, as we might say, the jack pot.

The youth of the hero is spent in an upstate New York town, which clearly is Ogdensburg, where Mayo was born in 1811. This part of the nation, I need hardly remind you, was known at the time as the "burned-over district," a region swept from end to end by a succession of religious revivals that culminated in the 1820's in the torrential whirlwind of Charles Grandison Finney, who introduced into the technique of whipping up zeal the ingenious device of praying for hardened sinners, or indeed for anybody who opposed the revival, by name in the church, giving a public catalogue of their offenses. *Kaloolah* relates that when this particular frenzy hit the hero's town, it brought to a halt not only all business but the local academy, for students and faculty alike deserted classrooms to confess their sins and to pray with gusto over those of their fellows.

It spread itself like an epidemic, and seemed to be governed by similar laws. Rapidly increasing in violence as it advanced, it attacked all classes, but evinced particular power over the very young, the very aged and the very vicious. No revival in that section of country had ever been more complete, or had been more strongly characterized by enthusiastic zeal and intense, wild, passionate excitement.

Published in *Religion & Freedom of Thought* (New York, 1954), pp. 9-23.

It emanated, Mayo significantly says, from all churches in the town—Baptist, Methodist, and Presbyterian—and engulfed virtually the whole population except the president of the academy, who was also pastor of the Presbyterian church. He set himself stoutly "against what his good sense led him to pronounce an unhealthy, if not an unholy excitement," and for this resistance he paid heavily. "A highly cultivated mind, refined taste, gentle manner and undoubted piety served not to save him from contumely and insult." His own congregation insulted him by praying for him, with clear allusions "to age, situation, connections, and prospects." Our minds inevitably leap ahead to practices recently reported from countries we call "totalitarian" when Mayo says that small children were used to work upon or to denounce their parents, and that pretty girls were employed to lead adoring swains to the anxious seat.

Now I think that there are two observations that must occur to any modern American who reads this description. One is the striking fact that in America of 1849 this terrifying episode could be presented as revolting only in a work of admittedly unrealistic fiction. Had Mayo made a full-dress, frontal attack on revivalism, his book would never have come anywhere near the best-seller list. We know that clergymen who did venture to attack revivals, not because they disapproved the end but because they disliked the methods, suffered even fouler abuse than Mayo's gentle Presbyterian in Ogdensburg. The student of religious periodicals of the 1840's finds things said, for instance, about Dr. John H. Nevin and his wonderfully sane book, *The Anxious Bench*, which he would hardly believe any professing Christian could utter about another, were it not that his incredulity has been dissipated by the spectacle of some investigating committees of the Congress of the United States.

The second, and more obvious, reflection invited by this passage takes the form of a question: Where, in this land that then, as now, boasted it had for the first time in world history achieved complete religious liberty—where was the freedom?

As a matter of fact, Mayo proceeds to tell us precisely where it was. I dwell upon this description not because *Kaloolah* is another *Moby-Dick,* but precisely because it was popular in 1849 and was still popular in 1851 when the public ignored *Moby-Dick*. With his school disrupted, the hero fled to the woods. He went to Nature. He stretched himself upon a sunny bank or sat upon a prostrate giant of the forest; there he "turned with shuddering and loathing from the sight and sounds of the distant village," and found himself persuaded "that cant and rant are utterly inconsistent with the true worship of God." So, for several pages Mayo chants the religion of Nature with which his romance is suffused. "How soft, and low, and calm, yet deep and full of meaning and power are the hymns sung to His Praise in the great temple of Nature." And indeed, not only is Nature in repose preferable to the raucous tumult of a revival, but in its awful and destructive might it is more so, even in the tempest.

> Stand forth, and enjoy it! Quail not! Bare your brow to the storm—
> look with a steady eye upon the lightning's flash—listen to the awful
> chorus and feel alike the infinity of God and the greatness of the soul.

As a piece of prose, this bears no comparison with Captain Ahab's address
to Nature's furious fire in the neglected book of 1851, but Melville's message is much the same:

> Here again with haughty agony, I read my sire. Leap! leap up, and
> lick the sky. I leap with thee; I burn with thee; fain would be welded
> with thee; defyingly I worship thee!

These two writers—the lesser and popular one, the great neglected one—
were not cloistered scholars; both had a large experience of American life.
Both managed to say, through the indirections in which they were obliged
to hide themselves, through romantic fictions, that freedom of the mind is
not to be found in a sniveling church which humiliates a man by advertising
his sins, but in the sublimity of Nature, even though that sublimity slay him.

Melville found in man's embrace of Nature a terror so titanic that his
masterpiece frightened his contemporaries; yet just because it does plunge
so deeply it can be called the most profound reading of the American mentality achieved in its day, and its rediscovery in our own time is proof that
its diagnosis remains valid. Certainly the cult of Nature became in the first
half of the nineteenth century a conspicuous manifestation of the American
mind. It can be found on all levels of culture, from the novels of Cooper,
the poems of Bryant, the landscapes of the Hudson River School, down to
the mawkish gift-books and annuals. It even flourished on the frontier,
in the face of floods, forest fires, the ague, and the camp meeting. As has
often been remarked, Emerson's little book of 1836 is a central document
for the epoch if only for its title, *Nature*. Though at first Emerson caused
alarm by too cavalierly dispensing with the last pretense of a specifically
Christian revelation, by proclaiming the utter sufficiency of Nature to supply
the life of the spirit, yet by his own saintliness and by the eupeptic proper-
ties of his doctrine, he won an astonishing acceptance even among those
church-goers who thought themselves impeccably orthodox. "Self-reliance"
was just what a nation needed that had before it the enormous task of con-
quering a continent, and consistency could be happily scorned as an unnatural hobgoblin by busy men who no longer wanted to be checked by petty
divines. In the second half of the century, Emerson along wtih Longfellow
was quoted from innumerable American pulpits in order to clarify the more
enigmatic utterances of the gospels.

This cult of Nature had its vogue, we should remark, among the better
educated, the sort of people who shared and who came increasingly to share
Mayo's distaste for the antics of revivalism. One would hardly expect to
find much of it among the leaping shouters, the yelping and jerking converts at the mammoth Cane Ridge meeting. Anyone who knows the New
England peasantry—whom we never call peasants but always "natives"—

knows that you can never get an authentic Vermont farmer to admire the view, but when the New Englander, even at evangelical Amherst, has risen in the cultural scale to that of Squire Dickinson, he will seize the rope and ring the church bell like mad to call the townspeople's attention to an especially gorgeous sunset.

Now we must always remember that this ubiquitous cult of Nature has its efflorescence just at the moment when this country—the first, as we have said, in world history to make the experiment—is feeling the full effects of realizing in a body politic the ideal of complete religious liberty. It had indeed become the proudest among all America's proud boasts, that here a man can worship as he chooses. Here is no established church, no tithe, no ecclesiastical court; here there is a wall of separation between state and church. Any group of persons can come together and form any kind of church, believe in anything they fancy (except, of course, in polygamy!), and as long as they obey the civil laws and do not get the notion that religion means sharing the wealth of John Jacob Astor, they can go their way unmolested. If this is not freedom of the mind, what in Heaven's name is?

It was a problem for patriotic and liberal historians like George Bancroft —whose *History,* by the way, is a major exhibit in the cult of Nature, for in it natural guidance has finally and utterly replaced supernatural providence—to explain just how Americans acquired their passionate devotion to the principle of religious liberty. Scholars hesitated to give all, or even any, of the credit to Thomas Jefferson, because while he had venerated nature, his was the nature of the Newtonian scientist, not Nature spelled with capital N, which Cooper celebrated, Thomas Cole painted, and to which Mayo's hero fled for relief from the din of the revival. When they went back to the pre-Revolutionary churches, especially those historians who were members in good standing of one of the principal denominations, they had trouble not only with the original, and "misguided," philosophies of their forbears, but in discovering the reasons for the churches' conversion to what had now become the realized American dream. Descendants of the Puritans inevitably had particular difficulty, for it was no easy task to convince themselves that churches that had exiled Roger Williams and Anne Hutchinson, had whipped Baptists and indubitably hanged Quakers, were prophets of the First Amendment. Presbyterians and Anglicans were almost as embarrassed, and while the record of the Baptists before the Revolution was good, still they had been small and despised groups who clearly had advocated toleration in order to get out from under their oppressors. The Methodists had come so late on the scene that they had no colonial past to plague them, but no one quite had the temerity to present John Wesley as a pioneer of the American conception of religious liberty. The history of colonial New York was a puzzle beyond a puzzle, because there, where English rule had tried to keep both the Dutch Reformed Church and the Church of England established, diversity of sects had come in such bewildering profusion that the ultimate triumph of religious liberty seemed rather an exhausted and a cynical resignation to the inevitable than any upsurge of positive conviction. True, the Quakers could claim that from the beginning William Penn welcomed all Christians to his emporium. Bancroft, as a matter of fact, dared to hold up Penn to admiration, in explicit contrast to his own maniacal ancestors, as one prematurely inspired by that spirit of Nature which, emanating in Bancroft's day in the form of Kantian philosophy, had taught America the categorical imperative of freedom. Still, the Quakers were only one, and a relatively small, group; nobody could seriously argue that the fathers of the Constitution and framers of state constitutions had arrived at the conclusion of religious liberty by studying Quaker precedents.

Actually, if for historians like Bancroft and Palfrey it was a bother to show exactly how the several denominations, starting with philosophies of exclusiveness and intolerance, had yet come in America to pride themselves on letting others live their own lives, for the historian of today, especially on such an occasion as this, it remains a vexation. For a long time there was a disposition, particularly among historians glorying in the name of liberalism, to search the American past in order to pick out and to laud the few figures who can be said to have pointed the way. Penn still receives unstinted praise, although I suspect that the terms employed in the lavish encomium might astonish and even dismay that benevolent autocrat. The most unfortunate obfuscation compounded by well-intentioned but historically inappropriate adoration has been that which buried in verbiage the majestic figure of Roger Williams. I have lately made a small effort to excavate him, and I must confess that, as notices of the book come to me from all over the country, I am amazed to see with what startled amazement reviewers greet the news that the founder of Providence was named Williams and not Thomas Jefferson. Perhaps even more mischievous has been the attempt of American historians and orators—a generation ago it might be said to have amounted to a conspiracy—to prove that somehow, in the very genes of the Protestant churches, and despite anything they may have said or done in the seventeenth century, the principle of liberty was latent. In this view, American history is seen as a steady translation into actuality of a potentiality inherent in the covenanted churches of Massachusetts, in Presbyterian synods of Philadelphia, in the vestries of Virginia, although neither New Englanders nor the Scotch-Irish nor even the genial planters of the Old Dominion had the slightest suspicion of its existence. If to this version of man proposing but God disposing, we can somehow add a conviction that the Almighty was especially conducting America by the hand of His Providence, we then manage to put ourselves into a happier relation with our ancestors, even though at the same time we have made them into a collection of libertarian Typhoid Marys, carrying unwittingly the germs of a contagion to which they themselves were immune.

To take a concrete example, loyal Harvard men are always seeking to unriddle how Harvard College, founded, at least so the founders said, in order that a literate ministry should continue in the churches after the present ministers lay in the dust—which took its motto "Veritas" to mean not an anthropologist's truth about marital rites in Timbuctoo or a physicist's parodoxical truth about the propensity of certain esoteric materials toward fission and toward fusion—but to mean simply and entirely "Christo et Ecclesiae"—it is a riddle, I say, how from this theological acorn grew the oak which today is in certain quarters reputed to be godless.

I think what happened with Harvard is, in slight measure, a help toward comprehending what happened in America. Loyal Harvard men like to insist that even under Puritan rule no loyalty oath was exacted from student or teacher, but this is to ignore the fact that any member of the college who then broached a heretical notion would have been immediately and summarily disposed of by the civil arm. They endeavor also to extract from the statement of the founders that, dreading to leave an illiterate ministry, they intended "to advance learning and to perpetuate it to posterity," the welcome conclusion that Harvard never was a mere "theological seminary." They forget that for these founders there was only one body of learning, the specified and codified liberal arts, which constituted "learning," and that there was no conceivably way this monolithic system could be subdivided, with some portion prescribed for secular students and the rest for theologians. Up to the B.A. all pursued the same curriculum; if a few, and then progressively more, left at that point, they merely stopped before coming to the queen of the sciences, and so did not take an M.A. But that there was any question of Harvard's being or not being a theological seminary was utterly unimaginable to the founders.

Without going into the long story of how history operated, it is enough to say that with the increase of knowledge, of new arts and sciences, and with the breaking-up of the old into "departments" and above all, with the demand made upon Harvard and then upon all colleges to send men into professions and into business, the unpredictable and unforeseeable thing happened: the Divinity School became a graduate school, along with Dentistry, Forestry, and (though not at Harvard) Hotel Management. It became a mystery for specialists, not required of ordinary students; it became a peculiarity in which one might indulge if he liked or wanted to earn a living (a modest one) that way. Thus was freedom of the mind achieved at Harvard University.

The point is, to put it baldly, that both in education and in religion, we didn't aspire to freedom, we didn't march steadily toward it, we didn't unfold the inevitable propulsion of our hidden nature: we stumbled into it. We got a variety of sects as we got a college catalogue: the denominations and the sciences multiplied until there was nothing anybody could do about them. Wherefore we gave them permission to exist, and called the result freedom of the mind. Then we found, to our vast delight, that by thus negatively surrendering we could congratulate ourselves on a positive and heroic victory. So we stuck the feather in our cap and called it Yankee Doodle. Revivalists, whether in Mayo's Ogdensburg or in Gopher Prairie, or more genteel ones in Westchester County, have always been enthusiastic celebrants of our God-given religious liberty. I think it was Mr. Justice Holmes who remarked that in the Boston of his boyhood, you could safely deny the divinity of Christ but you would be overwhelmed with the utmost social opprobrium if you advocated sports on Sunday.

But to come back to the cult of Nature: the period when it throve was that which witnessed the dramatic—we might say the melodramatic—working out of America's discovery that the freedom of the Christian man can be boiled down from the abstruse speculations of Augustine, Aquinas, Luther, Calvin, Edwards, to one simple and practical *modus vivendi,* which consists of letting everybody do what he likes. One might say of the Protestant churches up to and through the Civil War that they, too, were built, as Hosea Bigelow said the Confederacy was,

> on our bran-new politickle thesis
> That a Gov'ments fust right is to tumble to pieces.

Protestantism may carry in its loins the dissidence of dissent, but even a Bossuet would be hard put to chronicle and keep straight the splinterings, separations, schisms, broils, and divorces which constitute American church history from 1776 to 1865. I shall not inflict upon you the story of Unitarianism and then transcendentalism out of Unitarianism; of Bellamyites and Hopkinsians, New Lights and Old, and the explosive New Haven Theology; of the Cumberland Presbytery, the Missouri Synod, the trial of Lyman Beecher, the Disciples of Christ, the Millerites, and the Christian Adventists. I sometimes try to put on the blackboard for my students a chart of the fragmentation of the churches in these years, and I end up with something as labyrinthine as the genealogies of York and Lancaster, amid which even Shakespeare got confused. When you add to this maze the severances of the Civil War, you begin to understand why so many conscientious and Christian persons, why, indeed, so many of the clergy themselves, without (as they supposed) abandoning Christian belief, turned to the enduring, the consoling, the uncontentious verities of Nature. They all read Wordsworth, and he told them what they wanted to hear:

> One impulse from a vernal wood
> May teach you more of man,
> Of moral evil and of good
> Than all the sages can.

Surely there was no harm in thus exercising a Christian's freedom? Emerson might, for some queer Yankee reason, feel obliged, once he turned to the vernal wood, to get out of the church, but Wordsworth never did. And besides, even Emerson so expounded the new doctrine that a true believer could delight in it:

Therefore is nature glorious with form, color, and motion, that every globe in the remotest heaven; every chemical change from the rudest crystal up to the laws of life; every change of vegetation from the first principle of growth in the eye of a leaf, to the tropical forest and antediluvian coal-mine; every animal function from the sponge up to Hercules, shall hint or thunder to man the laws of right and wrong, and echo the Ten Commandments.

I am proposing a thesis which you may think too ingenious, but which I believe is not quite fantastic. Take the first decades of this republic as your testing ground—as a matter of fact, you can also take subsequent ones—and you will find that you must locate the tension between religion and freedom of the mind not amid the multitudinous jarring sects but between two definable extremes. On the one hand, there is a Biblicist and ineradicably revivalistic piety, saying with Thomas Campbell, "Where the Scriptures speak, we speak; where the Scriptures are silent, we are silent." On the other, there is a naturalism more or less spiritualized, becoming if anything more appealing to large numbers of Americans when, with the help of Darwin, Nature was found not so much to thunder the Ten Commandments as positively to yodel the Gospel of Wealth.

This dichotomy does become clear when we place in opposition Emerson and such infatuated revivalists as Peter Cartwright and Alexander Campbell. These exhorters were so intent upon working cataclysmic conversions —as Abraham Lincoln said, "When I hear a man preach, I like to see him fight bees"—that they were impervious to the forces even then sweeping their communities into Emersonian complacency. They were handicapped when confronting the new conceptions not only by their Biblicism but even more by their axiomatic retention of the empirical psychology of John Locke, by that sensationalism upon which Edwards had established the theory of revivalism, but which had become with them, as it had not been with him, mechanical. They may have read Byron and Scott, because everybody did, but they could not cope with Schleiermacher, Coleridge, or Newman. Here, I would contend, is the beginning of the division which later in the century became the fatal cleavage between what, for shorthand purposes, we may call fundamentalism and all the many forms of liberalism that found support for a genteel theism in evolution and in the "Higher Criticism." The line of battle was not so clear in 1850 as in 1900 only because the revivalists were still too busy fighting bees while the naturalists were still too vague or too little interested in ideas to lay down an open defiance of the dominant orthodoxy. Those who did perceive the dreadful rift—the most perceptive being Herman Melville—masked their dread in allegories uncomprehended by their contemporaries.

Fruitful analysis of the situation would be infinitely easier if only the mass of these innocent worshipers—one often wants to call them idolaters —of Nature had not all the time professed to be good Christians. Lowbrows and highbrows alike read Byron and Scott. Outside Concord, Massachusetts, those who embraced Wordsworth and Coleridge insisted that the new philosophy was authentic Christianity. The Rev. Caleb S. Henry, an Episcopalian but a student of German, strove valiantly in the only journal of the time which can be said intellectually to rival *The Dial, The New York Review,* to show that Coleridge was no transcendentalist in the Emersonian sense, "denying or refining away the historic truth of Christianity." The *Review* said that Emerson's writings, purporting to be ambrosial food, were in reality poison; in this pantheistic perversion of Coleridge it found a striking instance of the inherent lawlessness of the American mind—"the evil and punishment of our age and country." Yet this same *Review,* in less guarded pages, is full of hymns to Nature; it too forgets repeatedly that the Christian should admire in Nature only the handiwork of God, and treats the landscape as a self-sufficient source of morality and law.

There were only a few who perceived the problem and attempted to mediate between extremes. I think we ought so to interpret the Mercersburg theology of Nevin and Philip Schaff, but the man pre-eminently the hero and the victim of the predicament is Horace Bushnell. I am at a loss to comprehend why students of divinity in this nation are so ignorant of him; a few years ago Dean Weigle brought out through the Yale University Press an edition of Bushnell's *Christian Nurture* of 1847, but university presses, though commendably eager to print good books, are universally averse from stooping to anything so vulgar as selling them, and Dean Weigle's edition seems not to have been widely noted. However, one must say that Bushnell, along with his magnificent restatement of the atonement and the Trinity, also preached a kind of racist imperialism—what he called the "out-populating principle"—that makes him repugnant to those who today would hold to a complete freedom of the mind.

We are thus obliged to seek further into the reason why the cult of Nature made, and still makes, so tremendous an appeal to Americans. In the romantic era all Western culture found new charms in Nature, but there is something decidedly different between the appeal of Nature in Germany and in Paris and that which it developed in America. Actually, the reason is not far to seek. Nature assuaged persons like Mayo who were disgusted with a narrow and noisy revivalism, but more importantly it gave Americans a rationale for America. To take one example out of millions: in 1835 James Brooks, later editor of *The New York Express,* published in *The Knickerbocker Magazine* a series entitled "Our Own Country," which made a great stir and was reprinted across the country. America does unfortunately show a preference for things material over the mental and spiritual, said Brooks, but we should not despair: the time is coming when we shall wax great in culture. And how may we be certain of this? Because God Himself has told us. And how has God spoken?

God speaks this promise in the sublimity of Nature. It resounds all along the crags of the Alleghanies. It is uttered in the thunder of Niagara. It is heard in the roar of two oceans, from the great Pacific to the rocky ramparts of the Bay of Fundy. His finger has written it in the broad expanse of our inland seas, and traced it out by the mighty Father of Waters. The august TEMPLE in which we dwell was built for lofty purposes. Oh! that we may consecrate it to LIBERTY and CONCORD, and be found fit worshippers within its holy walls.

Nature therefore is not only God rebuking the hysteria of Charles Grandison Finney, it is the American TEMPLE. It means primarily freedom for the nation, only incidentally freedom for the mind. Concessions could be made to historic Christian doctrines, lip service paid to original sin, and occasional worries expressed about American lawlessness; yet in the exhilarating vision of the panoramic TEMPLE the last vestiges of Christian pessimism could be exorcised (except by a Hawthorne, or by a Melville who, in the full tide of irony, said of himself, "I was a good Christian; born and bred in the bosom of the infallible Presbyterian church"). I supposed when I was writing the second volume of *The New England Mind* that I was slyly exposing the temptations that beset, in modern times, prophets who, taking themselves for Isaiahs and Jeremiahs, try to pass judgment upon a social process in which they are inextricably involved. But an astute friend said he found the book a case history of "what happens to God in America." Perhaps he was only putting into more precise language what I had imagined I was saying.

It *is* a hard conundrum, isn't it? this liberty of the Christian man. It is tricky even in the exquisite analyses of Thomas Aquinas. In Protestantism it has always had to take the form of paradox. As Luther put it, the Christian is master of all, the Christian is servant of all. Our straightforward America has never been comfortable in the presence of paradox, refuses to allow that in our history there has been any trace of it, and becomes enraged when confronted with antinomy. Some may remember the dismay Reinhold Niebuhr spread when he propounded the paradox of moral man and immoral society. I know a clergyman who snarled at me that Niebuhr was ridiculing virtue and apologizing for sin. I remember thinking, but *not* saying, that if we take the word "apologia" in its highest sense, is not "apologia for sin," come to think of it, a fair working definition of Christianity?

The paradox is so hazardous to live with that men constantly seek a more plausible, a less torturing, freedom at one or the other of its extremities. The first we might call Quietism, if we may stretch the term to include unquiet revivalism: it says, "I am master by letting the all overwhelm me. I remain free amid persecutions, tempests, and the incessant bombardment of advertisers because I ̦keep my Christian liberty safe and snug inside me, knowing that despite persecutors and singing com-

mercials on television, I shall be gloriously free beyond the grave." The
second way we may call activism: I throw the function of servitude upon
the atonement so that, secure in the knowledge that it has been vicariously
won for me, I plunge into action—the action to which I am invited by
Nature. Thus I settle the continent, free the slaves, get votes for women,
buy the advertised toothpaste, and so become a citizen in the most powerful
nation on earth, all the time singing ecstatic hymns to the nation's holy
walls and calling myself free. Surely *this* is freedom? It is even *more* than
freedom: it is the American Way of Life.

Yet there does seem, somehow, an inadequacy in both these common-
sensical resolutions of the paradox. There appears to be a mysterious, an
ominous, complementary quality about the two, as though they belong
together even while they contradict each other. As my wise father-in-law
said when his small daughter asked what is the difference between
Unitarians and Universalists, "The Unitarians don't believe in Heaven,
the Universalists don't believe in Hell." And in some strange fashion, the
consequence of both seems to be that all responsibility is taken off the self
and put upon the group. If "they" hurl the hydrogen bomb at us, I am
obliged to insist it is none of my doing, "they" did it. But if "we" throw
it first at them, I still am not to blame, for "we" did it. When the child
spills the ink and is scolded, he says "I didn't do it, it did its own self." I
who live amid holy walls am my own master, am I not? To this sorry
and desperate pass, I sometimes think, has the popular conception of freedom
sunk in this our nominally Christian culture.

As many have noticed, the Protestant churches in America, even though
brought from Europe, show more qualities in common than any one retains
with its European stem. And they feel that in America the synagogue is
no longer an alien. Even the Catholic Church in America acquires a tone
unlike Catholicism in Europe. All have grown and prospered within these
holy walls. But a horrible thought keeps intruding itself: have these bodies
displayed on this magnificent continent the spirit of freedom, have they
fostered it, can the churches take *any* credit for it? Or have they not become,
and have they not in truth always been, groups of interest, class, race, or
consanguinity, elements in an evolution which is to be explained not from
within but from without, not by the spirit of Christ but by the natural
environment, not by the paradox but by economic and geographic circumstances. The two powers whom we had supposed contending for the
allegiance of America, both chanting the slogan of freedom—both the
Bible and Nature—turn out to have been hand-in-glove behind the scene.
Both, in the end, become sanctifiers not of fredom but of conformity. They
unite in order to condemn what is "un-American."

I need not remind an audience in Union Theological Seminary that the
Christian conscience of the republic has not been entirely silent before this
enormity. Nor has the Christian intelligence proved so obtuse as to be
wholly fooled. I have mentioned Niebuhr. I have lately witnessed the

intense delight with which students come to the ending of Paul Tillich's *The Courage to Be:* when they read his declaration that we must seek the God behind the God, they rejoice in the exercise of a freedom which in essence is that liberation from what the Germans call (or used to call) "Philisterhaft," that emancipation we most devoutly pray for.

The universities and churches of Germany, we know, have been put to a hard school to learn the lesson of freedom. I like to think that in the darkest of their days some of them might have remembered the University of Jena on November 7, 1825. That was the day on which Duke Karl-August of Saxe-Weimar held a civic celebration of the fiftieth anniversary of Goethe's coming to court. No doubt the University was disposed to please its patron, but its performance on this grandiose occasion was not obsequious. The Faculties of Philosophy and Medicine bestowed honorary degrees of Doctor; the Faculty of Law would have voted Goethe one did he not already have a doctorate from Strasbourg—this being a naïve time it was thought that one degree of each kind, even honorary, was enough! But the Faculty of Theology was in a bit of a quandary: somehow a Doctorate of Theolgy did not seem quite appropriate for Goethe. So they resolved to give him instead an inscribed diploma, which Goethe prized above all the gifts he received on that bountiful day. They said:

> Your Excellency has not only often elevated our peculiar branch of knowledge, and the principles on which it rests, by profound, enlightened, and awakening remarks, but, as creator of a new spirit in science and in life, and as lord of the domain of free and vigorous thought, has powerfully promoted the true interests of the church and of evangelical theology.

The vexed problem of religion and freedom of the mind might be immensely clarified if and when it can be stoutly declared in this country that the Faculty's statement is profoundly religious.

The pattern of American life and the clearly prefigured destiny of America seemed to the founders and to virtually all Americans for over a century thereafter to be the final simplification of history: liberty and concord within the holy walls of Nature. But the Christian insight has always discerned, even though dimly, that freedom is not a simple business. American society has moved from simplicity to complexity, even assuming that the early communities were actually as simple as we imagine. By its very paradoxicality, the Christian concept of freedom thrusts into the heart of the nation's struggle with itself a dimension which the nation might be happier, or at least more comfortable, could it be disregarded. The natural response is to cry, "Let us alone; what have we to do with thee? We're doing all right, aren't we?" But if the paradox perpetually causes self-dissatisfaction, it also imparts a curious glory; it has, even in this most prosperous of nations, thwarted our complacency, filled us with unrest, disturbed our sleep, and permitted us no peace of mind. It has constantly made us ask whether we really are doing all right. If the enigma of Christian liberty, the conundrum of the freedom of the religious mind, has remained obstinately insoluble, we may gratefully acknowledge that it will as surely continue to be stubbornly recalcitrant.

EMERSONIAN GENIUS AND
THE AMERICAN DEMOCRACY

R ALP H Waldo Emerson was a poor boy, but in his community his kind of poverty mattered little. Few of his classmates at Harvard had more money than he did, and they made no such splurge as would cause him to feel inferior or outcast. His name was as good as, if not better than, anybody else's. At reunions of the Class of 1821, Emerson and his fellows, without embarrassment, quietly took up a collection for their one insolvent member. In the logic of the situation, Emerson should have received the stamp and have embraced the opinions of this group—self-consciously aristocratic, not because of their wealth but because of their names and heritage, at that moment moving easily from the Federalist to the Whig party. In 1821 there could hardly be found a group of young Americans more numb to the notion that there were any stirring implications in the word "democracy."

Actually, Emerson did take their stamp and did imbibe their opinion. We know, or ought to know, that to the end of his days he remained the child of Boston; he might well have lived out his time like Dr. Holmes (whom he admired), secure in his provincial superiority, voting Whig and Republican, associating the idea of the Democratic party with vulgarity, with General Jackson and tobacco-chewing. In great part he did exactly that; for this reason he poses difficult problems for those who would see in him America's classic sage.

For reasons which only a sociological investigation might uncover, youths at Harvard College after the War of 1812 began to exhibit a weariness with life such as they fancied might become a Rochefoucauld, which, assuredly, was nothing like what the college in its Puritan days had expected of sons of the prophets. Perhaps this was their way of declaring their independence of Puritan tradition. At any rate it is exactly here that the pose of indifference commenced to be a Harvard tradition and to take its toll. But in the first days it was difficult to maintain; only a few resolute spirits really carried it off, and Emerson, of course, lost much of his Prufrock-ism in the enthusiasm of transcendentalism. Yet not all of it—he never got rid of the fascination he early felt for this first, faint glimmer of an American sophistication; unless we remember it, we shall not understand his essays on "Culture," "Manners," "Aristocracy,"

Published in the *New England Quarterly,* vol. XXVI (March 1953), pp. 27-44. Materials from the unpublished lectures are used with the permission of the R. W. Emerson Memorial Association.

or the bitterness of those who, like Parker and Ripley, had to look upon him as their leader even while hating just these aspects of him.

At the age of eighteen, in July 1822, Emerson was bored with the prospect of another Independence Day. (At this time he also found Wordsworth crude, and what he heard of German philosophy absurd.) We Americans, he wrote his friend Hill, have marched since the Revolution "to strength, to honour, & at last to ennui." There is something immensely comic—and sad—in this spectacle of a young American of intelligence and good family, in 1822, already overcome with lassitude. Suppose the event should prove—the disdainful youth continued—that the American experiment has rashly assumed that men can govern themselves, that it demonstrates instead "that too much knowledge, & too much liberty makes them mad?" He was already determined to flee from the oratory of the Fourth of July to the serenity of cherry trees: "I shall expend my patriotism in banqueting upon Mother Nature."

However, events and ideas in Europe were already indicating that nature was a dangerous refuge for a nice young Bostonian. In America they were soon to demonstrate just how dangerous: the crisis in Emerson's intellectual life, which he endured for the next several years, coincided with those in which the natural politician—General Andrew Jackson— rose by nature's means, certainly not those of culture, to the Democratic presidency.

With part of his brain—a good part—Emerson reacted to the triumph of Jackson as did any Bostonian or Harvard man. He informed his new friend, Carlyle, on May 14, 1834, that government in America was becoming a "job"—he could think of no more contemptuous word—because "a most unfit person in the Presidency has been doing the worst things; and the worse he grew, the more popular." Nothing would be easier than to collect from the *Journals* enough passages about the Democratic party to form a manual of Boston snobbery. In 1868, for instance, meditating upon the already stale transcendental thesis that beauty consists largely in expression, he thus annotated it: "I noticed, the other day, that when a man whom I had always remarked as a handsome person was venting Democratic politics, his whole expression changed, and became mean and paltry."

This was the Emerson who, in his last years, escaped as often as he could from Concord to the Saturday Club. I believe that students of Emerson get nowhere unless they realize how often Emerson wished that the cup of transcendentalism had not been pressed to his lips. Had he been spared that, he might comfortably have regarded the Democratic party as a rabble of Irish and other unwashed immigrants, and could have refused, as for long he did refuse, to find any special virtue in democracy as a slogan.

But he could not thus protect himself; other ideas forced themselves upon him, and he was doomed to respond. He lacked the imperviousness that armored State Street and Beacon Street; intellectually he was too thin-skinned. To the friends about him, and I dare say also to himself, the reason was obvious: he was a genius. This was his burden, his fate, and the measure of his disseverance from the ethos of his clan.

He emerged into literature as the castigator of the genteel, the proper, the self-satisfied; he aligned himself with forces as disruptive of the Whig world as Jacksonianism was of the world of John Quincy Adams. He called for a stinging oath in the mouth of the teamster instead of the mincing rhetoric of Harvard and Yale graduates, who stumbled and halted and began every sentence over again. He called the scholar decent, indolent, complacent. When he cried that the spirit of the American freeman was timid, imitative, tame, he did not aim at Democrats but at the fastidious spirits who made up Boston society. He meant the corpse-cold Unitarianism of Harvard College and Brattle Street. Or at least he said that is what he meant (whether he really did or not may be argued), wherefore he seemed to uphold standards as uncouth as those of that Democrat in the White House.

The first of these, notoriously, was the standard of self-reliance, but behind it and sustaining it was the even more disturbing one of genius. Emerson had to have a flail for beating those who stammered and stuttered, and he found it in the conception of genius; he pounced upon it, and spent the rest of his life vainly struggling with its political consequences.

It is a commonplace of literary history that the cult of genius came to a special flowering in the early nineteenth century. (We cannot possibly employ the word today with a like solemnity; half the time we use it as an insult.) Wherever it prospered—whether with the Schlegels and Tieck in Germany, with Hugo and George Sand in France, with Byron and Coleridge in England—it meant revolt against convention, especially the kind of social convention that made up Harvard and Boston. "If there is any period one would desire to be born in," Emerson asked the Harvard Phi Beta Kappa, "is it not the age of Revolution?" This was precisely the sort of period many of his listeners did not want to be born in, for revolution meant Old Hickory. But to some Emerson opened alluring prospects which, he appeared to say and they wanted to hope, would have nothing to do with politics; leaving the political revolution aside, they responded to his exhortation and became, overnight if necessary, geniuses. The works of Emerson served them as a handbook; with him in one hand they learned to practice with the other the requisite gestures, much as a bride holds the cookbook while stirring the broth. But his own *Journals* show him as never quite so certain as he appeared from the outside, never entirely sure as to just what constituted genius or just how politically healthy it actually was.

Genius, he would write, consists in a trueness of sight, in such a use of words "as shows that the man was eye-witness, and not a reporter of what was told." (The early lectures are full of this idea.) Still, he had to admit at the beginning—and even more as he thought about it—that genius has methods of its own which to others may seem shocking or incoherent or pernicious. "Genius is a character of illimitable freedom." It can make greatness out of trivial material: well, Jacksonian America was trivial enough; would genius make it great? Genius unsettles routine: "Make a new rule, my dear, can you not? and tomorrow Genius shall stamp on it with starry sandal." Year after year, Emerson would tell himself—coming as near to stridency as he was capable—"To Genius everything is permitted, and not only that, but it enters into all other men's labors." Or again, he would reassure himself: "I pardon everything to it; everything is trifling before it; I will wait for it for years, and sit in contempt before the doors of that inexhaustible blessing." He was always on the lookout for genius; wherefore he sweetly greeted Whitman at the dawn of a great career, and was dismayed when this genius—who assumed that to him everything was permitted, including the attempt to make greatness out of a trivial democracy—used Emerson's endorsement in letters of gold on the back cover of the second edition of *Leaves of Grass*.

There the problem lay: it was pleasant to appeal to nature against formality, to identify religion with the blowing clover, the meteor, and the falling rain—to challenge the spectral convention in the name of the genius who lives spontaneously from nature, who has been commended, cheated, and chagrined. But who was this genius—if he wasn't Andrew Jackson, was he then Walt Whitman? Was he, whichever he was, to be permitted *everything*? An inability to spell or parse might, as in the case of genius Jones Very, be amusing; but suppose genius should find permissible or actually congenial sexual aberration or political domination? If before it all convention is trifling, must genius flout both monogamy and the social hierarchy? Suppose the youth did learn to affirm that a popgun is a popgun, in defiance of the ancient and honorable of the earth— and then chose as his guide to genius not the reserved sage of Concord but the indisputably greatest literary genius of the age, Goethe, or the outstanding genius in politics, Napoleon?

There were other dangerous geniuses, of course—above all, Lord Byron. He, said Andrews Norton (who clearly thought Emerson no better), was a corrupter of youth, a violator of "the unalterable principles of taste, founded in the nature of man, and the eternal truths of morality and religion." But Emerson and the New England geniuses were not too perturbed by Byron; he did indeed exhibit that love of the vast which they thought the primary discovery of their times, but, as Emerson said, in him "it is blind, it sees not its true end—an infinite good, alive and beautiful, a life nourished on absolute beatitudes, descending into nature to behold itself reflected there." The moral imperfections of geniuses— including the obscenities of Shakespeare—could likewise be exculpated. But the early nineteenth century, more acutely conscious of its peculiar identity than any age yet recorded in history, could not permit itself to tame the two greatest geniuses it had produced, the two who above all others, in the power of nature and of instinct, shattered the "over-civilized" palace of artifice. An ethic of self-reliance could not pretend that such reliers upon self as Goethe and Napoleon were blind. They were the twin "representatives of the impatience and reaction of nature against the *morgue* of conventions,—two stern realists, who, with the scholars, have severally set the axe at the root of the tree of cant and seeming, for this time, and for all time." But the point Emerson had to make, obstinately, was that if Napoleon incarnated "the popular external life and aims of the nineteenth century," then by the same token Goethe was its other half, "a man quite domesticated in the century,"—in fact, "the soul of his century."

The story of Emerson's lifelong struggle with Goethe has been often recounted. He could not give over the contest, for if Goethe had to be pronounced wicked, Emerson would become what Norton called him, an infidel. "All conventions, all tradition he rejected," says Emerson, in order to add that thus Goethe uttered "the best things about Nature that ever were said." The ancient and honorable of the earth—well, of Boston's earth—sneered that the man was immoral, but the New England geniuses dug in their heels and insisted with Margaret Fuller that Goethe was "the highest form of Nature, and conscious of the meaning she has been striving successively to unfold through those below him." Those below were demonstrably (like Andrews Norton) nongeniuses.

Life for geniuses would have been simpler could Goethe have been separated from Napoleon. But the two giants met at Erfurt—and recognized each other. (Emerson punctiliously copied into his *Journals* what Goethe said about Napoleon: it was as though he kept hitting himself with a hammer.) Emerson came back from Europe to start his brave adventure as a free-lance lecturer with a series entitled "Tests of Great Men." To judge from the notes, he spent much time explaining that Napoleon was beneath contempt: he was "the very bully of the common, & knocked down most indubitably his antagonists; he was as heavy as any six of them." Measure him against any of the tests young Emerson proposed, and Napoleon failed on every count. One test was whether a man has a good aim: "Well, Napoleon had an Aim & a Bad one." Another was whether he be in earnest: "Napoleon was no more a believer than a grocer who disposes his shop-window invitingly." The lectures held up to American admiration Luther, Washington, Lafayette, Michelangelo, Burke, Milton, Fox, but the constant moral was this (Emerson came back to it from every angle): "Of Napoleon, the strength consisted in his renunciation of all conscience. The Devil helps him." Emerson delivered this statement on January 29, 1835—eleven months after he had assured Carlyle that "a most unfit person" was President of the United States, when that person was still in office.

There is no better gauge of Emerson's progress into sophistication than the contrast between this moralistic lecture and the chapter published in

1850 in *Representative Men*—although that too has its ambiguities. No one would call it a paean of praise to Bonaparte, but still, the conscienceless devil of 1835 has become one who "respected the power of nature and fortune, and ascribed to it his superiority, instead of valuing himself, like inferior men, on his opinionativeness, and waging war with nature." But if Napoleon was now on the side of the meteor, against the timidity of scholars, what of the democracy in America? What of our own Napoleons— Jackson and Van Buren? Neither Napoleon nor they could be consigned to the Devil, for in that case there would exist in the universe of the Over-Soul a foreign, an extraneous, element, something uncontrollable; in that case, for children of the Devil to live from the Devil would be really demonic, really unnatural—as it often did seem to cultured New Englanders that Democrats lived.

There was a great temptation to identify this upsurging of democracy with nature. (Brownson was willing to risk it, but not for long; except Bancroft, hardly an American before Whitman dared—that is, after Jefferson's nature became "romantic" nature.) If the stinging clarity of a teamster's oath was worth paragraphs of Harvard prose, was not Jackson a rod of nature reproving the timid, the imitative and tame? Emerson sometimes made this identification, or almost made it; but he was still the Bostonian, ninth in a line of ministers, and by no stretching of his conception of nature could he learn to look upon the naturals who composed the Jacksonian rabble with anything but loathing. The soliloquy—the endless debate with himself—runs throughout the *Journals;* it turns upon a triangle of counterstatement: democracy raises the problem of genius; genius the problem of Napoleon and the American politician; they in turn raise the problem of democracy and of America. The pattern is not always quite so explicit, but over and over again any mention of genius is sure to be followed, within an entry or two, by a passage on democracy, the Democratic party, Napoleon. The inconclusiveness of the inner meditations makes a striking contrast to the seeming serenity of the published oracles. The art—or should we call it the artfulness?—of Emerson is nowhere more charmingly revealed than in the fashion in which he managed to separate in the *Essays* the three themes that in the *Journals* were constantly intertwined. Yet even his great ingenuity could not keep genius, Napoleon, and democracy from coming together and forming knotty passages in the *Essays,* and especially in *Representative Men.*

Surely he ought, did he respect logic, to have been like Whitman a democrat, and therefore a Democrat. Returning from Europe in 1834, having seen how monarchy and aristocracy degrade mankind, he could write:

> The root and seed of democracy is the doctrine, Judge for yourself. Reverence thyself. It is the inevitable effect of that doctrine, where it has any effect (which is rare), to insulate the partisan, to make each man a state. At the same time it replaces the dead with a living check

in a true, delicate reverence for superior, congenial minds. "How is the king greater than I, if he is not more just."

But the fact remained that, in the America of Jackson or of Polk, democracy in the abstract could not be dissociated from the gang of hoodlums who showed nothing more, to Emerson's view, than withering selfishness and impudent vulgarity. The boy had fled from the ranting of orators to the cherry trees; the man of 1834 sought the same comfort: "In the hush of these woods I find no Jackson placards affixed to the trees."

Yet, the literature of the new age, the revolt against "upholstery," gave a hollow sound to the names of king and lord because it voiced the forces "which have unfolded every day, with a rapidity sometimes terrific, the democratic element." Today "the Universal Man is now as real an existence as the Devil was then." At the mention of the Devil, if not of the king, Emerson must recollect himself: "I do not mean that ill thing, vain and loud, which writes lying newspapers, spouts at caucuses, and sells its lies for gold." He meant only "that spirit of love for the general good whose name this assumes." A man need not be a transcendentalist to find this ill thing disgusting: he need only to have gone to Harvard. Viewed from this angle, there was nothing to be preferred in Abraham Lincoln over General Jackson. After the assassination, Emerson tried to atone; but in 1863 the President caused him to reflect that people of culture should not expect anything better out of the operations of universal suffrage:

> You cannot refine Mr. Lincoln's taste, extend his horizon, or clear his judgment; he will not walk dignifiedly through the traditional part of the President of America, but will pop out his head at each railroad station and make a little speech, and get into an argument with Squire A. and Judge B. He will write letters to Horace Greeley, and any editor or reporter or saucy party committee that writes to him, and cheapen himself.

In the clutch of such reflections, Emerson was frequently on the point of making democratic naturalism signify an open, irreconcilable war between genius and democracy. Genius, he said in 1847, is anthropomorphist and makes human form out of material, but America—"eager, solicitous, hungry, rabid, busy-bodied"—is without form, "has no terrible and no beautiful condensation." Had he let himself go in that direction, we could summarize him in a sentence: America's philosopher condemned America's democracy as something unnatural.

He came perilously close to this way out: he dallied with the solution that was always available for romantic theorists, that some great and natural genius, out of contempt for the herd, might master them. A man of strong will "may suddenly become the center of the movement, and compel the system to gyrate round it." Cromwell was never out of Emerson's mind. Such an actor would settle the problem, would redeem both nature and the ideal, the stability and the security of the commonwealth:

We believe that there may be a man who is a match for events,—one who never found his match—against whom other men being dashed are broken,—one of inexhaustible personal resources, who can give you odds, and beat you.

The rest of us could even tell ourselves that we did not abdicate self-reliance should we follow such a genius: "We feed on genius."

Still, Emerson had to add, we "have a half-belief." There was always the danger that a resolution of the political question into the personality of the great man would be like trying to resolve the poetic problem into the personality of Byron. Genius has laws of its own, but in the workings of a commonwealth neither whim nor demonism should be permitted. "Politics rest on necessary foundations, and cannot be treated with levity."

Levity! There was indeed the devil. It would be levity to give way to looking down one's nose at Jackson and Lincoln, to turn from them to the great man who promised to bring mediocrity to heel. For suppose this genius should prove a demon of the only plausible devil, of levity?

Here Emerson was back again with Napoleon. Upon his mind, upon the mind of his generation, was indelibly impressed the spectacle of that meeting in Erfurt. The Goethean genius met with and subscribed to the Napoleonic. Henceforth it was impossible to lift the standard of the epicurean, civilized Goethe against the leveling thrust of Napoleon, or to rally around him against Jackson. Assuredly Napoleon was unscrupulous, selfish, perfidious, a prodigious gossip: "his manners were coarse." So was Jackson, so was Lincoln. But Napoleon fought against the enemies of Goethe: timidity, complacence, etc., etc. If Goethe had sided with Bonaparte, how then ought an American intellectual act toward the Democratic party? After all, as Emerson in "Politics" was obliged to say, "Democracy is better for us, because the religious sentiment of the present time accords better with it."

He hoped that the rhetorical balance of his famous sentence would remove his anxiety, that while the Whigs had the best men, the Democrats had the best cause. The scholar, philosopher, the man of religion, will want to vote with the Democrats, "but he can rarely accept the persons whom the so-called popular party propose to him as representatives of these liberalities." On the other hand, the conservative party was indeed timid, "merely defensive of property." No wonder that men came to think meanly of government and to object to paying their taxes: "Everywhere they think they get their money's worth, except for these."

This was a miserable prospect, an intolerable dilemma, for the author of *Nature*. Yet Emerson was never more the spokesman for nature, and never more the American, than when he added, "I do not for these defects despair of our republic." He might have mourned with Henry Adams and every disillusioned liberal, with every disgruntled businessman, that the country was going to the dogs, that there was no hope left (there being no longer hope in a compensatory Christian heaven) except in the great man, the political genius, the dictator. There was everything in Emerson's philosophy to turn him like Carlyle into a prophet of reaction and the leader-principle.

But he did not go with Carlyle, and he meant what he said, that he did not despair of the republic. Why not? Was it merely that he was stupid, or mild-mannered, or temperamentally sanguine? Was it dogmatic optimism for the sake of optimism? Perhaps it was partly for these reasons, but the play of his mind kept hope alive and vigorous by circling round and round, by drawing sustenance from, the inexhaustible power of genius. However odd, fantastic, or brutal might be the conduct of genius, it does submit to laws. Levity gets ironed out. So in society: "No forms can have any dangerous importance whilst we are befriended by the laws of things." Emerson's historical perspective was deeper, richer than that of a Cooper— great historical novelist though he was. Cooper had Natty Bumppo to give grandeur to the sordid scene of *The Pioneers,* but no philosophy of genius to sustain him once he entered into conflict with *Home as Found.* Cooper let himself dream of violent catastrophe, a devastating judgment not of Jehovah but of nature, as an ultimate solution to the ills of democracy, and prophesied it in *The Crater.* But Emerson could comprehend democracy in a larger frame of reference, as a phase of western society, and see its connection, where the *rentier* could not, with the new kind of property. Emerson could point out that it was not something a gentleman could afford to despise and then expect still to have the refuge of being a gentleman. In other words, Emerson understood the portent not alone of Goethe but of Napoleon.

For this reason, Napoleon figures in the carefully planned structure of *Representative Men* as a prologue to Goethe, as the next-to-the-last. There is some perversity—one might say almost levity—in the other choices (Swendenborg most obviously) or in the arrangement, but Emerson was pushing his way through the book to the two problems which, his genius informed him, constituted one problem: that of genius in modern society, where the bad manners of democrats would not be sufficient reason for consigning them, on that ground alone, to the limbo of levity.

Representative Men had its origins in a few simple ideas which took hold of Emerson in the 1830's, of which he was the prisoner but which, for as long as possible, he held off from publishing. The secret record of his life with these ideas is the *Journals,* but there was a public record before his fellow countrymen: the lectures, those discourses he gave for audiences and for money, out of which he mined paragraphs for what became *Essays* but which, guided by some obscure impulse, he never translated directly from the platform to the page. (From the beginning of his career as a lecturer down to his last series at Harvard in 1871, there was always a discourse on "Genius"; materials from one or another recasting of this draft found their way into "Self-Reliance," "Art," "Intellect"— but never into a full-dress essay on genius.) With the lecture of January

1837 (entitled "Society"), Emerson had already gone so far beyond 1835 that he could define the genius as one who has access to the universal mind and who receives its influx in wise passivity. He could employ terms he was to use throughout many subsequent lectures, but which, at least in this same and revealing language, he would never print:

> Genius is never anomalous. The greatest genius is he in whom other men own the presence of a larger portion of their common nature than is in them. And this I believe is the secret of the joy which genius gives us. Whatever men of genius say, becomes forthwith the common property of all. Why? Because the man of genius apprises us not so much of his wealth as of the commonwealth. Are his illustrations happy? So feel we [that] not *his* mind but *the* mind illustrate[s] its thoughts. A sort of higher patriotism warms us, as if one should say, "That's the way they do things in my country."

Thus early the problem took shape in his mind—never to leave it—of genius and "my country." All men share in "*the* mind," and all men are the democracy; genius must be, in some sense, a patriotic triumph. But Napoleon was a threat to the conception of a "good" genius; his American aliases, Jackson and the Democrats, were a threat to State Street. Writers are often obliged to ask themselves exactly who they are, and fear to find out that they may be the most evil of their creations. Was Emerson, in his heart of hearts, a Napoleon? If not, were the Over-Soul and all its spokesmen, all the geniuses, to be counted in the Whig column? Obviously Whiggery was no home for genius. Maybe one would have to admit that Jackson was a genius? Maybe one would have to confess—as the easiest way out—that Lincoln was a genius? Lincoln was, nominally, a Republican, but before 1865 Emerson saw him only as the creature of universal suffrage; the assassination and the rapid canonization undoubtedly helped, but Emerson was still feeling his own way and not merely moving with the times when in 1871 he told his Harvard audience, "John Brown and Abraham Lincoln were both men of genius, and have obtained this simple grandeur of utterance."

Years before he was thus able to reconcile himself to Lincoln, Emerson tried to reconcile himself to the whole panoply of genius, and the result was *Representative Men.* The value of the book is not that it invents a way out of the quandary which we now confront as terribly as did Emerson. It is not a guide for the preserving of personality against mass pressures. Too many of his terms are altered; few of us can accept his metaphysics, and many of the geniuses we admire do not seem so clearly to contribute wealth to any commonwealth. But the exhilaration of the book consists in the fact that Emerson here got his many-sided perplexity in hand, sacrificed no one aspect to any other, and wrote a book not about heroes and how to worship them, but about how an intelligent and sensitive man lives, or must learn to live, in a democratic society and era.

By calling great men not heroes but representatives, Emerson, in the most American of fashions, put them to work; the first chapter is slyly entitled "Uses of Great Men." He divides geniuses as a genus into subordinate species, whereupon for each type a specific set of laws can be worked out. Thus the individual genius, even when seemingly lawless, adheres to a pattern of coherence in relation to the sum total of the parts. If it be necessary—as we are compelled to recognize—that all sides of life be expressed, then each genius has a function, be he good or evil; what each incarnates we recognize as an accentuated part of ourselves—because all men are one, and any one man is all men.

Likewise, genius is fragmentary, and so deficient on several sides. Sometimes the moralizing Emerson appears to line up his great men like naughty children and to tell them wherein they all fall lamentably short of what teacher expects of them. But you forgive him some (although not all) of this didacticism not so much because he was a New Englander but because behind it lay the intense moments recorded in the *Journals,* such as that in which he had taken the very existence of such a person as the Democrat Hawthorne to signify "that in democratic America, she [nature] will not be democratized." Therefore in this book Emerson can go far—as far as clear sight can see—toward making genius democratic. The genius is great not because he surpasses but because he represents his constituency. His crimes and foibles are as much a part of the record as his triumphs and nobilities; Napoleon belongs to genius not as a child of the historical Devil whom Emerson foolishly invoked in 1835, and not even as a creation of the metaphorical devil, levity, but as a serious, real, and terrifying power in modern western civilization.

Wherefore something more should be required of the scholar, the poet, the man of religion, than timid antipathy to a blatant democracy. Napoleon was "the agent or attorney of the middle class of modern society"—of those in shops, banks, and factories who want to get rich. He represents "the Democrat, or the party of men of business, against the stationary or conservative party." And—Emerson here plunges to the bottom of his insight—"as long as our civilization is essentially one of property, of fences, of exclusiveness, it will be mocked by delusions"—against which some Bonaparte is bound to raise the cry of revolt, for which men again will die.

What Emerson most gained, I believe, by this analysis was an ability to comprehend, even while never quite reconciling himself to, the vices of democracy—whether with a small "d" or a capital "D." He did not need to blind himself by patriotic fanaticism; by the same token he did not need to despair. He could confess his mistake about Lincoln without retracting his contempt for Franklin Pierce. He could criticize his country without committing treason, without having to demand, as did an irate Cooper, that they become like himself or else go to hell. The example and the laws of genius might work, would work, even in the ranks of the Democratic party.

Of course, Emerson trusted the self-operating force of moral law more than do most of us today. Napoleon (for him read Jackson, Lincoln, the boss, the district leader) did everything a man could do to thrive by intellect without conscience. "It was the nature of things, the eternal law of the man and the world, which balked and ruined him; and the result, in a million experiments, would be the same." Emerson was fully aware of what the lesson cost: "immense armies, burned cities, squandered treasures, immolated millions of men, . . . this demoralized Europe." He did, we must confess, look upon the desolation with what seems to us smugness, we who have seen Europe infinitely more burned and demoralized; but these things are relative, and he was happy to note that out of the destruction arose a universal cry, "assez de Bonaparte."

Emerson was too often chilly. But had he been only that, *Representative Men* would have been for him the end of a theme, would have put a period to a chapter in his *Journals*. It was nothing of the sort. No sooner was it published than the debate was resumed, and many of the most fascinating combinations of the triple meditation on genius, Napoleon, and democracy occur in later entries. The Civil War was for him as for others an excruciating ordeal, the more so as during the worst years he believed Lincoln the example of democratic incompetence. But in the darkest moments he never quite lost his bearings. The sanity (the chilly sanity, if you will) that sustains the essay on "Politics" and informs *Representative Men* never deserted him—the levelheadedness which is his most precious bequest to a posterity that is understandably exasperated by his unction. In 1862, although not yet respecting the President, he was able to keep the personality from obscuring the issue:

> A movement in an aristocratic state does not argue a deep cause. A dozen good fellows may have had a supper and warmed each other's blood to some act of spite or arrogance, which they talk up and carry out the next month; or one man, Calhoun or Rhett, may have grown bilious, and his grumble and fury are making themselves felt at the legislature. But in a Democracy, every movement has a deep-seated cause.

This was written by no flag-waving, tub-thumping patriot shouting, "My country right or wrong." This is no campaign orator mouthing the word "democracy" even while desecrating it by his deeds. It was written by a great American, a serious man who could finally run down the devil of politics and declare that his name is levity, who understood as well as any in what the difficult ordeal consists, that magnificent but agonizing experience of what it is to be, or to try to be, an American.

THOREAU IN THE CONTEXT OF
INTERNATIONAL ROMANTICISM

IN 1842 Emerson made a special trip to the State House in order to secure a set of reports recently published by the commonwealth itemizing the flora and fauna of the state. Then, he says, he "set Henry Thoreau on the good track of giving an account of them in the Dial, explaining to him the felicity of the subject for him as it admits of the narrative of all his boatcraft & fishcraft." The young Thoreau meekly followed his master's directive—as a few years later the recalcitrant Thoreau emphatically would not. Margaret Fuller, who did not share Emerson's admiration for the rustic genius, had given up the editorship of *The Dial* at the beginning of 1842, and so Emerson was able to print Henry's first original piece in the July issue, under the title "The Natural History of Massachusetts."

Emerson, like many later Thoreauvians, thought of Thoreau as being primarily a naturalist, a rural poet of the meadows and woods, a preternaturally accurate observer (as Emerson was not) of phenomena. Emerson was never to disabuse himself of this misconception, though he had momentary glimmerings of bewilderment and at times almost recognized that Thoreau had a mind. But in the funeral oration for Thoreau, published in the *Atlantic* in 1862, Emerson made an enduring incubus out of his own prejudice by such sentences as "He knew the country like a fox or a bird, and passed through it as freely by paths of his own." If even the sensitive Emerson, with all his chances of firsthand knowledge, held this to be the essential Thoreau, it is no wonder that later admirers, who oddly enough have often taken on some characteristics of a sentimental cult, construe any effort to submit him to a more critical or intellectual analysis as a denigration of their hero.

Yet "The Natural History of Massachusetts" should have warned Emerson, as it still should warn us. Thoreau did indeed demonstrate his vast familiarity with the concrete, the specific, but he pronounced the official reports to be limited and imperfect volumes because they were merely factual. As far as they went, they were admirable, and he was the last to condemn them; yet he was obliged to add "Let us not underrate the value of a fact; it will one day flower in a truth." If Emerson paused over this sentence, he probably smiled with the pleasure of seeing an ingenious variant on one of his favorite themes. Those who like Margaret

Published in *The New England Quarterly*, vol. XXXIV, no. 2 (June 1961), pp. 147-59.

Fuller or James Russell Lowell dismissed Henry as a bungling imitator of
Emerson—even, according to some of them, modeling his nose on Emerson's
—would have concluded that here he was commencing his career of stealing
neighbor Emerson's apples. Few if any at that time could comprehend,
and today the awareness even for the most devoted student is hard to
acquire, that this sentence was prophetic of Thoreau's whole artistic
endeavor. Yet understanding dawns when we read further into the paragraph and find him saying, ominously, "He has something demoniacal
in him, who can discern a law, or couple two facts." What? we should
ask at this point—if we are sufficiently jolted—do facts sweetly flower
into truths by and of themselves? If so then what need is there of
demoniacal assistance? And if it is demoniacal to couple two facts, where
does the demon dwell? Could it possibly be that he inhabits what Wordsworth called, and all Yankee transcendentalists repeated after him, "our
meddling intellect" which, according to the high priest of Romantic
Naturalism, botanizes on grandmother's grave and murders to dissect?

The story of America's initial hostility to Wordsworth—manifested in
virtually all departments of the indigenous intelligence—and then of his
gradual acceptance as the foremost poet of the age, is a familiar tale. Emerson himself had, in the 1820's, been repelled by him, but in a lecture of
1838 he declared to Boston, and he was later to make the point even more
emphatically in *The Dial,* his conversion. Whether Thoreau heard this
particular lecture or not, the passage is worth repeating, because it indicates what Thoreau would start with, he never having to learn, by a long
process of overcoming an inherited opposition, what Emerson with great
difficulty had finally grasped but on which Emerson's hold was never to
be as tight as Henry's:

> The fame of Wordsworth is one of the most instructive facts in modern
> literature when it is considered how utterly hostile his genius at first
> seemed to the reigning taste, & I may add with what feeble poetic talents
> his great & steadily growing dominion has been established. More than
> any poet his success has been not his own but that of the Idea or
> principle which possessed him & which he has rarely succeeded in
> adequately expressing.

The last sentence is the heart of the drama. In our perspective we may
indeed say that Wordsworth succeeded in adequately expressing his great
"Idea" only in *The Prelude,* which was not to become public property
until after his death in 1850. Yet magnificent as that statement is, and
fundamental though it be for *our* understanding of Wordsworth, it is
astonishing how in 1850, when it was at long last revaled, the meaning
of it had already been absorbed. Thoreau does not often mention Wordsworth, but the very opening segments of the *Journal* show that he hardly
needed to. He was already a Wordsworthian, and in that sense a child
of the Romantic era.

The original draft of the sentence about the fact flowering into truth was entered in December 1837, when Thoreau was twenty and just out of Harvard College. Even more revealing is a praise of Goethe in the same month which approves of his being satisfied "with giving an exact description of objects as they appear to him." This, Thoreau pontificates, is the trait to be prized, and its skill consists in the device whereby "even the reflections of the author do not interefere with his descriptions." For Thoreau had thus already completely comprehended one of the major problems of the Romantic movement—for that portion of Romanticism preoccupied with the new interpretation of nature it was the major problem—of striking and maintaining the delicate balance between object and reflection, of fact and truth, of minute observation and generalized concept. There can be no doubt that Thoreau was made aware of the problem at least in part by Emerson's *Nature,* which with its Platonic ascent from the lowly level of "Commodity" into the intellectual vistas of "Prospects" sought to offer an original method for combining the two poles of the Romantic dilemma. But it does seem to me that from the beginning Henry possessed an insight which, though it too must be located within the larger framework of Romantic Naturalism, is very different from Emerson's. The contrast becomes vivid if you put Emerson's famous sentences about becoming a transparent eyeball and about the currents of universal being circulating through him alongside this entry of Thoreau's, of March 3, 1839, on "The Poet":

He must be something more than natural—even supernatural. Nature will not speak through but along with him. His voice will not proceed from her midst, but, breathing on her, will make her the expression of his thought. He then poetizes when he takes a fact out of nature into spirit. He speaks without reference to time or place. His thought is one world, hers another. He is another Nature,—Nature's brother. Kindly offices do they perform for one another. Each publishes the other's truth.

It was from this duality of vision—what in *Walden* he would call "double-ness" and which, he would say, often made its possessor a bad neighbor—that he was able to extract from the *Journal* and put into "The Natural History" such contradictory assertions as, on the one hand, "Nature will bear the closest inspection; she invites us to lay our eye level with the smallest leaf, and take an insect view of its plain," and then, on the other, invoking in full awareness of its intellectualized nature one of the grand conceptual techniques of Biblical scholarship, this remark, "When I walk in the woods, I am reminded that a wise purveyor has been there before me; my most delicate experience is typified there." If at one and the same time nature is closely inspected in microscopic detail and yet through the ancient system of typology makes experience intelligible, then Thoreau will have solved the Romantic riddle, have mastered the destructive Romantic irony. Seen in such a context, his life was an unrelenting exertion to hold this precarious stance. In the end, the impossibility of sustaining it killed him. But not until, at least in *Walden,* he had for a breathless moment held the two in solution, fused and yet still kept separate, he and nature publishing each other's truth. Surely, it was a demoniacal enterprise from start to finish. This is why, it sems to me, Thoreau can at long last be seen as a major writer of his century, not because he also happened to know boatcraft and fishcraft.

When *The Prelude* was published, the by then great host of Wordsworth's followers found in Book XII a passage which they might well wish he had published in the first decade of the century (when it actually was written), for it would have saved them a great deal of trouble in groping their way to what Emerson called his "Idea." In a magnificent apostrophe to the "Soul of Nature" Wordsworth condemns anew what he held to be the vice of the eighteenth century, its lust for comparing scene with scene, pampering the taste with novelties of color and proportion, and so rendering taste insensible to the spirit of a particular place. He himself had once let his eye tyrannize over him, so that for awhile even he went about seeking for the picturesque,

> Still craving combinations of new forms,
> New pleasure, wider empire for the sight,
> Proud of her own endowments, and rejoiced
> To lay the inner faculties asleep.

Yet all this while he had beside him his sister Dorothy, who finally showed him how to be an enthusiast without permitting the eye to become mistress of the heart.

> She welcomed what was given, and craved no more;
> Whate'er the scene presented to her view
> That was the best, to that she was attuned
> By her benign simplicity of life.

Yet probably this passage would not have been really too helpful to such a creature as Henry because Wordsworth says that Dorothy's freedom from false notions of the picturesque in nature was a feminine trait, that she was content to remain passively receptive because she was "wise as women are." However, we have become of late increasingly aware that in many of the most characteristic figures of the Romantic movement there flourished a special type of exquisite emotional sensibility, a warmth of temperament and a disposition to let experience come to them rather than that they should go forth, sword in hand, to conquer it. Goethe's *Werther* is the prototype of them all, which the supreme man of action in the era, Napoleon, read and reread. We may think also of Constant's *Adolphe,* of Keat's *Endymion,* of the cult of Chatterton, of the personality of Robert Schumann. It would be too much to say that these creations or the creators were "feminine" in nature, but they are not robustly masculine as had been Dr. Johnson or Fielding. Each of them, whether an imagined creation or an imaginative creator, is what Thomas Mann (whose comprehension of the Romantic spirit was profound) called a "delicate child of life." In all American literature Henry Thoreau is the one to whom this characterization perfectly applies. Let us remind ourselves, one of the earliest and most appealing of Thoreau's poems is, of course, "Lately, alas, I knew a gentle boy."

So it was not necessary that the example of Dorothy Wordsworth be put before the young Transcendentalists in order that they should learn the inner secret of Romantic receptivity. They had such tuition as Wordsworth's lines on "Tintern Abbey," and on the superiority of an impulse from the vernal wood over all intellectual instruction if only they would learn to come forth from science and art "with a heart/That watches and receives." Above all, they had the "Preface" to the 1800 edition of *Lyrical Ballads*. I do not propose to argue that Thoreau found the origin of his own "Idea" in this document, or even to insist that he read it (though the chances are all on the side that he did). Even if he never looked at it, we can find in it the most precise exposition of his ambition as a writer and his aspiration as an artist.

To read the "Preface" with Thoreau in mind is to realize anew how different was the situation of the Romantic revolutionary in England (as indeed in all Europe) from that of the American. The chief thrust of Wordsworth is against the poetic diction of the neoclassical age, the formalized and stereotyped abstract adjectives of Pope and Johnson. His great plea is that poetry use "the real language of men." We comprehend from his fervent argument how terribly dominating neoclassical verse had been in literary England. Provincial America endeavored to imitate the mode—witness Freneau and the Connecticut Wits—but we never had a poet who so tyrannized over our native taste as did Pope in England. Hence when youths like Emerson felt the impulse from the vernal wood stirring in their hearts, they had to exert themselves not so much in dethroning a vested interest in technique as merely in liberating themselves from a culture that they now perceived was prosaic and uncreative.

Hence what meant the most to them in Wordsworth's "Preface" were the hints he threw out about a new kind of utterance—he was talking about poetry but his prescriptions would apply as well to prose—in which the writer would strive by might and main to look steadily at his subject. The most thrilling paragraph to the generation of Thoreau would be that wherein Wordsworth rejected as idle and unmanly the faintness of heart which, despairing of ever producing a language as fitting for expression of the passion as the real passion itself, abjectly concluded that the artist should become a translator and substitute excellencies of another kind for those which are unattainable in speech. By this specious attempt to surpass his subject, said Wordsworth, the writer condemns his material to an inferior status, and thus slyly exalts himself over it. No, no: fidelity to the thing, strict application to the object, no underestimation of the value of the fact—these convictions and only these will create a literature "not standing upon external testimony, but carried alive into the heart by passion; truth which is its own testimony, which gives competence and confidence to the tribunal to which it appeals, and receives them from the same tribunal."

As we know, Wordsworth had a long struggle explaining to his contemporaries that by his phrases "the language really spoken by men" and "looking steadily at the subject" he did not mean what we would term photographic reproduction of the scene or of the human face. Romantic nature was not—for better or for worse—what the next generation would salute as "Realism." Wordsworth never taught the neophyte that a daguerreotype of Walden Pond should be esteemed more highly than a truly poetic rendition of it. He insisted that poetry have form, that it cast into metrical arrangements the materials carried alive into the heart, that passion come into literature not as animal cries or exclamations of pain, but as emotion recollected in tranquility. This meant that while no a priori concept of the picturesque, or of dignity or of excellence, should be imposed from without, that there would be an organic growth of the concept out of a fervent devotion to objective truth. The fact, in other words, would flower into a truth—if, that is, the poet could bring an adequate passion to his portraiture. Thoreau, therefore, would not be betraying or patronizing or insulting his material when he openly admitted that he was "for convenience putting the experience of two years into one." That was not illegitimate manipulation of reality, it was a way of being "something more than natural," of becoming "Nature's brother."

By the time Thoreau graduated from Harvard, this Romantic aesthetic had been widely domesticated in America. The principal agent in reconciling a suspicious public to what had at first seemed a nonsensical or even subversive paradox was landscape painting. In terms comprehensible to the average intelligence the Hudson River School, as historians now label them, were dramatizing Wordsworth's great "Idea." Indeed, I am convinced that one immensely helpful way to deepen our appreciation of what Thoreau was seeking is to look closely at certain pictures of Thomas Cole (not his grandiose tableaus but his smaller scenes), Asher Durand, or Thomas Doughty. Especially I would say Durand, for in him appears that union of graphic detail and organizing design which the disciple of Wordsworth ever strove to attain. An influential periodical of the time, the *Knickerbocker,* said of him in 1853—just as *Walden* was receiving its last revision—that "His compositions, while faithful to the truth of detail, combine a beautiful *sentiment,* which is felt by the observer, and it is in this in which his true greatness consists." All the implications of this sentence, advertised by its use of "while" along with "combine," show how, even in the complacent circles which subscribed to the *Knickerbocker,* the Romantic "Idea" had become an orthodoxy. Hence the more opulent in these circles paid high prices for the landscapes of Durand and his fellows.

We might surmise that by the same token they should have recognized in *Walden* a prose counterpart to their beloved painters. But, as is a matter of record, they bought the paintings but never the book.

There are a hundred reasons why comfortable citizens of the republic in 1854 would hang over their fireplace a landscape by Durand or Doughty, at whose wildness they might gaze without perturbation, and still be horrified at the wildness of *Walden*—if indeed they so much as heard of it. Among these reasons, however, must be enumerated—or at least I shall venture to list it—the fact that Thoreau managed so radical a penetration into "the truth of detail," and then so blatant an assertion of what the *Knickerbocker* called "sentiment," that the "combination"—to use again the catchword of the era—seemed either grotesque or truly demoniacal. Or another way to put it is to say that Henry Thoreau took the basic premise of the Romantic Age more seriously than most romantics were able to accept.

I would not unduly belabor this point, yet I would like to suggest that it indicates the perennial and never quite definable fascination of *Walden*. Thoreau spoke it as bluntly as possible in the chapter he called "Sounds," and most succinctly in the first sentence. Books, he there said, are things in dialect and are provincial, and if we are confined solely to them, "we are in danger of forgetting the language which all things and events speak without metaphor, which alone is copious and standard." Consequently *Walden* is one of the supreme achievements of the Romantic Movement— or to speak accurately, of Romantic Naturalism. Mr. Shanley has proved beyond the shadow of any doubt that it was a conscious, a deliberate creation; it was not and is not some spontaneous impulse from the vernal wood, although unfortunately many of its modern champions pretend that it was. No, it is truly emotion, but emotion ostensibly recollected in tranquility. Yet it is assuredly emotion, passion. There is no substition for the original experience, there are no excellencies of diction contrived so as to suggest an inferiority of the original to the narration. Still, it is not a mere recital, item by item, atomic moment after moment, of two years beside the pond. It is a magnificent autobiography, faithful in every detail to the setting, arising to the level of a treatise on imagination and taste, and all this without ever becoming didactic. When seen in such a perspective, it can be placed beside *The Prelude*. It is the "growth of a poet's mind," and despite all its wealth of concrete imagery it is centered not upon nature, but upon nature's brother, the intelligence of the artist.

I need hardly observe that in this century the entire philosophy of what I call Romantic Naturalism has been attacked from innumerable sides and is generally thought to be completely discredited. In painting, the Hudson River School of representation gave way to a succession of infinitely more sophisticated methods until eventually the object disappeared altogether and an artist simply painted his idea. In poetry the creative impulse for several decades has been calling for a repudiation of the identification of mind with thing, for the formulation of a poetry which shall be entirely intellectual, metaphorical, artificial. That disposition which in recent English writing has been expressed in Yeats, in Ezra Pound, in T. S. Eliot, sees in the artist a manipulator, an inventor of symbols and images, who severs himself from nature, who deliberately violates her, pillages her for schemes of his own devising. And even Robert Frost, who like Wordsworth insists that poetry must keep close to the language of ordinary human talk, reminds us again and again that we must avoid the pathetic fallacy of assuming any correspondence between human emotions and natural fact. If one is versed in country things, he memorably says, one does not suppose phoebes weep over the desolation of an abandoned farmhouse. Indeed, in one of his most powerful proclamations, "The Most of It," Frost seems to be deriding all the Henry Thoreaus of his past by describing a "he" who kept the universe alone, who wanted from nature "someone else additional to him" and who received in answer only the sudden eruption from the woods of a great buck, an utterly inhuman beast.

If the twentieth-century judgment of the Romantic aesthetic is correct, then Henry Thoreau is one of its monumental failures and martyrs, along with Shelley and Novalis. Neither he nor they were able to answer the terrible question of whether, once they committed themselves to the proposition that their most delicate experience was typified in nature, they were thereafter actually writing about nature—about Walden Pond, for instance —or about nothing more than their delicious experiences. If in reality they were only projecting their emotions onto the natural setting, if the phoebes do not weep for human miseries, then their effort to find someone additional to themselves was doomed to ghastly defeat. In this view, the career of Henry Thoreau is as tragic as that of King Lear. He too sacrificed himself needlessly to a delusion.

In his first organized statement, Thoreau could say, with all the confidence that a Lear had in the love of his daughters, that when he detects a beauty in any recess of nature he is reminded of the inexpressible privacy of a life, that he may rest content with nothing more than the sight and the sound. On the premise of that doctrine, he may properly say no more than "I am affected by the sight of the cabins of muskrats," or than "I am the wiser in respect to all knowledges, and better qualified for all fortunes, for knowing that there is a minnow in the brook." In the glowing confidence of these aphorisms lurks the assumption that moral law and natural law contain analogies, and that for this reason the writer may safely record facts without metaphors, since truths are bound to sprout from them. The later portions of Thoreau's *Journal,* those after 1854, with their tedious recordings of mere observations, of measurements, of statistics, seem to attest not only the dwindling of his vitality but the exhaustion of the theory upon which he commenced to be an author in the first place.

He immolated himself on the pyre of an untenable concept of literary creation.

And yet, he refuses to be consumed. Expound *Walden,* if you will, as a temporary and so an empty triumph of the Romantic dream, as a work doomed to diminish with the recession of that dream, yet the book refuses to go into the archeological oblivion of, shall I say? Shelley's *The Revolt of Islam.* Robert Frost, while objecting with all his Yankee soul to Thoreau's epistemology, still proclaims that with him Thoreau is a "passion." The obvious answer, or rather the easy one, is that Thoreau was a great writer, and so his pages survive in spite of changes in metaphysical fashions. But that is truly an easy, a luxurious way of salvaging our poet. The more difficult, but I believe the more honest and, in the final accounting, the more laudatory way is to say that the Romantic balance, or its "Idea" of combination, of fusing the fact and the idea, the specific and the general, is still a challenge to the mind and to the artist. Thoreau was *both* a transcendentalist and a natural historian. He never surrendered on either front, though the last years of the *Journal* show how desperate was the effort to keep both standards aloft. He said, in the central conceptual passage of *Walden,* that he wanted to drive life into a corner, to publish its meanness if it proved to be mean, but that if it should turn out to be sublime, then to give a true account of its sublimity. "The universe constantly and obediently answers to our conceptions" was his resolute determination. For what more sublime a cause, even though it be a questionable thesis, can a man expend himself?

MELVILLE AND TRANSCENDENTALISM

H ERMAN MELVILLE, like Pierre, conned his "novel-lessons," wherein life's beginning gloom concludes with wedding bells. In all romances the hero is tempted by an exotic brunette—Rebecca, Cora, Zenobia—who comes from the regions of sophistication, foreignness, money-changing, the city, or from miscegenation. She is "unnatural." The hero, being natural, resists her enticements, to subside into marriage with the blonde heroine, with unsullied nature, Rowena, Alice, or Priscilla. Scott candidly admitted that Ivanhoe might still be troubled by memories of the dark Jewess; Melville went Scott one better: the profounder emanations of the mind, he said, do not thus unravel their intricacies, they have no proper endings.

Melville's development from *Typee* in 1846 through *Pierre* of 1852 can be presented as the effort of an inexperienced writer to master the formula of the age—perfected by Scott and adapted to the American scene by Cooper, Simms, and a hundred romancers. From the beginning he was schooled in the convention; like Jack Chase, he "had read all the verses of Byron, and all the romances of Scott." He was indignant to his English publisher, Murray: "Bless my soul, Sir, will you Britons not credit that an American can be a gentleman, & have read the Waverly Novels, tho every digit may have been in the tar-bucket?" Uncle Peter Gansevoort was a friend of Cooper, and in 1849, when Cooper was still considered too critical of America, Melville boldly called him "our National Novelist." Melville spoke truth when he said in 1851 that Cooper's works "are among the earliest I remember, as in my boyhood producing a vivid, and awakning power upon my mind." A month after the printing of *Moby-Dick* Melville used "awakning" to describe the impact of Cooper!

The letter to Murray also makes clear that, when he found *Mardi* taking off from the solid "facts," he could recognize what was happening: "I went to work heart & soul at a romance." The word was self-explanatory; he was seized by an impulse "to plume my powers for a flight," he was "irked, cramped & fettered by plodding along with dull common place." To him it seemed an augury of success that "the romance & poetry" of the work were daily increasing, that it would be "a story wild enough I assure you & with a meaning too." Murray might (and did) think it unwise to follow two books for which he had claimed that they were entirely "truthful" with "an acknowledged *romance*," but Melville, becoming himself a Romantic hero, scorned to think in terms of dark

Published in *The Virginia Quarterly Review*, vol. XXIX (Autumn 1953), pp. 556-575.

calculation: "Instincts are prophetic, & better than acquired wisdom." Instincts, in the romance, live in the heart, that organ which, fighting against the head, led Ivanhoes through the mazes of Rebeccas to the security of monogamous Rowenas.

Scott sharply distinguished the romance from the "novel" (as written by Jane Austen), and his dicta can be extracted from Melville's plots as easily as from his own. The final wedding bells proclaimed not so much a marriage as a victory of nature over culture, of simplicity over complexity, of country over city. In America, the romance vindicated nature's nation, land of Natty Bumppo, against the artificiality of Europe. Melville was prisoner of the theme no less than Cooper, for to an awareness of it Cooper "awakned" him.

Yet we know that Melville, unlike Cooper, employed the pattern of the romance to explode the Romantic thesis. The inner history of his mind, from 1846 to 1852, seems to be a mounting loathing of his own premises, until at last he is flagrantly abusing those very devices by which other romancers attained proper endings. *Pierre* thus appears to be the climax of satanic rebellion; because *Moby-Dick* marks a stage halfway between *Mardi* and *Pierre,* it rises far enough out of the formula to be free of the stereotype, and yet is not so far gone into conceptualism as to become a rigidified tract: hence, on this assumption, its success.

I think this a superficial view, but there are advantages in considering even *Moby-Dick* in the light of contemporaneous fashions. Such an examination may put a brake upon what has become the scandal of Melville scholarship; Elmer Stoll attacks devisers of "symbolic" interpretations, and quotes T. S. Eliot: "Our critics are often interested in extracting something from their subject which is not fairly in it." But are we more likely to reach what Stoll calls "adequate appreciation of the story" by following those later researchers, already dubbed the "externalists," who construct so prosy a biography of Melville as to show indubitably that the poor man could never have written an imaginative book? I am wary of becoming overhistorical, but we need help in understanding how Melville's masks became pasteboard; no reader can be let off the duty of striking through them with whatever harpoon he can handle, if only one of the period.

Historians too seldom ask what conventions really mean in the life of a culture. It is easy to lament that youthful writers reproduce the Hemingway hero according to specifications, but he does exist and he is a symptom—if you will, a "symbol"—of our epoch. The Byronic hero— Manfred, Cooper's Pilot, Metamora as Forrest played him, or Captain Ahab—was not just a stock or slick character. Textbooks treat him as a mere vogue; to those for whom he was authentic he was the heroic natural man at odds with the unnatural, with civilization, with convention, with hardness of heart. He destroyed himself in an unequal combat, which the Ivanhoes of this world shrewdly evaded.

Today the rivalry of the blonde and dark heroines seems Hollywood type-casting, but then it posed the issue of the nineteenth century. Wherefore readers breathed sighs of relief when the gloom concluded with wedding bells—for the blonde. She was Wordsworth's Lucy, and also Melville's; Bryant had her born in forest shadow instead of growing in sun and shower, but even when Americanized her infant eye met only green boughs and glimpses of the sky. She was nature against city, moribund convention, dull fact, pedantry, vice, impurity of blood, and she guaranteed the future of the race. In America, she also stood, hardly feeling the burden, for the new nation against Europe, and so contended against the brunette, who always turned out to pertain to the head. The blonde's virtue had to be jealously guarded; the dark heroine might be, often was, debauched. Considering what a stake mankind had in the contest, what it meant to the nation, we may exclaim of all romances as did Melville upon his own, "Wonder ye then at the fiery hunt?"

Contemporaneous reviewers are not final judges, but even when stupid they appeal to rubrics within which the artist worked. Fitz-James O'Brien was obviously not up to divining Melville, but he wholeheartedly accepted the assumptions of the romance. He wrote upon Melville in *Putnam's Monthly Magazine* for February 1853, and again in April 1857; he acknowledged that Melville was a "genius"—magic word in all romances —and that genius has its royal rights, but Melville's progression seemed to him a perverse, a wanton surrender of natural genius to the unnatural enemy. *Typee* was "healthy," *Omoo* "nearly so," *Mardi* was "excusable wildness," but *Moby-Dick* and even more *Pierre* were "inexcusable insanity." Let Melville "stay his step in time," was the advice of 1853, for "he totters on the edge of a precipice." In 1857 O'Brien mourned that this advice had not been taken; Melville was an example of the pernicious effect of "the metaphysical tendencies which belong so eminently to the American's mind." By indulgence "in a trick of metaphysical and morbid meditations" (activity of the head), he "has perverted his fine mind from its healthy productive tendencies" (the heart). The prescriptions of the romance were available: "We desire him to give up metaphysics and take to nature."

O'Brien could see that Melville, unlike Poe, had not actually renounced nature; all the more reason, he said, why we should know what Melville did "mean" in *Moby-Dick*. "He carried us floundering after his great white whale, through all manner of scenes, and all hints of company— now perfectly exhausted with fatigue and deafened with many words whereof we understood no syllable, and then suddenly refreshed with a brisk sea breeze and a touch of nature kindling as the dawn." O'Brien, generous to a fault, insisted that Melville was basically orthodox: "Nature says to Herman Melville" that he should report what he has seen "in a warm, quick, nervous style, and bring the realities of life and man before your readers in such a way that they shall know your mind without calling on you to speak it." There was the wonderful thing about the romance, that it did not have to speak its moral; the blonde defeated the dark, and wedding bells rang out.

Twenty years earlier Emerson preached what many called infidelity when he said that nature is "to us, the present expositor of the divine mind." Henry Thoreau, appearing under Emerson's imprimatur, deduced that "there is neither harm nor disappointment in the natural world. . . . The universe will bear the closest inspection." Consequently, when he announced, "Let us not underrate the value of a fact; it will one day flower in a truth," ought not men like O'Brien agree?

Melville tried to explain to Murray that the writing of *Mardi* was a fact flowering into truth: "It opens like a true narrative—like 'Omoo' for example, on ship board—the romance & poetry of the thing thence grow continuly." But, he added, it will thus have a "meaning." His explanation was that his audience, although supposedly familiar with the conception of natural truthfulness, had goaded him to this fatal step by accusing him of being "a romancer in disguise." All right, he would put the question to nature. Short as was the first divergence, Melville was conscious enough of the issue to recognize the chasm: "I have long thought that Polynisia furnished a great deal of rich poetical material that has never been empl[o]yed hitherto in works of fancy." But to employ nature is not to grow in sun and rain, but to impose a design of the head upon it. "Truth is mighty & will prevail," Melville cried to a dismayed Murray, "& shall & must."

So O'Brien saw the root of the problem: while nature had given the good counsel, "Obstinate cultivation rejoins: 'No! You shall dissect and divide; you shall cauterize and confound; you shall amaze and electrify: you shall be as grotesquely terrible as Callot, as subtly profound as Balzac, as formidably satirical as Rabelais.' " The first deviation of *Mardi* toward the insidious conception of a romance full of "meaning" led irresistibly to that "impossible and un-understandable creature," *Pierre*. The only hope, said O'Brien and the dominant spirit of the age, would be a frantic scramble back to nature, to romances that tell themselves and end with wedding bells. However, Melville was so far gone, it might already be too late.

We are astonished that the American mind in the days of President Millard Fillmore was reputed to be "metaphysical," supposed to be corrupted by a "love of antic and extravagant speculation, the fearlessness of intellectual consequences, and the passion for intellectual legislation." But virtually all such pronouncements spring from a deep, a pervasive fear; they are anxious previsions of that terrifyingly ruthless march of the peoples across the continent which De Tocqueville found so awesome, of obstinate culture invading the pristine natural simplicity. And culture exerted a baneful fascination, if only because it accused natural America of boorishness and provinciality. Cooper's work, from the chapter in *The Pioneers* on the slaughter of the pigeons to the end, is a threnody on the succumbing of the wilderness to the advance of civilization. He would be the last to flee in person before it, and certainly the last to retreat to Walden Pond, but he sent Natty Bumppo into the sunset, grieving as might one who had seen the blonde heroine ravished. So there was a certain bravado in yielding to the inevitable, a temptation to out-Byron Byron. There was an irresistible excitement in adventuring into the treacherous region of meaning, of cutting one's ties to nature and unawareness.

Furthermore, we must remember that those apostles of nature who accused the American mind of being metaphysical and analytic had, as they thought, one supreme example: Emerson. He and his followers presented themselves to their countrymen not as recipients of an impulse from the vernal wood, but as diseased victims of a fearlessness of intellectual consequences. The young men, said Emerson, "were born with knives in their brains, a tendency to introversion, self-dissection, anatomizing of motives." He dared to salute those vigorous souls who "conceive a disgust at the indigence of nature: Rousseau, Mirabeau, Charles Fox, Napoleon, Byron," and then horrified all good Americans by continuing, "I could easily add names nearer home." He seemed positively to glory in these "raging riders, who drive their steeds so hard, in the violence of living to forget its illusion: they would know the worst, and tread the floors of hell." To those who had staked their lives and the country's welfare upon the power of nature to heal and conserve, Emerson was a fiendish Enceladus leading an analytical assault upon the citadel of nature.

The easiest way for defenders of the citadel to repulse these raging riders was to heap upon them the ridicule of being "German." Duyckinck had ready to hand a critical scheme by which to explain away the un-American extravagances of *Moby-Dick:* like *Mardi,* it appears under a "double character." Both are simultaneously "romantic fictions" and also "statements of absolute fact." It was then easy to explain why a young writer was misled into this doubleness: "Something of a parallel may be found in Jean Paul's German tales." The German method called for "realities of some kinds at bottom, but veiled in all sorts of poetical incidents and expressions." Duyckinck had no difficulty in seeing "a bit of German melodrama" in Ahab as the Faust of the quarter-deck, while Queequeg, the renegades, and castaways were Walpurgis Nacht revelers in the forecastle. He seemed to be trying to persuade readers to concentrate on the statements of fact and the realities at bottom, upon the natural, but he ended lamely that *Moby-Dick* was "an allegory on the banks of the Nile."

Other reviewers were less restrained by friendship. The chorus commenced upon *Mardi:* "An overstraining after anti-thesis and Carlyleism," said *The Albion;* the disillusioned transcendentalist, George Ripley, called it "A monstrous compound of Carlyle, Jean-Paul, and Sterne." In June 1849 Melville confessed to Richard Bentley that "the metaphysical ingredients" had justifiably repelled readers, but promised, full of repentance, that the next book would have "no metaphysics, no conic-sections, nothing but cakes & ale." Reviewers at once recognized in "Redburn" a return to sanity. "Indebted less for its interest to the regions of the fantastical and the ideal, than to the more intelligible domain of the actual and real," said *Bentley's Miscellany. The Athenaeum* found it a welcome relief "in a writer who has hitherto gone on *crescendo* in the way of mysteries and madnesses of many kinds."

But alas! "Redburn" was only a momentary check. In 1857 O'Brien hoped that Melville might come home from "the Old World" ready "to give us pictures of life and reality." He did not know that in 1849 Melville had left America on a quest for reality, but had been regaled all across the Atlantic by the "high German metaphysics" of his friend George Adler, a vigorous rider "on the German horse." On that trip or soon thereafter Melville read Chateaubriand and Rousseau—engenderers of the German madness. In February 1850 he borrowed from Duyckinck Richter's *Flower, Fruit & Thorn Pieces,* and in the summer, along with Thoreau's *Week,* Carlyle's *German Romances.* A little of this goes a long way.

So the chorus swelled over *Moby-Dick* and became strident—with both fear and hatred—over *Pierre*: these were German affectations. "A species of New York Werther, having all the absurdities and none of the beauties of Goethe's juvenile indiscretion." "A repulsive, unnatural and indecent plot [the string of adjectives is revealing], a style disfigured by every paltry affectation of the worst German school, and ideas perfectly unparalleled for earnest absurdity." A writer in the London *Leader* was less skittish about the German contagion, and so did damage to Melville's reputation in America by saying that he and Hawthorne were carrying on the work of German romancers. "To move a horror skillfully, with something of the earnest faith in the Unseen, and with weird imagery to shape those phantasms so vividly that the most incredulous mind is hushed, absorbed—to do this no European pen has apparently any longer the power—to do this American literature is without a rival. What *romance* writer can be named with Hawthorne? Who knows the horrors of the seas like Herman Melville?" Well-meaning commendation could hardly have come at a worse time, or in worse form.

I am not saying that Melville and Emerson have a common source in German Romanticism. What links Melville with Emerson is not that they necessarily acquired anything from the "high German metaphysics," but that they were both aware of a configuration of ideas which, popularly identified with Germany, challenged the regnant ethic and aesthetic of nature. Both he and Emerson knew that this Devil's child could not be silenced by the conventions of the ordinary romance; Emerson therefore gave over reading romances as a waste of time, but Melville had no recourse but to write romances that would destroy romance.

Poe memorably declared, "Terror is not of Germany but of the soul." He would not have had to say this had he not known that American audiences held terror and Germany to be synonymous—and so both foreign to America. Emerson made the point more laboriously but more cogently in 1848:

> How impossible to find Germany! Our young men went to the Rhine to find the genius which had charmed them, and it was not there. They hunted it in Heidelberg, in Göttingen, in Halle, in Berlin; no one knew where it was; from Vienna to the frontier, it was not found, and they very slowly and mournfully learned, that in the speaking it had escaped, and as it had charmed them in Boston, they must return and look for it there.

Thoreau, who knew this much from the beginning, went to Walden, prepared, if he found life mean, to publish its meanness. Melville lived in New York, had a wife and family, a living to get, and only the romance to publish.

On April 16, 1852, Melville tried to convince Bentley that his new book would have novelty—and be calculated for popularity—"being a regular romance, with a mysterious plot to it, & stirring passions at work, and withall, representing a new & elevated aspect of American life." Cooper might so have described *The Spy* or Simms *The Yemassee,* but again, their romances spoke for nature against civilization without straining to be "new & elevated." A writer who talked in this analytical vein might be trying to appear a regular fellow, but he was clearly far gone with the German disease.

German literature gave to the word "titan" a peculiar and lurid connotation; as the character explains himself in Jean Paul's *Titan,* "I would calculate and dissect from very pride; whatever came of it I would abide, and I should be ashamed to be unhappy about it. If life, like the olive, is a bitter fruit, then grasp both with the press, and they will afford the sweetest oil." A titan is capable of experiencing a violent storm at sea while overhead the sun looks on in majestic tranquility; out of nature he extracts the unnatural injunction: "So be thou! The heart is the storm; self is the heaven." We know the American titan:

> I own thy speechless, placeless power; but to the last gasp of my earthquake life will dispute its unconditional, unintegral mastery in me. In the midst of the personified impersonal, a personality stands here. Though but a point at best; whencesoe'er I came; wheresoe'er I go; yet while I earthly live, the queenly personality lives in me, and feels her royal rights.

This did not need, in order to be written, familiarity with Richter; as Emerson said, seekers after the German genius had to come home. There were certain stylistic manifestations which proclaimed to all the world that the thing had been found; these had been succinctly enumerated by Carlyle:

Figures without limit: indeed, the whole is one tissue of metaphors, and similes, and allusions to all the provinces of Earth, Sea and Air; interlaced with epigrammatic breaks, vehement bursts, or sardonic turns, interjections, quips, puns, and even oaths! A perfect Indian jungle it seems; a boundless, unparalleled imbroglio; nothing on all sides but darkness, dissonance, confusion worse confounded!

Initiated readers could hardly fail to recognize that Melville progressively emulated this Teutonic formula. American readers also knew that it was not a formula on which to bring up husbands-to-be of the blonde heroine.

Again let us remind ourselves that Emerson struck these readers, at first, as an unnatural imbroglio. In those days, Bryant was later to recall, "a very serious alarm was manifested lest the literature of our own language should become distempered and spoiled by the contagion which threatened it from Germany." Emerson said that a writer should give not cause and effect, but a cause and then an effect thrice removed; was not this to create on all sides dissonance and confusion? He said that the modern poet is no longer content to cry, "Fair hangs the apple from the rock," but must also demand, "What is the apple to me?" This, he explained, quieting no apprehensions, "is called subjectiveness, as the eye is withdrawn from the object and fixed on the subject or mind." He said this just when Bryant, the Hudson River painters, Cooper, and a myriad romancers had persuaded the American public that natural impulses translate themselves into the innate piety and chivalry of Natty Bumppo, that He who guides a waterfowl will guide instinctive steps aright.

Emerson's disciples—Jones Very, Margaret Fuller, Henry Thoreau—did nothing to allay suspicion. Emerson said that the "Genius" of the German nation, "spreading from the poetic into the scientific, religious and philosophical domains, has made theirs now at last the paramount intellectual influence of the world, reacting with great energy on England and America," and then publicly advertised that if he was the Devil's child, he would live from the Devil. As his first comments on Emerson show, Melville was cautious; he would hang himself, not oscillate in anybody's rainbow. Transcendentalism seemed obtuse to the problem of the duel between blonde and brunette—possibly because transcendentalists knew little about women. Still, they made immense sense on one theme of the romances, on the opposition of nature to the city. Their lingo might be a little weird compared with the speech of Bryant or the devices of Cooper, but here it was spelled out:

The City delights in the Understanding. It is made up of finites: short, sharp, mathematical lines, all calculable. It is full of varieties, of successions, of contrivances. The country, on the contrary, offers an unbroken horizon, the monotony of an endless road, of vast uniform plains, of distant mountains, the melancholy of uniform and infinite vegetation; the objects on the road are few and worthless, the eye is invited to the horizon and the clouds. It is the school of Reason.

Hence it is not surprising that Emerson, on the alert to record the few and worthless objects that invite the eye to the horizon, listened in his coach on February 19, 1834, to the talk of a sailor, and so, on reaching home, told his *Journal* about a giant whale known as Old Tom, "who rushed upon the boats which attacked him, and crushed the boats to small chips in his jaws." As Thoreau was soon to say, a fact will one day flower into a truth. Mr. Jay Leyda further reminds us that on May 10, 1847, while *Omoo* was a best-seller, Emerson wrote from Nantucket the tale of a sperm whale who twice charged with full speed against the *Essex* and sunk her in a few minutes.

Emerson did not moralize upon these leviathans. He disposed of the "noble doubt" of Immanuel Kant by asserting that the laws of nature answer to those of mind as image to the glass; he would not be left in "the splendid labyrinth" of his perceptions, and therefore declared nature not "foreign." The young Thoreau, secure in this assurance, was willing to risk everything upon the certainty that there is nothing in the closest of inspections which nature cannot safely bear. In the conduct of his own life and mind, Emerson observed a measure of prudence, but he did say, "The only way into nature is to enact our best insight."

Modern research has surprisingly discovered that much of *Typee* is "factual," but even so, we don't take it for mere autobiography. It is a flight from civilization, and is saturated with Cooper; it was a success as much because the boy confirmed accepted conventions as because the scene was exotic. The age of Cooper and Scott found nothing more as it should be than that the beauty of nature should exert "a soothing influence upon my mind," that the "tranquilizing influences of beautiful scenery" should be a "consolation," that a flight to the primitive should confirm the superiority of the natural Reason over the civilized Understanding.

A gentleman in Typee could bring up a family with less anxiety and toil than he expends in striking a light; a "poor European artisan," though he has ignition matches, is at his wits' end to provide food for his children. Life in Typee, "surrounded by all the luxurious provisions of nature," was less intellectual than life in Europe, but less "self-incomplacent." Fayaway was no problem to civilized readers: she was a Marquesan Lucy, although few were astute enough to notice that she was a brunette.

Melville possibly exaggerated, but when he said, "Until I was twenty-five I had no development at all," we take him to mean that when he started writing he began to give close inspection to the doctrines to which Cooper had already "awakned" him. "From my twenty-fifth year I date my life." In February of 1849 he wrote Duyckinck that up to then he had only glanced at one book of Emerson's and that, despite the usual reports, the man was "quite intelligible." In these months (*Mardi* was appearing) he was reading Shakespeare, commenting on a passage in *King Lear*, "The infernal nature has a valor often denied to innocence." On March 3 he wrote upon Emerson, "Any fish can swim near the surface, but it takes a great whale to go down stairs five miles or more." Even as he was scribbling in his Shakespeare that "this Shakespeare was not a frank man to the uttermost," and was posing the histrionic question, "Who in this intolerant universe is, or can be?"—even then he refused to oscillate in Emerson's rainbow, preferring "rather to hang myself in mine own halter than swing in any other man's swing." Self-reliance, being a function of "Reason," might be an alien in the city, but to New York Melville had returned. "I would to God Shakespeare had lived & promenaded in Broadway." Innocence among rural glades might be altogether admirable, but did it have valor? Was not some dissociation from nature required, in the name of naturalness, in order that nature be inspected? Would not this require a disseverance by the writer from the conventions he accepted (those of the romance), and a resort to direct address? "I should not talk so much about myself if there were anybody else whom I knew so well," began Henry Thoreau. "Call me Ishmael," Moby-Dick commenced. By mock-heroic candor could be conveyed an inability to accept at face value, as in every opening chapter a Cooper or Simms did, the supposedly natural frame within which the narrative would flow to a proper ending.

In this perspective, the conclusion of Mardi is indeed the turning point in Melville's artistry. He positively used the romance to assert the ambiguity of nature. The blonde Yillah is lost in the dark Hautia: "It will show thee, Taji, that the maidens of Hautia are all Yillahs. . . . In some one of her black-eyed maids, the blue-eyed One was transformed." The machinery creaks, the writing is melodramatic, but Taji is in a labyrinth. "From side to side, in frenzy, I turned; but in all those cold, mystical eyes, saw not the warm ray that I sought."

We pardon the fustian of Mardi because it points ahead to Moby-Dick, but we must study Pierre in order to look backwards. In exasperation Melville let go at those ideologues with whom the regular romance was officially at war: "Plato, and Spinoza, and Goethe, and many more belong to this guild of self-imposters, with a preposterous rabble of Muggletonian Scots and Yankees, whose vile brogue still the more bespeaks the stripedness of their Greek or German Neoplatonical originals." The jibe is certainly directed toward Emerson; the book sneers at "amiable philosophers of either the 'Compensation' or 'Optimist' School." It heaps insult upon injury by calling utilitarians the better transcendentalists, because they translate maxims into deed, whereas transcendentalists treat their transcendentals as "but theoretic and inactive, and therefore harmless."

One is tempted, thus, to read Pierre as simply a critique of transcendentalism. It is a case history of a mind enacting its best insight, to find that by obeying the categorical imperative it has destroyed the idea of nature as "her own ever-sweet interpreter," and is left with "the mere supplier of that cunning alphabet, whereby selecting and combining as he pleases, each man reads his own peculiar mind and mood." Nature will not bear inspection; the natural theology of transcendentalism is a monstrous ambiguity: "All the world, and every misconceivedly common and prosaic thing in it, was steeped a million fathoms in a mysteriousness wholly hopeless of solution." Yes, this makes the book a blast against the shallowness and smugness of transcendentalism—or seems to, until we remember that it is not a treatise; it is a "romance."

All this is not the full story, or even a profound one. There was, we might note, available to him a frame of reference within which he could have redeemed, or else justified the condemnation of, Ahab and Pierre; he could have judged them guilty of the sin of pride. "Why," cries Starbuck, "why should any one give chase to that hated fish?" But neither in *Moby-Dick* nor in *Pierre* is there any "escape" or "retreat" into Christianity.

There is a school which interprets Melville as bitterly anti-Christian, covertly attacking Jehovah as a demon. Another answers this by describing a man trying to make a living. Both these, and many others, identify Melville with his characters, and all solemnly forget that he wrote romances. His terms are those of the romance, not of Calvin. The fundamental premises, those of Scott, Cooper, Byron, Rousseau, and that "inconceivable coxcomb of a Goethe," are those that lead Ahab and Pierre to destruction; but they are never declared, by Melville the author, to be false. They are not so reassuring as in the compensation or optimist versions, but they are the same; they are, dare I say, precisely those of transcendentalism?

Research has recovered a volume of Emerson's *Essays* that Melville read in 1862 and *The Conduct of Life* that he bought in 1870. His markings may, of course, throw no light on the creative years. Sometimes he applauds the pontifical Emerson with "Nothing can be truer or better said," or simply, "True & admirable! Bravo!" The passages he so approves seem to be scored mainly for their relevance to his own desperate plight; the annotations tell more about his self-pity than about his grasp of Emerson. (What he finds true and never better said is Emerson's assertion that man learns humanity by humiliations, defects, loss of sympathy, and "gulfs of disparity.") There is also dissent: Emerson says that the sailor who buffets the storm all day finds his health renew itself as a vigorous pulse under the sleet; Melville scrawls: "To one who has weathered Cape Horn as a common sailor what stuff all this is." Yet in these marginalia there is nothing of the radical break we might expect—that is, if we take *Pierre* too naïvely. The nearest Melville comes to repudiation in 1862 is revealing: "His gross and astonishing errors & illusions spring from a self-conceit so intensely intellectual and calm that a first one hesitates to call it by its right name." A few pages later, he calls it by the right name: Emerson's errors proceed "from a defect in the region of the heart." Ten years before, Pierre was represented as plunging into folly by becoming "the heart's annointed," and the book was judged a failure because the author, by imposing meaning upon it, tried to write a romance out of his head instead of out of his heart!

No, Melville never got free of the incubus of Emerson. He will object, when reading "Spiritual Laws," to the dictum that artists who lived a life of pleasure deteriorated, and cite Titian and Byron, but he rallies to Emerson's side: "He keeps nobly on, for all that." Oddly enough, the London *Leader,* when hailing him along with Hawthorne, also linked with them Emerson as making up the "German Americans." *La Revue des Deux Mondes* in February 1853 surmised astutely that Melville like Hawthorne was imbued, "peut-être plus qu'il ne faudrait, de la prestigieuse philosophie dont Emerson est l'apôtre inspiré." In 1866, Colonel Henry Gansevoort, who like many in the family was by this time annoyed with Cousin Herman, praised what he could of *Battle-Pieces* but regretted that "he has so much of Emerson & transcendentalism in his writing that it never will really touch the common heart." Touching the common heart was exactly what the romance was designed to do, as long as transcendentalism did not seduce it into confusing the symbolism of the blonde and the brunette.

In *Pierre* explicitly (in *Moby-Dick* implicitly), the issue lies not between heaven and hell but between country and city. "The pavements, Isabel," cries Pierre, "this is the town." Nature's simple Delly chimes in like an echo: "It feels not so soft as the green sward, Master Pierre," requiring the young master to explain, "The buried hearts of some dead citizens have perhaps come to the surface." "Think'st thou, Pierre, the time will ever come when all the earth shall be paved?" Pierre's whole soul is in the answer, "Thank God, that never can be!" In the depths of degradation, the dupe of the heart is never blamed; not "practical unreason" is at fault, but only the old enemy of transcendentalism: "Civilization, Philosophy, Ideal Virtue! behold your victim!"

The point is tediously belabored. "Among the evils of foreign travel" is that it "dislodges some of the finest feelings of the home-born nature." When city-bred and European-cultured Glen Stanly expels his country cousin from the glittering parlor, he coolly patters on to another returned traveler, "The statues you saw in the Louvre are not to be mentioned with those in Florence and Rome. . . ." Like Ahab, Pierre was cradled in nature, "by scenery whose uncommon loveliness was the perfect mold of a delicate and poetic mind." "Nature intended a rare and original development in Pierre," who, prompted by the natural heart and in defiance of the iconography, takes the side against society of his natural sister, the dark Isabel. Utter reversal of the formula follows fast thereafter. The blonde Lucy, instead of waiting amid nature like Rowena for the return of Ivanhoe, *pursues* him to the city! Enacting the best insight leads not deeper into nature, but to that most artificial of rituals, an art gallery; there are the shattering portraits, the Cenci of Guido, which proves that profanation can double-hood "so sweetly and seraphically *blond* a being," and "The Stranger," which proclaims that the intuition of the heart was deceptive. The dark heroine proves (Melville had said that this would be a "regular" romance) to be a creature with "an unequivocal aspect of foreignness, of Europeanism."

But the point is never that the fiery quest is wrong—not even in the Plinlimmon pamphlet, which deceives those who do not understand what Carlyle meant by the boundless imbroglio. Melville could see that the tendency of those elements which the romance maintained, superficially, along with transcendentalism was bound, if allowed full scope, to negate the romance. In the process of destruction, he employed that same confidence in the ability of the mind to give laws to nature—to impose a plot upon it—which Emerson called the knife in the brain but which the orthodox said was an illicit importation from Germany. Melville, "awakened" by Cooper, understood the meaning for his age of the Romantic conventions, but also perceived that the intellectual assumptions were so linked with contrary propensities that the form itself was self-consuming.

Emerson could allow to lie side-by-side generalizations which seemed not to contradict each other. He would say that Napoleon did not value himself on his own opinionativeness and so never waged war with nature; then he would also say, "We may, therefore, safely study the mind in nature, because we cannot steadily gaze on it in the mind." In flat prose, there was no way to test the congruity of these statements. A disbeliever might insist that the two were mutually exclusive (in which case virtuous expediency, according to Plinlimmon, would become the rule of conduct), or else nature should again be viewed as the handiwork of God, inaccessible to man (in which case prayer would be man's only resort). But in the creatures of romance, Ahab and the Whale, Pierre and the ambiguous maidens, it would be possible to give a more accurate diagnosis of the eternal tension between the advices of nature and of the mind. There might come disaster or the collapse of form, but there would be no surrender. Melville alone could confront this ambiguity, for he alone had memories of tropical maidens who, authentic children of nature, exhibited "soft and light blue eyes, with an extremely fair complexion, vailed by funereally jetty hair."

Moby-Dick and *Pierre* are not Christian works, but they have more urgent business to perform than feuding with the Christian God. They do not yield to temptation, they confront a challenge. Man in nature may meekly accept the universe, but only if he pretends that the dark European is a foreigner against whom he is quarantined, or at least protected. But to embrace her, whatever the risk, even unto the realm of fancy—would not this be the most strenuous enactment of the transcendental imperative? Then would the hero prove himself, so long as he did not fear or fawn, so long as he would never repent. In the two books there is compassion, but there is no intercession, and no forgiveness. The fundamental terms are not God and man, but man in nature. In the vulgar use of the word they are "tragic," but in the proper meaning they reject tragedy. They are, to the end, implacably, defiantly, unrepentantly, transcendental.

THE ROMANTIC DILEMMA IN AMERICAN
NATIONALISM AND THE CONCEPT
OF NATURE

On MAY 8, 1847, *The Literary World*—the newly founded vehicle in New York City for the program of "nativist" literature—reviewed an exhibition at the National Academy. The magazine had just undergone an editorial revolution, and the new management was endeavoring to tone down the strident nationalism of the first few issues; still, the exuberant patriotism of the reviewer could not be restrained, for he had just beheld two exciting landscapes of Staten Island painted by J. F. Cropsey.

This artist, said the reviewer, must be ranked along with the acknowledged masters, Thomas Cole and Asher Durand—and this was high praise in 1847. And as do these masters, young Cropsey illustrates and vindicates the high and sacred mission of the American painter:

> The axe of civilization is busy with our old forests, and artisan ingenuity is fast sweeping away the relics of our national infancy. What were once the wild and picturesque haunts of the Red Man, and where the wild deer roamed in freedom, are becoming the abodes of commerce and the seats of manufactures. Our inland lakes, once sheltered and secluded in the midst of noble forests, are now laid bare and covered with busy craft; and even the primordial hills, once bristling with shaggy pine and hemlock, like old Titans as they were, are being shorn of their locks, and left to blister in cold nakedness in the sun. 'The aged hemlocks, through whose branches have whistled the winds of a hundred winters,' are losing their identity, and made to figure in the shape of deal boards and rafters for unsightly structures on bare commons, ornamented with a few peaked poplars, pointing like fingerposts to the sky. Yankee enterprise has little sympathy with the picturesque, and it behooves our artists to rescue from its grasp the little that is left, before it is for ever too late.

Students of the history of art recognize in this passage a doctrine that had, by 1847, become conventional among landscape painters in Europe, England, and America: that of a fundamental opposition of nature to civilization, with the assumption that all virtue, repose, dignity are on the side of "Nature"—spelled with a capital and referred to as feminine—against the ugliness, squalor and confusion of civilization, for which the pronoun was simply "it." However, though this passage proceeds from a

Published in the *Harvard Theological Review*, vol. XLVIII, no. 4 (October 1955), pp. 239-53.

premise as familiar in Dusseldorf as in New York, still it takes the form of an exhortation that is seldom, if ever, encountered in the criticism of Europe. In America the artist has a calling above and beyond an accurate reporting of scenery: he must work fast, for in America Nature is going down in swift and inexorable defeat. She is being defaced, conquered—actually ravished. Civilization is leading us into a horrible future, filled with unsightly structures, resounding with the din of enterprise. All too soon we shall become like Europe. In the old world artists may indeed paint only such "garden landscapes" as are dotted here and there in a setting that man has mastered; but our noble Hudson and "the wild witchery of our unpolluted inland lakes and streams," this Nature is not man's but "GOD'S." American artists return from Europe, "their hands cramped with mannerism, and their minds belittled and debauched by the artificial stimulants of second-hand and second-rate creations." This was what America must resist, debauching artificiality. Yet if history is so irresistibly carrying the defiling axe of civilization into our sublime wilderness, will it not be merely a matter of time—no matter how furiously our Coles, Durands, and Cropseys, our poets and novelists, strive to fix the fleeting moment of primitive grandeur—before we too shall be cramped into mannerism, before our minds shall be debauched by artificial stimuli?

The reader may object that I am talking nonsense. This was the expanding, prospering, booming America of the 1840's; here, if ever in the annals of man, was an era of optimism, with a vision of limitless possibilities, with faith in a boundless future. There was indeed some fear that the strife of North and South might wreck the chariot of progress, but the more that threat loomed the more enthusiastically the nation shouted the prospects of wealth and prosperity, if only in order to show the folly of allowing politics to spoil the golden opportunity. Dickens and other foreign visitors report a republic constantly flinging into their faces preposterous vaunts about what it would shortly become, and then steadily making good its wildest boasts. Surely this society was not wracked by a secret, hidden horror that its gigantic exertion would end only in some nightmare of debauchery called "civilization"?

The most cursory survey of the period does indeed display a seemingly untroubled assurance about the great civilization America was hewing out of the wilderness. This faith, with its corollaries of belief in progress and republican institutions, might be called the "official" faith of the United States. It was primarily an inheritance from the eighteenth century: back in 1758, the almanac-maker, Nathaniel Ames, writing from Dedham, Massachusetts, dreamed that within two hundred years arts and sciences would transform nature "in their Tour from Hence over the Appalacian Mountains to the Western Ocean," and that vast quarries of rocks would be piled into cities. On the whole, despite the Jeffersonians' distrust of cities, I think it fair to say that the founders had no qualms about doing harm to nature by thrusting civilization upon it. They reasoned in terms of wealth, comfort, amenities, power, in terms which we may conveniently call, though they had not been derived from Bentham, "utilitarian."

Now in 1840, in 1850, the mighty tread of American civilization was heard throughout the Ohio Valley, across the Mississippi, and the advanced guard was rushing into California. But the astonishing fact about this gigantic material thrust of the early nineteenth century is how few Americans would any longer venture, aside from their boasts, to explain, let alone to justify, the expansion of civilization in any language that could remotely be called that of utility. The most utilitarian conquest known to history had somehow to be viewed not as inspired by a calculus of rising land values and investments but (despite the orgies of speculation) as an immense exertion of the spirit. Those who made articulate the meaning of this drama found their frames of reference not in political economy but in Scott and Byron, in visions of "sublimity." The more rapidly, the more voraciously, the primordial forest was felled, the more desperately poets and painters—and also preachers—strove to identify the unique personality of this republic with the virtues of pristine and untarnished, of "Romantic," Nature.

We need little ingenuity to perceive that behind this virtually universal American hostility to the ethic of utilitarian calculation lies a religious mood—one that seventeenth-century Puritanism would not have understood, and which was as foreign, let us say, to the evangelicalism of Whitefield as to the common sense of Franklin. We note, first of all, that this aversion to the pleasure-pain philosophy became most pronounced in those countries or circles in which a vigorous Christian spirit was alive. In the long run, a host of the emotions excited in the era we call Romantic were mobilized into a *cri du coeur* against Gradgrind. A host of nameless magazine writers uttered it on the plane of dripping sentiment, of patriotic or lachrymose verse, but on higher levels the poet Bryant, the novelists Cooper and Simms, the painters Durand and Cole—and on still more rarefied heights the philosopher Emerson—denounced or lamented the march of civilization. In various ways—not often agreeing among themselves—they identified the health, the very personality, of America with Nature, and therefore set it in opposition to the concepts of the city, the railroad, the steamboat. This definition of the fundamental issue of life in America became that around which Thoreau, Melville, and Whitman organized their peculiar expression. They (along with the more superficial) present us with the problem of American self-recognition as being essentially an irreconcilable opposition between Nature and civilization—which is to say, between forest and town, spontaneity and calculation, heart and head, the unconscious and the self-conscious, the innocent and the debauched. We are all heirs of Natty Bumppo, and cannot escape our heritage. William Faulkner, notably in "The Bear," is only the most dramatic of recent reminders.

Now, in this epoch, American Protestants were especially hostile to utilitarianism, even to the conciliatory form promulgated by John Stuart Mill. In England there were elements in the general situation which supported him, which could rally to his side a few sensitive and intelligent Christians. Sensitive and intelligent Christians in America were so constantly distressed by the charge that America was utterly given over to the most brutal utilitarianism that they in effect conspired to prevent the appearance of an American Mill. The more their consciences accused them of surrendering historic Christian concerns to the rush of material prosperity, the more they insisted that inwardly this busy people live entirely by sentiment. A review of the gift-books and annuals of the 1830's and 1840's—if one can bring himself to it—will tell how, at that pitch of vulgarity, the image of America as tender, tearful, dreaming noble thoughts, luxuriating in moonlit vistas, was constructed. These works were produced in huge numbers for the predominant middle class—if the term be admissible; they reposed on the parlor tables of wives whose husbands spent all day at the office pushing the nation on its colossal course of empire. But the more sophisticated or learned disclaimers of utility said about the same thing. An organ of Episcopalian scholarship, *The New York Review,* declared, for instance, in 1837 that utilitarianism is a "sordid philosophy." And why? Because it teaches that virtue is the creature of the brain, whereas true righteousness is "the prompt impulse of the heart." Yet this review, with no awareness of inconsistency, was at the same time rigorously preaching that because of the fall of Adam the impulses of the natural heart are suspect!

There is one truism about the early nineteenth century which cannot too often be repeated: in one fashion or another, various religious interests, aroused against the Enlightenment, allied themselves with forces we lump together as "Romantic." In England the Established Church was surprised, and momentarily bewildered, to discover that Scott, Wordsworth, and Coleridge started new blood pulsating through its veins, expelling the noxious humors of indifference, deism, and skepticism. At Oxford, Romantic religiosity indeed swung so far to the other extreme that it carried Newman all the way to Rome. (His conversion so shattered the ranks of Episcopalian naturalists in America that *The New York Review,* finding itself unable to speak for a united body, had to discontinue.) On the Continent there appeared a Romantic Catholicism which could afford not to answer but to disregard the *philosophes* as being no longer relevant. However, this ecstasy of Romantic piety did not always require institutions; it could amount simply to a passionate assertion against the Age of Reason. Carlyle and Chateaubriand might have little love for each other, but they could embrace on one piece of ground: they could dance together on the grave of Voltaire.

Everywhere this resurgence of the Romantic heart against the Enlightened head flowered in a veneration of Nature. Wordsworth did speak for his era when he announced that he had learned to look on her not as in the hour of thoughtless—that is, eighteenth-century—youth, but as one who heard through her the still, sad music of humanity. This was not the nature of traditional theology: neither the law of nature of the scholastics, nor the simple plan of Newtonian apologists. It was Nature, feminine and dynamic, propelling all things. With so many Americans severally convinced that this had become ultimate truth, was not a further reflection bound to occur to a nation that was, above all other nations, embedded in Nature: if from vernal woods (along with Niagara Falls, the Mississippi, and the prairies) it can learn more of good and evil than from learned sages, could it not also learn from that source more conveniently than from divine revelation? Not that the nation would formally reject the Bible. On the contrary, it could even more energetically proclaim itself Christian and cherish the churches; but it could derive its inspiration from the mountains, the lakes, the forests. There was nothing mean or niggling about these, nothing utilitarian. Thus, superficial appearances to the contrary, America is not crass, materialistic: it is Nature's nation, possessing a heart that watches and receives.

In American literature of the early nineteenth century, this theme is ubiquitous. Social historians do not pay much attention to it; they are preoccupied with the massive expansion and the sectional tensions. Probably John Jacob Astor and the builders of railroads gave little thought to the healing virtues of the forests and swamps they were defiling. The issue I am raising—or rather that the writers themselves raised—may have little to do with how the populace actually behaved; nevertheless, it has everything to do with how the people apprehended their conduct. If there be such a thing as an American character, it took shape under the molding influence of these conceptions as much as under the physical impositions of geography and the means of transport.

So, let me insist upon the highly representational quality of an essay by one James Brooks, published in the *Knickerbocker* in 1835, which so phrased the theme that it was reprinted over the whole country. Manifestly, Brooks conceded, this country *seems* more dedicated to matter than to mind; there is indeed a vast scramble for property, and no encouragement is given the arts. But, though foreigners may sneer, we need not despair; we do not have to reconcile ourselves to being forever a rude, Philistine order. In the future we shall vindicate our culture, if only we can preserve our union. For this confidence, we have the highest authority:

> God has promised us a renowned existence, if we will but deserve it. He speaks this promise in the sublimity of Nature. It resounds all along the crags of the Alleghanies. It is uttered in the thunder of Niagara. It is heard in the roar of two oceans, from the great Pacific to the rocky ramparts of the Bay of Fundy. His finger has written it in the broad expanse of our Inland Seas, and traced it out by the mighty Father of Waters! The august TEMPLE in which we dwell was built for lofty purposes. Oh! that we may consecrate it to LIBERTY and CONCORD, and be found fit worshippers within its holy wall!

Walt Whitman had for years been drugging himself upon such prose; in him the conception comes to its most comprehensive utterance, so self-contained that it could finally dismiss the alliance with Christian doctrine which Romantic Christians had striven to establish. However, he was so intoxicated with the magniloquent idea that he had to devise what to contemporaries seemed a repulsive form, and they would have none of it. Nevertheless, Whitman's roots reach deep into the soil of this naturalistic (and Christianized) naturalism. Today a thousand James Brookses are forgotten; Whitman speaks for a mood which did sustain a mass of Americans through a crucial half-century of Titanic exertion—which sustained them along with, and as much as, their Christian profession.

That is what is really astounding: most of the ardent celebrators of natural America serenely continued to be professing Christians. Or rather, the amazing fact is that they so seldom—hardly ever—had any intimation that the bases of their patriotism and those of their creed stood, in the slightest degree, in contradiction. Magnificent hymns to American Nature are to be found among Evangelicals and Revivalists as well as among scholarly Episcopalians. If here and there some still hard-bitten Calvinist reminded his people of ancient distinctions between nature and grace, his people still bought and swooned over pseudo-Byronic invocations to Nature. It was a problem, even for the clearest thinkers, to keep the orders separate. For example, *The New York Review* in January 1840 devoted an essay to foreign travelers, saying that their defect was an inability to behold in America not the nonexistent temples and statues but the "Future":

> A railroad, a penitentiary, a log house beyond the Mississippi, the last hotly-contested elections—things rather heterogeneous to be sure, and none of them at first glance, so attractive as the wonders of the old world—are in reality, and to him who regards them philosophically, quite as important, and as they connect themselves with the unknown future, quite as romantic.

For some pages the *Review* keeps up this standard chant, and then abruptly recollects its theology. Confidence in the American future, it remembers barely in the nick of time, must not betray us into the heresy of supposing man perfectible: "Tell a people that they are perfectible, and it will not be long before they tell you that they are perfect, and that he is a traitor who presumes to doubt, not their wisdom simply, but their infallibility." Assuredly, the American Christian would at this point find himself in an intolerable dilemma, with his piety and his patriotism at loggerheads, did not the triumphant ethos seem to give him a providential way out: America can progress indefinitely into an expanding future without acquiring sinful delusions of grandeur simply because it is nestled in Nature, is instructed and guided by mountains, is chastened by cataracts.

It is here that errors are rebuked, and excesses discountenanced. Nature preserves the identity and the individuality of its various races and tribes, and by the relation in which each stands to her, and the use which each makes of her, she becomes both a teacher and an historian.

So then—because America, beyond all nations, is in perpetual touch with Nature, it need not fear the debauchery of the artificial, the urban, the civilized. Nature had somehow, by a legerdemain that even Christians so highly literate as the editors of *The New York Review* could not quite admit to themselves, effectually taken the place of the Bible: by her unremitting influence, she would guide aright the faltering steps of a young republic.

Here we encounter again the crucial difference between the American appeal to Romantic Nature and the European. In America, it served not so much for individual or artistic salvation as for an assuaging of national anxiety. The sublimity of our natural backdrop not only relieved us of having to apologize for a deficiency of picturesque ruins and hoary legends: it demonstrated how the vast reservoirs of our august temple furnish the guarantee that we shall never be contaminated by artificiality. On the prairies of Illinois, Bryant asked the breezes of the South if anywhere in their progress from the equator have they fanned a nobler scene than this?

> Man hath no part in all this glorious work:
> The hand that built the firmament hath heaved
> And smoothed these verdant swells, and sown their slopes
> With herbage, planted them with island-groves,
> And hedged them round with forests.

Goethe might insist in ancient Germany that he devoted his life to Nature, but in Europe this meant that he became an elegant genius domesticated in the highly artificial court of Weimar. What could Europe show for all of Rousseau's tirades against civilization but a band of Bohemians, congregated amid the brick and mortar of Paris, trying to keep alive a yearning for such naturalness and spontaneity as any child of the Ohio Valley indubitably flaunted without, like them, becoming outcast from society? America, amid its forests, could not, even if it tried, lose its simplicity. Therefore let Christianity bless it.

But—could America keep its virtue? As *The Literary World's* exhortation to the artists reveals, almost as soon as the identification of virtue with Nature had become axiomatic, the awful suspicion dawned that America was assiduously erecting the barriers of artifice between its citizenry and the precious landscape. If God speaks to us in the sublimity of Nature, then was not the flood of pioneers a devilish stratagem for drowning the voice of God? In the same issue that printed Brooks's "Our country," the *Knickerbocker* also carried an oration on the Mississippi River, declaring that no words can convey what an American feels as he looks upon this moving ocean, because he sees not only the present majesty but the not distant period when the interminable stretch of vacantness shall become bright with towns, vocal with the sounds of industry: "When the light of civilization and religion shall extend over forests and savannahs." Or, as the same magazine vaunted in 1838, "Nature has been penetrated in her wildest recesses, and made to yield her hidden stores." But how could we at one and the same time establish our superiority to artificial Europe upon our proximity to Nature, and then view with complacency the rapidity of our despoiling her? And furthermore—most embarrassing of questions—on which side does religion stand, on Nature's or on civilization's? Once the dichotomy had become absolute, as in American sentiment it had become, then piety could no longer compromise by pretending to dwell in both embattled camps.

Once more, in Europe the problem was personal, a matter of the individual's coming to terms with himself, absorbing a taste for Nature into his private culture. Here it was a problem for the society—and so for the churches. Goethe had put it for Europe: the young revel in those aspirations of the sublime which in fact only primitive and barbaric peoples can experience; vigorous youth pardonably strives to satisfy this noble necessity, but soon learns circumspection:

> As the sublime is easily produced by twilight and night, when forms are blended, so, on the other hand, it is scared away by the day which separates and divides everything, and so must it also be destroyed by every increase of cultivation, if it is not fortunate enough to take refuge with the beautiful and closely unite itself with it, by which these both become immortal and indestructible.

By recognizing that the sublime is ephemeral, for a nation as for a person, Goethe inculcated the necessity of a mature reconciliation to the merely beautiful, in order to preserve a fugitive glory, one which might, by adroit cultivation, survive into a weary civilization as a memory out of the natural sublimity of youth. But the beautiful is only ornament, amenity, decoration. A nation cannot live by it, neither can a faith. It is far removed from the voice of God thundering out of lofty ridges and roaring waterfalls. Even the painter Cole in 1841 published "The Lament of the Forest," by which, he seemed to say, he found at the end of his self-appointed task only a tragic prospect. The forest stood for centuries, sublime and unsullied, until there came man the destroyer. For a few centuries thereafter, America was the sanctuary; now, even into it comes artificial destruction:

> And thus come rushing on
> This human hurricane, boundless as swift.
> Our sanctuary, this secluded spot,
> Which the stern rocks have guarded until now,
> Our enemy has marked.

It was this same Thomas Cole, this master interpreter of the American landscape whose death in 1848 was, according to the *New York Evening Mirror,* "a national loss," who most impressed his generation by five gigantic canvases entitled "The Course of Empire." The first shows the rude, barbaric state of man; the second is a perfect symbolization of that pastoral conception with which America strove to identify itself. Presiding over each scene is a lofty and rocky peak, which patently represents Nature, but in the pastoral panel, and only in this one, the point of view is shifted so that there can be seen looming behind and above the peak of Nature a still more lofty one, which even more patently is the sublime. In the third cartoon the perspective returns to that of the first, but the entire scene is covered with a luxurious civilization, only the tip of mountain Nature peering over the fabulous expanse of marble. In the fourth, barbarians are sacking the city, and the picture is a riot of rape, fire, pillage; in the fifth, all human life is extinguished, the temples and towers are in ruin, but the unaltered mountain serenely presides over a panorama of total destruction.

The orator who in the *Knickerbocker* anticipated the civilization to arise along the Mississippi was obliged to warn the young empire to learn from the history of the past, from the follies of the old world: it must so improve the condition of the *whole* people as to "establish on this continent an imperishable empire, destined to confer innumerable blessings on the remotest ages." Yet like so many vaunters of American confidence in this ostensible age of confidence, by admitting the adjective into his exhortation he indirectly confesses the lurking possibility of the perishable. Cole's "Course of Empire" was exhibited over and over again to fascinated throngs of the democracy; the series ought, said George Templeton Strong in 1838, "to immortalize him." Cole made explicit what the society instinctively strove to repress: the inescapable logic of a nationalism based upon the premises of Nature. (Many, even while forced into admiration, noted that the drama as Cole painted it, he being both a pious Christian and a devout Wordsworthian, left out any hint of Christianity; the "Empire" is wholly material, and there is no salvation except for the mountain itself.) The moral clearly was that a culture committed to Nature, to the inspiration of Nature and of the sublime, might for a moment overcome its barbarous origins, take its place with the splendor of Rome, but it was thereby committed to an ineluctable cycle of rise and fall. The American empire was still ascending, rising from Cole's second to his third phase. But if this rationale explained America, then was not the fourth stage, and after it the fifth, inescapable?

The creator of Natty Bumppo and of Harvey Birch (who was a vestry-man and a close friend of Cole) grew worried. As Cooper reissued *The Spy* in 1849, he could only marvel at the immense change in the nation since 1821, when the book had first appeared. America had now passed from gristle into the bone, had indeed become a civilization, and had no enemy to fear—"but the one that resides within." In his mingling of anxieties and exultations, Cooper is indeed the central interpreter of his period; even while glorifying the forest-born virtue of America, he had also portrayed the brutal Skinners in *The Spy* and the settlers in *The Pioneers* who wantonly slaughter Nature's pigeons.

It would not be difficult to show how widespread, even though covert, was this apprehension of doom in the America of Jackson and Polk. Of course it was so elaborately masked, so concertedly disguised, that one may study the epoch for a long time without detecting it. Yet it is there, at the heart—at what may be called the secret heart—of the best thought and expression the country could produce. So much so, indeed, that some patriots sought escape from the haunting course of empire by arguing that America was no more peculiarly the nation of Nature than any other, that it had been civilized from the start. For instance, in 1847 *The Literary World* noticed a work on the prairies by Mrs. Eliza Farnham which once more appealed to the piled cliffs, the forest aisles, the chant of rushing winds and waters in the West against the decadence of Eastern civilization. The New York journal, conscious of the city's daily growth, had to ask if this tedious declamation was not becoming trite. After all, the *World* demanded, when men go deeper and deeper into wild and sublime scenes, do they in fact put off false and artificial ways? Do they become spontaneously religious? Unfortunately, we must admit that some of the fairest portions of the earth are occupied by the most degraded of mankind; even sublimity works no effect on the rude and thoughtless, and so, instead of following a fatal course from the primordial to the metropolitan, perhaps we should try to stabilize this society at the merely decent and sane. "Moral and aesthetic culture require something more than the freest and most balmy air and mellow sunshine."

The *World* did not quote Goethe to justify this escape from the cycle of naturalism, but Emerson, who did know his Goethe, could never successfully resolve within himself the debate between Nature and civilization, solitude and society, rusticity and manners. In fact, something of the same debate went on through most of the fiction and poetry, and markedly among the architects and landscape gardeners, of the time. Very few of those who found themselves impelled in both directions consciously tried to find their way into civilization because, thanks to Cole, they had peered into the frightful prospect of Nature. Still, I think it can be demonstrated that some vague sense of the doom was at work in all of them, as it surely was in both Cooper and Simms. As the implications of the philosophy of natural destiny forced themselves upon the more sentient, these were obliged to seek methods for living in civilization, all the more because civilization was so spectacularly triumphing over the continent. A growing awareness of the dilemma informed the thinking of Horace Bushnell, for instance, and he strove to turn American Protestantism from the revival, associated with the lurid scenery of Nature, to the cultivation of "nurture" which could be achieved only in a civilized context.

Of course, there was also the possibility of escape from the cycle of empire in another direction, opposite to that chosen by Bushnell. The nation could resolutely declare that it is invincibly barbaric, that it intends to remain so, and that it refuses to take even the first step toward civilization. Or at least, if the nation as a whole shrunk from such audacity, if Christians fled for protection to older sobrieties they had come near to forgetting, a few brave spirits might seek the other spiritual solution, though they had to defy the palpable evidence of economic life and to renounce a Christianity that was proving itself incapable of mediating between forest and city. They would refuse to be content with the beautiful, they would defiantly wear their hats indoors as well as out, and would sound a barbaric (and American) yawp over the roof of the world. Possibly there were, in sum, no more than three Americans who chose this violent resort, and in their time they were largely ignored by their countrymen. Yet Whitman, Thoreau, and Melville speak for this society, and to it, in great part because, by making their choice, they thrust upon it a challenge it cannot honestly evade. In 1855 Melville pictured John Paul Jones in Paris as a jaunty barbarian in the center of the very citadel of civilization; exclaiming over his incorruptibility amid corruption, Melville apostrophized: "Intrepid, unprincipled, reckless, predatory, with boundless ambition, civilized in externals but a savage at heart, America is, or may yet be, the Paul Jones of nations."

Possibly the fact that America came to its first essay in self-analysis and self-expression in the period we call Romantic is only fortuitous. But perhaps there is a deeper conjunction. The suspicion that we are being carried along on some massive conveyor belt such as Cole's "Course of Empire" is hard to down. It is more nagging today than it was around the year 1900, when for the moment America could give up the dream of Nature and settle for a permanently prosperous civilization. It more pesters the religious conscience in our time, when a leading theologian expounds the "irony" of American history, than it did when the most conscientious were absorbed in "the social gospel." So, it is no longer enough to dismiss the period of Romantic America as one in which too many Christians temporized their Christianity by merging it with a misguided cult of Nature. No scorn of the refined, no condescension of sophisticated critics toward the vagaries of Romance, can keep us from feeling the pull: the American, or at least the American artist, cherishes in his innermost being the impulse to reject completely the gospel of civilization, in order to guard with resolution the savagery of his heart.

In that case, the savage artist poses for the Christianity of the country a still more disturbing challenge, as Thoreau, Melville, and Whitman posed it: if he must, to protect his savage integrity, reject organized religion along with organized civilization, then has not American religion, or at any rate Protestantism, the awful task of re-examining, with the severest self-criticism, the course on which it so blithely embarked a century ago, when it dallied with the sublime and failed to comprehend the sinister dynamic of Nature?

AN AMERICAN LANGUAGE

I. A COLONIAL DIALECT

IN THE course of the last century, or indeed of the last two centuries, within the confines of American discourse, the word "Puritan" has taken on a wholly American connotation. When, for instance, in 1826 John Randolph of Roanoke denounced the combination between John Quincy Adams and Henry Clay which, the previous year, had made Adams President, as a conspiracy of "the Puritan and the blackleg," he was not associating Adams with the majestic figures of Milton and Cromwell. He was stigmatizing Adams by an adjective that had already become in many quarters of the country, especially among Southern gentlemen, synonymous with hypocritical self-righteousness, moral snobbery, and the peddling of wooden nutmegs.

In much of literary discussion, especially since the heyday of H. L. Mencken, the term has generally been used pejoratively to mean those Americans who are afraid of life, who would impose moralistic restraints on free expression, who for long enforced the sway of the "genteel" over both creation and criticism, and who have at last been put utterly to rout by the upsurge of a vigorous, liberal, outspoken literature. Even sympathetic attempts to find meanings for our age in such "Puritanical" writers as Nathaniel Hawthorne and Emily Dickinson, or in the Puritan strains of Melville and Mark Twain, are apt to treat Puritanism as a thing of wholly native growth. They assume that it sprang full-grown from the soil of New England with the first planters of Plymouth and Massachusetts Bay, that having thus become rooted in America it has grown like some insidious poison ivy from whose roots stifling tendrils have coiled around the American soul.

It is perhaps useless to protest that originally the name "Puritan" was applied to those who wanted to purify the institution established by the Elizabethan Settlement in the Church of England of the remnants of medieval ritual and polity. It is still more idle to insist that these English Puritans were not a peculiar English sect but that they were members of an international movement which is best subsumed under the term "Calvinist." English Puritanism no doubt took on distinctive characteristics

The three sections of "An American Language" were delivered as the Samuel Harris Lectures in Literature and Life at the winter convocation of the Bangor Theological Seminary in 1958. The third, "Huckleberry Finn," was originally published in *The Alumni Bulletin* of the seminary (vol. XXXIII, April 1958, pp. 12-21), under the title "Mark Twain and His Successors," and is here reprinted with permission.

because of the special situation in England, but essentially it was at one with the Protestantism of the Continent—that Protestantism which could not rest with what it considered the halfway measures of Lutheranism or Anglicanism. In contemporary Britain, whether in the *Times Literary Supplement* or over the BBC, the word "Puritanism" is seldom or never used with the same implications as in America. Several surrogates have taken over—most notably "the Nonconformist conscience" or "evangelicalism"—which indicate how, in English society, Puritanism after 1660 diffused itself into a frame of mind rather than remaining an ecclesiastical program. For the English, "Puritanism" signifies that historical party which rose in rebellion against Charles I, reached its crest of power under Cromwell, disintegrated during the Restoration, and dissolved under the Act of Toleration. It has little modern relevance, except as its descendants have retained a few vestigial traits.

Insofar as a religious motivation propelled Englishmen to emigrate to New England, that impulse was not theological but ecclesiastical. The colony intended first of all to set up a New Testament polity, to follow the New Testament prescription of how a pure church should be instituted, and to the realization of this true Christian polity, all other purposes, political and social, were to be subordinated. Hence the major literary productions of the first generation in New England are treatises on polity—those of Cotton, Davenport, Richard Mather, Norton, and above all Thomas Hooker's *Survey of the Summe of Church-Discipline*. It was only as events in England—the ironic developments of the Civil Wars, or the utterly unpredicted workings-out of strife on the Continent, where concrete programs of church polity had to be relegated to matters indifferent—left the New Englanders with no countries to convert except their own, that this literature eventually became the badge of a colonial eccentricity.

In England, for the whole complex of bibliolatry, Nonconformism, evangelicalism, Matthew Arnold in 1869 coined the term "Hebraism," which, he declared in *Culture and Anarchy*, inculcates "strictness of conscience" as against "spontaneity of consciousness," and to "the book which contains this invaluable law they call the Word of God" attributes "a reach and sufficiency co-extensive with all the wants of human nature." I do not know whether in 1869 English Nonconformists to any sizable degree accepted Arnold's charge that they took the Bible as adequate to meeting all the wants of human nature, but in America the heritage of colonial Puritanism worked in a quite different setting. Historians are still not clear just how far the Great Migration of 1630 really intended to go toward setting up a pure "Bible Commonwealth." When codification of the first statutes became imperative, John Cotton drew up a digest in 1641, usually known as "Moses His Judicials." It is about as close to literal Biblicism as one can come, but already there were forces in the tiny community that could not stomach it; so Nathaniel Ward, who had studied the common law as well as divinity, framed the "Body of Liberties," which the General Court did officially adopt and which, severe though it may seem by our standards, is as much indebted to secular precedents as to the Old Testament. Furthermore, the fact of the matter was that all the while these Puritans were staking their lives and fortunes on a vindication of the authentic church polity, they were also deeply implicated in the Parliamentary struggle against the Stuarts.

I have elsewhere tried to describe the vast concourse of ideas and systems of thought the Puritans brought with them into the wilderness which in actuality was derived not, as they supposed their polity was, by direct deduction from the Bible but from the contemporaneous world of the intellect. They carried with them not only the Bible itself but that elaborate superstructure which we call Calvinism and which for them found ultimate formulation in the *Westminster Confession*. Above all, they brought with them an organon of logic which they assumed was so simple and obvious as to be beyond question, and which they serenely employed for the exposition of sacred texts without the slightest awareness that the results which men extract from these texts vary inversely to the squares of the number of methods used in interpretation. Without the slightest suspicion that they were doing anything but taking at face value the words of the Bible, they translated these into the terminology of a complex psychological conception—that of the "faculties"—which had come down to them not from Hebrew sources but from Aristotle and scholasticism, and which, even as they were perfecting their expositions, was already shattered by Descartes and would soon be interred by John Locke. Here again we can see what the process of colonization means: in the realm of matter, it requires subduing a wilderness to towns and agriculture; in the realm of the mind it leads to being subdued by the emptiness of explicit victory, with the consequent necessity, which can be extremely painful, of having to construct a coherence out of implicit assumptions.

As the core of bibliolatry shrank, particularly as the argument for a strict application of New Testament polity became irrelevant, even meaningless, the Puritan intellect was reduced to digging for clues as to its meaning among the shards and remnants of what had originally been these vast, majestic assumptions. And because in the general debacle of strict Biblicism it also lost its apparatus of logical discourse—the dialectic of both Aristotle and Ramus could not long survive Descartes and Locke—and by the same token saw the dissolution of its doctrines of the human faculties, American Puritanism had in fact only one tool left with which to explore the secret caverns of its soul. But Puritanism still possessed the trusty spade with which it had from the beginning dug its foundations: the word. Though the universe might change from Ptolemaic to Copernican, and from an intricate machinery of faculties into a Lockean creature of pure sensation, the word would still serve this culture, because it had always seen the word as primarily a serviceable thing. In Europe and in England life was so complicated that even Calvinists learned to speak and write with baroque flourishes. But this society, thanks to its colonial isolation, which for so long had seemed an affliction, could now perceive the hand of providence. The founders had dedicated it irrevocably to what they called the "plain style." Through thick and thin, through wars, plagues, revolutions, they had never, or seldom, yielded to the temptation to use the word to ornament their woes. If their dialect had to be provincial, very well, but let it be their own: let it be defiantly plain!

This term, "the plain style," is not something that I have devised or that some ingenious historian has invented, like "metaphysical," "Augustan," or "Victorian," as a convenience in narration. It was consciously used by the Puritans themselves. In their minds it was a shorthand expression for a vast body of rhetorical, psychological, and theological conviction, all of which centered on a doctrine of how the word, spoken or written, should properly be managed. For instance: during several years John Cotton was renowned as one of the most eloquent preachers at the University of Cambridge; crowds came to revel in his erudition and fancy, much as other crowds came to admire the spectacle of John Donne at St. Paul's in London. But John Cotton underwent a conversion; he became a Puritan. He advertised this event not by announcing a change of opinion but simply by abruptly, on a particular Sabbath, commencing to speak in the plain style. He had uttered no more than five sentences before his auditors knew what had happened. The difference between "the *mode* of the University" and the Puritan mode was so striking that it was almost as though he had suddenly started to speak in another language. The founders of New England thus brought to these shores not only a highly developed theology, cosmology, logic, psychology, and a sophisticated concept of state and society: they also brought a doctrine of the word. Because they utilized this doctrine to make themselves understood both in their congregations and ceremonial observations, and in their publications, either through the presses of London or else, later, through their crude presses in Cambridge and Boston, they bequeathed their principles to America.

To be sure, Puritan writers were not irrevocably bound to employ it on all occasions. Nathaniel Ward deliberately shoved it aside for *The Simple Cobler of Aggawam in America,* of 1647; Captain Edward Johnson tried to cultivate a more ornate manner in telling of *The Wonder-Working Providence of Sions Saviour* in 1654; Cotton Mather risked and almost achieved bathos by casting his *Magnalia Christi Americana* of 1702 in a curiously hysterical prose which, however it may be characterized, is assuredly not "plain"; while Edward Taylor, as we have only recently become aware, struggled in the solitude of his study in frontier Westfield to subdue the sensuous impulses of a "metaphysical" technique to the rigorous impositions of his creed.

However, the existence of these sports amid the orthodox utterances merely serves to reinforce the moral that on occasions where the Puritan position most required exposition—which is to say, in the sermon, the treatise on polity, the history, the explanation of political theory—the Puritan spokesman picked up the plain style as readily as he picked up a hoe instead of an axe. Governor William Bradford, who had lived through the grim drama of Plymouth, instinctively and surely recounted it according to the canons of simplicity, and if one wants to comprehend most immediately what the concept of the plain style meant to Puritans, he has only to read any paragraph of Bradford's *History of Plimouth Plantation*.

One may select almost at random. For an example of the plain style at its finest, there is Bradford's account of what the separatist exiles confronted once they had escaped from England and were striving to hold their community together in Leyden, in Holland:

> Being now come into the Low Countries, they saw many goodly and fortified cities, strongly walled and guarded with troops of armed men. Also, they heard a strange and uncouth language, and beheld the different manners and customs of the people, with their strange fashions and attires; all so far differing from that of their plain country villages (wherein they were bred and had so long lived) as it seemed they were come into a new world. But these were not the things they much looked on, or long took up their thoughts, for they had other work in hand and another kind of war to wage and maintain. For although they saw fair and beautiful cities, flowing with abundance of all sorts of wealth and riches, yet it was not long before they saw the grim and grisly face of poverty coming upon them like an armed man, with whom they must buckle and encounter, and from whom they could not fly. But they were armed with faith and patience against him and all his encounters; and though they were sometimes foiled, yet by God's assistance, they prevailed and got the victory.

Note the haunting couplings, nearly yet never quite becoming redundant, so obvious, so generalized that they seem at first sight to tell little about the situation, but which upon second reading tell everything about exile and forlornness: "goodly and fortified, " "walled and guarded," "strange and uncouth," "wage and maintain," "grim and grisly," "buckle and encounter." What saves Bradford's prose from tedium is the way in which this device is used to restrain the passion. The very abstractness of the couplings holds experience at arm's length, thus insuring that the real point is not lost in the glitter and rush of sensation. The rhetoric folds back upon the substantive purpose; out of these pairs comes the didactic proposition, not mechanically affixed but inherently rising from the analyzed experience of the faith and patience which, with divine assistance, do prevail and gain the victory.

Puritan writings are full of theoretical expositions of the plain style, and it may be worth our while to note one or two of these theoretical statements. Thomas Hooker composed his *Survey of the Summe of Church-Discipline* just at the moment when, by accounts arriving from London, the argument between Presbyterians and Independents had come to such a dire pass that the polity vindicated, as the colonists believed, in New England seemed on the point of becoming a mere colonial experiment rather than what the founders had gloriously intended, a model for the fulfillment of English reformation. Hooker was a man who, a panegyrist said, could put a king in his pocket, but when he sent the manuscript of this work to London (where it was printed in 1648), he was already bewildered. What was happening there made no sense to him: his fellow-Congregationalists in England, now known as "Independents," were not only resisting Presbyterianism—which he could understand—but were seeking allies among heretics whom they should have despised, the enthusiastical Anabaptists and Antinomians, glossing over their apostasy with a newfangled notion of religious liberty. Hooker would have none of this: he offered a philosophy of Biblical polity within the rubrics of the old Puritan logic, but especially within the framework of solid Puritan rhetoric.

The *Survey* is a technical treatise on the polity, but what Hooker announced in his preface may also stand as the canon of composition he followed in his sermons; it provides a perfect summation of the ideal of the plain style as it was brought to New England and there made the presiding rule of American prose:

> As it is beyond my skill, so I professe it is beyond my care to please the niceness of mens palates, with any quaintnesse of language. They who covet more sauce then meat, they must provide cooks to their minds. It was a cavill cast upon Heirom, that in his writings he was *Ciceronianus non Christianus:* My rudeness frees me wholly from this exception, for being *Logos Idiotes* [ignorant of the Word], as the Apostle hath it, if I would, I could not lavish out in looseness of language, and as the case stands, if I could answer any mans desire in that daintinesse of speech, I would not do the matter that Injury which is now under my hand: *Ornari res ipsa negat.* The substance and solidity of the frame is that, which pleaseth the builder, its the painters work to provide varnish.

Ornari res ipsa negat—"the thing itself refuses to be ornamented"! There in a nutshell is the principle by which the Puritan word, the spoken or written word, must be regulated. Or as the compilers of *The Bay Psalm Book* strikingly phrased it in their preface of 1639: "If therefore the verses are not always so smooth and elegant as some may desire or expect; let them consider that Gods Altar needs not our pollishings." For the "Altar" of God was in the Puritan view not only verses in the Bible but the propositions of theology and polity, the factual record of divine providences in biographies and histories, or of the natural environment about them, the vast sea and the terrible forest. These were things in themselves; to ornament the handiwork of the Almighty was a presumption of inherent depravity: it was to set daintiness, looseness of language, above the objective facts of creation. Occasionally even Puritan writers might try to enjoy a holiday from such rigorous objectivity, and indulge themselves in a thin varnish of wit; the great ones, and even the lesser ones when dealing with the great themes, submitt.d themselves to the inexorable rule of substance and solidity.

This is not the place to attempt a defense of the Puritan aesthetic. Many in our age may see in Hooker's contemptuous relegation of the painter to mere provider of varnish an illustration of aesthetic starvation. In our own time there has arisen a new interest in the prose and poetry contemporaneous with Hooker and Cotton which these worthies condemned as frivolous niceness—the richly tessellated discourse of Donne, Launcelot Andrewes, and the Laudian clergy, and the densely intellectualized poetry of those we lump together as "metaphysicals." I am sure that anyone at all sensitive to the nuances of religious expression may, from time to time, even though he admires Bradford's simple majesty, cry out for the richer vocabulary and the more intricate patterns of the Anglican mode, just as one may pardonably grow weary of a steady diet of Bach and in revolt turn to Berlioz. In such moods we are not reconciled by the assurance that the Puritan plain style was far from being a crude style, that it was the result of a lengthy training in formal rhetoric, that it was a highly conscious art in which the supreme virtue was to conceal the art. The Puritan writers, within the limits determined by their creed, took pride in writing well and pleasure in their achievements. There is an excitement in the passage quoted from Bradford which, once the nature of the enterprise is appreciated, becomes quite as communicable to us as the beauty of any periods of John Donne. But the argument over whether the Puritans did or did not experience aesthetic delight in words or in nature is a stale one; fortunately we are not obliged, as they were, to embrace the one standard and repudiate the other. What at this juncture we are concerned to note is that for better or worse the Puritans did bring a completely rationalized theory of the plain style to America, and because they wrote and published so much, and because their descendants carried on their instruction, we must realize how they fastened it upon the literary conscience of America so securely that virtually all our writers, even though they come from Mississippi rather than from Connecticut, or were brought up as Catholics rather than as Puritans, have had to contend with its consequences.

To the extent that this generalization is even partially true, then there are two further aspects of the Puritan cultivation of their art which we should briefly note. Here again Thomas Hooker's preface goes straight to the point. The nature of this particular volume required him to use logical and scholastical terms, such as he would not employ in the pulpit. Even so, he was not addressing his treatise exclusively to the learned; however technical the material, it was of vital concern to all Christians, no matter how simple. Wherefore Hooker voices what is always a primary consideration in the plain style: it must address the vulgar.

Plainesse and perspicuity, both for matter and manner of expression, are the things, that I conscientiously indeavoured in the whole debate: for I have ever thought writings that come abroad, they are not to dazzle, but direct the apprehensions of the meanest, and I have accounted the chiefest part of Iudicious learning, to make a hard point easy and familiar in explication.

We have learned to be cautious, as often pietistic celebrants of the nineteenth century were not, about hailing the Puritan founders as in any purposive sense contributing to the development of American democracy. The first Congregationalists did not consider democracy a virtue; they rejected every charge that they were in the slightest measure inclined toward egalitarianism. Still, in their concept of the uses of the word there was a democratic implication more pregnant for the future than in their idea of the covenanted church: the word in the mouth of the learned must be addressed to the "capacity of the common Auditory," to use Increase Mather's phrase. The aim of the learned was not social, it was religious; they had the tremendous responsibility of making "an ignorant man understand these Mysteries in some good measure." What they could not foresee was that eventually, after they had drilled this thought into the philosophy of American education, the rule of comprehensibility to the common man would continue to weigh upon the American writer long after he had ceased to be a preacher of theological mysteries.

Second, let me cite Hooker again to give us one of the first hints in our literature of a boast which was steadily to resound through later writings. The ideal of plainness in style was, of course, formulated among European Protestants, and Hooker needed to say no more in his preface than that he was obeying the precepts of the same academic masters which both they and he had studied; however, he began his passage with an apology which would strike them as astonishingly novel:

> That the discourse comes forth in such a homely dresse and course habit, the Reader must be desired to consider, It comes *out of the wildernesse,* where curiosity is not studied. Planters if they can provide cloth to go warm, they leave the cutts and lace to those that study to go fine.

Hereafter, we have an augmenting iteration of this plea, through the prose of Benjamin Franklin, through the cultivated rusticities of the epistles of several Revolutionary "farmers," into the very language of the Declaration of Independence. We are plain speakers not so much because we learned simplicity in European universities, but because we have to do with the wilderness. It was, let me repeat, no part of the original Puritan conception that ministers should make eschatological conundrums clear to the common auditory because those peoples dwelt in a savage land. Puritan divines were to speak to yeomen in Lancashire, to shepherds in Northumberland, yet also to such gentry as Winthrop and Bradstreet. But out of New England first arose, and subsequently grew, the argument that an immigrant stock no longer had time to heed "cutts and laces." In a wilderness setting, the plain style, without changing a single syllable of its formal profession, subtly, rapidly became no longer a manifesto of the scholars but a method of dealing with the environment.

The mere fact that Thomas Hooker, in so elaborately "scholastic" a work as the *Survey,* smuggled this plea into his preface is an eloquent confession of how even the first generation, educated in England and Holland, were already losing contact with the great world they had virtually rejected, though they had never intended the rejection. Their sons, their grandsons, those who never knew Cambridge, Leyden, Strasbourg, unless by report, would find themselves insisting upon a hearing not because they wrote a Protestant rhetoric but because they were Protestants in the wilderness. In this development, one fact stands out: in rhetoric the *result* of a once highly elaborated doctrine could survive, could prove its utility. In virtually every other department of thought and expression, the original assumptions, the machinery of proof, fell away and can hardly be recovered by modern research. The ancient cosmology yielded to the triumph of Newton; patterns of logic were replaced by those of eighteenth-century speech. Even in the vital business of political theory, Governor Winthrop's expositions of the social compact in 1645 had become archaic language by 1745 and were utterly ignored in the patriotic sermons of 1776. Indeed, by the time the plain style becomes the instrument, the wonderfully effective instrument, for stating a Revolutionary case against the government of George III, hardly any practitioner of the method has the slightest memory of Petrus Ramus, of Omer Talon, or of the host who instructed the first Puritans. The intellectual revolution of the seventeenth century—in cosmology, logic, psychology—had in effect obliterated the philosophical premises of the Puritan migration. In all these areas, inhabitants of an American wilderness had been obliged, bit by bit, to make their adjustments. But in one respect they did not need to change: they might forget the rhetorical methods inculcated at early Harvard, but when the task descended upon them of speaking out, plainly and as citizens of the wilderness, they had no problem about finding a mode of utterance. The consequence of their seventeenth-century discipline remained with them long after the tuition had faded, and in the language of Revolutionary ardor, determined to speak to the common auditory and glorying in their rusticity, spokesmen of the Revolution conveyed the plain style into the extending vistas of American self-expression.

II. WALDEN AND MOBY-DICK

"I believe in the forest, and in the meadow, and in the night in which the corn grows." Henry Thoreau, of Concord, Massachusetts, wrote this sentence somewhere toward the end of his life; it was published in an essay entitled "Walking" in *The Atlantic Monthly* in June 1862, shortly after his death on May the sixth at the age of forty-four. Since the "plain style" has become my subject, let me call attention to Thoreau's sentence as constituting an indubitable triumph of the mode. What indeed could be plainer, and yet what phrasing could more effectively employ the impact

of surprise, the arresting of vulgar attention, which in the Puritan aesthetic
had ever been the aim of the manner?

Thomas Hooker did not always publish in the style of logical argumentation of the *Survey.* For example, in a series of sermons published in London
twelve years after his death (in 1647) under the title *The Application of
Redemption,* he too appealed to the symbolism of the corn. While addressing
the momentous question of wherein a true sight of sin properly discovers
itself, "But alas," he wrote, "all this wind shakes no Corn, it costs more
to see sin aright than a few words of course." If you will remember that
"of course" in this connection means not what we now intend by the
phrase but rather the conventional enumeration of the signs of human
depravity in formal sermons, those which are wearisomely adduced in the
"course" of a standard explication, you will sense how effective in the seventeenth-century context was Hooker's invocation of a wind which "shakes
no Corn."

Corn! We must understand that what the settlers meant by corn is
what we call wheat; what Thoreau means by corn is American corn, Indian
corn. The natives of New England had learned this transubstantiation precisely as they had learned how to employ the plain style for purposes not
foretold in the prospectus of the founders: in that beginning, nobody had
intended to declare a "belief" in the American night in which the maize
grows.

But the prose of Hooker was ready for some such translation. He was expounding, within the rubrics of the imported theology, what constitutes an
authentic realization of inherent depravity. Yet look at how a metaphor
preoccupies him:

> There is great ods betwixt the knowledge of a Traveller, that in
> his own person hath taken a view of many Coasts, past through many
> Countries, and hath there taken up his abode some time, and by Ex-
> perience hath been an Eye-witness of the extream cold, and scorching
> heats, hath surveyed the glory and beauty of the one, the barrenness and
> meanness of the other; he hath been in the Wars and seen the ruin
> and desolation wrought there; and another that sits by his fire side, and
> happily reads the story of these in a Book, or views the proportion of
> these in a Map. The ods is great, and the difference of their knowledge
> more than a little: the one saw the Country really, the other only in the
> story; the one hath seen the very place, the other only in the paint of
> the Map drawn.

Henry Thoreau did not, I shall promptly acknowledge, see many coasts
except that of Cape Cod, nor pass through many countries beyond eastern
Massachusetts, though he did journey unfruitfully to Montreal, New
York, and Duluth; yet he never sat beside his fire and read only a painted
map of Walden Pond.

Then let us join with him another young American who did indeed experience a view of many coasts, who took up his abode there some time, who knew the extreme cold of the Straits of Magellan and the scorching heats of the tropical Marquesas: Herman Melville. I think it fair to say—though I do not wish here to contest the merits, possibly in some respects the commanding merits, of Emerson, Poe, Whitman, Hawthorne—that these two strangely do stand out as the great practitioners of the Puritan heritage, the supreme confronters of the double-edged, the razor-edged, challenge of the plain style. In their utterly different ways, Thoreau and Melville were those Americans who had been eyewitnesses, had been in the wars, had seen the ruin and desolation, the glory and the barrenness. One traveled much in Concord and the other in the South Seas, but from the point of view of the plain style, mere dimension is a relative quantity. The crucial difference is between him who sees a country of the spirit really and him who sees it only in story, in the paint of a drawn map. Walden Pond or Tahiti—wherein is one to choose? Either is a subject for language: the style is everything.

We should commence by noticing in Thoreau's sentence the barely disguised blasphemy: it is a parody of confession of belief in the Trinity: the "forest" (God the father), the "meadow" (Christ the Savior), and a "night in which the corn grows" (assuredly this, if anything, is the Holy Ghost). Something curious had happened to the concept of the use of the word between the time of Hooker and of young Henry Thoreau—or at least in Thoreau's brain something had happened to the concept. And also, we are bound to say, in the brain of Herman Melville: "Talk not to me of blasphemy, man," cries Ahab to the mate who calls Ahab's quest for vengeance on a dumb brute blasphemous. "I'd strike the sun if it insulted me." To which the captain adds the question that Puritan discourse had been invented to ask, and then the answer for which, it had been assumed, the prose would supply the precise signification: "Who's over me? Truth hath no confines."

It would be entirely incorrect to call the Puritans of New England Utilitarians, with a capital "U," implying any philosophical or temperamental affinity with Jeremy Bentham. Yet in every aspect of life Puritan Calvinism was strongly determined that things should be made use of. In the business world the ethic of laboring in one's calling, though it was a religious obligation, meant making full use of one's time and talents. Furthermore, while government was an ordinance of God, only that government was good which contributed to the welfare of the community. *Salus populi suprema lex* was the axiom which eventually would be found to be the basic stone in the legal foundation, so that when an English government struck deeply at it, the head of a King would be severed or the red coats of British regulars be stained with the deeper dye of their own blood.

Likewise in the business of the word. The rhetorical doctrine which inculcated simplicity was a sufficient rationale in and by itself; there was no need to invoke the further consideration that the word must also reach the lowest and meanest capacity, even though that contention was a welcome reinforcement. On both scores, therefore, on the theoretical and the utilitarian, the case was clear: as William Ames had written in the textbook which for over a century was the main content of Puritan education, *The Marrow of Sacred Divinity,* "The efficacy of the holy Spirit doth more cleerly appeare in a naked simplicity of words, then in elegancy and neatness. . . . So much affectation as appeares, so much efficacy and authority is lost."

Now it is certainly true that the mass of Puritans did not intend, all the time they were agitating for purification of the Church of England, ultimately to gain their end by beheading their sovereign and setting up a republic. They were loyal subjects who were brought to these extremities by forces beyond their control, which they could interpret only as the guiding hand of an inscrutable providence. Once they did have control of a situation, as in Massachusetts Bay under Winthrop, the Puritans showed that beyond the limits of their ecclesiastical reformation they had no intention of embarking upon radical experiments in society, economics, or metaphysics. If we forget how Winthrop and his fellows were aligned in England against Canterbury and Whitehall, if we consider only how they organized their society in America, then we may properly say that they were conservatives. Therefore, to the extent that the plain word was put to the use of explaining the principles of this society and its theology to the multitude, it has a basically conservative motive. Cotton Mather said of the preaching of his father, Increase Mather, "He was very careful to be *understood* and *concealed* every other *Art,* that he might Pursue and Practise that one *Art* of *Being Intelligible."*

But though the Puritans hardly ever so much as suspected the fact, and when they did they were rendered acutely uncomfortable, the truth is that a prose stripped of elegancy, neatness, affectation, and harnessed to making intelligible to a populace the nature of authority, is bound to show radical and disruptive tendencies. As long as the principles which constitute an authoritative orthodoxy remain intact—which is to say, as long as they are kept in vigorous and healthy congruity by the other arts and sciences, not only by theology but by physics and logic—then rhetoric can go dutifully about its menial function. It can piously devote itself to making mysteries halfway intelligible, to reducing hard points to the vulgar comprehension. But what happens when a comprehensive revolution in all the realms of the mind takes place—such an overturning as we discover in the seventeenth century? With such an uprising, the very concept of authority is emptied of meaning. What thereafter does the plain style do? Its mission had at first been precisely designated; now it was left adrift. The one thing it could not do was take refuge in elegance, mannerism, fantasy, drama. It could not, for instance, follow Goethe through *The Sorrows of Young Werther* and *Wilhelm Meister,* because by the nature of the beast, the plain style is obliged to expound, even though there may be confusion in higher headquarters as to whether there is any longer an authority to be expounded. After all, though the American form of outspokenness was in the beginning a code with a dignity of its own, it survived because, and in the process only because, it was socially effective. As a rhetorical method, therefore, it was left to operate on its own, aware of its isolation, its disseverance from theology and cosmology. The word itself, and by this I must include also the practitioners of the word, had eventually, however reluctantly, to ask, "Who's over me?" The moment it admitted that question to the new context wherein the scholastic rubrics had vanished, it had no option but to insist, "Truth hath no confines."

A tradition of prose thus irrevocably committed to making all things, even the most impenetrable mysteries, comprehensible to the democracy would, almost of necessity, be courting perilous adventures. As also, I might remark in passing, would poetry: at his most subtle, Robert Frost adheres to the Puritan canon, whereas Mr. T. S. Eliot has (he asserts) rejected it. In either vein, the risk of losing touch with the audience is equally grave; from both, from either Frost or Eliot, comes the ironic disclosure so long hidden within the Puritan code: as the queer consequence of the Puritan's proud willingness to try all things and to prove all things by the plain style, the rhetorical discipline, left to itself, would turn into an instrument not of a conservative utility but of a reckless subjection of historical certitudes to corroding examination. The forthright method proved to be, once it survived as a method, the most subversive power that the wicked could invoke against those generalities it had, long ago, been designed to protect.

Repelled by the memory of a decadent fifteenth-century scholasticism, in which the flowers of rhetoric were encouraged to blossom with a tropical fecundity, Puritan theorists summoned an obsequious bondservant who, obedient to the Apostle Paul, would, as Samuel Willard put it, begin with matters doctrinal, and then always descend "to things practical." Willard could thereupon conclude, as though for all time, "Practical application is the life of preaching." Neither Willard nor any of the Puritan formulators could possibly have foretold that a child of the Puritans, he who in an utterly altered context would remain most faithful to the ideal of the plain style—that this Henry Thoreau would someday write, "Give me a wildness whose glance no civilization can endure." Even less would they have foreseen, though they might object that the Puritan stream in Herman Melville was muddied by an admixture of Dutch Calvinism, that out of a serious consideration of their Calvinism in relation to the spoken word might burst such a declaration as, "I know thee, thou clear spirit, and I now know that thy right worship is defiance." What I would like to say, though I fear I may be spoiling the truism in so bluntly saying it, is simply that the plain style was, by its inherent character, a defiant style. Our Puritans kept the defiance in check; Emerson strove to but never quite did loose the demon; in our literature it was Henry Thoreau and Herman Melville who released the blast. Both of them endeavored to achieve, through the plain style, explication to the common auditory, and both of them missed their public. With them, therefore, we are bound to ask, of publicists and of theologians alike, what kind of speech really does find its mark with the ranks of the American commonalty?

At this point I resist the impulse to discourse on the prophetic contrast between Jonathan Edwards and Benjamin Franklin. By our acceptance of these opposites, we often surrender the effort to think further about our culture. I shall therefore eschew the problem of what Jonathan Edwards attempted to achieve with the plain style, once he realized that the Puritan cosmology and psychology had been eradicated. Let me say merely that he did make the gallant effort to maintain the canons of the Puritan plain style that the speaker be clear, simple, direct, and that he communicate to the common auditory. Whatever Edwards had to say after 1740-1741 to account for his gigantic failure, we may be assured that in his revival preaching of those years of crisis, he rigorously adhered to the rhetorical rules. The documents which survive from that time are marvelous exemplifications of what the style could accomplish, without embellishment, without mitigation, succeeding by virtue of no arts other than stark explication.

Benjamin Franklin is quite another story, and yet part of the same story. At the risk of doing violence to a great career—above all to a career achieved primarily by use of the word—let me crudely put it that Franklin concentrated his genius upon the plain style in its purely utilitarian implications. He wrote for the common auditory, not to explicate authoritarian mysteries, but to clarify the confusions of men's ordinary existence. It has been said before, but one may say it again, that it was pre-eminently through Benjamin Franklin that the utilitarian version of Puritan eloquence carried over to the language of American business. "Keep your shop and your shop will keep you," a clear translation, into provincial economic terms, of the doctrine of predestination. But let us not accept this translation too definitively, and we should not be surprised that those who still remembered the pristine meaning of calling, even though they themselves had no clear spiritual vocation, invoked the mighty plain style of the founders against those who, as they believed, prostituted its utility to the ethic of success. In the seventeenth century, the argument had rested upon a cosmological premise; what should the writer do now, whether harpooning whales or wattling a hut, but to rely upon the plain spoken word, and so to persuade the common auditory that we, as a people, have not remained eccentric precisionists, that we are doing our utmost to obey the will of God? And this despite the Almighty's having become for us, beyond the utmost anxiety of the Puritan imagination, *absconditus?*

Even though the mere mention of Benjamin Franklin's name in itself is enough to remind us of what he did by way of converting the plain style to wholly utilitarian purposes, we may refresh ourselves with the flavor of one or two of his utterances. There is in the record of American literature hardly a writer so fully aware of what he was about. As he remarked in discussing a taxation problem in Pennsylvania, "In matters of general concern to the people, and especially where burthens are to be laid upon them, it is of use to consider, as well what they be apt to think and say, as what they ought to think." By implication, this surrender of the tutorial function marks the complete secularization of the plain style; Franklin's prose cultivates and cherishes all the virtues of Puritan writing except the Puritanism, so that these could now be harnessed to an expanding economy and worldly ambition. In a successful piece of composition, he says—and everything he wrote became in his hands, as did every article of merchandise in his shop, a profitable undertaking—

> The words used should be the most expressive that the language affords, provided that they are the most generally understood. Nothing should be expressed in two words that can be as well expressed in one; that is, no synonymes should be used, or very rarely, but the whole should be as short as possible, consistent with clearness; the words should be so placed as to be agreeable to the ear in reading; summarily, it should be smooth, clear, and short, for the contrary qualities are displeasing.

Here, put as neatly as anyone ever expressed it, is the aesthetic of utility.

Obviously it would be absurd to label Benjamin Franklin, the religious liberal, the far-ranging questioner of nature, the serene revolutionary that he became, a "conservative." As we must do with Governor John Winthrop, we have to evaluate his career (and his writing) against the dominant ethos of Europe in his day. Though historians rightly point out that during the eighteenth century the "middle class" in western nations was steadily gaining power over the remnants of feudal aristocracy, yet, even in that era, the progress of the tallow-maker's son from Boston through the printer's shop of Philadelphia to apotheosis at Versailles was in truth a radical triumph. Viewed as it must be in relation to the period, Franklin's success is the archetypal victory for the common man; in the intellectual race, as well as in the financial and political, he won, without any advantages from high birth or education. And, as he was always ready to confess, he made his advance primarily by his skill as a writer. In Paris he wore his coon-skin hat, and let the ladies suppose him a Rousseauistic child of the wild frontier, because he had prepared the role for himself by the sententious platitudes of *Poor Richard's Almanac*.

All this is possibly obvious, yet it needs to be said in view of the symbolic character that Franklin has assumed in the American imagination. In fact, the image of the Philadelphia apprentice, who eventually stood before several kings and with one of them, the King of Denmark, sat down to dinner, had already given powerful sanction in the early nineteenth century to the American business ethic. In that sense, the idea of Benjamin Franklin operated in the days of Thoreau and Melville even more compulsively than did religious instruction to impose upon young men the imperative that they should early find themselves a job and stick to it, accumulating wealth and dignity as they went along. So that equally, for the one who would run away from responsibility aboard a whaling ship and for the other who would escape to self-absorbed indolence two miles south of Concord, the figure of Franklin would embody that conservative order against which they protested. Yet Franklin would also be a problem for them because, conservative emblem as he had become, he was no tyrant, no artistocrat, no theocrat; he was first and last one who wrote in common speech, who succeeded superlatively in reaching his audience.

Three years after Herman Melville had consumed his emotions in the ordeal of *Moby-Dick*—he wrote to Hawthorne, "I have written a wicked book and feel spotless as the lamb"—and two years after he had wantonly alienated his audience by *Pierre,* he made an unsuccessful effort to prove his respectability by sending forth a historical novel about the American Revolution, entitled *Israel Potter.* A good part of it is devoted to a sketch of Benjamin Franklin—a portrait limned in venom, anger, contempt. Franklin appears niggardly, calculating, vain, utterly Philistine, sly. Yet Melville's satire, which is surely as embittered as anything he ever wrote, attests his awareness that Franklin had triumphed at the game of life principally by what Melville considered a profanation of simplicity.

It may be of interest to observe just how Melville leads up to his excoriation of the patriot-philosopher: he finds in Franklin a modern parallel to the Patriarch Jacob. The history of the younger of Rebekah's twins, Melville notes, his tongue entirely in his cheek, "is interesting not less from the unselfish devotion which we are bound to ascribe to him, than from the deep worldly wisdom and polished Italian tact, gleaming under an air of Arcadian unaffectedness." Only upon reflection do we recollect that the simple shepherd Jacob twice perpetrated swindles of such cool effrontery that western culture still holds them to be exemplars of gulling: the one upon his brother Esau, the other on his uncle Laban the Syrian. Melville siyly alludes to how Jacob's father Isaac, who in fact was the real victim of the first ruse, characterized the son: "Thy brother came with subtilty, and hath taken away thy blessing." He stole the blessing—true, we must acknowledge, with the help of Rebekah, for Jacob would not have had the wits to contrive the disguise if left to his own resources—which was intended for Esau, "a cunning hunter, a man of the field." Which is to say, a denizen of the wilderness. All this gives spice to Melville's characterization of Jacob: "A tanned Machiavelli in tents."

But, as Melville mischievously continues, we may be assured that even though he thus became lord of the pastoral manor, his raiment was of homespun! Indeed, Genesis 25:27 tells us: "and Jacob was a plain man, dwelling in tents." Whereupon Herman Melville springs his trap, all the more devastating for seeming to be the artless observation of Israel Potter:

> Franklin all over is of a piece. He dressed his person as his periods; neat, trim, nothing superfluous, nothing deficient. In some of his works his style is only surpassed by the unimprovable sentences of Hobbes of Malmsbury, the paragon of perspicuity. The mental habits of Hobbes and Franklin in several points, especially in one of some moment, assimilated. Indeed, making due allowance for soil and era, history presents few trios more akin, upon the whole, than Jacob, Hobbes, and Franklin; three labyrinth-minded, but plain-spoken Broadbrims, at once politicians and philosophers; keen observers of the main chance; prudent courtiers; practical magians in linsey-woolsey.

Few paid attention in 1854 to *Israel Potter,* and of these none seems to have perceived the barb on Melville's harpoon. All good Americans of that soil and era knew, if they knew anything, that Thomas Hobbes was the satanic apologist for the most brutal political absolutism, arguing from the premise of an inherent depravity which was a caricature of Christian pessimism; Hobbes was the complete opposite, in every respect, to the democratic idealism of America, in which hagiography Franklin figured as a saint of liberty along with Washington. What curious sleight-of-hand was Melville enacting by linking Jacob, who indubitably wore homespun in Beer-sheba (as did Franklin in Philadelphia) and presumably wore the same when he came as ambassador to Padan-aram (as did Franklin in Paris), along with Hobbes, the "unimprovable" paragon of perspicuity, to the classic apostle of American individualism? Well, we discover soon enough that during Israel Potter's stay in Franklin's house, the rustic boy is deprived by Franklin's imposition upon him of the maxims of ascetic prosperity—sobriety and chastity—of a bottle of excellent wine and of an accommodating chambermaid. " 'Every time he comes in he robs me,' soliloquised Israel, dolefully; 'with an air all the time, too, as if he were making me presents.' " Then we remember, with a flash of illumination, how Jacob defrauded Esau and how he bamboozled Laban out of cattle, sheep, and goats. And immediately thereafter we bethink us that Jacob, as a consquence of his dubious but highly profitable transactions, was blessed with the name of "Israel," and that the twelfth child he begot, the only full brother to Joseph, was Benjamin.

Put in another way, though in a cruder fashion than Melville would approve, what he charges against Franklin is that by his manipulation of the plain method to the support of his calculations, following the precedents of Jacob and Hobbes, he becomes the master hypocrite. In Melville's view, Franklin's is the most reprehensible of hypocrisies because in the guise of simplicity, symbolized by his garb, Franklin cheats his admiring readers as viciously as ever Jacob hoodwinked Esau and Laban. He perverts the art which conceals art to the magian schemes of linsey-woolsey; the more successful he waxes, the more he plays a game, taking secret satisfaction in cozening the common auditory, whether his fellow-tradesmen in Philadelphia or sentimental ladies at the court of Louis XVI. His affectation of homespun prose periods is a conceited masquerade, and so a betrayal of the majesty of the truly plain style.

There are few if any mentions of Benjamin Franklin in Thoreau's writings or in his *Journal*. From one or two oblique references, we can be sure that he also considered Franklin a formidable opponent, who challenged him not at all by presenting him with a reactionary doctrine but by threatening to outdo him in asceticism. I believe I am not the first to point out that the opening chapter of *Walden,* that entitled "Economy," is a parody of Poor Richard's linsey-woolsey ethic, a reduction to absurdity of Franklin's *Autobiography.* The meticulous calculation of debit and credit, leaving him a deficit of $25.21 and ¾, is a goatfooted parody of Franklin's account of his rise to prosperity, naughtily made more ludicrous by Thoreau's dead-pan assurance that he is far from jesting: "Economy is a subject which admits of being treated with levity, but it cannot so be disposed of." Yet oddly enough, we here most directly confront Henry Thoreau's determination to reach what Increase Mather called the "common auditory," because while minutely listing, to the last penny and quarter-penny, the expenses of his house, he explained, in the tradition of the plain style, "I give the details because very few are able to tell exactly what their houses cost, and fewer still, if any, the separate cost of the various materials which compose them."

I confess that I am not playing entirely fair by adducing *Moby-Dick* as a masterpiece of the plain style. Melville's heritage was only half that of New England, and he was no such student of the Puritan literature as was Thoreau. What little he could learn about the art of writing he acquired in New York, where standards of elegance were ostentatiously cultivated; he spoke as a New Yorker in his scorn for the prosaicness of Franklin. Also, he studied Shakespeare, Milton, and the English metaphysicals of the seventeenth century, and in several of the more orotund passages of his book strove to recapture a prose that owes more to Sir Thomas Browne than to Governor Bradford. But I think even a casual reader of the book feels that these purple orations are pumped up, that Melville was never so instinctively at home with surcharged rhetoric as were, let us say, his supposedly more "realistic" contemporaries, Dickens and Thackeray. Captain Ahab's most histrionic orations are closer to the rhythms of Thomas Hooker's metaphors than to the melodrama of Bill Sikes's murder of Nancy. What, in any event, must always fascinate us is the combination in the book of efforts at heightened eloquence with insistence upon the mundane ordinariness of the actors. "But Ahab, my Captain," Melville exclaims, "still moves before me in all his Nantucket grimness and shagginess: and in this episode touching Emperors and Kings, I must not conceal that I have only to do with a poor old whale-hunter like him; and, therefore, all outward majestical trappings and housings are denied me." At this point, even though not at any other, Thomas Hooker would have nodded approval.

Assuredly, one is on safer ground when he adduces Thoreau's *Walden* as essentially a continuation, into a radically altered universe, of the Puritan determination to speak plainly, using art to conceal art, and metaphor suited to the common understanding. Almost any sentence of Thoreau's will stand as the essence of the style, and some of them, by their brusqueness, have become famous: "I never dreamed of any enormity greater than I have committed. I never knew, and never shall know, a worse man than myself." This, you will perceive, was the confession toward which the plain style was always driving. In Puritan congregations, the ministers never quite asked candidates to venture upon so positive or sweeping a self-condemnation; they trusted that some more "hopeful," some modest signs of election might be disclosed. Of course, they expected a repentant sinner to confess the enormity of his unregeneracy, but they never quite envisioned confession, full confession, by a recalcitrant child of the covenant who would glory in his participation in the community of sin. Hence, would they not be doubly confused, while recognizing him as a grandson of their loins, that he outdid them all, outdid even Benjamin Franklin, in an ascetic way of life, eschewing meat and alcohol, spurning marriage, molding himself to the implacable rules of a Divinity in whom he no longer believed? And would they not then be trebly bewildered to find in him, amid the calculated efforts of his Puritan contemporaries, the one writer in whom the ideals of strict conformity to the injunction of plainness were most energetically followed?

We are brought back to what these two great works of the American imagination are really about—*Moby-Dick* in 1851 and *Walden* in 1854. Historians have demonstrated how little, how abysmally little, contemporaneous reviewers appreciated their significance. We have to say that each of them was, in commercial terms, a failure; we have thereafter to note how they persist in maintaining their place in serious American thinking, how we today are thrown back upon them. If we attempt surmise about ourselves—and who among us today does not worry a bit about who or what he is?—then we turn to *Moby-Dick* and to *Walden*. We have learned not to be put off by the attitudinizing of the former, as we should no longer be put off by the posturing of the latter. These are American works, both of them operating in an established vein of metaphorical symbolism, both of them striving to make their point in all humble simplicity, and both of them utilizing the resources of the plain style to appeal to a common auditory. In their own day they failed of communication, and even today are not widely familar to readers. Lay the responsibility as you may to the authors' eccentricity, perversity, egotism; the fact remains that both are major books which reach only a limited audience because both, however different they may be in conception and execution, are primary examples in American writing of the word compelled to operate as a word by and in itself, without the prior sanction of a mission. Each is the work, beyond any writing America had known up to that time, of a writer in search of a meaning, or rather of a theology, of a meaning to be derived out of nothing but his prose.

To substantiate my case, I must, of course, fall back upon familiar passages. There is, for example, Thoreau's arabesque upon the first answer in the Westminster Catechism: "What is the end of man?" the interrogation runs, and the reply follows, "To glorify God and enjoy him forever." Thoreau was haunted by this dialogue; he comes back to it repeatedly, always wringing some ironic scandal out of it, nowhere more pointedly than in the second chapter of *Walden*. He quotes the Catechism with a bit of preface, noting that men are in a strange uncertainty about whether life be of the devil or of God, and so have (italics his) "*somewhat hastily concluded*" that man's end is to glorify the Creator and enjoy Him. To Thoreau, after two centuries of ritual reiteration, it was high time that a Puritan conscience should arouse itself against this "hasty" Puritan tenet. There was no other instrument for him but the plain style, the only disruptive implement the Puritans had left to generations after them.

Thus armed, both in authority and in rebellion, Thoreau stated the purpose of his book, and again we perceive the links with Hooker:

> I went to the woods because I wished to live deliberately, to front only the essential facts of life, and see if I could not learn what it had to teach, and not, when I came to die, discover that I had not lived. I did not wish to live what was not life, living is so dear; nor did I wish to practise resignation, unless it was quite necessary. I wanted to live deep and suck out all the marrow of life, to live so sturdily and Spartanlike as to put to rout all that was not life, to cut a broad swath and shave close, to drive life into a corner, and reduce it to its lowest terms, and, if it proved to be mean, why then to get the whole and genuine meanness of it, and publish its meanness to the world; or if it were sublime, to know it by experience, and be able to give a true account of it in my next excursion.

Leaving aside for the moment the fact that *Walden* does seem to assert at the end that life is sublime, the point we have to confront is the sincerity of Thoreau's invitation to life to prove itself mean, and his readiness thereupon to publish that meanness "to the world." Egocentric as he was, he still thought he should address "the world." This was ever the Puritan intention; where are we if the world pays no heed?

The world paid not much more heed to Captain Ahab. Again I say, Thomas Hooker would have comprehended Ahab's language, though he would have held it a sad distortion of the Westminster Confession. When the ship is ablaze with St. Elmo's fire, Ahab takes up the chains, inviting the destructive current to pass into himself, and thus addresses this symbol of the Omnipotent:

Oh! thou clear spirit of clear fire, whom on these seas I as Persian once did worship, till in the sacramental act so burned by thee, that to this hour I bear the scar; I now know thee, thou clear spirit, and I know that they right worship is defiance.

Hooker, Cotton, and company had not, it is true, made a virtue of defiance; but let us say that they did perfect a prose and a use of metaphor within the confines of their intensity which could easily become, on the one side, the smooth efficiency of Franklin, on the other, the strenuousness of Thoreau and Melville.

I shall not detain the reader with detailed discussion of *Walden* and *Moby-Dick*. I trust my contention is clear, even though not fully substantiated, that these are the two most insurgent works in American literature. And I hope that my thesis is somewhat plausible, that their relation to the Puritan utterance of the seventeenth century is not so much a matter of a theological genealogy as of their inheritance of a mode of prose narration. Even though both Thoreau and Melville would have disowned any debt to Thomas Hooker, these two volumes as they stand belong to a pattern of explication which bestows, from afar, a blessing upon their failures, which indeed confers on their failures a measure of achievement. Renouncing all recourse to the utilitarian purposes that had brought success to the Puritan preacher, they strove to invest the pure word with full power to expound both the "marrow of life" and "right worship." Belatedly, we pay a sort of homage to them; but these master-Puritans come down to us as cryptic geniuses. We placate them endlessly, but we have yet fully to realize, if indeed we ever shall, how they beseech us to consider the way in America that words, the beautiful and terrible words, must serve us, all by themselves, without any adventitious assistance from generalized profession, to comprehend our peculiar position in history. We have every reason, in the inheritance of Benjamin Franklin and of the Revolutionary documents, to insist that our words mean only what they say; however, as long as we have also in our memory the sentences of Thoreau and Melville, we have the task of realizing how our words signify more than they say. We have no choice but to drive life into a corner, we have no option but to greet omnipotence with defiance. This in reality is the true literature of America.

III. HUCKLEBERRY FINN

In *Green Hills of Africa,* Ernest Hemingway permitted himself to deliver a dictum upon his contemporaries: "All modern American literature comes from one book by Mark Twain called *Huckleberry Finn*. . . . It's the best book we've had. All American writing comes from that. There was nothing before. There has been nothing as good since."

As far as I know, Mr. Hemingway was never induced further to explain what he meant. It is probably just as well. Those of us who are concerned with the import of modern American writing, including the works of Ernest Hemingway, are thus left at liberty to speculate. Exercising that freedom, I have no hesitation in saying wherein Hemingway's declaration is true: Mark Twain's *Huckleberry Finn* is the originating point for modern American literature because of its mastery of language.

We are all, I suppose, if we give any thought to the matter, in some doubt about Mark Twain's intellect. There are those who insist he had no mind. But if for one single moment we suppose this to be the truth, we have a problem on our hands. Can Americans imagine that they would be what they take themselves to be if the record of Mark Twain, and especially of *Huckleberry Finn,* were expunged from the national recollection? How, without that book, would even those of us who have never seen the Mississippi River know who we are? *Walden* tells only a few of us—possibly fewer and fewer as the decades unroll. *Moby-Dick* assuredly speaks to young intellectuals, who write their own versions of it voluminously; yet I doubt that, in spite of all the modern ballyhoo, it actually addresses the American common auditory. We have no doubt about Huck: if any "classic" figure in our literature carries himself to ordinary readers, to children as well as to men, he is that one. In this book we have, to our bewilderment, an address to the populace in a language which they immediately understand, and a work of art which, even more contrived than *Walden* and *Moby-Dick,* commands respect from the most sophisticated. If we had only *Walden* and *Moby-Dick* to work with, we would have to say that the American public is incapable of appreciating the greatness it engenders. Since, however, we also have *Huckleberry Finn,* whom both highbrows and lowbrows can love, we happily have the issue of expression in America kept alive. The plain style asserted that it would find ways of touching the common auditory. Thoreau and Melville were defeated. Mark Twain succeeded, and succeeded without vulgarizing or demeaning himself. If he did it, we have to ask, can the trick not again be turned? Dare we again have a writer who, speaking to all men as one among them, will at the same time satisfy the aristocratic requirements of form? But who will work the miracle without becoming a plain-speaking Broadbrim?

By raising these questions I am taking us back to the curiously contradictory implications of the apparently self-consistent ideal of the plain style. Let me repeat: there is no particular reason why this Puritan code should have been fastened upon America. To begin with, it was a sophisticated doctrine, using the arts in order to conceal the arts. Thoreau and Melville converted it into an artful method of defying the arts. Mark Twain, whose intellect could never be sullied by reflections as to whether he was radical or conservative, ultimately employed simplicity of style for fecundity of effect; without retaining any such vestiges of scholastical theory as clung to Thoreau and Melville, he wrought the purely stylistic triumph. The irony is, the mystery is, that precisely because he did this, we are obliged, along with Ernest Hemingway, to acknowledge that the viable modern American literature comes out of *Huckleberry Finn*.

There is no end to the debate about how much Mark Twain comprehended of the intellectual issues of his America. For him to serve as the supreme dramatizer of them, he may never have needed to comprehend; it may have been enough that he merely saw and recorded. Yet I suspect that however much we give the artistic conscience a freedom to disregard the theological and sociological, we are forced to hold Mark Twain responsible for an abstraction which he might and did abhor. I am inclined to feel that biographers and critics have grossly exaggerated the importance in his youthful training of his mother's "Calvinism." They exaggerate because they know little or nothing of what a true Calvinism would mean to a sensitive youth—to one brought up as, let us say, was Jonathan Edwards, within the formulated creed—or else because they object to certain residual forms of Protestantism which Samuel Clemens did retain out of his typically American experience. For the purposes of literary explication, he probably made these lessons most clear in the epigraphs he put before the chapters of *Pudd'nhead Wilson*—those observations which have little or nothing to do with the story, and which we may plausibly take as Mark Twain's personal revelations. I would not contend that this is the only proper way to read these wisecracks; I am still in a quandary about him. However, permitting him to exploit his ambiguity, let us note that he commences *Pudd'nhead Wilson* with a moralism that might well have been improved, beyond Benjamin Franklin's admission, out of the premises of Poor Richard: "Tell the truth or trump—but get the trick." At that point, I take it, conscience would be obliterated; should this injunction alone prevail, nobody would be left to drive life into a corner. Yet wonderfully enough we have, at the beginning of Chapter 11, another exhortation, and with it the ethic of the plain style comes again to life: "As to the Adjective: when in doubt, strike it out."

Strike out the adjective—this in the Puritan aesthetic had been the practical conclusion, though as we have seen in Thomas Hooker's prose the stubborn creature forced itself into the sentences. The plain style puts a terrible requisition upon the speaker, as Thomas Hooker confessed. Thoreau and Melville tried to meet the obligation by talking through masks (the "I" of *Walden* is as much a disguise of the author as is Captain Ahab); thus they attracted few in their community. Melville had difficulty eliminating the adjective; Thoreau did better at the excision. But we have to say that neither of them ever quite told on the American imagination as did Mark Twain when he had the child of the river decide to protect Nigger Jim and so announce to the Puritanical divinities, "All right, then, I'll *go* to hell."

We are only casually alarmed, or rather quietly amused, by this declaration. We know that slavery was abolished by Mr. Lincoln's Proclamation, and we know that Mark Twain wrote his book at a comfortable distance, in 1884, some two decades after Lincoln's decision. Nobody can hold Mark Twain responsible for our taking Huck's radical resolution literally, in the way in which we must believe Governor Winthrop meant what he told the town of Hingham, that government is set over men for their own good. Mark Twain did not propose to undermine the regulations of society. Still, he did let his hero utter this defiance. And let us note, it contains no adjectives. We have the plain style triumphant.

The adjectives are, of course, the crux of the business. There are not many of them in the passage from Hooker which I have quoted as a fair example of the plain method. Such adjectives as intrude are generalized: "many coasts," "many countries." What is emphasized are the facts of the case: "He hath seen what sin is and what it hath done, how it hath made havoc of his peace and comfort, ruinated and laid waste the very principles of reason and morality, and made him a terror to himself." Let us admit the whole progression of mentality, and happily confess that Hannibal, Missouri, is not Hartford, Connecticut (where, strangely enough, Sam Clemens came to roost); so let us see what Huckleberry Finn made out of the spectacle of innate depravity. Several dawns break over Walden Pond, and in *Moby-Dick* the sun rises over the Pacific Ocean; but had the plain style ever before so woven together the mystery and the depravity? Surely not in any American writing!

> Not a sound anywheres—perfectly still—just like the whole world were asleep, only sometimes the bullfrogs a-cluttering maybe. The first thing to see, looking away over the water, was a kind of dull line—that was the woods on t'other side; you couldn't make nothing else out; then a pale place in the sky; then more paleness spreading around; then the river softened up away off, and warn't black any more, but gray; you could see little dark spots drifting along ever so far away—trading-scows, and such things; and long black streaks—rafts; sometimes you could hear a sweep screaking; or jumbled-up voices, it was so still, and sounds come so far; and by and by you could see a streak on the water which you know by the look of the streak that there's a snag there in a swift current which breaks on it and makes that streak look that way; and you see the mist curl up off the water, and the east reddens up, and the river, and you make out a log cabin in the edge of the woods, away on the bank on t'other side of the river, being a wood-yard, likely, and piled by them cheats so you can throw a dog through it anywheres; then the nice breeze springs up, and comes fanning you from over there, so cool and fresh and sweet to smell on account of the woods and flowers; but sometimes not that way, because they've left dead fish laying around, gars and such, and they do get pretty rank; and the next you've got the full day, and everything smiling in the sun, and the song-birds just going it!

As in the prose of Hooker, the problem is to make the semicolons carry the thrust. Except that in seventeenth-century typography, printers depended more heavily on the comma: the intention is still the same, to make the prose move. Listening to Mark Twain's flow, we may likewise remember Hooker:

> Meditation is not a flourishing of man's wit, but hath a set bout at the search of truth, beats his brain as we say, hammers out a business, as the Gouldsmith with his mettal, he heats it and beats it, turnes it on this side and then on that, fashions it on both that he might frame it to his mind; meditation is hammering of a truth or poynt propounded, that he may carry and conceive the frame and compass in his mind, not salute a truth as we pass by occasionally but solemnly entertain it into our thoughts; Not looke upon a thing presented as spectator or passenger that goes by: but lay other things aside, and look at this as the work and employment for the present to take up our minds.

The fantastic requirements of the plain style, whether in the Puritan sermon or in *Huckleberry Finn,* is simply that language as printed on the page must convey the emphasis, the hesitancies, the searchings of language as it is spoken. Compared with this objective, purely literary speech is an easy achievement. Almost anybody who puts his mind to it can write in the periods of Dr. Johnson or Macaulay; it takes hard work to hit off the cadences of Hooker, and in the late nineteenth century, when literary form is highly codified, it takes the ruse of speaking through the tongue of a Huck Finn for a master stylist to put into print a prose that conforms to the irreducible plainness of the word spoken.

The Adventures of Huckleberry Finn is a challenging work in the history of American expression because more than anything that had come before it, the story pretends to be not only secular but trivial. Many reviewers, in the year it appeared, greeted it as "a boy's book." To a large extent this is what it was and what it remains; there is no better book to give a boy, none he will read with greater avidity. Despite the few efforts made at the time, most notably by William Dean Howells, to call attention to the undertones of the romance, it won its reception, almost overnight, by its appeal to the boyish strain in all mankind. I imagine that nothing would more surprise Mark Twain's contemporaries, and possibly nothing would more surprise Mark Twain himself, than to perceive the amount of portentous, solemn critical analysis which has been devoted to exposing the hidden meanings of *Huck Finn.* Although we cannot be too sure. We just do not know whether he himself understood that he was saying more than appears on the surface, or whether he builded better than he understood, being driven by subliminal forces deep within his own being, hardly realized in his conscious mind.

I think we may safely say that he was apprehensive, that he was even a bit dismayed by what he had done. True, he could keep up his public character as an American "humorist" by prefacing the book with a "Notice," but I suspect that most of us are alerted by this pantomime of the "funny man" to an awareness of something other than mere joking at work:

> Persons attempting to find a motive in this narrative will be prosecuted; persons attempting to find a moral in it will be banished; persons attempting to find a plot in it will be shot.

At first sight we may declare this about as far removed from the tone of Thomas Hooker's preface to *A Survey of the Summe of Church-Discipline* as any spokesman for a culture could possibly travel in a little over two centuries. Yet when we listen to it more attentively, noting that this jape is prefixed to the immense majesty of Huck's voyage down the Mississippi, we remember Hooker's plea that his discourse appeared in a homely dress and coarse habit because it came "out of the wilderness." The theologian trained in the logic of schoolmen thus made one of the first gestures in our literature toward repudiating the disciplines of European scholarship in the name of a wild simplicity. Of course, Hooker was not creating a thing of imagination, and in a sense, because he was defending Congregational polity, he was drawing out a moral, even a "plot." Yet he was also explaining in advance that there were some things he would not say too openly; he would content himself whenever he pleased with indirection, with understatement, with a deliberate neglect of "curiosity." Though Mark Twain was not a New Englander, and probably never paid any attention to the name of Hooker, it is still fair to say that his apology develops the theme which Hooker first propounded, that the writer in America has the privilege of using a European method of expression in order to observe certain reticences.

Following this observation we come face to face with an irony, one with which I freely confess I cannot entirely cope. Ostensibly the Puritan concept of style professes to deal with all human concerns; it asserts that the orator or the narrator must not take refuge in verbal embellishments to communicate his emotion. "My care and study," wrote Samuel Willard of the Old South Church in Boston, "was to accommodate it to the meanest hearer, chusing with the Apostle, to speak five words intelligibly, than many more in an unknown manner of expression; and I hope these truths will relish never the worse to those that love truth for its own sake, because they are not garnished with florid language." However, what the Puritan literature eventually makes clear is that while through it the truths are made supremely manifest precisely because they are not garnished with florid language, there are certain aspects of truth which have to go without being said at all. Thus we come directly to Huck's understatement at finding Buck Grangerford murdered by the Shephersons:

> When I got down out of the tree I crept along down the river-bank a piece, and found the two bodies laying in the edge of the water, and tugged at them till I got them ashore; then I covered up their faces, and got away as quick as I could. I cried a little when I was covering up Buck's face, for he was mighty good to me.

Here we assuredly have no florid language. And here is truth for its own

sake, the truth of sheer terror. Huck, let us notice, observes the slaughter
from the safe refuge of a cottonwood tree—much as a famous serpent is
reputed to have lurked in a tree and from its false security to have hissed,
"Ye shall not surely die." Huck spares us none of the agony simply by
not being too precise: "I ain't a-going to tell *all* that happened—it would
make me sick again if I was to do that. I wished I hadn't ever come ashore
that night to see such things. I ain't ever going to get shut of them—lots
of times I dream about them."

I would like to believe that the time has long since passed when we
have to blame some fabricated monster of "Puritanism" for a blight that
has supposedly fallen upon the American spirit. We have heard the charges
that it starved our sexual appetites, that it tried to deprive us of the
consolations of alcohol. In rebuttal, several historians, of whom I suppose
I am one, have pointed out that the Puritans enjoyed a vigorous and
productive sexuality, that they drank staggering quantities of rum. By
now this topic for recrimination has, I hope, worn itself out. It is not
necessary to insist any longer that the Puritans could love their wives,
their children, or that they could spend pleasant evenings with the neighbors. There is no longer any reason for pretending that the Puritans' living
in daily confrontation of the overwhelming issues of predestination and
eternal salvation did not prevent them from indulging in petty animosities,
village gossip, and displays of sheer spite.

Perhaps, then, a better way of confronting our paradox is to say that
the Puritan influence upon American literature came to be a curse, grew
into a repression against which the literary conscience had to revolt, because
it ceased to be genuinely Puritan and instead became merely didactic. In
this process a double disaster was enacted: on the one side, the splendor
of the Protestant conception of life as an ordeal was watered down to a
comfortable moralism of good cheer; on the other, the meanness, the
brutality, which Calvinism always recognized in the ordinary conduct
of Christians, was covered over with a gauze of sentimentality. The
triumph of this twofold modification was the popular verse of the New
England "household poets" of the mid-nineteenth century, Longfellow
and Holmes, Whittier and Bryant, with their invariable proof that life
is real and life is earnest. They so pervaded the schoolroom conception of
literature by the end of their century that rebellion could no longer be
stifled, became in fact irresistible. We encounter Ernest Hemingway saying, just before he makes his salute to Mark Twain, that the New England
classics—he includes Emerson and Hawthorne along with "Whittier, and
Company"—were all gentlemen, all respectable, with small, dried wisdoms.
"They did not use the words that people always have used in speech, the
words that survive in language. Nor would you gather that they had
bodies. They had minds, yes. Nice, dry, clean minds."

The Puritan founders also had minds, but not nice, dry, clean minds.
Such a man as Thomas Hooker did not work up his metaphors in order

to prove himself a gentleman. The hazards of living were too important for him (as for Thoreau) to bother about that consideration. In this regard, Hooker's language is alive, where Longfellow's stanzas are not. Yet all their lifetime, Longfellow, "Whittier and Company" were serenely persuaded that they derived legitimately from the Puritans, that though they had become Unitarians or, as Hemingway calls them, "Quakers with a sense of humor," they were continuing the high ethical devotion of their ancestors, and were composing in a manner compatible with the lofty purposes of edification. They never realized how fatally they had lost the innermost secret of Puritan expression: they made everything explicit, they propounded the inexpressible moral, and so announced that the grave is not life's goal. As compared with Huck Finn, they had no reticences. They tried to make truth so solid that it no longer had any resonance in the minds of the common auditory. Never for a moment did they confess that they were not a-going to tell *all,* for nothing they had to tell would make them sick again in the telling, if only because they had never been sick in the first place. The result was that they became the orthodox poets of American households, while Melville and Thoreau, who did have horrors to relate even by indirection, were disregarded. All of which makes our debt to Mark Twain infinitely greater: by pretending to write a boy's book, he captured an American audience; under the guise of protesting he had no moral and no motive, and not even a plot, he hymned the dawn over the Mississippi and allowed one beautifully sentient being to reconcile himself to going to hell.

Huckleberry Finn would not be the masterpiece it is had not Mark Twain, by speaking through the person of the boy, been able to respect the reticences which had originally been calculated devices of plain discourse. When in later life Mark Twain strove to become more explicit in his pessimism, in his castigations of the "damned human race," he waxed merely tedious. Many of the aphorisms of *Pudd'nhead Wilson* are already boring. One may sympathize with his black moods, may see in them testimonies to his inherent nobleness of spirit, but the speech is monotonous. The beauty of Huck Finn is that the boy sees all there is to see about human depravity, violence, skulduggery, as well as virtually all which is noble, lovely, self-sacrificing, and that he tells about both without ever yielding to florid language. Or, to put it another way, he never draws the moral, he lets the language show what is better left unsaid. The mock "Notice" is as serious in intent as Hooker's preface: in the altered cultural context, it says the same thing.

There is no doubt a fine bravado about flying directly into the face of the sun. In New England we are apt to suppose this propensity somehow allied to a "Latin" or a "Mediterranean" upbringing—at least to a youth closer connected with the sun. We think, perhaps, of Pickett's charge at Gettysburg as the last suidical surge of the operatic style. No American writer who had firsthand reason to understand the facts has been more caustic than Mark Twain about the romanticism of the Confederate mentality. He went so far as to say that Sir Walter Scott caused the Civil War. His denunciation of the feudal fantasy of the South, most eloquent in *Life on the Mississippi,* is the cry of a soul in torment, who feels himself betrayed by the stupendous rhetoric on which he was weaned. Accordingly, the linguistic realism of *Huckleberry Finn* comes from something far deeper than a desire to reproduce several dialects accurately. Mark Twain did permit himself to boast that in the book he had caught the differences in inflection among Missouri, Arkansas, Louisiana; we may thus consign the book to philologists, who have not yet plumbed the recesses of his astoundingly clever ear. As Puritan preachers first suggested, mimicry is a telling way to inform men about the things they casually say. But mimicry, after a short time, becomes a dead routine. How to make the words that survive in language, those used in speech, also words that spring from the printed page—here was the challenge to the Puritans, here was the invitation to Thoreau and Melville, here was the mission Mark Twain took upon himself in *The Adventures of Huckleberry Finn.* He did not have to assume so strenuous a job. He had already written a facsimile boy's book, *Tom Sawyer,* in which he spoke not through the boy's mouth but through the author's. He could have repeated that *ad infinitum,* or just have written dialect and earned royalties. Even when he congratulated himself on getting the various lingos right in *Huckleberry Finn,* he knew that this was not the reason for his having written the book. He would be the last to say it, but we may say it: what he really did was write a romance, a grandiose adventure story, within the strict limitations of the plain style. He said more than he ever would attempt to say openly by imposing upon himself the restrictions of partial statement. For this reason he becomes, as Mr. Hemingway rightly proposes, the progenitor of modern American literature.

I am aware that when one speaks thus broadly, and invokes sweeping definitions of national characteristics, he is apt to speak nonsense. William Faulkner, for instance, has also confessed his debt to Mark Twain, but I suspect that many of the more convoluted portions of his novels could hardly be cited as modern exemplars of the plain style. Yet even there, Faulkner curiously observes the reticence. At the end of *Absalom, Absalom,* after Quentin Compson has kept his Canadian roommate awake through what must have been a more interminable night than ever Marlow needed to relate the tragedy of *Lord Jim,* this Southerner moans out the withheld significance of his story of the Sutphens in dramatic understatement. "Why," Shreve asks, "do you hate the South?"

"I don't hate it," Quentin said, quickly, at once, immediately; "I don't hate it," he said, *I don't hate it* he thought, panting in the cold air, the iron New England dark; *I don't, I don't! I don't hate it! I don't hate it!*

Neither did Mark Twain. Neither did Thomas Hooker hate the clearing in the wilderness he called Hartford. Nevertheless, in order to prove the point, Hooker, Mark Twain, and William Faulkner are compelled to assert the obvious. What rings in the consciousness of their readers is what lies, unsaid, behind their compulsion. To let be said these things which otherwise are not to be spoken at all, this is the purpose of the plain style. This is why it has in general become, for reasons which may be historically sketched, but which still remain psychologically baffling, the characteristically American manner.

It must always be accounted to the credit of William Dean Howells that he, more than any other of Mark Twain's contemporaries, perceived the profound literary importance of the book which most people at the time took to be simply clever clowning. Yet fine as were Howell's tributes, we are obliged today to reflect that even he did not peer as deeply as he should have into the subterranean springs of *Huckleberry Finn.* Twain, Howells said, was the "Lincoln of our literature." This would have been indeed perceptive had Howells gone on to see the analogy in the fact that these two inspired raconteurs used comedy, even slapstick, to mask a black melancholy that coiled around the base of their spirits. The Lincoln who read Artemus Ward's "goaks" to his cabinet as a preliminary to telling them about the Emancipation Proclamation was the man who found never-ending consolation in chanting to himself, "Oh, why should the spirit of mortal be proud?" The same Mark Twain who could do a hilarious burlesque of Emmeline Grangerford's mortuary poetry would let Huck meditate upon the tarring and feathering of the king and the duke, "Well, it made me sick to see it; and I was sorry for them poor pitiful rascals, it seemed like I couldn't ever feel any hardness against them any more in the world. It was a dreadful thing to see. Human beings *can* be awful cruel to one another."

What Howells did stress by his comparison with Lincoln amounted to something a bit less complicated, namely, that Twain's books, particularly *Huckleberry Finn,* embodied on one side the "vast kindliness and good-will" of the American character and on the other its "shrewdness." This balance of attributes is assuredly there, and something of the same balance enters into the personality of Melville's Ishmael and also into the image that Henry Thoreau projected of himself in *Walden,* though there the effort to hide the kindliness often effectively conceals its presence. However, these three would hardly have increased so rapidly in stature, as lately they have indeed grown upon our horizon, had they presented only some Lincolnesque version of an Uncle Sam, kind and yet shrewd. And in the case of *Huckleberry Finn,* the labor of penetrating the surface has been the most difficult. There was a time, in the years after Twain's death in 1910, when the very fact of its immense popularity among the generality of readers inspired a hostility to it among intellectuals. In 1920 Van Wyck Brooks voiced this mood with *The Ordeal of Mark Twain.* If there has grown up a more profound reading of Mark Twain it is in great part because of the sustained campaign for deeper insight conducted by the late Bernard De Voto. In his blunt, outspoken way, Mr. De Voto may have uttered too many hyperboles, but his shock tactics succeeded in forcing all to realize that when the humorist went back to memories of his youth in Hannibal, "he found there not only the idyl of boyhood but anxiety, violence, supernatural horror, and an uncrystallized but enveloping dread."

The popularity of Mark Twain among those possessing only what Howells called "ordinary minds" was a great consolation to Howells himself, because it confirmed his democratic trust that the American people would welcome a literature which ceased to lie about life, which told the truth. The immense factuality has certainly been an element in its appeal; we can, if we wish, go back to it again and again for its panoramic documentation of a civilization. It is not actually a very long book; hence we marvel anew at how much of the river, how many ways of living, how many people it presents us. But then, while *Moby-Dick* is indeed longer, still what a staggering array of minute detail it gives, and then think for a moment of the wealth of fact contained in *Walden!* One reason why I like to think of these three as the finest achievements of the plain style in America (again admitting that there are rhetorical flourishes in *Moby-Dick* which almost disqualify it from being so accounted) is that they use words to stand for things, objects, concrete entities. On this score, *Huckleberry Finn* is the most dense of the three; indeed, Mark Twain's reveling in things for and in themselves frequently becomes an ecstatic inventory, nowhere more exuberant than in the catalogue of loot Huck and Nigger Jim take out of the house afloat on the river:

> We got an old tin lantern, and a butcher-knife without any handle, and a bran-new Barlow knife worth two bits in any store, and a lot of tallow candles, and a tin candlestick, and a gourd, and a tin cup, and a ratty old bedquilt off the bed, and a reticule with needles and pins and beeswax and buttons and thread and all such truck in it, and a hatchet and some nails, and a fish-line as thick as my little finger with some monstrous hooks on it, and a roll of buckskin, and a leather dog-collar, and a horseshoe, and some vials of medicine that didn't have no label on them; and just as we was leaving I found a tolerable good currycomb, and Jim he found a ratty old fiddlebow, and a wooden leg, though it was too long for me and not long enough for Jim, and we couldn't find the other one, though we hunted all around.

On first reading, we laugh at the sheer incongruity of the assemblage. On a later reading we suddenly become aware of how pitiable, how forlorn, how heartbreaking is the portrait of a culture which this aggregation summons vividly before us. This is someone's house, a typical house in that semipioneer condition, washed away by the mighty river, and these miserable artifacts tell their sordid story. It becomes impossible to laugh; we are on the verge of bitter tears.

In a stimulating study of *The American Novel and Its Tradition,*

Professor Richard Chase makes an astute observation upon the several dialects used in *Huckleberry Finn:* while the book pretends to be the natural speech of an uneducated boy, it is all the more a "literary" performance because, says Mr. Chase, "it is always conscious of the traditional English—notably of the Bible and Shakespeare—from which it is departing." The fact that it exorcises traditional literary English allies it irrevocably with what it exorcises. I think that this device is a stylistic element in what I have called Huck Finn's reticences. He seems to be writing everything out, just as it occurs to him, holding back nothing; but all the time he looks on the panorama of people and things with an objectivity that is terrifyingly surgical, and never, even in what purports to be the most direct address to the reader, explicitly tells the secret of his book. So Mark Twain richly deserves the praise both Hemingway and Faulkner have bestowed upon him, and their work pre-eminently exhibits what later American novelists did learn from *Huckleberry Finn.* A transparent simplicity, one which does not throw the reader off with florid language, is effective to the extent that it forces the reader to perceive for himself that which the clarity of statement can only imply. In this respect, then, *The Adventures of Huckleberry Finn* is the supreme victory in our literature of that ethic of the plain style which Protestants brought to colonial America and which Puritans in New England first exemplified.

Wherever the topic of religion figures in the book, it is almost always organized religion and churchgoing, and it is invariably a subject for ridicule. "Sivilized" life in the Widow Douglas' house is made intolerable for Huck by her piety. "When you got to the table you couldn't go right to eating, but you had to wait for the widow to tuck down her head and grumble a little over the victuals." Miss Watson tells him that if he will pray every day, he will get what he asks for: "But it warn't so. I tried it. Once I got a fish-line, but no hooks. It warn't any good to me without hooks. I tried for the hooks three or four times, but somehow I couldn't make it work." A Sunday school picnic is fair game for a raid by Tom Sawyer's gang; at the Grangerfords' Huck tries to read *Pilgrim's Progress,* "about a man that left his family, it didn't say why. I read considerable in it now and then. The statements was interesting, but tough." Or, most pointed, when Miss Sophia sends him back to the church to get her Bible, he finds nobody in the building that afternoon but several hogs, and Huck moralizes at his shrewdest, "If you notice, most folks don't go to church only when they've got to; but a hog is different."

So, then, the formal religion of America is a target for comic demolition. The theology of Bunyan and the rigors of Sunday school, the efficacy of prayer and the doctrine of divine providence all come in for a wholesale reduction to absurdity. Is the book then a covertly antireligious tract disguised as the voyage of a raft down the Mississippi? In a sense, yes, it is. But then one has to learn in what sense. Again Mr. Chase's insight assists us: in relation to true Christianity, Huck's religious naïveté stands in much the same relation that the dialect stands to the English of Shakespeare and the Bible. This is once more a device of the plain style, which confronts the mystery of the faith by indirection. And as several students have variously pointed out, the link that takes us to a faith which is not a ritual or a cramping of life's joys is the bondman, Nigger Jim. It is a ghastly mistake Huck commits, letting the raft get past Cairo; Jim, being carried deeper and deeper into the land of bondage, is the one who will suffer for Huck's iniquity. Huck cries out in anguish; he wishes he had not transgressed. "It ain't yo' fault, Huck; you didn't know," says Jim. "Don't blame yo'self 'bout it." Somewhere in the heart of this book, but well hidden, is a benediction of forgiveness. The unspoken secret behind the ragamuffin's relentless objectivity in viewing the human comedy is that he functions as the avatar of a charity which, though no supernatural warrant is ever claimed for it, far transcends all the conventional levels of morality.

THE ROMANCE AND THE NOVEL

I

IN 1846, Herman Melville scored an immense success with an account of what purported to be his adventures in the South Seas, entitled *Typee*. He was an utter novice, had received little education, and was equipped to become an author only by his gusto and his fund of experience. Intoxicated by his unexpected fortune, he turned out a sequel, *Omoo,* which was also profitable. With, as far as we can tell, not the slightest conception of what in his America it meant to set up as a professional writer, Melville married Elizabeth Shaw, daughter of the monumental Chief Justice of the Commonwealth of Massachusetts, took a house in New York City, and prepared to support both her and himself by turning out a third best-seller.

Although widely praised and purchased, the two narratives had also been attacked. Not so much because they showed Protestant missionaries as despoilers of a Polynesian Eden as because, while claiming to be truthful narratives of real escapades, they were so full of improbabilities that Melville could be accused, in the language of the day, of "romancing." His New York sponsors were embarrassed by this charge, and his English publisher—he had had the good fortune to be taken up by the great John Murray—was dead set against printing fantasies of the imagination. So as Melville sat down to produce his third book, the injunction lay heavy upon him to keep it factual. He strove manfully. He got through thirty-eight chapters of a story about a whaling ship and two sailors who desert a tyrannical captain. Though not presenting itself as another piece of autobiography, up to this point it was plausible, matter-of-fact, compatible with the realities of ships and the sea. Then something hit him, just what we do not know. On March 25, 1848, he wrote Murray that while he had indeed promised "a bona-fide narrative of my adventures in the Pacific, continued from Omoo," still—this is the reason he gave an astonished Murray—the reiterated charge of his being a romancer so galled him that he had determined to show his critics what a *"real* romance" was. Therefore, he reported, "suddenly abandoning the thing altogether, I went to work heart & soul at a romance." He knew, even though in his folly he did not sufficiently estimate, Murray's contempt for Romances. It would be new and original, he pleaded; then he blurted out his mad resolution: "My *instinct* is to out with the Romance, & let me say that instincts are prophetic, & better than acquired wisdom."

These three essays were delivered as the Jacob Ziskind Lectures at Smith College in 1956.

Instinct in this case proved sadly lacking in prophetic insight. Murray promptly rejected the substitution, but Richard Bentley in London took a chance on *Mardi,* as the romance was now entitled, while Harper and Brothers, gambling on the pull of Melville's name, risked it in New York. The result in both cities was disaster. But what concerns us at the moment is not the history of Melville's reputation but the fact that, once he decided to change course, he had at hand precisely the term to describe his new direction. The "thing" he abandoned was a novel, "a true narrative"; what instinct drove him to could be immediately designated, with a capital letter, as "Romance." The distinction between the two was as precise in the mind of an untutored Melville as that between, let us say, an epic and a sonnet, simply because it was equally present to every even semiliterate consciousness in the era.

Some thirty-six years later, in 1884, while Melville was still alive, Henry James published in London an essay on "The Art of Fiction." This by now celebrated piece was a reply to Walter Besant, who had outraged James (if so violent a verb can be said ever to have pertained to him) by laying down rules by which one could say "definitely beforehand what sort of an affair the good novel will be." James answered that all such a priori theorizing is illegitimate, because the novel "lives upon exercise, and the very meaning of exercise is freedom." In denouncing artificial prescriptions James sweeps away the once "celebrated distinction between the novel and the romance." This, he acknowledges, had been supposed a reality in the days of his youth, but to him it appeared "to have been made by critics and readers for their own convenience, and to help them out of some of their occasional queer predicaments." He could think of no obligation to which the "romancer" would not be held equally with the novelist: "the standard of execution is equally high for each." He would not make exception even for Hawthorne, who, James insisted, tacked the word *Romance* onto his *Blithedale* "simply for the pleasantness of the thing." As far as we know, James, for all that the "small boy" in New York took in virtually all the literary phenomena of the place, quite disregarded Melville.

Upon the failure of *Mardi,* Melville endeavored to rehabilitate his fame by two sober narratives which might pass for novels—*Redburn* in 1849 and *White-Jacket* in 1850: the former he himself called "beggarly." In 1850 he apparently started another novel, but somewhere in the tumultuous composition, this project, even more peremptorily than *Mardi,* took off into the empyrean of Romance. Since even Hollywood honors *Moby-Dick's* importance, we are justified in pausing in our admiration to ask just how much of its present acclaim as one of the six or seven indubitable masterpieces of the century is owing to its being conceived as a "Romance." Even though the term be pronounced irrelevant to modern criticism—as to James—Melville's letter to Murray shows that to him it was very much alive. It was not something made up for his own convenience, but figured for him as a way out of a "queer" predicament. Again he was disappointed. Although *Moby-Dick* found a few more or less tepid defenders, it too failed of success.

By this time, Melville was insensate. In a fury he threw upon paper another book, and almost hysterically pleaded with Bentley to publish it. *Pierre*, which he had called a "regular romance," was not even a disaster; it was catastrophe. Though after 1852 Melville did some work which modern resurrectors find absorbing, his career as a writer of public stature was shattered by *Pierre*.

Pierre scandalized its few reviewers and fewer readers for a variety of reasons, but all of these can be subsumed under the charge that, far from being a regular Romance, it was a vicious perversion of a formula so universally worshipped as to be in effect sacrosanct. A generation had grown up breathing the atmosphere of the Romance as naturally as they breathed the air of America. And there can be little doubt that this intermingling of the literary form with the consciousness of the nation was wrought in the early decades of the century, not by an American, but by the Wizard of the North, "the Author of *Waverley*."

In England, if not elsewhere, a critical separation of the Romance from the novel had been evolving during the three or four decades before Sir Walter Scott confirmed it. Indeed, the German distinction between "Classical" and "Romantic" shows a parallel movement, though English theorists were as yet fairly ignorant of the language and owed little to this discrimination of the Schlegels. That the recognition was becoming common at the turn of the century can be discerned in the writings of others beside Scott, notably Hazlitt. Still, it was Scott who validated the currency, who established it as substantially an ineluctable law of nature, and he did this by both precept and example. In 1823 he wrote for the *Encyclopedia Britannica* "An Essay on Romance," which quickly circulated as a separate publication. Scott directed his erudition to the metrical romances of the Middle Ages, but his generalizations applied not only to the verse narratives with which he won fame in the first decade of the century but also to the prose fictions by which in the second decade he acquired an infinitely larger audience. Dr. Johnson, Scott noted, had been dimly aware of the difference between a Romance and novel: he defined the Romance as "a military fable of the middle ages; a tale of wild adventures in love and chivalry," as opposed to the novel, which, ruled Johnson, is "a smooth tale, generally of love." But now Scott, with all the insight a passionate study of the Middle Ages had imparted to him (and in his case probably with some tuition from Germany), contradicted the great polymath. The novel, he said, should more properly be described as "a fictitious narrative, differing from the Romance, because the events are accommodated to the ordinary train of human events, and the modern state of society," whereas, the Romance—as *Waverley, The Antiquary, Rob Roy, Ivanhoe, Quentin Durward* had made splendidly clear—is "a fictitious narrative in prose or verse; the interest of which turns upon marvellous and uncommon incidents."

The triumph of the Waverley Romances was so complete—from the very first years when an elaborate guessing game was conducted on each side of the Atlantic as to who the mysterious Wizard might be—that sober persons brought up on Alexander Pope and accustomed to regard Fielding, Smollett, and Fanny Burney as the glories of English fiction, those trained to consider marvellous and uncommon incidents as the vulgar trappings of such gothic sensationalists as Mrs. Radcliffe and Monk Lewis, were overwhelmed by the tide. The response in America was as immediate as in England. Scott overcame even the cool distrust of rational Unitarians in Boston; more spectacularly, he conquered by a wave of his wand the deepseated objection of orthodox Protestants to wasting precious time on fiction. Catherine Beecher's fiancé died in 1822, leaving her his library; her father Lyman forbade the children to touch a single volume until he had inspected the lot. After reading *Ivanhoe* he emerged from the ministerial study with the fiat: "You may read Scott's novels. I have always disapproved of novels as trash, but in these is real genius and real culture, and you may read them." Scott's Romances were devoured in Virginia and New Orleans, were carried—and treasured—by pioneers on their migration to Kentucky, and they formed the staple of culture in Hannibal on the banks of the Mississippi in Missouri.

Waverley was published in 1814, the other volumes following with bewildering rapidity. In a matter not of years but of months such literary journals as strove for existence in the infant republic were asking why we Americans had nothing to match them. Is it true, they asked, that we are, as the British charge, such a "down-right, inflexible, matter-of-fact sort of people" that our land is utterly destitute of romantic associations? Are there here no "materials for the higher order of fictitious composition"? In 1821 the answer came ringing clear: James Fenimore Cooper produced *The Spy*. It was received as avidly as any of the Waverley series, and Cooper, much to his disgust, was hailed as "the American Scott." Even the staid *North American Review,* which as a Boston voice begrudged any praise of New York and as a Unitarian vehicle had little enthusiasm for the imagination, had to concede to Cooper, despite his slovenly grammar, the glory "of having struck a new path—of having opened a mine of exhaustless wealth—in a word, he has laid the foundations of American romance, and is really the first who deserves the appellation of a distinguished American novel writer."

Though the critical terms were still so new to this country that the *North American,* like Lyman Beecher in the same year, was confused as to which was which, the series of Romances that Cooper thereupon threw off with a fecundity equal to Scott's—*The Pilot* in 1823, *The Last of the Mohicans* in 1826, *The Prairie* in 1827—so instructed the American public in the genre that any who could read at all came to take its features for granted. The success of Cooper inevitably showed others how to exploit the market he and Scott had opened. Catherine Sedgwick in New England, Richard Montgomery Bird in Philadelphia, James Hall in Cincinnati, John Pendleton Kennedy in Baltimore, Charles Fenno Hoffman in New York, even John Lothrop Motley in Boston, Daniel Thompson in Vermont, Nathaniel Beverly Tucker and William Caruthers in Virginia—one and all they turned out Romances, each seeking to do for his region what Cooper had done in making the Hudson Valley "Romantic." The most prolific of them, in his day considered the rival of Cooper, was William Gilmore Simms of Charleston, South Carolina. When a friend in New York City, where it may be noted that a kind of underground resistance to the Romance hung on, expressed mild dissent from one of Simm's books, he replied that the reviewer had not grasped the essential character of the Romance, "the standards of which are as different from those of the novel, as its characteristics are." Were you to determine, Simms insisted, the merits of *Ivanhoe* by the rules that govern a judgment of *Tom Jones,* then indeed his own books were trash. But they must be evaluated in their terms; as he said of his most successful, *The Yamassee,* published in 1835, the modern Romance "differs much more seriously from the English novel than it does from the epic and the drama, because the difference is one of material, even more than of fabrication."

This battalion of Romancers is mostly forgotten today. Although until the day before yesterday boys continued to read Cooper, Simms is known only to antiquarians. However, if we look objectively at the literary mentality of America before the Civil War, we realize that it was dominated by the then throbbing conventions of the Romance. These books were not dime novels, they were not amusements for idle ladies (though there were of course cheap imitations by the score); they were serious efforts to put the meaning of America, of life in America, into the one form that seemed providentially given, through the exemplum of Scott, for expressing the deepest passions of the continent. Thus we may justifiably accuse Henry James of confusing the issue—as we shall see, he did it deliberately—when he insists that the term Romance really has no relevance to an understanding of Hawthorne. James's brilliant study of Hawthorne, published in 1879, pointedly ignores Hawthorne's prefaces, most wantonly that to *The House of the Seven Gables,* of 1851. Therein Hawthorne is exceedingly explicit:

> When a writer calls his work a Romance, it need hardly be observed that he wishes to claim a certain latitude, both as to its fashion and material, which he would not have felt himself entitled to assume, had he professed to be writing a Novel.

So Hawthorne begged his readers to take the book "strictly as a Romance, having a great deal more to do with the clouds overhead than with any portion of the actual soil of the County of Essex." Neither can we suppose that he gave his title to *The Blithedale Romance* in 1852 only for the pleasantness of the thing, or that he was not in earnest when he insisted that his treatment of Brook Farm, insofar as it served as model for his setting, was "altogether incidental to the main purpose of the romance." He still knew in 1860 what he was doing as he subtitled *The Marble Faun* "A Romance of Monte Beni," and explained that Italy served him "as the site of his Romance" because there "actualities would not be so terribly insisted upon as they are, and must needs be in America." And so we are likewise duty bound to respect the precision of Melville's instinct—Melville who worshipped Hawthorne, who lived beside him and conversed with him —when it drove him to what he could consciously call a Romance. *Moby-Dick* was dedicated to Hawthorne; and Melville's friend and patron in New York, Evert Duyckinck, dismayed by the book but endeavoring to help it along, could do no better for it than to call it "an intellectual chowder of romance." Though there are innumerable perspectives from which *Moby-Dick* may be viewed—indeed, in recent years we have been offered rather too many—yet none of them is looking at the object itself unless it proceeds on an awareness that the book is the supreme thrust of the Romance in America. The secret of *Moby-Dick*—or rather the innermost secret behind the myriad lesser secrets—is that it pushes the Romance to extremities which exhaust the form. As Ishmael meticulously expounds it, Captain Ahab holds the crew in his demonic power despite the sordidness which in Ahab's opinion is "the permanent constitutional condition of manufactured man," and thus can drive them on to their "one final and romantic object."

Today when we speak of the Romance or of romantic fiction, we think merely of the lonely horseman in the dark woods, the flight, pursuit, the daring leap, the secret cave, the timely rescue, the tournament, the villain foiled, and the fade-out with hero clutching heroine. And in truth, many of the vulgar Romances of the time were nothing more. An English hack, who published as G. P. R. James ("alphabet James," he was called), turned out reams of such confections, which were greedily consumed by the masses as the more substantial members of society devoured Scott and Cooper. It remains true, however, that the contrived dash and charge are indispensable elements in the Romance. When Simms criticized Cooper for defective management of plot, saying that in him there was "none of that careful grouping of means to ends, and all to the one end of the denouement, which so remarkably distinguished the genius of Scott, and made all the parts of his story fit so compactly as the work of the joiner," we are inclined to reply that what Simms found a deficiency in Cooper we now salute as a virtue he displayed despite himself. Though he tried to manipulate the action according to the standard pattern, he had so much feeling for life and landscape that he often smothered the plot with extraneous material drawn from his rich experience, and informed by his broad, manly sympathies. In this respect *The Pioneers,* published in 1823, is perhaps his worst failure as a Romancer; yet because the wooden plot is only an excuse for his poignant threnody of the passing of the frontier with which Cooper had grown up, the Lake Oswego region, it comes through to any who will give himself to the reading, as it did to D. H. Lawrence, as "marvellously beautiful."

Yet there is a curious circumstance to be noted when we go back to the contemporaneous reception of both Scott and Cooper: first Scott, then Cooper, then other popular practitioners of the form, were saluted not so much for their adventurous plots as for the amount of truthful and accurate detail by which they made their adventures plausible. In fact, when Scott found that he had *Waverley* on his hands, he did not know quite how to classify it. In his playful "Introductory" he endeavored to distinguish it from then existing modes. It was not, he said, a gothic tale like one of Anne Radcliffe's; it was not a German fantasy (at this time he applied the term "romance" to this form) of daggers and trap doors and *Doppelgängers;* it was not a sentimental story in the manner of Goldsmith; it was not a novel of contemporary life as written by Jane Austen. What then could he call his venture? Without at the moment adopting the word, Scott proclaimed the thesis which soon became the recognized definition of the Scottian Romance: "It is from the great book of Nature, the same through a thousand editions, whether of black-letter, or wire-wove and hot pressed, that I have venturously essayed to read a chapter to the public." Nature with a capital N—Nature as meaning both universal human nature and natural landscape—this is what for Scott and his adulators his sort of fiction signified. And if Scotland and medieval England presented a tableau of uncorrupted human nature amid unspoiled mountains and rills, then what splendid opportunities did America offer the Romancer! Ruined castles, old traditions, ancient wrongs—these were not necessary; the only materials required for the "higher order" of composition were natural men and maidens amid the virgin forest. These materials America could furnish in abundance.

Because Scott was scholar as well as Wizard, he took immense pains to "get up" the manners, speech, costumes, legal procedures, superstitions, table manners of his periods, whether eighteenth-century Scotland as in *Waverley* or twelfth-century England in *Ivanhoe*. This union of opposites in happy synthesis is what chiefly conquered his readers. "With his love of the picturesque and romantic," said the *North American Review*, "the author unites a singular intimacy with men in the practical, common pursuits." Whereupon the reviewer—Edward Tyrrel Channing, who taught rhetoric at Harvard to such students as Emerson and Thoreau— beautifully confesses the reason why Scott's triumph was so complete and so universal: while in these Romances the imagination is never straitened by the perpetual reality of things, neither "does it lose itself in endless and vain illusions." In other words, Scott provided a holiday excursion into the excitements of flight and pursuit without seducing readers into fantasy. Because he documented his plots with authentic facts and actual scenes, he was pre-eminently *safe*. In the final analysis, this is what Scott meant by insisting that he went to the great book of Nature. "No man," agreed Channing, "will be made an idle visionary by the union between life and poetry in these works, for it is just such a union as is established by nature." Let us remark that in America of 1820 or 1830, with a million or more square miles of Nature to the west of it, there was no place whatsoever for the idle visionary.

In the critical terminology of the era a word soon came into general usage to connote just what was aimed at by this Romantic naturalism: *vraisemblance*. This did not mean in the slightest what fifty years later became the rallying cry of "realism." It conveyed that minuteness, that fidelity which come from an author's surrendering himself passively to the impress of Nature; it meant, for instance, that he did not presume, even though a Wizard, to invent landscapes. Scott maintained, says another of his American disciples, "that whoever copies truly what is before his eyes, will possess the same variety in his descriptions, and exhibit apparently an imagination as boundless as the range of nature in the scenes he records," whereas he who trusts only his imagination will find his mind contracted to a few repeated images, will produce that monotony "which always haunts descriptive poetry in the hands of any but the patient worshippers of truth." *Vraisemblance* at bottom is a conserving, not to say a conservative, conception: it lets imagination roam into the farthest reaches of daring-do, but in the end brings emotions back to the sanity of a stable society. Scott's language, his celebrators constantly insisted, is beautiful in its simplicity: it is of the eye, not of diseased reflection, "there is nothing abstract, nothing undefined in his pictures—all is imaged, colored, moving—and not only so, but the succession of images in his narratives, is in the same order as that of events in the scene—they rise, move, and pass, as they do to a spectator's eyes." Once we get a sense of how resolutely, how nervously, the Romancers belabored this argument, we are driven to the somewhat surprising awareness that in the orthodox Romance of the early nineteenth century there was a strong, a half-concealed but pervasive antiromantic moral. Seen in this perspective, the Romance becomes a method for exorcising the demonic, not by preaching and not by the genial satire of common sense, but by giving the demon full play, and then letting the eternal verities subdue it by the obstinacy of inertia.

So, for example, Cooper defended his portrait of Natty Bumppo, no doubt the finest creation of Romantic genius in American literature. "Imagination," Cooper said in the general preface to the five-volume Leatherstocking epic, has no great task conceiving a being removed from civilized life who finds the impress of the Deity in the wind and the forest. But were this being presented without "any of the drawbacks of humanity," the picture would be false. It would not teach true piety, it would make natural piety chimerical. Therefore, "in order to preserve the *vraisemblable*," Cooper added the prejudices, manners, weaknesses of the man. That is, he let us see Natty's discolored teeth and had Natty wipe his nose on his sleeve. Thus Cooper was assured, not that he had devised a frontiersman such as one might actually encounter on the frontier—for that was not his concern—but that he had avoided offering the spectator "a monster of goodness." To provide the interest of adventure without resorting to monsters, either of goodness or of evil, this was the secret, the relentless determination, of what we may call the orthodox Romance.

The devices by which this purpose was accomplished have been chronicled in textbooks. The most obvious to our perception is the hero who lacks a particular identity. Compare Tom Jones or Humphrey Clinker with Ivanhoe or Quentin Durward, or with the stock heroes of Cooper—those whose names one never can remember, Heyward of *The Last of the Mohicans* and Griffith of *The Pilot*. They are simply heroes, moved about like blocks of wood by an author; they are never, in the slightest degree, Gatsby or Quentin Compson, they are not even David Copperfield. Their most heroic performances are a mechanical routine, and would have struck readers even in that period as dull had not these manikins been accompanied by, aided by, instructed by, and at last united to the heroine by, the tutelary genius who speaks the voice of Nature. Again and again this figure appears in Scott—Fergus MacIvor in *Waverley;* Meg Merrilies, Dominie Sampson, Captain Dirck Hatteraick, Dandie Dinmont in *Guy Mannering;* Bailie Nichol Harvie and Andrew Fairservice in *Rob Roy;* Gurth the Swineherd in *Ivanhoe*—and he is dutifully repeated in almost every American Romance. Here again Natty Bumppo is the master creation. Without him the Heywards and Effinghams would be lost in the wilderness, scalped twenty times over; without him the heroine would be ravished or massacred. To the faceless "lad" this simple son of Nature expounds the piety and the craft of the woods, and ranges the benign forces of the primeval on the side of virtue, so that at last Ivanhoe can settle down to civilized monogamy with his Rowena, Heyward with his Alice. Readers did not object to these arrangements, they reveled in them; as an American reviewer noted in 1815, all of Scott's "spirit and originality is concentrated in the inferiour characters, who are indeed the most important in the conduct of the story, and the principal agents in bringing about its denouement."

We cannot help wondering why this peculiar inversion of the relation of Don Quixote to his squire Sancho Panza, this entirely altered version of the eighteenth-century hero's partnership with his clever lackey, so captivated the nineteenth-century audience. Perhaps the Romances themselves give us whatever clue we need if we will turn from the heroes to the heroines. Just as Scott seems to have blundered into inventing the new form with *Waverley* and only afterwards to have realized what he had wrought, so in that work he adumbrated the duality with blonde Rose Bradwardine and dark Flora, the wild Highland maid. By 1820 he was sure of himself; in *Ivanhoe* he presented the Saxon Rowena and the Jewess Rebecca to figure forever as the archetypes of the Romantic opposition. Cooper, whom even contemporaries found sadly inept in devising women, lumbered along with the golden Frances and the brunette Isabella in *The Spy,* flaxen Alice and raven-haired Cora in *The Last of the Mohicans.* But Cooper knew very well what to do with his figurines, even if he could not put life into them: the dark ones entertain passions which, if gratified, would upset the order of Nature, so they are killed off, tragically, nobly, but nonetheless killed. Then, with the help of the tutelary divinity who bestows the sanction of Nature upon suitable marriages, through the untutored wit and instinctive perception of Harvey Birch and Natty Bumppo, the blondes are bedded down with the impeccable heroes, to bring into society strong and healthy children.

Everywhere the dark heroine is foreign, strange. She is a Jewess; she is, like Cora, the product of miscegenation; and frequently in America she is an Indian maiden who for hopeless love of the hero betrays her own people. The point she makes is that she intrudes into the equilibrium of Nature by proffering love where love is not wanted. However, the sinister element in her character is that she too is natural, as natural as a daughter of white and black can be, as a Jewess can be, above all as an Indian can be. Therefore there must be shown to operate in Nature itself some process by which she is eliminated. Here the tutelary genius intervenes. No hero can cope with this delicate balance and still remain a gentleman, but Natty Bumppo can and does; and so the Romance of wild adventure leads back, through his skillful guidance, to the mild serenities of the hearth. As Cooper openly boasted, the aim of Romance is to deal "poetic justice" all around, and thus in the end prove truer than ordinary mundane truth. And when the Romance has a historical setting, then it is a more truthful representation of reality than a plodding chronicle—for in actual history, of course, too many heroes marry the wrong girls.

Violent and disruptive passion in the female could thus be conveniently disposed of. But did the demonic, disruptive power of Nature never assume a masculine guise? Villains, of course, were no problem. They were simply evil, raised no perplexing theological issues, and could be defeated, generally slaughtered in the end. Again, the tutelary genius does the trick, either producing the evidence that undoes the wicked, or killing him. Cora is stabbed by a nameles Huron: the villain Magua stabs the noble Uncas, who disdains resistance now that his beloved is dead, but as Magua climbs the cliff to escape, Natty Bumppo draws a bead on his long rifle: "The surrounding rocks, themselves, were not steadier than the piece became, for the single instant that it poured out its contents." Villains therefore were expendable. However, the vogue of Scott in these decades was equaled by the cult of Byron. The Romance could not blink the fact that Childe Harold, Manfred, Conrad, were as much the children of Nature as Gurth the Swineherd or Natty the Leatherstocking. What to do with them?

There was only one answer: let the demonic figure serve—tortured, tormented being that he is—the cause of righteousness by becoming for the moment the ally, even the commander, of the tutelary divinity; let him bless the union of hero and blonde, and then go off to a lonely, desolate fate. Since he could not be tamed into matrimony, he must perish bravely in the final encounter, or else remove himself into mysterious exile. King Richard in *Ivanhoe* sketches out the role, but in America the aloof, brooding, gaunt figure of John Paul Jones in Cooper's *The Pilot* demonstrated how the Romance would incorporate a Byronic Manfred within the texture of Nature and then amputate him when the fabric was complete. Remote, unconcerned, buried in his own unfathomable anguish, he stands apart until the moment of exquisite danger; then he springs into action like a tiger, his voice rises above the tempest as he thunders forth his orders, and both the hero Griffith and Long Tom Coffin (who in *The Pilot* is a sea-going Natty) instinctively obey him with absolute devotion. The ship saved, the battle won, peace come again, the haunted genius withdraws into the impenetrable vastness of Russia. The comfortably domestic hero and heroine can then complacently moralize: "He was a man who formed romantic notions of glory." The mystery of him is never solved, but why should it be? As Griffith tells his blonde Cecilia, "It is enough to know that he was greatly instrumental in procuring our sudden union, and that our happiness might have been wrecked in the voyage of life had we not met the unknown Pilot of the German Ocean."

By such manipulations of plot the satanic egoist was somehow both given his due and yet robbed of his poison. Seldom or never is he consigned to the arms of the dark heroine, as might seem to those not initiated into the purpose of the Romance an obvious way to get rid of them both. No, she must pay the price of aspiring to the place she has no right to, and he must remain gigantically alone, in order to demonstrate to the heroes and heroines that only gall and wormwood are the lot of those who let natural genius run riot. The techniques by which the "regular romance" coped with the Byronic Titan constitute a parallel to those arguments by which moralists contrived to salvage the nobility of Byron himself, by which they converted him from arch immoralist of the age into a lesson in piety. When he first became the rage in America, guardians of the public morality attacked him as pernicious, but in a very few years the standard chant became that he was one who sinned from excess of virtue. As an influential critic of the time, H. J. Tuckerman, discreetly put it: "He continually preaches hopelessness; but the actual effect of his poetry is the reverse. No bard more emphatically illustrates the absolute need we all have of love and truth." Indeed, said the *Knickerbocker Magazine* in 1833—no journal in the country so reflected the sentiment of polite society—Byron was scorched, withered, wrung—but also he was "bold, intrepid, soaring, and irrepressible;—dauntless as the fabled stormers of heaven, and Promethean as the fire which destroyed them." By that time fathers who would not permit their daughters to read Bulwer or Goethe's *Werther* somehow allowed *Manfred* to repose on the parlor table, assured by the *Democratic Review,* voicing the regnant opinion, that an "intense and absorbing sense of moral power" pervades the drama. This exculpation of suffering Byron, once he was happily dead, went even so far that these sheltered daughters were allowed to read *Don Juan.* By and large, the satanic effluvia of Byron had been efficiently disinfected; while the apologetic interpreters did their part in working this sleight-of-hand, Romances in the wake of *The Pilot* made it commonplace.

It would strain the limits of space and patience were I to call the role of all the dark ladies in the American Romances who, from *The Last of the Mohicans* to the eve of the Civil War, expired for a love that could not be requited, or of the glowering Byrons of the forest who stalked majestically into the sunset. Here and there a writer might attempt a bit of variety by leaving out one or another of the standard cast of characters, or by allowing the heroine to exhibit a brown instead of a golden head. By and large they remained faithful to the conventions, for in their eyes these were not conventions but indispensable symbols for setting forth the true burden of Romance in America, which was not at all the love story. What all of them were basically concerned with was the continent, the heritage of America, the wilderness. *The Pilot* advertised that the American adventure could be enacted on that other expanse of Nature, the sea, thus giving a strong hint to younger aspiring Romancers; yet for obvious reasons the forest provided the more congenial setting. With a machinery for mounting the action furnished by the formula, American writers could devote themselves heart and soul to portraying the uniqueness, the glory, the ordeal of America. Dark, savage, brutal the wilderness might at first appear to a civilized view; that it dragged immigrants down to barbarism might be the report of foreign observers. Nevertheless, Romantic imagination could assure the Republic that these were but superficial appearances. Into undefiled Nature went the characters of Romance; within it the dark forces were exorcised, and out of it the creatures of light, male and female, emerged—strengthened, purified, exuding a native virtue that not only needed no instruction from European sophistication but could proudly scorn the culture of the Old World as a mask of depravity.

One of the most popular of these exonerations of Romantic America was Charles Fenno Hoffman's *Greyslaer,* first published in 1840. It rings a slight change on the conventional iconography by letting the blonde heroine die early in the book, thus laying on the hero the mission of leading the dark Alida—who at first is as proud and tempestuous as the darkest of them—back to female docility. The lawless genius takes the form of Joseph Brant, the Mohawk chief who turns against the patriots of the Revolution, commands the Cherry Valley Massacre in 1778 and the harrying of Wyoming in 1779, but who turns out, in Hoffman's treatment, to be an instinctive Byron of the forest, torn by inward remorse. The tutelary divinity is cut to specifications in the form of a noble frontiersman,

Balt, who shoots the Tory villain and in the end unites hero and heroine.
They are married in the autumn, the most glorious season of "our American climate," when the bluebird carols, the squirrel pranks on the chestnut
bough, the doe loiters in the woods—"when Nature, like her own wild
creatures, who conceal themselves in dying, covers her face with a mantle
so glorious that we heed not the parting life beneath." Thereafter, though
one might suppose that the violent adventures they had run through would
leave them with a lingering taste for excitement, Hoffman informs the
reader that "the current of their days was as calm as it had hitherto been
clouded."

Greyslaer, unlike *Mardi* or *Moby-Dick,* went through edition after
edition, that of 1848 being greeted by *The Literary World* of New York as
fully substantiating Hoffman's claim that his "Forest Romance" was so
constructed

> as to display a perfect unity in its design and action; that a great moral
> truth is continually exhibited in its changing incidents, and that at
> last its result is conformable to the principles of art that governed all
> the developments of the action.

The *World* continued to set forth Hoffman's merits in phrases that tell
everything as to why this sort of artificial epic, presenting itself as
artless Nature and as a sustained hymn to natural America, proved irresistibly attractive to the Jacksonian era:

> He claims that he has endeavored to fuse the romantic feelings called
> up by the stirring times of our American Revolution here, on the soil
> of our own State, and the native land of the Knickerbockers, amid the
> freshness of the almost untouched forest-glades, by the brooks of the
> Hudson and the Sacondaga, the mountain barriers of the Adirondack,
> with the pioneer, the discoverer, and the aboriginal; with the majesty,
> the simplicity, and the unbending vigor classic literature requires; where
> one idea like the great soul of nature informs the whole mass, and turns
> each incident to a likeness, or a part of the final catastrophe, the decree
> of fate.

For the moment, then, it would be joyfully proclaimed from every throat
in the land (or almost every one) that the American Romance had accomplished a hazardous mission, that it had won a double victory, both artistic
and patriotic. On the one hand it proved that in this commonplace
republic, with no hoary medieval traditions to guarantee its identity, a
form of narration could be perfected which merged the skill of classical
construction with the vastness and featureless expanse of our landscape.
On the other hand, it demonstrated that the sublimity of our forest glades,
brooks, mountains, waterfalls, the aboriginal and the primitive, could be
mobilized into the service of order, sobriety, steady virtue, and incorruptible
purity. Though the Americans took their cue from Scott, they went to
Nature not simply to mount picturesque settings for exciting deeds but to

pronounce upon the nation a benediction which, even to a people who generally professed to be Christian, had become for them more than divine.

This was indeed a stupendous achievement. All should have been serene in the realm of Romance, with blonde heroines invariably marrying their spotless heroes, scoundrels and Tories endlessly meeting deserved doom, superhuman Titans working their good and going on to a panoplied immolation, while Nattys and Balts ranged swiftly through the leafy shadows. But from its very inception the American Romance had, though with the greatest reluctance, to recognize that there was a fatal dread it could not entirely lay to rest. At the end of *The Pioneers,* Cooper could do nothing with Natty but dispatch him deeper into the West before the advancing march of civilization. In *The Prairie* of 1827 even the expanding imagination of James Fenimore Cooper was obliged to perceive that, in reaching the foothills of the Rockies, Natty Bumppo must come to the end of his tether. Gazing back to the East, the aged scout saw in his mind's eye the once glorious wilderness of New York: "Natur' then lay in its glory along the whole coast, giving a narrow strip, between the woods and the ocean, to the greediness of the settlers." But where am I now? Natty asks. "Had I the wings of an eagle, they would tire before a tenth of the distance, which separates me from the sea, could be passed; the towns and villages, farms and highways, churches and schools, in short, all the inventions and deviltries of man, are spread across the region." The garden of the Lord, he keens, was the forest then, and remains the forest still, but America sends forth choppers and loggers to humble the wilderness: "then the land will be a peopled desert, from the shores of the main sea to the foot of the Rocky Mountains; filled with all the abominations and craft of man, and stript of the comforts and loveliness it received from the hands of the Lord!"

In the very hour of glowing success, the Romance in America confronted inescapable defeat. As it strove with might and cunning to create the American epic by tearing down the dull flag of the novel and nailing its standard to the mast of Romantic Nature, just when it might exult in the assurance that by identifying American destiny with the destiny of the forest, it was paralyzed by the realization that in America Nature was steadily being first defiled and then destroyed by the inexorable march of civilization.

II

Moby-Dick was published in 1851. For a historian this date is beautifully convenient because it turns out to be exactly thirty years after *The Spy.* In that year, again suiting our convenience, Cooper died. The year before, Melville had removed himself and his family to a country house in Pittsfield, Massachusetts, and there so immured himself in solitude that his New York friends, who deplored such (to them) unnatural seclusion, attributed to this isolation his regrettable tendency to engraft a "speculative character" upon his writing. To them as to most of the reading public, the regular conventions of Romance imparted all the "philosophy" a sensible man need bother about. The rivalry of blonde and brunette, the melodrama of the self-consuming genius, the stabilizing sanity of the good-hearted denizen of the forest, the defeat of the villain, and always an ever-refreshing presence of environing Nature—all these added up to a system which hung so beautifully together as to require no further explication. Indeed, to translate into abstractions the propositions thus dramatized in narrative was contrary to the spirit of the thing; to indulge in further speculative flights was to desecrate what over the three decades had become a sacred formula.

Thus buried in rusticity, Melville was unable to attend the memorial meeting in honor of Cooper held in New York City, but he sent a letter to the chairman to be read aloud. In an earlier review Melville had addressed Cooper as our "national Novelist"; now he wrote that Cooper was "a great, robust-souled man, all whose merits are not even yet fully appreciated," and recollected that in his boyhood Cooper's works produced "a vivid, and awakning power upon my mind." That awakened power had just been infused into *Moby-Dick;* the next year what energies were left in him were pumped into *Pierre,* which critics and readers alike denounced as the work not of a man awakened but of a madman in a nightmare.

In 1850 Hawthorne published *The Scarlet Letter,* in 1851 *The House of the Seven Gables,* and the next year *The Blithedale Romance.* Thus Hawthorne's major works, Melville's masterpiece, and his delirious mystery come at the conclusion of three decades during which a host of American writers had cultivated, perfected, formalized the Romance. A hundred years later Hoffman's *Greyslaer,* along with some forty Romances of William Gilmore Simms and many, many similar ornaments of the period, have withered and disappeared like the autumnal leaves that blessed the union of Hoffman's hero and heroine. If Cooper is still read, it is mainly out of historical curiosity. So, then, the only works out of this once great endeavor that speak livingly to us are those which mark the termination of an epoch. True, a few writers still turned out Romances in the 1850's: Simms kept on until the Civil War, and one or two other Southerners, John Esten Cooke most conspicuously, strove to argue the Southern case in the fashion in which Cooper had justified the American Revolution, but the fiction of that decade suddenly rings hollow. No longer sound the authoritative accents of Leatherstocking or of Hoffman's Balt. There still are, of course, innumerable potboilers, but they are pale shadows even of G. P. R. James. Hence we are driven to the conclusion—and this observation needs much emphasis—that Hawthorne and Melville do not inaugurate a "renaissance" in American literature: they constitute a culmination, they pronounce a funeral oration on the dreams of their youth, they intone an elegy of disenchantment.

Neither gave up without a struggle. Hawthorne found enough stimulation in Italy—away from the commonplace prosperity, the broad and simple daylight of America, in a land full of antiquity, mystery, and gloomy wrong —to get through one more Romance, *The Marble Faun,* complete with a villain and the two heroines, more patently derived from Scott than any he had yet introduced, Miriam being in every particular a Rebecca and Hilda a New England version of Rowena. Yet even he, upon revising the book, was dismayed to perceive how much he had propped up his creaking plot by inserting a guidebook to Rome. He came home in 1860, to expend the last four years of his life in a futile struggle with four attempted Romances which he could not master or bring to conclusion. Melville managed several short stories and sketches for magazines, and in 1857 *The Confidence Man,* which, if it was in any sense a child of the Romance, was so misbegotten a monstrosity as to be unrecognizable by his contemporaries. Both men, as they themselves acknowledged, were being crushed before the juggernaut of the novel. They went down—Hawthorne with stubborn stoicism, Melville with a cry of defiance—keeping the ensign of the Romantic still flying, even though in order to hold it aloft they had to turn the standard Romance inside out. In their separate ways—and the differences of their temperaments are great—they had realized by 1850 that, in the mortal extremity of the form, they were called upon to let loose the beast which Scott and Cooper had supposedly caged within the wooden bars of "poetic justice." They at last could see that there was a savage thrust in the center of the Romance which the genteel either had not been conscious of or had discretely ignored (in 1923 D. H. Lawrence startled us by pointing out that if Natty Bumppo is, as we like to suppose, the symbol of the essential American, then his soul "is hard, stoic, and a killer").

Hawthorne and Melville reverse and so deliberately wreck the balance of the orthodox form. They take their stand with the dark heroine and against the blonde, with the Byronic Titan and against the faceless hero. Before the advancing legions of realism, before the serried ranks of the obsequious copyists of civilization, they fling their sacrificial victims, the unrepentant children of Nature, dark Hester and still darker Zenobia, and most furiously Pierre, the victim of "Civilization, Philosophy, Ideal Virtue." "What we did," says the adulteress Hester, "had a consecration of its own." "She is a pretty little creature," says Zenobia of the brown-haired Priscilla, "and will make as soft and gentle a wife as the veriest Bluebeard could desire. Pity that she must fade so soon! These delicate and puny maidens always do." Foremost among the Titans Pierre recognizes his own features on the face of Enceladus, "a moss-turbaned, armless giant, who despairing of any other mode of wreaking his immitigable hate, turned his vast trunk into a battering-ram, and hurled his own arched-out ribs again and yet again against the invulnerable steep." This Titan Pierre most thoroughly outraged all the righteous of his time by wilfully abandoning Lucy Tartan, his golden-haired fiancée of pastoral Saddle Meadows, fleeing to the city with the black seductress Isabel, and then dragging both of them with him into a maelstrom of death.

It was this *Pierre* which Melville had endeavored to sell in advance to Richard Bentley on the plea that it would be calculated for popularity, that it would be "regular," with a mysterious plot and stirring passions, "and withall, representing a new & elevated aspect of American life"! And it was this *Blithedale Romance,* in which the suicide Zenobia is borne from the Black River with her arms "bent before her, as if she struggled against Providence in never ending hostility," her hands "clenched in immitigable defiance," which Hawthorne blandly offered as a sweet Romance, an affectionate memorial of his stay at Brook Farm, "certainly the most romantic episode of his own life"! In either enterprise, how far had these two Americans traveled since the time Sir Walter Scott had genially explained that the Romance was drawn from the great book of Nature, ever the wholesome and sanitive same through a thousand editions.

It may be worth our while to pause, as we gaze upon this lurid sunset of the Romance in America, to note what books in these years, around 1851 and 1852, were coming into the country, unhindered by international copyright, from Europe and, most massively, from England. *Pickwick Papers* found a delighted audience in the United States almost as soon as it did in England. *Martin Chuzzlewit* was not at all concerned with the elevated aspects of American life, but despite the shrieks of patriots Americans read it with avidity, as they did *Dombey and Son* in the next year. *David Copperfield* in 1850 and *Bleak House* in 1853 with their smoking realism of the London streets, and *Hard Times* in 1854 with the grime of the Midlands upon it, won more and more attention. Disraeli's *Sybil* in 1845, setting forth a social conflict with a minimum of Romantic trappings, excited more readers than ever glanced at *Moby-Dick*. Running Dickens a close race for popularity was Thackeray's *Vanity Fair* in 1848, which made explicit its rejection of the Romance by advertising on the title page that it was a novel without a hero. Bulwer-Lytton, who in the 1830's had charmed hundreds with *The Last Days of Pompeii,* abruptly turned to the novel in 1849 with *The Caxtons* and followed this in 1853 with *My Novel;* his American followers stayed with him. Elizabeth Gaskell's *Mary Barton* in 1848 was not quite so popular, but it was taken seriously, and her *Cranford* in 1853 immediately became a classic. In 1855 Trollope turned out the first of his decidedly antiromantic forays, *The Warden.* As Hawthorne foundered with his last, desperate efforts, he sighed that he himself would never read his own books did he come across them by another hand, that could he write as he really wanted to write, he would, like Trollope, deal with "bully beef and ale."

These English writers constitute the advance phalanx of what historians call, or used to call, "Victorian realism." Though to our taste many of them still trail bedraggled clouds of the Romance, as compared with *Greyslaer, The Scarlet Letter,* and *Moby-Dick* they are emphatically novels, not

Romances. Scott had died in 1832, universally lamented. For a decade English fiction remained hypnotized by his example, but in the 1840's the spell was broken, the Wizard's wand become a dead stick.

For the historian of taste—and I would insist equally for the purely literary critic—this makes a problem. Here is a flood of English realism sweeping over the American market, and being relished with enthusiasm by American readers, while our few practicing writers wearily persist in turning our Romances, and our two major artists produce *The Scarlet Letter* and *Moby-Dick*. It is not enough to say that provincial Americans still nourished such an inferiority complex that they would take anything that London gave, no matter what its nature. We get a little further by checking this phenomenon off as one more example of that "cultural lag" about which historians talk, even though in the cities pirated copies of English authors were on the streets so soon after the originals appeared in London that the lag, as far as the public was concerned, was of the briefest. There were, it should be noted, a few efforts in this country, if only by a small coterie of New York journalists, to break away from the Romance and to treat the city and the town in somewhat the manner of Dickens. But courageous as these ventures were, they wrought little effect on native production. Possibly we come as near as we can to explanation in sociological terms when we say that before the Civil War there simply was no material for the nascent realist to work upon. In England we can see how the rapid urbanization and industrialization forced upon the generation of Dickens and Thackeray themes arising from the turmoil of London, the black smoke of Manchester and Birmingham, the social competition of Barchester and Grosvenor Square. But the creative imagination of this country had taken shape amid the single reality of vast, unsettled tracts of wilderness. Crowded and noisy as New York seemed to country visitors in 1850, it was still not sufficiently a pile of "civilization" to make imperative a writer's forsaking the wilderness for the urban scene. The dream of Arcadia died hard. A Civil War was required to shatter it.

Possibly American writers would have turned away from the Romance even though there had been no war. In one sense, we are astonished that the conflict wrought so little effect on the imaginative life of the people in general. Youths on both sides went into battle conceiving themselves heroes of Romance. We may wonder how, by the end of it, after the wholesale butchery of the Wilderness, Cold Harbor, and Petersburg, after Sherman's ravaging of Georgia and Sheridan's devastation of the Shenandoah, any participants could still think of the business as a gallant tournament. Astonishingly most of them did just that: Sidney Lanier sang of it as a joust between Head—the North—and Heart—which is of course the South! No sooner had John Esten Cooke ridden from Appomattox Court House to his impoverished plantation in the Shenandoah than he proceeded to feed the war into the grinder of Romance, just as before he rode away he had been feeding colonial Virginia into the same hopper.

The very titles of his postwar efforts show how unshaken remained his fidelity to the genre: *Surrey of Eagle's-Nest, Hilt to Hilt, Mohun: or the Last Days of Lee and His Paladins*. Northern treatments may not have been quite so flamboyant, but they never approach the realism of Whitman's *Specimen Days* or remotely suggest the brutality and terror that Stephen Crane and Ambrose Bierce were to recreate some thirty years later. The one realistic treatment of the stench of battle that did come out of the struggle, John W. De Forest's *Miss Ravenel's Conversion,* was utterly ignored by the public, despite Howells' determined efforts to advertise it. De Forest is the first, Howells wrote in the *Atlantic* for July 1867, "to treat the war really and artistically": in 1895 he was to lament as a discredit to our taste the neglect of De Forest, and to doubt "that I shall ever persuade either critics or readers to think with me."

So it can hardly be said that the horrors of war rudely detached American youth from their devotion to the Romance's idealization of conflict, not even those who had seen the dead and writhing wounded carpet Marye's Heights at Fredericksburg, not those who had watched amputated legs and arms pile up outside steaming hospital tents. Once the stillness settled upon northern Virginia, the commercial and industrial pace of life in the preserved republic accelerated so dizzily that few had time to read long tales, not even the supposedly idle wives of brokers. But magazine fiction flourished beyond anything Poe had dreamed. The public at once displayed an insatiable receptivity to what literary historians call "local color," the nostalgic sketch that looks back within some particular region to the idyllic and vanished days "Befo' dah Wah." California, Indiana, Vermont, Maine, central Pennsylvania were thus explored and longingly caressed, but the desolated South offered sentimental attractions beyond any other region. The industrial North, which had wrought the desolation, displayed no tendency more striking than an eagerness to escape, in its rare moments of leisure, into a dream world of old marster sitting on the veranda drinking mint juleps while the happy pickaninnies sang at their work in the cotton fields. Nobody would pay any attention whatsoever to the bitter reports Albion W. Tourgée was putting into such novels as *A Fool's Errand* and *Hot Plowshares,* which painfully revealed how, once the Northern troops had been removed, Southern Bourbons went about circumventing the thirteenth amendment.

These local colorists took over the Romantic cast of characters. The tutelary divinity became the cowboy or the forty-niner, always with a heart of gold, always a diamond in the rough. He was Kentuck in Roaring Camp, clinging to the dead baby: "He's a-taking me with him. Tell the boys I've got The Luck with me now." In Southern versions he is Sam, the faithful body-servant. And almost everywhere the iconography of the blonde and brunette remains unaltered. "Miss Anne," reminisces old Sam, "wuz puttin' her hyar up like old missis use' to put hers up, an' 't wuz jes' ez bright ez do sorrel's mane when do sun cotch on it, an' her eyes wuz gr't big dark eyes, like her pa's, on'y bigger an' not so fierce, an' 'twarn' none o' do young ladies ez purty ez she wuz." Villains were foiled and shot with the old regularity, and a special care was expended on painting accurately, in minute detail, the natural backdrop.

And yet, for all the infinitely greater pains taken by local colorists to render the amphitheater of Nature with photographic fidelity, the role of the landscape in their creations was nothing like what it had been in the Romance. *Vraisemblance* required the Romancer to portray actual scenes, not to make up fictitious ones as did that renegade from the Romance, Edgar Allan Poe; but it was far from intending that the writer should simply produce a daguerreotype of Lake Georgia or of Glens Falls. *Vraisemblance* presupposed as its major premise that the Romance brought into dramatic play the union of mind and setting, of the human spirit and the panorama of Nature. Scott does not take us into the wilderness merely because it is new and attractive, said Walter Channing in the *North American Review* of 1818, showing how quickly Americans had got the point: he transports us because "he there finds man in harmony with the landscape, and at home, in the presence of objects that were about him in infancy, which have grown into his soul, and are now secretly incorporated with all he feels of pride and sorrow and happiness." Francis Parkman, who learned much from Cooper, insisted again and again that Cooper's woods-paintings are not to be thought of "as mere rendering of material forms": "they breathe the somber poetry of solitude and danger." The Romance was hostile to systematic metaphysics, regarding it as one of the deadening weights of civilization. Yet implicit in the treatment of Nature, under the sanction of *vraisemblance,* lay an assertion essentially similar to Emerson's conception of "correspondence." The Romance maintained through Long Tom Coffin and Natty Bumppo that there is a positive, creative, joyous union, active on both sides, between the virtuous soul and beautiful Nature, between the heroic soul and sublime Nature. The American writer, Simms never wearied of proclaiming, must be imbued with sympathies caught from the surrounding aspects of his infant horizon: "the heart must be moulded to an intense appreciation of our woods and streams, our dense forest and deep swamps, our vast immeasurable mountains, our voluminous and tumbling waters." All such epistemological assurance has strangely evaporated from the local-color landscape; they are paraded before the readers as though the guide of a conducted tour were stopping the charabanc for a moment to point out a graceful grouping of objects before resuming his description of historic monuments through his megaphone.

Few if any of the authors in the age of Bret Harte and Thomas Nelson Page had sufficient generalizing intelligence to explain why they turned away from the contemporary world to seek solace in a past that lay on the far side of the Battle of Bull Run. Even so fine a sensibility as Sarah Orne Jewett, with all her deep love for the pointed firs, could not critically enunciate the reason why her exquisite landscapes were something apart from the mentalities of her characters, why the two created no such union of action and picture as did Glens Falls in *The Last of the Mohicans.* But all of them, and their public, seem to have felt in some obscure way, about the middle of the century, and in America coincident with the Civil War, that the magic link of subjective and objective which the Romance had maintained became irrevocably sundered. Indeed, there are signs that the quicker minds were beginning, under the guidance of the new realists, to suspect as much even before the war. George Templeton Strong, the highly literate Wall Street lawyer whose diaries are an invaluable addition to American literature, perceived the portent upon reading *Vanity Fair.* Thackeray, he gratefully mused, excludes any sort of idealism in character, plot, or catastrophe, and satisfies us by a fiction replete with features that never rise above our own experience of the world.

And it is a preference no one need quarrel with. Every commonplace man, woman, and child on earth has hopes and fears and destinies and trials and latent powers of good and evil that no human artist can do justice to. The elements of what we call Romance are but a cheap substitute, after all, for the awful interests of everyday realities.

The greatest painters, Strong further reflected, found their noblest expression in portraits of real persons. Why then should democratic America indulge in dreams of theatrical heroics: *"Every* character is ideal." I need not point out that at the touch of this straightforward dogmatism, *vraisemblable* portraits of Gurth the Swineherd and Natty Bumppo become crayon drawings from the kindergarten.

Lawyer Strong is, in truth, a sure-footed guide through this period of transition, all the more because as a perceptive layman he was attached to no literary creed and so could reflect the subtle changes working throughout the society. In 1837, at the age of seventeen, he had told himself that no one ever "combined so large a quantum of talent and genius with so much of personal lovability" as did Scott. By 1856 the cosmos of Scott and Cooper had collapsed into a heap of rodomontade: "How do you know," Strong asked himself, "that hillside and river and forest are entitled to awaken in you these emotions of joy and veneration?" Homer and Dante never went into raptures over a mountain gorge or a woodland clearing; the whole complex of feeling was unknown, he calculated, until about seventy years before. It may be genuine with those who profess it, "but is not its very reality a sign of sentimentalism, a badge of unfruitfulness and of incapacity to bear fruit, and does it not stamp your nature as unable to do works of righteousness, and as substituting for efficient action the aesthetic contemplation of the works of God?"

The moment this question was so much as whispered, the fire that illuminated the Romances of Hawthorne and blazed through *Moby-Dick* was extinguished, the embers no longer even smoldering. The former could be ranged on glazed shelves, along with the poetry of Longfellow, as sweet classics of New England's Arcadian phase; the latter be forgotten as having been only the ravings of a maniac. At the end of *The Blithedale Romance,* Hawthorne had Hollingsworth and Coverdale stand beside the grave of Zenobia, she of whom, while she lived, Nature had been proud. "Will not Nature shed a tear?" "Ah no!" muses Coverdale, though the voice we may be sure is Hawthorne's: "She adopts the calamity at once into her system, and is just as well pleased, for aught we can see, with the tuft of ranker vegetation that grew out of Zenobia's heart, as with all the beauty which has bequeathed us no earthly representative except in this crop of weeds." And the critical chapter of *Moby-Dick,* we can now perceive, is that entitled "The Whiteness of the Whale," wherein Melville, pushing to the utmost the fearful reflection that white is no color of itself and yet all colors at once, finds a blank, heartless void at the center of Nature, so that all the trappings of color, "the sweet tinges of sunset skies and woods; yea, and the gilded velvets of butterflies, and the butterfly cheeks of young girls; these are but subtile deceits, not actually inherent in substances, but only laid on from without." The crescendo rises: "all deified Nature absolutely paints like the harlot, whose allurements cover nothing but the charnel-house within." Thus this mightiest of American Romances defied the sacrosanct divinity of all Romance: the palsied universe lay before it like a leper, and the infidel who refuses to wear the painted glasses of Romance "gazes himself blind at the monumental white shroud that wraps all the prospect around him." Of these things, Melville could say, the Albino Whale was the symbol, and so could rhetorically ask, "Wonder ye then at the fiery hunt?" But the meditation at Zenobia's grave became a merely casual observation as soon as righteous citizens of the Republic like George Strong discarded as rubbish the doctrine of a mystical union of mind and Nature. Melville's question became an empty scream as soon as the issue of a moral and aesthetic correspondence between human emotion and the earthly hues of sunset skies was relegated to the bog of sentimentalism. Romantic counterstatement ceased to be meaningful even as blasphemy when there no longer was an orthodox Romance to blaspheme against. Zenobia's and Ahab's immitigable defiance became only tedious aberrations when nobody was any longer interested in deifying Nature.

It becomes a fact of immense import, therefore, that the four major American writers of the postwar epoch—Henry James, William Dean Howells, Mark Twain, and Henry Adams—came of age during the years of that blood-bath with a variously conceived resolution to have done with the Romance and all its works. Curiously enough, these four were noncombatants; they never saw the carnage with their own eyes; yet more than any of the soldiers, such as John Esten Cooke, they intuitively determined to declare unrelenting war upon the deification of Nature, to turn from the wilderness to the city, to declare that Natty

Bumppo *was* a monster and that Hawthorne was sadly misguided in dallying with allegory. They were instinctively and passionately intending, if they wrote prose fiction at all, to produce novels.

Howells, James, and Adams had, of course, a sophisticated knowledge of recent European literature to guide the translation of their instinct into a conscious literary program. In some respects Mark Twain does stand apart, but not so far as is often represented. He like the others had been a boy when the Romance was still enthroned as the highest form of fiction, yet like them he had received from the early Victorian realists a glimmering of the impending revolution. James, who learned from many masters, beheld the revolution accomplished by George Eliot, and she carried him far beyond Dickens and Thackeray. Once and for all she demonstrated that the adventures and histories of her characters— that is to say, "the author's subject-matter all"—were determined by the feelings and the quality of their minds. For James this became the great technical lesson. Out of it he drew his matured counterstatement to the Romance's allegiance to a master idea informing the whole mass like some fancied "spirit of Nature." With Dorothea and Lydgate of *Middlemarch* before him, he would never again see a hero in a featureless Ivanhoe or a blank Major Heyward. And as for Natty Bumppo—well, peasants are only peasants. And likewise for the blonde and brunette—Dorothea is raven black while Lydgate's silly, petulant little wife is a Rowena in crinoline. She is named Rosamund; she is the spoiled daughter of a small-town tradesman, and her only real passion is an ambition to be received by the aristocracy.

Howells and James met in 1866. They kept each other up nights with animated conversations about their grand futures. They were resolved to "do" America, and were convinced that nobody had as yet touched the subject, least of all Cooper. They were acutely aware, as were also Adams and Twain, that the Civil War cut a wide, deep gash across the national history, that the region on the other side, though charmingly pastoral, offered no great objects to examine save, as James put it, "forests and rivers." "Life was not the least spectacular," he continued, "society was not brilliant; the country was given up to a great material prosperity, a homely *bourgeois* activity, a diffusion of primary education and the common luxuries." Hence the utterances of Hawthorne were relished because he took a picturesque view of one's internal responsibilities and found in the landscape of the soul "all sorts of fine sunrise and moonlight effects." James, in short, so completely put aside the whole cult of Nature as a quaint "moral passion" that even so sensitive a historian as he could see in the demonic rebellions of Hester and Zenobia nothing but a moonlight effect.

For all these four spokesmen of the decades after Appomattox, the problem of determining just how they stood in relation to the years of their childhood was to be gnawingly insistent. In their maturity and old age they would come back to it again and again, trying to settle what in 1866 or 1870 they had supposed was settled for them. The supreme examination of the insecurity to which, in final retrospect, it appeared they had been foredoomed, is *The Education of Henry Adams;* in the light of that ultimate recognition, we are privileged to note the ambivalence that had lurked in the most confident assertions of their youth. On the other side of the gulf lay an era bathed in a beautiful faith, said James, "in the light of which it appeared that the great American state was not as other human institutions are, that a special Providence watched over it, that it would go joyously forever, and that a country whose vast and blooming bosom offered a refuge to strugglers and seekers of all the rest of the world, must come off easily, in the battle of the ages." But the victory of the North, James continued in his 1879 study of Hawthorne, marks a new era in the chronicle of the American mind; at the rate things were then going, there would soon be more "good Americans" than ever, "but the good American, in days to come, will be a more critical person than his complacent and confident grandfather." These burgeoning novelists were enthralled at the prospect of becoming the best of Americans, they were exhilarated with a self-congratulatory certitude that they were fore-warned against complacency, and they felt themselves sobered, as their grandfathers never had been, by a critical awareness of the complexities of the task. They were all four to live long enough to confess that in the beginning they had formed no notion of how appalling were the difficulties that they so blithely undertook to surmount.

Howells assigned himself the function of composing the theoretical statement of the insurgent novelists, through his reviews in the *Atlantic* and other magazines and his extended discussions in *Harper's* of the late 1880's, from which he made a book, *Criticism and Fiction,* in 1891. James liked to picture himself, as he showed in the reply to Besant, as the one who banished from critical discourse all abstract terms, who called for life in the novel, and only life and freedom. In the end, ironically enough, the reviews and critiques that James was publishing in these years, to which were added in 1908 the stately prefaces to the New York edition, make him today our pre-eminent analyst, so that out of him doctrinaires of a type he scorned derive systematic formulations which would immeasurably distress him. However, in the decades when the two were waging a campaign on behalf of the novel, it was primarily Howells who lectured the public and expounded the program which was the all-important concern to both of them.

Far from pooh-poohing the distinction between Romance and novel as a chimera, Howells took it for an ontological reality—which is probably one reason for James's wishing Howells would "quit" talking about the novel as it ought to be and concentrate upon writing it. In an earlier day, Howells would handsomely admit, the Romance made a vigorous fight against effete classicism; it sought to widen the bonds of sympathy, to level every barrier against aesthetic freedom, to escape from the paralysis of tradition. Now it has exhausted itself. Consequently, today realism is making the same attack on "effete romanticism" that the Romance had made on classicism, by asserting "that fidelity to experience and probability of motive are essential conditions of a great imaginative literature." Those who denounce the new tendency as sordid, who are horrified and resentful at having their literary saints dethroned, represent a "petrifaction of taste," and strive "to preserve an image of a smaller and cruder and emptier world than we now live in." Patiently he led "the purblind worshippers of Scott" to listening to, and many of them to accepting, his famous exhortation:

> Let fiction cease to lie about life; let it portray men and women as they are, actuated by the motives and the passions in the measure we all know; let it leave off painting dolls and working them by springs and wires; let it show the different interests in their true proportions; let it forbear to preach pride and revenge, folly and insanity, egotism and prejudice, but frankly own these for what they are, in whatever figures and occasions they appear; let it not put on fine literary airs; let it speak the dialect, the language, that most Americans know—the language of unaffected people everywhere—and there can be no doubt of an unlimited future, not only of delightfulness but of usefulness, for it.

Herman Melville was still alive when Howells penned these words, but nobody, not even he, gave a thought to *Moby-Dick*. Why should anyone? Think for a moment of the fine literary airs of the pseudo-Shakespearean dialogue, the high-flown language of the ordinary sailors, the passions out of all measure to those we know, the pride, revenge, folly, insanity, and above all the egotism! If Howells was to win his cause—and around 1890 a disinterested observer of the American literary scene would have judged that he had won—then surely *Moby-Dick* was buried past all recall.

By the time Howells and his followers perfected their credo, by the time James was well on the way to working out the lesson of George Eliot, the novelists had so far defined their quarrel with the Romance that in their perspective even Dickens and Thackeray seemed to belong more to the universe of Scott and Cooper than to that of Turgenev. In Turgenev, Howells gladly proclaimed, they found their supreme justification: he let the effects in his novels flow naturally from the characters; he stood aside from the whole affair; he completely dispensed with the impertinent moralizing of Thackeray, the stage-carpentering and lime-lighting of Dickens, with "even the fine and important analysis of Hawthorne." Again and again, in allusions within his novels and more militantly in the prefaces, James puts Scott and Dickens under the same rubric. In order to indicate how Hyacinth Robinson, the child of the London streets in *The Princess Casamassima* of 1886, acquired false and grandiose notions of life, James has him as a boy spend hours with Scott and Dickens. What James aimed at in the novel, and what he unrepentantly insisted he had accomplished, was the story of Hyacinth's shedding of these tinsel illusions. A hero of Scott's—Edgar Ravenswood, for instance, in *The Bride of Lammermoor*—"has a black cloak and hat and feathers more than he has a mind"; but Hamlet, "while equally sabled, and draped and plumed, while at least equally romantic, has yet a mind still more than he has a costume." The Romance, even when "presented with great romantic good faith," showed us the passion only in a secondary, a confused and disfigured aspect. It therefore sacrificed "intensity," and this virtue James was resolved to impart to the literature of his native land, just as Howells was determined to take its mind off painted dolls worked by springs and wires.

There is one fact of the utmost importance for us to bear in mind while re-enacting the assault which Howells and James led against the Romance: it sprang from a devoted patriotism. Theirs was not at all—or so they believed—like the flamboyant nationalism of the Romancers. They had only scorn for the resounding boasts of their predecessors that American literature should roar with the voice of Niagara and echo with the sublimity of the prairies and the Rocky Mountains. James allowed the untutored sculptor Roderick Hudson to mouth this rhetoric: "I mean to do the Morning; I mean to do the Night! I mean to do the Ocean and the Mountains, the Moon and the West Wind. I mean to make a magnificent image of my Native Land." In that case, says the practiced and disciplined European artist, "You'll have at any rate to take to violence, to contortions, to romanticism, in self-defence. Your beauty, as you call it, is the effort of a man to quit the earth by flapping his arms very hard. He may jump about or stand on tiptoe, but he can't do more." James lets us know that Roderick is doomed to a destruction as absolute as Captain Ahab's when he has him respond, "My colossal 'America' shall answer you!" but the point is that Roderick is an uncivilized brute, and his debacle is not something with which we have any degree of sympathy. He is rather the subject of a sermon, the moral of which is that America should grow up and put aside the childish gigantism of Romance.

And it was his deep concern for the country that led James to this theme for his first full-length novel. In 1867 he wrote to Thomas Sergeant Perry, who shared his dreams, that while he admired Sainte-Beuve, still that critic was a man of the past, of a dead generation, and "we young Americans are (without cant) men of the future." We are ahead of the European races in that we can deal freely with forms of civilization not our own; that we have no national stamp has hitherto been considered a drawback, but think what a unique opportunity is thus afforded us: "I think it not unlikely that American writers may yet indicate that a vast intellectual fusion and synthesis of the various National tendencies of the world is the condition of more important achievements than any we have seen." What this meant at bottom was that by ridding ourselves of our preoccupation with the Romance we could divest ourselves of the insidious confrontation of Nature with civilization. No longer obliged to fasten our national aspiration to a "colossal America" which was every day perishing before the railroad and the city, we could seize a still more glorious place amid the civilized communities by becoming the synthesizer of universality. For the winning of this breathtaking position, the destined weapon was clearly the novel.

There was, however, a slight complication in the apparently easy road to success. As James, even at the age of twenty-four, felt obliged to add in his letter to Perry, "We must of course have something of our own— something distinctive and homogeneous." He thought we might find this in the American moral consciousness, "our unprecedented spiritual lightness and vigour." Perhaps he and Perry should expect nothing great during their lifetimes, said Henry, Jr., already committed to greatness, but his "instincts"—shades of Herman Melville!—looked "to see something original and beautiful disengage itself from our ceaseless fermentation and turmoil." And there stood the question of questions. It was easy enough to let drop the cloak and feathers of Edgar Ravenswood, to substitute Hyacinth Robinson and Silas Lapham for Major Heyward; it was equally easy, with the help of George Eliot and Turgenev, to discern in advance the original and beautiful that must disengage itself from American existence. But if the novel was to accomplish all this, then it had first of all to cope with the ceaseless fermentation and the turmoil. The Romances of yesteryear might no longer seem in the least original and not at all beautiful; but those "large loose baggy monsters," James had to confess, did incontestably contain life. While he might ask what did they artistically *mean,* the fact remained that they had once upon a time given a form to the fermentation of war and the wilderness, the turmoil of Zenobia's pride and of Ahab's vengeance. Did these civilized novelists, James, Howells, Adams, really *know* enough about the new America arising out the Civil War to confront and master, anywhere nearly as effectively as had Cooper, Hawthorne, and Melville in their day, the ferment and tumult of an age that was not so much colossal as it was colossally Gilded?

III

In 1955, William Faulkner replied to questions addressed to him by Japanese students at a seminar in Nagano: "In my opinion," he said, "Mark Twain was the first truly American writer, and all of us since are his heirs, we descended from him. Before him the writers who were considered American were not, really; their tradition, their culture was European culture."

Hemingway as well as Faulkner has, on occasion, made grudging exception for *Moby-Dick.* Occasionally, Hemingway concedes, it is a good book; however, he adds, it wraps its good things in rhetoric like plums in a pudding: "the people who praise it, praise it for the rhetoric which is not important. They put a mystery in it which is not there." Faulkner told the Japanese that he read *Moby-Dick* every four or five years. But he read *Don Quixote* every year. As for Poe, both agree that he was basically European, and Hemingway adds that his writing is dead; Hawthorne is lumped along with Emerson, Longfellow, Whittier. "Hawthorne, the others," gestures Faulkner, "they were Europeans, not Americans."

These pronouncements are nothing like so new as they may sound. The vast audience which Mark Twain commanded in 1869 upon the publication of *Innocents Abroad*—so astronomically larger than any Henry James was ever to reach, many times over as numerous as Howells could attract even at his peak—rejoiced that at last an authentic America voice had been raised. Readers in Europe no less than in America chortled to hear the Cathedral of St. Mark described as irresistibly ugly, resembling nothing so much as a gigantic warty-bug out for a meditative walk. Then in 1876, the year in which Roderick Hudson (in book form; the serial ran the previous year in the *Atlantic*) was rushing to Romantic doom with impossible conceptions of a colossal America, Tom Sawyer inveigled his schoolfellows into whitewashing a fence for him—and on a Saturday! In 1885, just after James had officially disallowed the distinction between Romance and novel, Huck Finn took off on a raft down the Mississippi. Except, of course, that 1885 is the date when "Mr. Mark Twain" told about him in a book. The actual year in which, according to the story, that voyage took place was in the halcyon period before the war, a time when supposedly novelists had nothing to depict but a simple society, nothing to look upon but forests and rivers. This was the period in which Hawthorne discovered Zenobia, and Melville stared until blinded into the Lapland whiteness of the whale.

Both Hemingway and Faulkner had their contemptuous quarrels with critics of their work. Hemingway jeered at writers who pay attention to critics, and when readers found symbolism in his writing, Faulkner ingenuously marveled: they discover something "that I had no background in symbolism to put in the books." He could only surmise that what they took for symbolic "is evidently instinct in man, not in man's knowledge but in his inheritance of his old dreams, in his blood, perhaps in his bones, rather than in the storehouse of his memory, his intellect." So let us, remarking in passing how it was Melville's "instinct to out with the Romance" and how James's "instinct" assured him that something original and beautiful would emerge from the turmoil, consider a fact which stares us in the face throughout the work of Mark Twain. From *Innocents Abroad,* through *Tom Sawyer, Life on the Mississippi, Huckleberry Finn,* down to *The Mysterious Stranger,* we are subjected to one sustained, unremitting forensic attack on the Romance. The indictment is repeated so vehemently, so apoplectically, so tediously, that in the final reckoning it seems an obsession more monomaniacal than Ahab's comparatively mild delusion. If this rancor springs originally from instinct, by the time the tale is told, it has certainly been repeatedly dredged up to the plane of consciousness. If, then, Hemingway and Faulkner speak truth, the purely American writers, those uncontaminated by "European culture," are condemned by the father of them all to unrelenting assault on the Romance. Yet the one consideration which our Nobel prizewinners neglect to mention is that Mark Twain, arch-opponent of the Romance, was himself a Romancer whom Cooper and Hawthorne and Melville might easily have welcomed as blood-brother—or at least cousin-german. Mark Twain protested, but he protested too much. He conducted a strenuous campaign all his life long, and expended himself to the utmost, waving what he believed to be the standard of the novel; he was never to look aloft at it long enough to notice that it was a double-faced banner, that on the reverse side it sported the old tapestry of Romance. What he would have demolished, he loved; what he loved, he hated. If it be that Mark Twain is indeed the "first" American writer, and that Hemingway and Faulkner— not to mention Fitzgerald, Dreiser, Sinclair Lewis, Thomas Wolfe—are his heirs, then to the progeny of his literary loins Mark Twain bequeathed an ambivalent—Melville would have called it an "ambiguous"—inheritance.

Hemingway tells Kandisky in *The Green Hills of Africa* that if he reads *Huckleberry Finn,* he must stop when Nigger Jim is stolen from the boys: "That is the real end. The rest is just cheating." It is rather an odd predicament for us, is it not, to have to explain to Europeans and Japanese that the last quarter of *the* central American novel is a swindle. That is to say, the last hundred pages, where Huck masquerades as Tom, where Tom pretends to be his half-brother Sid and so superintends the liberation of Jim according to the elaborate rules of all the "authorities" of Romance. "He could out-superintend any boy I ever see," marvels Huck; it all has to be done according to the "regulations." No such easy method as simply unlocking the door and letting Jim go free—that would be "old maidy." So, all the painful claptrap—Jim must carve exalted sentiments about his lonely heart upon a grindstone, construct a rope ladder out of stolen sheets, let his cell be filled with spiders and rats, escape in female dress just as the countryside is forewarned by anonymous letters— "nonnamous" as Huck gets it—and Tom ecstatically receives a bullet in the calf of his leg. "It 'uz planned beautiful," admires Nigger Jim, "en it 'uz *done* beautiful; en dy ain't *nobody* kin get up a plan dat's mo' mixed up en splendid den what dat one wuz." Jim and Huck demur at all the elaborate folderol; they don't see the sense of the underground passage, the rag-ladder, the spiders. Tom keeps the children of Nature up to scratch: "The thing for us to do is just to do our *duty,* and not worry about whether anybody sees us do it or not. Hain't you got no principle at all?" It isn't the glory of Tom's scheme that cows Jim and Huck; it is Tom's high moral dignity: "He was always just that particular. Full of principle." Never was Tom Sawyer in such high spirits: "He said it was the best fun he ever had in his life, and the most intellectual."

Criticism cringes before this protracted bore. There are actually efforts to prove, in the teeth of Ernest Hemingway and despite the chagrin of even the most charitable readers, that this nonsense makes a fitting climax to the splendid Odyssey of the raft: it is a boy's story, says the defense, and why should boys not be allowed to behave like boys? But this plea generally overlooks the real point of the wearisome fanfaronade: the rescue conducted according to the strictest regulations of Romance, meticulously faithful to exalted principle, is a phony from the beginning. Tom knows all the time that Miss Watson had died two months before and that in her will she had set Jim free. Why on earth, then, did he go through these shenanigans? "Why, I wanted the *adventure* of it; and I'd'a' waded neck-deep in blood. . . ."

By the time a reader has battered his way through these pages he has almost forgotten that the real climax of the voyage came when the fraudulent duke and king sold Nigger Jim "for forty dirty dollars," when Huck, after a soul-searching struggle, decided on his own realistic basis to rescue the Negro, recognizing that the decision consigned him, unreformed and unreformable, to hell. "For a starter I would go to work and steal Jim out of slavery again; and if I could think up anything worse, I would do that, too; because as long as I was in, and in for good, I might as well go the whole hog." That was a terrible resolution, but it was rational: Huck knew he was no good anyway, so he might as well consent to being damned. Therefore, once Tom's Romantic masquerade is exposed, Huck's sense of rational decorum is appeased: Tom took all that trouble to set a free nigger free—"and I couldn't understand before, until that minute and that talk, how he *could* help a body set a nigger free with his bringing-up." And we are supposed to smile in condescending amusement as we recognize that this solution of Huck's puzzlement restores his feeling for the social proprieties, but thereby prevents him from comprehending he has been duped into playing a role in a Romantic farce.

This is the obvious though unspoken moral of the concluding escapade. But plain as it may seem to us, the implication was too subtle to impress itself upon Twain's contemporaries, even on the sympathetic Howells. They persisted in reading it as a comic charade played by normal and healthy boys. In fact, there is an even larger question, which I would rather not go into, as to whether Samuel Clemens himself was not the one most pitiably fooled. If William Faulkner says that he does not know enough about symbolism to put into his books the symbolic configurations critics find there, then it may be that in more senses than one he is in truth a spiritual descendant of Mark Twain, who conceivably said more in his novels than Samuel Clemens realized. There always remains, however, the disturbing wonder as to how far these truly American novelists— uncontaminated by European culture—may be romancing about themselves. They boast their native originality, yet take care to dissociate themselves from writers on the eastern slopes of the Alleghenies—all, that is, except the mythologizing Melville. They pointedly ignore Cooper. Thus they cover their tracks, and in practicing such literary woodcraft they, like their acknowledged master, conceal their own secret. For once we step outside *Huckleberry Finn* to consider less guarded statements of Mark Twain, or once we cast a cold eye upon the less subtle *Tom Sawyer,* we see the source of the animus that could carry him through the dreadful play-acting of the *finale* to his masterpiece, under the euphoric persuasion that he was slaying the dragon who had haunted him from the dawn of his consciousness—namely, the Romance.

You cannot read any ten pages of Mark Twain without sensing the rebellion festering in his spirit. The target of this revulsion has been variously identified—his father, his mother, the Main Street of Hannibal, John D. Rockefeller, Theodore Roosevelt, the genteel restrictions of his wife and of Hartford, the Jehovah of Calvinism, sex, or the mere physical existence of Europe. Huck Finn, in his own narrative, manages to take a pot shot at all these enemies except the mother; however, in *Tom Sawyer* Huck had already disposed of his mother by recollecting that when Pap and she were married they did nothing but fight. There is little reward in tracking Twain's grudges through the wilderness of his psyche; it is much more rewarding to take an aerial survey, to listen for the snarl arising from every quarter of the underbrush, the accents of his hatred for the Romance. And let us, while listening, catch the mumbled phrases that punctuate the snarl: "But Tom Sawyer," reports Huck, "he hunted me up and said he was going to start a band of robbers, and I might join if I would go back to the widow and be respectable. So I went back." The sum and substance of Twain's compulsive barrage against the Romance was just this: it is inherently dishonest because everywhere it is a lie told by the respectable and civilized in order to glorify and delude themselves. "But Huck," reasons Tom, "we can't let you into the gang if you ain't respectable, you know." In other words, far from setting up a real opposition, as it pretended, of Nature to civilization, the Romance took an insured holiday into the forest, as little risking life or limb as when Tom played at Robin Hood, at piracy, or at jail-delivery, secure in the knowledge that he could and would return to the foregone conclusions of respectability. Launched upon self-gratifying adventure, the Romantic of genteel cultivation becomes reckless not only of blood but of the credulity of Huck Finn, and so perpetrates, on Jackson's Island, along the majestic course of the Mississippi, a desecration of Nature fouler than any of which the Romance accused civilization. The sun rises upon Jackson's Island: "the marvel of Nature shaking off sleep and going to work unfolded itself to the musing boy"; Tom and his fellow "pirates" swear they will never return to "civilization." But Tom Sawyer, the Black Avenger of the Spanish Main, and Joe Harper, the Terror of the Seas, grow homesick— "Even Finn the Red-Handed was dreaming of his doorsteps and empty hogsheads." They go back to town, to hear their own funeral sermon, and then to posture as heroes. Tom decides it is better after all to play at robbery than piracy: "It's close to home and circuses and all that."

Mark Twain was given, and coyly accepted, the laudations of a grateful public when he published "Fenimore Cooper's Literary Offences." Cunningly hidden but unmistakable implications in *Huckleberry Finn* had put his audience into a receptive mood, but they had hesitated to draw the clear deduction. Cooper was still a revered classic; they were ready to hear, but they needed Mark Twain to tell them, that the emperor had no clothes. He made certain that *hoi polloi* would side with him by first setting up for refutation the fulsome praises of two professors; then he tore *The Deerslayer* to shreds: "It is not a tale, and accomplishes nothing and arrives nowhere, the episodes have no rightful place in the work, since there was nothing for them to develop." Making hay with Cooper's diction —Twain's list of Cooper's misuse of words could be a handbook for instructors in Freshman Composition—he ridiculed the whole of the Leatherstocking Tales, calling them "the Broken Twig Series" (in his two major works Twain some four or five times employs the snap of a twig under foot!), and slashingly summarized *The Deerslayer* as typical of the entire body of Romance:

> It has no invention; it has no order, system, sequence, or result; it has no life-likeness, no thrill, no stir, no seeming of reality; its characters are confusedly drawn, and by their acts and words they prove that they are not the sort of people the author claims they are; its humor is pathetic; its pathos is funny; its conversations are—oh! indescribable; its love-scenes odious; its English a crime against the language.

Counting all these elements out, Twain concluded, what remains may be admitted to be "Art." Amid the guffaws that greeted this disquisition, nobody so far recovered himself from laughter as to remark that Twain's piece is actually not at all funny: it is written in deadly earnest, out of white hatred, out of a cold and ferocious determination to blast not only the Romance but all the stultifying profusions which the respectable Tom Sawyers of this world, in the name of authoritative and regular "Art," impose upon vagrant lovers of American Nature, upon Huck Finn and Sam Clemens.

Sam Clemens, we should remember, was a Southerner. I have called him, along with Howells, James, and Adams, a noncombatant in the Civil War. His brief flurry with a Missouri volunteer company, which he turned into slapstick in "The Story of a Campaign That Failed," does not qualify him for veteran's rights; he stayed out of the draft as effectively in Nevada as Howells did in Venice. Even so, the general rebellion in his soul, which obliquely pours its scorn upon Tom Sawyer, aimed its vehemence more precisely against the romantic folly of the Confederacy. The reason was not far to seek: the respectable South, like Tom Sawyer, had been brought up on Sir Walter Scott.

Twain's rancor come out most explicitly, far more than his "humorous" method usually permitted, in Chapter 44 of *Life on the Mississippi* in 1883, revealingly entitled "Enchantments and Enchanters." The French Revolution and Napoleon, he declares, whatever their crimes, broke the chains of the *ancien régime,* leaving the world their debtor for mighty services to liberty, humanity, and progress. Then came the enchanter Scott, to set the world "in love with dreams and phantoms; with decayed and swinish forms of religion; with decayed and degraded systems of government; with silliness and emptinesses, sham grandeurs, sham gauds, and sham chivalries of a brainless and worthless long-vanished society." Had it not been for Sir Walter, the character of the Southerner—"or Southron, according to Sir Walter's starchier way of phrasing it"—might have become wholly modern, but Scott so debauched the mentality of the region that "he is in great measure responsible for the war." Cervantes had swept the "chivalry-silliness out of existence"; *Ivanhoe* restored it. For the South, and as a proud Southerner Mark Twain could never cease to lament, the work of Scott was unqualifiedly "pernicious." In case any should miss the point, in 1889 he caused the Connecticut Yankee to plant nineteenth-century mines under the mail-clad hosts of medieval chivalry and blow them to pieces. Howells thought *A Connecticut Yankee in King Arthur's Court* a charming "Romance"!

I present this hasty review of Twain's work as it appears to me in the light of the historic contest in American literature between the Romance and the novel. However, in the modern celebration of Mark Twain, these historical considerations seldom figure. It seems strange to me that the symbolism—if symbolism is what the critic searches for—of the wrecked steamboat's being named the *Sir Walter Scott* in *Huckleberry Finn* is not more widely appreciated. What further confuses the issue, apart from the critics' ignorance of earlier American fiction, upon which both Clemens and Tom Sawyer fed, is the love Twain bore for the pristine American landscape, a passion which ranges him, in this particular, on the side of the Romance he despised, and which makes it impossible to classify *Huckleberry Finn* as a novel in the sense that James, Howells, and Adams gave the term. It is this love which involves him in ambivalence in his attitude toward the American adventure, and, indeed, is the very attribute which qualifies him for the role assigned him by Hemingway and Faulkner, that of progenitor of all modern American literature—at least, of its fiction.

Any direct approach to the beauty of the continent in the manner of Cooper's descriptions or Natty Bumppo's apostrophes (or I must say in the manner of such landscape painters as Durand and Thomas Cole) embarrassed Mark Twain, struck him as an indecent exposure of private emotions. This uneasiness further accounts for the violence of his attack on the Leatherstocking Tales; when Natty wails that if the settlements spread inland from the Hudson, then both war and hunting will lose their beauty, Mark Twain's inner monitor knew precisely what the scout meant, but publicly he responded by wisecracking that nothing improves scenery like ham and eggs. The Nature passages in *Tom Sawyer,* such as the sunrise over Jackson's Island, avoid becoming hymns to natural beauty by being turned to ironic purposes, serving as commentary on the absurd romanticism of the boys. But in *Huckleberry Finn* Twain found the device by which, with calculated indirection, he could let the poetry of his own heart gush freely forth as the quaint and supposedly naïve observations of a ragged rapscallion as he watches at dawn how the great river "softened up," and the "nice breeze springs up," bringing with it the far sound of voices and the "fresh and sweet" smell of woods and flowers. The early Romancers and their apologists said that the problem confronting the American writer was how he could adapt an imported vocabulary and structure of language, which had been devised for the description of English meadows and London Bridge, to the depicting of Niagara and the boundless prairies. "Now I feel sure," Twain lectured the professors, "that Cooper wrote about the poorest English that exists in our language." What Huck does to the English language makes it something far remote from the standards of an Oxford Commonroom (where his speech was so relished that the University gave the boy from Hannibal an honorary degree), but in the process it had become a perfect voice for the colossal river.

The difficulty for his contemporaries was that they had never seen a sunrise on the Mississippi. Howells was later to tell how he once tried to become a reporter for a Cincinnati newspaper, but that one round of the police courts early in the morning so appalled him that he took flight for Boston. He and James might swear an oath to "do" America, but both were quickly to discover that when they tried to peer into the vast and formless jungle west of the Appalachians they found themselves depressed, as James put it, by the poverty of their categories. James says that he would have despaired entirely had he not, upon examining the popular literary treatments of this wild garden of the "unconventional," found that their stock in trade was nothing more than dialect. "The key to the *whole* treasure of romance independently garnered was the riot of the vulgar tongue." The local colorists, he perceived, were in an intrinsically false position: they were writers of urban sophistication, of the schools, yet they raised their monuments "to the bastard vernacular of communities disinherited of the felt difference between the speech of the soil and the speech of the newspaper." Inevitably they proved capable only "of taking slang for simplicity, the composite for the quaint and the vulgar for the natural." Was he then to regret his own failure to contribute even a pebble to these monuments? "Perish, and all ignobly, the thought!"

By that sweeping exclusion, his problem, or the problem of every anti-romancer in America, was, though narrowed, far from solved. James faced up to it by spending the winter of 1882-1883 in New York, and then had to confess himself beaten. He could not penetrate the world "down-town," the monstrous labyrinth from Canal Street to the Battery, any more than he could invade the dialect-ridden interior. He found himself incarcerated, "at the very moderate altitude of Twenty-Fifth Street," to spend his days with the ladies and children, the music-masters and French pastry-cooks, the whole dull order of society testifying "to the extraordinary absence . . . of a serious male interest." Prophetically he had told Perry in 1867 that very likely the special American *cachet* would turn out to be "our moral consciousness, our unprecedented spiritual lightness and vigor." Refusing to be put off by such a raucous account of the American lack of spiritual lightness as Twain's and Warner's *Gilded Age* in 1873, or by Henry Adams's anonymous and dour report in *Democracy* of 1879, James amplified the teaching of George Eliot, and at the end could congratulate himself, even though few others would do so, for having conducted, from *Roderick Hudson* in 1876 to *The Golden Bowl* in 1904, a fairly steady march toward defining that "interest which consists in placing advantageously, placing right in the middle of the light, the most polished mirrors of the subject." The "all-objective" Newman of *The American,* he liked to think, had at least this virtue; assuredly Isabel Archer in *The Portrait of a Lady* had it—the preface James wrote for this volume of the New York edition is his most aggressive assault on the Romance—and at last he satisfied even his own highest requirements with Lambert Strether in *The Ambassadors*—he is, James notes with almost insufferable satis-faction, "a mirror of miraculous silver and quite pre-eminent, I think, for the connexion."

However, the prefaces also wryly confess that his progress was not quite so steady as he might have wished. Though the essay of 1884 denied that any such formulation as the separation of the Romance from the novel ever had existed, the prefaces use the word "Romance" as signifying exactly what it had stood for in his father's time. In that perspective he could eventually make out that *The American* was an arch-Romance which he had constructed without knowing what he was doing; had it been a novel, the noble French Bellegardes would have positively jumped at the chance of marrying the daughter of their house to this "rich and easy American." Likewise he had to concede, after several women friends had called his attention to how American girls do actually conduct themselves in Europe, that *Daisy Miller* was also a Romance: "My supposedly typical little figure was of course pure poetry, and had never been anything else."

Despite these lapses, Henry James, as by now is generally allowed even by those who still find him "difficult," devised a way to vindicate, within the confines of his experience, a form of the novel which, if not precisely about America, is indubitably about Americans. He was providentially assisted on his course by the hostility aroused in America by *Daisy Miller*— it was denounced as "an outrage on American girlhood"—and by the unanimous refusal of American readers to see anything at all in *The*

Bostonians. Howells waged his war against the Romance with somewhat larger public support through a sequence of novels now more honored in historical surveys than by any conspicuous eagerness on the part of readers. That his experience was restricted to a particular segment of American society he was the first to acknowledge, and the anemic quality of the result has become a commonplace of criticism. He did indeed make the first gallant effort in our literature to get the novel into the businessman's office with *The Rise of Silas Lapham,* and, galvanized by his horror over the Haymarket Riots and the legal murder of the accused, he attained the distinction of presenting a panoramic view of megalopolis with *A Hazard of New Fortunes* in 1890. Though American literary production during all these years continued to be in large part local color, with its riot of the vulgar tongue, still an objective observer around 1890 might well have decided that the vestigial remains of Romantic convention were withering away.

Then, in the decade of the 1890's, there struck what the novelists could only regard as disaster. The Romantic miasma again spread its vapors. On the vulgar level revulsion took the form of a sudden craze for the flimsiest kind of Romance, of a sort that Cooper and Simms would have despised, a farrago of cloaks, duels, golden-haired heroines, and rescues in so close a nick of time that Natty Bumppo's seem by comparison stately. These were escapes into the never-never land of *When Knighthood Was in Flower, In the Palace of the King,* and the histrionics of an utterly implausible Graustark. Nor need I remark how the species has remained with us, down through *Gone With the Wind* to the profitable lucubrations of Mr. Yerby and Kenneth Roberts. However, this retrogression might have been endured, even though the new Romance was a degeneration from even the basest of local-color sentimentality. But a more serious challenge emanated from France, in the person of, as James characterized him, "the coarse, comprehensive, prodigious Zola." James and Howells could quickly perceive that "le roman experimental" was essentially the old Romance redraped in garments collected out of *The Origin of Species* instead of in the cloaks and plumes of Sir Walter Scott. It too portrayed man in Nature, except that now Nature, instead of humming the still sad music of humanity, thundered the redness of tooth and claw; of the writer it demanded, just as had the earlier Romance, that he construct his narrative according to an a priori metaphysic, that he organize it around one idea which would inform the whole and govern each event according to a preconceived abstraction. It turned the artist into the enunciator of some supposedly overpowering decree of fate, and required him to subordinate the continuity of experience to some (from the novelist's point of view) arbitrary dictum. Still worse, it invested him with the arrogant pretension that his plan was not a mechanical device of his own contriving, but the objective law of life. Naturalism re-imposed the tyranny of Nature; it abrogated the freedom for which the novelists had striven so patiently and so doggedly.

For a time Howells, noting that Zola was not at all the realist some thought him but was instead "full of the best qualities of the romanticism he has hated so much," took comfort from the thought that Zola would never have any effect "among people of our Puritanic tradition." Then, with the appearance of Stephen Crane and Frank Norris, Howells saw the handwriting on the wall; to his credit he defended these young naturalists as best he could, though sorrowing that the day had come when it was dangerous to leave the American novel within the reach of young girls, when we should have to recognize that it too was suitable only for men and "married women," just as in corrupt Europe. The naturalists, in the person of Frank Norris, repaid his generosity by sneering at "the drama of a broken teacup, the tragedy of a walk down the block, the excitement of an afternoon call, the adventure of an invitation to dinner." Norris was not afraid of the hated word; he took it up, he gloried in it. "Romance," he said, "is the kind of fiction that takes cognizance of variations from the type of normal life." Realism stultifies itself, becomes merely somnolent, "but to Romance belong the wide world for range, and the unplumbed depths of the human heart, and the mystery of sex, and the problems of life, and the black, unsearched penetralia of the soul of man." In 1901 Norris's *The Octopus* announced the formation of a new and much more powerful cult of the colossal.

Naturalism as exemplified in Norris's doctrinaire application to fiction of the law of survival of the fittest proved as transitory a fashion as did the attempt to impose upon prose fiction a Marxist dialectic in the 1930's. Even Theodore Dreiser, who in 1900 commenced his literary career with the blessing of Norris, came to more complex and humane insights when he created Clyde Griffiths in *An American Tragedy* of 1925. Virtually all the fiction of what now appears to have been the second great period of American expression, roughly the decade of the 1920's, owes obvious debts to the reforms wrought by late nineteenth-century novelists, American and European. Their central figures are not the faceless heroes and stereotyped females of Cooper and Simms; they are personages—Clyde Griffiths, Carol Kennicott, Sam Dodsworth, Robert Jordan, Jay Gatsby, Quentin Compson. Also, the World Wars, the force of social anxieties, the radical departures in form of such influential writers as Joyce and Proust and Gide, do make any rigid aligning of recent authors into romancers and novelists about as pointless as James fondly hoped the division had become in the 1880's. However, one can hardly say of the majority of these storytellers that they conceive of the novel in terms that would satisfy James and Howells, that they have not admitted into fiction all the elements which Norris declared would become the substance of the new Romance, or that as compared with contemporaneous European literature, they do not exhibit an unmistakably Romantic tendency. In many cases the heritage of nineteenth-century American writing may account for the curious persistence of patterns of the Romance into even the most hard-boiled and resolutely disillusioned of them, though it is difficult to imagine Cooper as a formative influence on Hemingway and Faulkner. Perhaps a more pertinent observation would be that the Romance, for all its highfaluting bombast, did so reflect the predicament of the human spirit in this country that the later novelists, those who deliberately broke through the genteel restrictions to which Howells and James had bowed, found themselves perforce recreating Romance.

Our fiction was born when the two standards, of the novel or of the Romance, marked out the whole field between them, when the craft of storytelling had to grow by professing either one allegiance or the other. To examine the ways in which the tensions between the two have relevance for the best of our modern fiction would become a long story, one that for the moment I am content to leave in abeyance. I would, however, contend that this is where the symbolic as well as the tutelary importance of Mark Twain resides. For it is Mark Twain, the arch-foe of Romance, he who would blow the knight-errantry of chivalric legend into kingdom come, who lives as the wildest Romancer of them all.

SINNERS IN THE HANDS OF A
BENEVOLENT GOD

In VAIN expounders of Jonathan Edwards plead that he was not the cruel, sadistic preacher of torment and terror which popular legend makes him. Asa Turner, graduated at Yale in 1827, and all the redoubtable "Iowa Band" from Andover, who ultimately established the college of Grinnell, would have emphatically repudiated the notion that their master, Jonathan Edwards, was a monster. In vain they pointed out, as do we, that the majority of his sermons came out of a calm and beautiful, an ecstatic, serenity. In vain we demonstrate from his own "Personal Narrative" that he was a man of rare sweetness, of gentleness, of love. In vain we beg students to pause, to listen how in his exalted moods he went forth into the meadows, solitary and enraptured:

> I often used to sit and view the moon for continuance; and in the day, spent much time in viewing the clouds and sky, to behold the sweet glory of God in these things; in the mean time, singing forth, with a low voice my contemplations of the Creator and Redeemer.

In vain we plead these considerations, because, in the agonies of the Great Awakening, in 1740 and 1741, he did indeed preach "terror" sermons. Because he was, among the clergy of his day, or of any subsequent day, a supreme master of words, these discourses live in the memory of mankind. They remain the arch-symbols of the grim Calvinism against which the humanitarian, liberal, progressive nineteenth century is supposed to have steadily fought. By overcoming the barbaric cruelty of Edwards, the argument runs, American Protestantism entered into the euphoric phase of Christian optimism.

Above all, Edwards is identified with a sermon he delivered at Enfield, Connecticut, on July 8, 1741, published to the world under the title *Sinners in the Hands of an Angry God.* It drove the congregation to a frenzy. One witness described the convulsion: "There was a great moaning & crying out through ye whole House—What shall I do to be Saved —oh I am going to Hell—Oh what I shall I do for Christ." Many of the colossal camp meetings and frontier revivals of the early nineteenth century staged scenes of greater mob hysteria; even so, the figure of gaunt, tall, relentless Edwards—standing in the pulpit of Enfield, speaking with a quiet logic that seemed more fiendish than Christian, and so driving

Lecture given at the convocation in 1958 celebrating the one hundredth anniversary of the founding of Grinnell College.

these simple folk to distraction—this would remain the American emblem of a conception of life in which men figure as contemptible sinners while Almighty God stands aloof, a being compacted essentially of wrath.

The Edwards image endures in our memory because no other spokesman for this philosophy ever put the central idea in such simple, unflinching, unforgettable rhetoric:

> The God that holds you over the pit of hell, much as one holds a spider, or some loathsome insect, over the fire, abhors you, and is dreadfully provoked; his wrath towards you burns like fire; he looks upon you as worthy of nothing else, but to be cast into the fire; he is of purer eyes than to bear to have you in his sight; you are ten thousand times so abominable in his eyes, as the most hateful and venomous serpent is in ours.

Edwards goes on to explain, with his strangely moderated ferocity, that nothing but the hand of God holds you from plunging into hell at any moment, that there "is nothing else that is to be given as a reason why you do not at this very moment drop down into Hell."

We may safely figure that on that eighth of July there were in Enfield no rival attractions to the visit of Mr. Edwards. There were no theaters to be closed, no television sets to be snapped off; there was not even a carnival to be hushed. Farmers milked their cows in the morning, and left their plows and hoes in the shed. We gather that the two or three shops at the crossroads were shut. On this day the sermon was not simply the main attraction, it was the only attraction.

A student of the spiritual history of this republic is bound to derive a certain amusement, not to say stupefaction, from conning the pages of a recent the New York Sunday *Times* devoted to "amusements." For example, on August 18, 1958 on the second page, in the upper right corner, was a box heralding *Around the World in 80 Days,* proclaimed to be "the greatest show now on earth." Two spaces below this were advertisements for Rockefeller Center, picturing chorus lines of Rockettes who dance with such machine-like precision that both their beauty and their sense of timing endlessly astound their congregations. Beside this was the announcement of "Ice Capades of '58," "the greatest show on ice," scheduled to perform at Madison Square Garden, which should present no terrors to anybody because this emporium sports "escalators to arena & balcony."

Between these gorgeous displays, the second insertion on the right side of the page told of the show that on this day and for several weeks past had been jamming Madison Square Garden. The performance went on nightly, except Mondays, at 7:30 P.M. The top line screams, "It's Teen Week at the Garden!" beseeching the teen-agers of New York to hear Billy Graham discourse on "With an accent on Youth." All seats were free. At the bottom was a P.S: "Bring your parents." Lest these adolescents quail in anticipation of being confronted with the fires of hell, the notice calms their trepidations by announcing that Madison Square Garden is air-conditioned.

It is, assuredly, easy to make comic comparisons between the simplicity of our colonial origins and the multifariousness of modern industrial, megalopolitan, automated civilization. One can force these contrasts to imply both an admiration for the good old days (without, however, any serious intention of getting back to them) and a passing query as to whether we really are any better off with all our physical comforts. But I hope that in setting up the obviously antithetical tableaus of Edwards in Enfield and Billy Graham at Madison Square Garden, I am reaching for a thought of somewhat deeper significance.

Anyone who pauses in the day's occupation long enough to meditate about the meanings of American experience over the last two centuries finds himself obliged to ask, "What became of the sinners?" And then, in his second breath, to inquire, "What became of the angry God?" If he pushes his questioning further, if he refuses to take the facile explanation that Americans have all become organization men, all other-directed, he asks in what body of expression he can get at least an insight into the mystery of the process. Thereupon he discovers that he is posing as a question what in fact is the major theme of American literature.

I do not deny that social history has much to say about the story, nor that—if one is fully to understand it—one would need to know the chronicle of the churches, of theology, of philosophy, or even of journalism. But in a manner which seems peculiar to this one of the modern nations, virtually all important American writers have, in one way or another, from the time of the Revolution, had to grapple with a single problem: if the God of wrath, step-by-step but irresistibly, becomes transformed in the American setting to a God of benevolence, how then does the artist cope with what society presents him? Especially when the panorama which the nation does offer him, which it thrusts upon him, is replete with the sort of behavior that for Edwards was consummately covered by the simple word "sin"?

Once I phrase the questions in this manner, you will recognize that they can also be addressed to other literatures. You will say that they are issues in the novels of George Eliot and of Thomas Hardy. You will note that they are the heart of *The Brothers Karamazov*. Some may note they are obsessive in recent French writing, and point to Camus' *The Fall* as conclusive evidence that Americans are not unique. Furthermore, it is true that many solid American writers have not been bothered at all by these metaphysical concerns. At first sight, for instance, they seem hardly to be present in the romances of James Fenimore Cooper—though even there I might argue that in fact they inform all the seeming superficialities of the Leatherstocking Tales.

Without endeavoring a digression into comparative literature, I still think it fair to contend that in the civilizations of Europe and Russia there remained, and still remains, so manifold a complexity that writers could and do put aside these problems; they can devote themselves to art as an end in itself, if not quite for itself. To make the point all too abruptly, we can hardly imagine an American in the nineteenth century writing a *Madame Bovary,* even though William Dean Howells genteelly tried it. We can not conceive an American's writing Zola's *Nana,* however a Frank Norris might suppose that he was doing something analogous. But we may assuredly assert that only an American could have produced *The Education of Henry Adams.* And it had to be an American (albeit he became a British citizen) who in 1922 posed all the religious questions anew in a language which still dominates our imaginations, in that tremendous revival sermon, *The Waste Land:*

> Unreal City,
> Under the brown fog of a winter dawn,
> A crowd flowed over London Bridge, so many,
> I had not thought death had undone so many.

In 1885 Mark Twain did not harm the popularity of *The Adventures of Huckleberry Finn* by centering the spiritual drama upon Huck's temptation to betray the fugitive Nigger Jim into slavery. Huck struggles with himself, you remember, and on the side of respectable betrayal are arrayed all the orthodox forces of his culture. For a moment, after he has written his letter to Miss Watson, "I felt good and all washed clean of sin." He knew, for only the moment, that he could pray, in the standard manner. But after that moment, benevolence assaults him: he remembers the devotion, the love, the service Jim has given him; impulsively he tears up the letter, crying to himself, "All right, then, I'll go to hell."

Hell was in 1885 still officially a reality. Even so, Mark Twain's readers were not offended; on the contrary, they loved Huck all the more. Can one imagine such a declaration achieving anything else in the Connecticut Valley of 1741 except a scandal! But in 1885 Mark Twain enlisted the Protestant conscience on the side of naïve Huck Finn because that conscience was long since assured that slavery had been sin. The most orthodox of churchmen would smile indulgently over Huck's crisis. All could rejoice in this triumph of instinctive benevolence over the ancient formalities of a crude society and a crude theology—and congratulate themselves upon their sophistication.

Mark Twain himself fought a losing battle with the angry God of his boyhood's Calvinism. We today appreciate that there are deeper layers of tension in the scene of Huck's decision than greet the eye. In his last years Mark Twain was wracked by a pessimism more ghastly than any implied by Edward's Enfield sermon. His blanket condemnations of "the damned human race" are more lethal than any that emerged from Puritan jeremiads. But when he chose to address his audience, at least in 1885, Mark Twain knew how to catch the changing temper. He rallied generous sentiments by showing Huck as proof positive that spontaneous human nature, in this progressive century, would find its way, despite the imported barbarisms of European theology, to a benevolence which bespeaks a deep, an indestructible, a natural morality.

We need to remark again that the larger part of Edwards' religious consciousness was not occupied with the terror of *Sinners in the Hands of an Angry God.* One of his shorter discourses, yet possibly his masterpiece, was written late in his exile at Stockbridge, in the 1750's. *The Nature of True Virtue,* he called it, and it was to have a profound, a disturbing effect upon Protestant theology in the United States for the next century; it is still a disturbing tract. His central thesis is that true virtue consists "in benevolence to Being in general." He distinguishes this impersonality from all forms of love for beauty or harmony, from those he called "secondary virtues"—those affections which extend benevolence to a private system of good, such as one's wife and children, one's nation, or even all humanity. No! It had to be, if it were "true," a disinterested benevolence toward the sum total of created being, to the ultimate star; it had to love the infinite universe itself, even those vast interstellar spaces which terrified Pascal. It had to become an individual's agreement with the nature of things.

Edwards strove to exalt this conception of universal benevolence so far above all utilitarian notions of sexual love, family loyalty, patriotism, aesthetic delight, as to prove that only by the gratuitous gift of Almighty God would a particular identity achieve the sense which transcends all finite senses. But he more than any of his colleagues made clear that if men had still to tremble before the God of wrath, there was in the absolute nature of things an ecstatic benevolence which some men might receive even within the stern mechanism of a Newtonian physics. They might— though from no more merit of their own than was claimed by a Huckleberry Finn—find it bestowed upon them.

Only eighty years after the Enfield sermon, Ralph Waldo Emerson, aged nineteen, having just graduated from Harvard College, communed with himself on the beauties of lakes, of the boundless ocean, of the plenitude of being:

> The air is fanned by innumerable wings, the green woods are vocal with the song of the insect and the bird; the beasts of the field fill all the land untenanted by man, and beneath the sod the mole and worm take their pleasure. All this vast mass of animated matter is moving and basking under the broad orb of the sun,—is drinking in the sweetness of the air, is feeding on the fruits of nature,—is pleased with life, and loth to lose it. All this pleasure flows from a source. That source is the Benevolence of God.

Obviously, young Emerson had left behind all thought that access to this realization of benevolence is limited only to those arbitrarily elected by a vengeful Deity. Yet no less than Edwards is he distressed that not all men experience it. His lifelong effort was to communicate the sense to as large a number as possible. But many appeared obtuse, dogmatic, pedantic; Emerson also had to recognize the fact of sin. However, in a universe which was truly and universally benevolent, the new definition of sin would soon emerge: "Sin is when a man trifles with himself, and is untrue to his own constitution." Emerson's ideal transcended the sublunary goods of the self or the local community as much as did Edwards'. Emerson admired a friend who could say that he never spent anything on himself until he was sure to derserve "the praise of disinterested benevolence."

Historians discern in the optimistic individualism, the eupeptic self-reliance, the consequent philosophical egotism of Emerson and his fellow transcendentalists, a distinctively American phenomenon. But we are apt to forget just how this individualism was indeed premised upon the conviction of a vast all-pervasive goodness in man and nature. This egotism was a *consequence* of the assumed universal benevolence. Henry Thoreau, having by the age of twenty-four caught the Emersonian enthusiasm, was thrilled to realize that obedience to God is "only to retreat to one's self, and rely on our own strength." "If by trusting in God," he wrote in 1841, "you lose any particle of your vigor, trust in Him no longer." Thoreau could afford to risk the exhortation because he was persuaded that by trusting in God he augmented his own vigor. His anger was directed against those who professed to trust in the Almighty but who, judged by his standards, really did not. He raged because the Commonwealth of Massachusetts issued a pamphlet for farmers entitled *Insects Injurious to Vegetation*. To Thoreau, the very idea of such a publication was an insult to the bounty of creation:

> Children are attracted by the beauty of butterflies, but their parents and legislators deem it an idle pursuit. The parents remind of the devil, but the children of God. Though God may have pronounced his work good, we ask, "Is it not poisonous?"

Emerson and Henry Thoreau discarded the traditional apparatus of Christian theology, going far beyond what the most "liberal" of their countrymen would admit. Even so, if we consider them in the larger perspectives of American development, they were not so far ahead of the procession, or so much outside it, as used to be supposed. On popular levels, the basic shift had begun with the American Revolution. The majority of the clergy in 1776 were patriots. One and all, even while doctrinally remembering the sinfulness of man and the need for Christ's intercession, they incorporated into their Christian apology for resistance an essentially optimistic philosophy, that of *The Declaration of Independence*. For instance, Samuel West, preaching before the General Court of Massachusetts on May 29, 1776, reinterpreted the Apostle Paul into something strangely different from what the first Reformers had found him saying. According to West, St. Paul declared that rulers were appointed to defend our just rights, and so should be resisted whenever they fail "to promote the good and welfare of the community." The Apostle's reasoning, in West's account, comes out very little like Luther's version; it appears to be one with that of the Continental Congress: rulers, he says, are "to carry on the same benevolent design towards the community which the great Governor of the universe does towards his whole creation."

Passages of similar tenor may be cited by the thousands out of the patriotic agitation of the Revolution; take them in the whole, they bespeak a revolution in the American mind infinitely more radical than any achieved on the battlefields. Jonathan Edwards expounded how disinterested benevolence would enhance the good of the community, but insisted that those who would truly aid the society were those who had larger conceptions in mind than merely the community. These would be the elect; the rest, whatever the fervor of the patriotism, were in the hands of a God of wrath. Bit by bit, almost imperceptibly, the benevolent God who led the Americans to independence was interpreted as a Being who shepherded this whole community into a heritage of social prosperity. Sinners might remain, but they were no longer in the hands of an angry God: they were in the midst of an ebullient America, before which extended the prospect of infinite expansion, unprecedented wealth. In this reach of vision, no creatures, not even spiders, were any longer poisonous by necessity.

The rank and file of the people remained Christians. They were children of, and practitioners of, the Revival. Yet it seems clear that as the revivals of the early nineteenth century grew and profited from experience, beginning in Connecticut in the 1790's and in Kentucky in 1801, through the powerful movement of 1858, they became more and more concerned with "making Christianity work," less and less with the technical subtleties of doctrine. In his recent and (to my mind) admirable study, *Revivalism and Social Reform,* Mr. Timothy L. Smith plausibly argues that Emerson and Theodore Parker could never reach the masses of this republic because they too rudely challenged traditional Christianity; yet out of revivals came the program which called for the consecration of baptized believers to building the kingdom of God. Another way of putting it, in my brief analysis, is that the revivals no less than transcendentalism summoned the energies of sinners into producing the benevolent program of American democracy. The few who dissented, who drew back, who tried to maintain that man was still finite, febrile, and damned, were disregarded, shunted aside into the Princeton Theological Seminary, disobeyed by their own students. They suffered bleak isolation. Of late we have realized that the most radical of these pessimists was Herman Melville, an untutored novelist more rigorous than any Old School Presbyterian. That he had to wait for rediscovery in our own time may be taken as evidence of the crisis in which we today find ourselves plunged—the crisis of well-intentioned American benevolence.

This is not to say that the American experience through the nineteenth century was all beer and skittles. Life on the frontier was hard; the building of the West cost health and lives; many were defeated and turned their faces to the wall. Then there was the mighty blood-purge of the Civil War, and the anguish of a defeated South. By the end of the century there were ominous rumblings in the cities, strikes and violence, and the Chicago anarchists. Still, the generalization may stand, that American society subscribed to—and on the whole vindicated—the benevolent thesis of Revolutionary patriotism. Emerson seemed to demonstrate that, even when traditional Protestant theology could be dispensed with, the economy of the universe was such that traditional morality was undisturbed. By trusting himself, Huck Finn comes out morally inviolate. Despite the ordeals of rude pioneering and civil strife, the steady progression of this society toward the goals of benevolence was unmistakable.

It is worth remarking, even though an aside upon a complex matter, that while in the literature, political oratory, and evangelical Protestantism of the nineteenth century, the American mind came to conceive of the human problem more and more as that of fallible man within a benevolent society, American Catholicism by no means was quarantined against these tendencies. In Father Walter J. Ong's *Frontiers in American Catholicism* you can find a brilliant statement of just how "American" the Catholicism of this country has become. He argues that American Catholics must think even more seriously than they yet have done about the "mystique" of American optimism, which he feels they have now assimilated more thoroughly than their Protestant neighbors—who originated it. "This American optimism," says the Jesuit, "is psychologically linked with the hopeful facing into the future which so far has marked the American mind." Here the Catholic seems to be in fundamental agreement with Protestant Timothy Smith: American experience proved that it was not at all necessary for the multitude to surrender the Christian conception of man as conceived in sin in order to join wholeheartedly in the American drama of realizing on earth Jonathan Edwards' vision of supernal benevolence. The mass of Christian believers did not need to follow Emerson. In fact, it would seem that energies generated out of a conviction of sin have proved more efficacious for society than those that arise from a rationalistic denial of it.

In 1913 George Santayana, who had just left Harvard and America, never to return to either, published an essay, "The Intellectual Temper of the Age." At the time, it was heeded only by a small band of aesthetes Santayana had gathered about him in Cambridge; if elsewhere noted, it was dismissed as the gloom of a queer, cold fish, who never had the least understanding of a country in which he had ever been a foreigner. We still cling, said Santayana, to fragmentary vestiges of Christian civilization; we still dogmatically assume that progress is inevitable, that the large moral principles are irresistible. But, he pointed out, the mind of the Orient is yet unconquered, and will remain unconquerable; Christianity is confronted with equal authority by the pagan past and the industrial, socialistic future.

"Our whole life and mind is saturated with the slow upward filtration of a new spirit—that of an emancipated, atheistic, international democracy."

In 1913, as I say, hardly anybody paid attention to what must now seem a highly prophetic diagnosis. By 1929 apostles of progress were reeling from the final shattering blow in a decade and a half of blows; guardians of the moral law were in bewilderment before an upsurge of pessimism, hedonism, egocentricity, and several forms of socialism, all of which seemed the utter negation of American experience. Moralists, preachers, exhorters, politicians could no longer speak to these youths. The new generation seemed to have no shred of benevolence left in their view either of the world or of themselves. In 1929 the voice of that generation spoke with measured vehemence in *A Farewell to Arms:*

> I was always embarrassed by the words sacred, glorious, and sacrifice and the expression in vain. We had heard them, sometimes standing in the rain almost out of earshot, so that only the shouted words came through, and had read them, on proclamations that were slapped up by billposters over other proclamations, now for a long time, and I had seen nothing sacred, and the things that were glorious had no glory and the sacrifices were like the stockyards at Chicago, if nothing was done with the meat except to bury it. There were many words that you could not stand to hear and finally only the names of places had dignity. Certain numbers were the same way and certain dates and these with the names of the places were all you could say and have them mean anything. Abstract words such as glory, honor, courage, or hallow were obscene beside the concrete names of villages, the numbers of roads, the names of rivers, the numbers of regiments and the dates.

The vocabulary of progressive, American benevolence had vibrated with the abstract words of glory and devotion—honor, courage, hallow—with repeated assurances that sacrifices were not made in vain. The American expression, sophisticated or evangelical (leaving out Herman Melville), had translated the Christian heritage into this ethos. But Ernest Hemingway declared, and the youth agreed, that these terms could no longer mean anything at all when for four years Western civilization did not even eat the meat slaughtered in the trenches; it just buried the corpses.

This is not the place, even in a paragraph, to summarize that sudden literary eruption that makes the decade of 1920 to 1930 a shock from which American complacency has not yet recovered. We may now perceive that the break with the benevolent past—the dissent from what William Dean Howells memorably announced in 1890 were the most American aspects of life, the "smiling aspects"—had begun even before the United States made its contribution to the wholesale stockyards of the First World War. An attack upon the criteria of moral security was launched around 1910 or 1912 by the early writings of Walter Lippmann, Randolph Bourne, Van Wyck Brooks, and was strengthened by the first American readings of Freud. In the 1920's, however, the attack became concerted, so as to

seem to the respectable a subversive conspiracy. Anderson, Fitzgerald, Dos
Passos, and a hundred others, some now forgotten, a few become classics,
joined the assault with a violence which bespoke the outrage that a generation felt, as in the lines of Ezra Pound, had been perpetrated upon it:

> There died a myriad,
> And of the best, among them,
> For an old bitch gone in the teeth,
> For a botched civilization.

Santayana's essay of 1913 now appeared to err, if at all, on the side of
mildness. Mankind had suffered beyond anything the imagery of Jonathan
Edwards had conceived; a spider thrown onto the flames shrivels and
dies in a merciful instant; he is not tormented month after month in the
gangrene of the trenches. But now, it appeared, there was not even the
consolation of an angry God to make the torture explicable. What could
the mangled soul do but turn in rage upon the speech of benevolent
optimism? What could the tender conscience cry but that the meaning of
the ghastly mess was that there is no meaning?

It has taken the corporate intelligence of this republic a long time to
realize that the inner burden of insurgent expression in the 1920's was
not pessimistic nihilism. In fact, one may pardonably ask whether the
average mind of the citizenry has still grasped what happened. At the
moment, for a variety of reasons, we stand in the field of the domestic
intellect, as in the area of international politics, in a posture of armed
neutrality. The public wonders—if it gives so much as thought to the
question—why this good America spawned such rebels against venerable
sanctities as Sinclair Lewis, Eugene O'Neill, Ernest Hemingway, William
Faulkner—and, one should mention, from its point of view, T. S. Eliot.
Americans generally are baffled when such men as these receive Nobel
Prizes. They do not appreciate how extensively the literature has been
translated, is read in Europe and Asia, how it stimulates young writers
in those continents, how it molds the image of the United States. In the
present literary doldrums, we know not whether the critical impulse has
spent itself. We are half afraid lest successors to Faulkner and Hemingway
should appear, half afraid that their vitality has left us. We want to hope
that civilization is something better than an old bitch gone in the teeth.
But we are not certain.

Critical opinion is assured that William Faulkner has proved a major
voice in American self-scrutiny. Even his most ardent admirers are not,
however, persuaded that *A Fable,* published in 1954, is an entirely successful work. It is an allegory of the passion of Christ, enacted on the
Western Front in 1917. It turns out that God the Father is the Allied
generalissimo, and that his Son is the silent and illiterate corporal who
leads the troops into mutiny. The general takes his son to the top of a
mountain crowned with Roman ruins, and shows him the wide world into

which he may escape; the Father begs his offspring not to court martyrdom. I know man better than you do, says the Almighty:

> Oh yes, he will survive it because he has that in him which will endure even beyond the worthless tideless rock freezing slowly in the last red and heatless sunset, because already the next star in the blue immensity of space will be clamorous with the uproar of his debarcation, his puny and inexhaustible voice still talking, still plannning; and there too after the last ding dong of doom has rung and died there will still be one sound more: his voice, planning still to build something higher and faster and louder; more efficient and louder and faster than ever before, yet it too inherent with the same old primordial fault since it too in the end will fail to eradicate him from the earth.

Mr. Faulkner used essentially these words at Stockholm in 1950 upon receiving the Nobel Prize. They rang around the world. We do not know whether, when he then used them, he had already ironically put them into the mouth of God the Father. Mr. Faulkner's allegory is painfully exact, but then so is that of *The Scarlet Letter* and *Moby-Dick*. There are those who think Faulkner's speech simply fustian; readers in 1851 thought Ahab's orations sheer bombast. Like these two of his predecessors, Faulkner sees no hope in a return to abject confession of sinfulness before the anger of Jehovah. As they foresaw, and as Faulkner seems more clearly to perceive, we in America have come so far along the road that, amid the higher, the faster, and the louder, sinful man, acknowledging anew his frailty and his anxiety, has somehow to triumph over the creations of his own benevolence. In a way, it seems to me, William Faulkner summarizes the innermost spirit which all along inspired the literature of American iconoclasm. "I don't fear man," says the Supreme Allied Commander, "I do better: I respect and admire him."

INDEX